IMPRISONMENT IN ENGLAND AND WALES

A CONCISE HISTORY

Christopher Harding, Bill Hines,
Richard Ireland and Philip Rawlings

CROOM HELM

London • Sydney • Dover, New Hampshire

© 1985 Christopher Harding, Bill Hines, Richard Ireland
and Philip Rawlings
Croom Helm Ltd, Provident House, Burrell Row,
Beckenham, Kent BR3 1AT
Croom Helm Australia Pty Ltd, First Floor,
139 King Street, Sidney, NSW 2001, Australia

British Library Cataloguing in Publication Data

Imprisonment in England and Wales: a concise history.
   1. Imprisonment—England—History
   I. Harding, Christopher
   365'.942   HV9649.E5

ISBN 0-7099-1294-3

Croom Helm, 51 Washington Street, Dover, New Hampshire 03820, USA
Library of Congress Cataloging-in-Publication Data

Main entry under title:
Imprisonment in England and Wales.

   1. Imprisonment—England—History. 2. Imprisonment—
Wales—History. 3. Prisons—England—History.
4. Prisons—Wales—History. I. Harding, Christopher, 1951–
HV9644.I47   1985   365'.942   85–14948
ISBN 0-7099-1294-3

Typeset by Columns of Reading
Printed and bound in Great Britain

CONTENTS

List of Illustrations   vii

Preface   x

Introduction   xi

Part One: The Middle Ages   1

1. The Structure and Organisation of Imprisonment   3
2. The Population and Conditions Within Prisons   35

Part Two: The Early Modern Period   53

3. Developments in Punishment   55
4. The Prison System   76

Part Three: The Period 1750 to 1877   107

5. The Rediscovery of the Prison   109
6. Reformation or Punishment?   143

Part Four: Modern Period, from 1877   185

7. The Organisation of a State Prison System   187
8. Types of Prison Sentence and the Prison Regime   205
9. The Social Functions of Imprisonment   236

Discussion and Concluding Remarks   264

Review of Literature and Sources   272

Chronological Table   291

Appendices   297

Index   305

ILLUSTRATIONS

Plates

1. *Boethius in prison*
   From a twelfth-century West of England manuscript (Bodleian MS. Auct. F.6.5. fol 1ᵛ), by permission of the Bodleian Library, Oxford.

2. *Sketch of Newgate Gaol in the fifteenth century*
   From the City of London Journals (Journal 4, fol 79b), by permission of the Corporation of London Records Office.

3. *'The Representations', 1728: conditions in the Marshalsea Prison*
   From the Report to the House of Commons, by permission of the Trustees of the British Library.

4. *Portrait of Howard visiting a prison*
   By permission of the Trustees of the British Library.

5. *Prisoners exercising at Pentonville Prison*
   Engraving from Mayhew and Binney's *Criminal Prisons of London*, 1862.

6. *Interior of the Surrey House of Correction, Wandsworth*
   Engraving from Mayhew and Binney's *Criminal Prisons of London*, 1862.

7. *Treadwheel at Pentonville Prison, c. 1890*
   By permission of the Hertfordshire Constabulary.

8. *Prisoners working on land reclamation on Dartmoor, early 1890s*
   By permission of the Hertfordshire Constabulary.

9. *Children shoe-shining at Upton House Industrial School, London, at the turn of the century*
   By permission of the Greater London Council Photograph Library.

10. *Prisoner working a hand crank at Wormwood Scrubs Prison, late nineteenth century*
By permission of the Hertfordshire Constabulary.

11. *Contrasting architectural styles: entrances to Dartmoor, Manchester (Strangeways) and Coldingley Prisons*
From the report on the Work of the Prison Department (HMSO, 1977).

12. *Sir Alexander Paterson*
From S.K. Ruck (ed.), *Paterson on Prisons* (Frederick Muller, 1951).

Figures

5.1 *Plan of Ipswich County Gaol*   132

5.2 *The Panopticon*   132

5.3 *Plan of Millbank Penitentiary*   133

5.4 *Plan of Pentonville Prison*   133

7.1 *Daily average prison population, 1880-1980*   197

8.1 *Convict uniforms*   229
From the autobiography of John Lee, 1908

To our Parents, Families and Friends

PREFACE

It was typical that when it came to writing the last words, Phil was not there but was, so far as we knew, over a hundred miles away. It was also typical that we should still be divided as to the genesis of the idea for this book: whether it lay in idle talk, in the garden of the Victoria in Llanbedr one evening in the summer of 1982, about a coffee table book on prisons; or in more scholarly ambitions for a work on the prisons at Montgomery. What was clear, however, was that the whole project had only proven possible through the collaboration of the four of us, based on what each could offer about the particular period in which he was interested and the interchange of ideas on the whole subject which developed as the writing progressed. Our primary debt is therefore to each other and in that sense it is a collective work and not four separate offerings.

Having said that, we have been supported and assisted by others along the way. Hopefully the text will make it clear that we have inevitably relied, given the nature of the work, on a certain amount of primary research and observation by other writers. Also, in the course of writing, specific items were brought to our attention by Mr Robert I. Ireland of University College, London, and Dr Susan Davies of the Department of History at UCW, Aberystwyth. Our thanks should go to Mrs Eileen Price who had to endure increasing harassment over the typing of much of the manuscript in the later days of 1984; to David Jenkins of UCW Library Photographic Unit; and to the British Library and the National Library of Wales for providing facilities for research. In various ways we have received support and encouragement from others, in particular David Freestone, John Richardson, Jenny Harding, Gwyneth Owen, Non Vaughan Thomas, and Margaret Llewelyn and from the ready response to our idea by Richard Stoneman at Croom Helm.

The Aleppo Merchant, Carno, January 1985

INTRODUCTION

The history of imprisonment is a subject which has attracted attention at a number of levels and for a variety of reasons, from a humanitarian concern about the way in which offenders have been and are treated to the less intellectual urge of the child when taken to visit a castle (or indeed any suitably large and antique structure) to visit 'the dungeons' before all else. For hundreds of years men, women and children have found themselves incarcerated, and the institution of imprisonment appears at first sight to be a sturdy monolith. Yet a moment's thought must reveal that the sorts of persons imprisoned, the reasons for that imprisonment, the location and conditions of that imprisonment, and the aims and justifications behind that imprisonment may have varied over centuries and even as between decades. A proper understanding of the use of imprisonment must involve an investigation of the institution in the context of the forces which create, mould and react to it.

Yet such a subject has not, until relatively recently, been conceived of as an appropriate area of historical research. With the recent increase in interest in legal and social history and a climate which allows the present 'state of the prisons' to be shown regularly on television and discussed frequently in at least some newspapers, more work, much of it excellent, has been done on this subject. With the studies of writers such as Sean McConville, Michael Ignatieff, and the late Ralph Pugh, as well as the works of those who have themselves been involved in shaping the prison system, all available to the reader, it may be asked why the present book has been undertaken.

The answer must be that we feel that there is a place for a work which aims to bring together in one moderately sized volume a history of imprisonment from earliest times to the present, a history which is neither too detailed to deter the non-specialist nor too superficial to be of any utility. It is, we hope, a book which will prove useful to anyone with an interest in its subject-matter and it presupposes no familiarity with the topic.

Whether it succeeds in these aims is for the reader to judge. For those who seek a fuller knowledge of particular aspects of the topic a bibliographical chapter has been included at the end of the volume. Without the works of the authors mentioned therein this book could not have been written or, if it had been, would have taken more than a lifetime to write. Yet we would hope that the end product might be viewed as more than simply the abridgement of the scholarship of others, for in our utilisation of sources, both primary and secondary, we have hoped to draw our own picture and have concentrated on areas which have seemed of interest and importance to us in so doing.

This leads to a further point. This book is the work of four writers, each with his own period of interest. It is not intended simply as a collection of independent essays for the whole may be taken together to provide an overall picture. Yet it retains, of necessity, differences of style and emphasis determined by the characteristics of both the writer and the period under study. We have not attempted to produce a spurious uniformity for there is, we feel, no 'correct' way to write a history of this subject. The scheme of the book then is as follows: in Part One Richard Ireland discusses the period from Anglo-Saxon times to *c.*1500, considering not only the facts of but also the reasons for the introduction and the nature of imprisonment; in Part Two Bill Hines looks at the period from *c.*1500 to *c.*1750 and discusses the introduction of the Bridewell and related ideas of labour discipline; Part Three by Philip Rawlings covering the period from *c.*1750 to 1877 considers the development of a centralised penological philosophy and its practical effects; while Part Four by Christopher Harding discusses the rise and fall of the idea of prison as a training institution within the modern period. There then follows a short discussion chapter in which we have attempted to draw some threads together.

Some more specific points need to be made. We have limited our inquiry to the prisons of England and Wales, save for occasional comparative references. Some geographical limitation was necessary and in view of both our own expertise and our desire to produce a book of manageable length this particular limitation seemed the most desirable. Wales, of course, originally had its own legal system but our researches have been restricted to those areas under English influence. The laws of that part of Wales which formed the subject of the conquest of Edward I were assimilated to those of England in 1284 and the process of the identification was completed in the reign of Henry VIII.

Another limitation should also be noted. As will become apparent within the ensuing chapters, imprisonment occupies a shifting position amongst a larger institutional framework which has been comprised at different times of a number of different places of disposition for those categorised as properly the objects of confinement. So we will refer to hospitals, asylums, workhouses and other institutions but must of necessity provide little in the way of discussion.

It should also be noted that for reasons of style the terms 'gaol' and 'prison' have been used as synonyms. In medieval terminology the two might mean different things, the 'gaol' being that part of the building or buildings reserved for the suspect offender as opposed to the debtor or convicted trespasser. So the imaginative fugitive, Richard son of Nigel, whose fate will be discussed later, could argue in 1225 that he had escaped 'from prison' but not from 'the gaol' (see page 22). The two terms have, insofar as 'gaol' is still used at all, long been treated as meaning the same and are so treated here.

PART ONE

The Middle Ages

1
THE STRUCTURE AND ORGANISATION OF IMPRISONMENT

The Use of Imprisonment

To attempt to discover the ultimate origin of the practice of imprisonment in England and Wales is an endeavour doomed to failure if that origin is conceived of as a specific statutory enactment or an isolated example recorded in an early chronicle. For some means of detention becomes necessary as soon as disputes over wrongs come to be settled in any but the most immediate and brutal fashion. Once one suspected of wrong is to receive some form of trial rather than find himself the object of the summary judgement of his community it will be necessary to provide some form of custody to ensure his appearance at that trial. It is in this manifestation, which Pugh[1] has called its custodial aspect, that the earliest use of imprisonment is probably to be found.

Detention before trial does not, of course, imply an organised or extensive system of purpose-built gaols throughout the countryside, for a man may be held for this purpose in a house under guard, in stocks or simply bound by ropes. Moreover at a time when society attaches a great significance to the role of the small communal grouping, originally the kindred and later the village, such means of physical restraint might be supplemented by the surety system under which such group undertakes, on giving surety, to produce the suspect for trial. In such a way custodial imprisonment is replaced by group responsibility or, if physical restraint should become necessary, it will be administered by the group itself rather than by the order of a court. In one of our first legislative enactments to mention prison, a law of Cnut from the late 1020s or early 1030s, the use of custodial imprisonment pending trial is expressly reserved for the foreigner or one without friends who can find no one to stand surety for

3

him.[2] As will become clear later it is often the outsider in the locality who is the one most likely to sample its gaol.

The release of suspects upon their finding surety for appearance at trial continues even for offences of considerable gravity for many years. It is not until the latter part of the thirteenth century that steps were taken by legislation to restrict the ready availability of bail.[3] References to the institution in Norman custom as 'le vifvre prison' ('the living prison'),[4] or in the English court records of the 1240s as being a handing over of an individual to others 'quasi in prisona',[5] indicate the view that the two forms of security for appearance, custody and surety, are regarded as alternatives although the phrases perhaps indicate that a change of emphasis has taken place within the system, for chronologically it is probable that the pledge system preceded custodial imprisonment.

Both methods of pre-trial treatment of suspects are mentioned in the Assize of Clarendon in 1166, but it is in respect of imprisonment that this most important piece of legislation is particularly significant. In legal terms 1166 is a date of greater immediate significance than 1066, for the Norman Conquest, profound as its effects were in many areas of life, had been accompanied by little new law-making; indeed its legitimacy depended on the continuity of the Anglo-Saxon legal tradition. A century later, however, the precocious English bureaucratic state was able to take a more active role in directing the emerging common law. Henry II, attempting to restore order over a realm which had been split by civil war, introduced much legal change. Feudal lords were to be restrained from abusing their positions, the position of the Church clarified and, at Clarendon, the problem of crime within the country was attacked. The provisions, supplemented by those made at Northampton ten years later, overhauled the methods of prosecution and trial of criminal offences, although the main method of proof — by submission to the judgement of God in the ordeal — was retained. A system of communal prosecution of serious crime by those who represent the local community — the system which was to develop into the later indictment process — was introduced or amended and offered an effective alternative to the initiation of criminal actions by an aggrieved individual. After dealing with these matters and a number of issues concerning the arrest of suspects the Assize goes on to state:

In the several counties where there are no gaols, let such be made in a borough or some castle of the king at the king's expense and from his wood, if one shall be near, or from some neighbouring wood at the oversight of the king's servants, to the end that the sheriffs may be able to guard those who shall be arrested.[6]

The statute's demand for a gaol in every county would seem to have been taken seriously and a building programme was swiftly undertaken. Many new gaols were added to those already in existence and, with the exception of a few recalcitrant counties, the first truly national network of prisons, the county gaols, was established.[7] From this time onwards the pre-trial detention of suspect felons was facilitated, but it took another century before more legislation was introduced to improve the procedure, by a review of the administration of the bail process. The immediate background to this tightened control over the bail decision, the abuse of which remained a constant problem throughout the Middle Ages, lay in a series of investigations into the subject undertaken in 1274. These inquiries revealed considerable maladministration in both the bailing and gaoling of suspects and legislation introduced at Westminster in the following year contained a catalogue of those types of putative offender to whom bail was to be denied. Release on bail remained common, as did its abuse, but an attempt had been made, within a statute which had much to say on the subject of prisons, to systematise the procedure.[8]

Those held in gaol upon suspicion of serious crime would be confined until the arrival of the king's justices at the gaol. The justices would supervise the trial of those held within the prison, the process being known as 'Gaol Delivery', from the thirteenth century the most common, although by no means the exclusive, method of bringing felony cases to trial. The gaol delivery system gradually become better organised and in a statute of 1330 it was declared that gaols were to be delivered three times each year.[9] The rule was not always adhered to, frequency of visitation being more effectively determined by the amount of business to be attended to and the degree of efficiency shown by the officials who operated the system. Nevertheless even where the thrice-yearly rule was strictly observed it was by no means certain that the suspect's pre-trial incarceration would be restricted to a maximum period of four months, for the prisoner would be remitted to gaol by the justices in the event of any procedural irregularity such as the not infrequent default of the relevant local official. In this way we can explain cases such as those from the fourteenth century of a man held pending trial for a period of two years on a charge of horse stealing on which he was eventually acquitted,[10] or the woman held in Guildford gaol for the death of her husband for over 20 years.[11] One of the most remarkable aspects of the medieval felony trial was the very low conviction rate. Analysis of the records of the thirteenth and fourteenth centuries suggests that between 70 and 80 per cent of those tried were acquitted.[12] Unless the defendant was taken in circumstances strongly indicative of his guilt, or was a stranger to the locality and hence both a legitimate object of suspicion and a convenient scapegoat, or indeed was a cleric (for whom, as will be seen later, procedural advantages would mitigate the consequences of conviction), the chance of being found guilty would seem to have been rather slight. This fact has led Hanawalt to suggest that the pre-trial confinement of suspects, or even the bail procedure where employed, may have been regarded as sufficient punishment in itself and the death penalty or mutilation, the appropriate legal sanctions for convicted felons, seen as an unnecessary further step.[13] The thesis is supported by the fact that conviction rates in the lay courts for clerics, on whom no death sentence could be imposed, were considerably higher, Hanawalt's own figure from her study of the early fourteenth century being 64 per cent.[14] Contemporary evidence as early as the mid-thirteenth century compilation of law known to us as '*Bracton*' similarly suggests at one point that pre-trial detention may be regarded as a 'punishment'.[15] If this argument is correct then the simple division which is often drawn between custodial and punitive imprisonment breaks down and a more widespread role than traditionally assigned for imprisonment as a punishment for even the most serious offences, the felonies, becomes apparent. That this was found acceptable in the thirteenth and fourteenth centuries, and the death penalty generally reserved for only the most notorious or suspicious felons, will also help to explain the growth in the use of punitive imprisonment in other areas as the Middle Ages progress.

What then of punitive imprisonment? To the reader whose understanding of imprisonment is largely in punitive terms a survey of the institution which begins with a discussion of the use of prison as pre-trial custody must look rather strange. Yet the use of imprisonment as a punishment for wrong is something which requires far more explanation than its use as a temporary detention for those awaiting trial. There are, to the medieval mind, much simpler and less expensive methods of dealing with someone who has confessed to or been found guilty of a crime. He may be disposed of, by execution or by being forced to leave the community; he may be incapacitated, by mutilation, the marks of which will provide a constant and public reminder of his offence; he may be made to pay money, either as compensation for his wrong or as a penalty; or, if his liberty is to be deprived, then this may be done in such a way that a tangible benefit is conferred upon someone, that is to say he may be enslaved. All these penalties were available before the Norman Conquest and all but the last long survived it. But lest it be assumed that post-Conquest England had a particularly highly developed notion of personal freedom, in the deprivation of which we see our modern notion of punitive imprisonment, it must be remembered that long after slavery ceased to exist the condition of villeinage, which bore with it rights in the lord to reclaim, by writ of naifty, the runaway villein, continued throughout the medieval period.

However this may be, it is clear that imprisonment was used as a punishment throughout the Middle Ages in England, and indeed it is in this guise that we come across our first legislative mention of the subject, in a law of Alfred dating from 892-3.[16] Imprisonment is prescribed in this law for one who breaks a pledge, and sits beside the more usual Saxon punishments, the payment of compensation ('wergild') and mutilation. During the tenth century royal control over crime was seen to increase and afflictive punishments, death or mutilation, gained ground at the expense of the idea of compensation. In this context a law of Aethelstan (who ruled from 925-39) which arose from a council at Whittlebury is noteworthy, for it uses imprisonment as a lighter form of punishment for juvenile thieves since the King, we are told, 'thinks it cruel to put to death such young people for such slight offences, as he has learned is the practice everywhere'.[17] The enactment recognises that a prison may not be available and accordingly makes alternative provision should this be the case. A feature of Aethelstan's use of imprisonment both for theft and other offences is that where it is enjoined an added requirement is imposed, namely that surety is to be given for future good conduct. Prison then is to be a penalty, but it is not to stand as the sole consequence of conviction.

The incidence of punitive imprisonment in post-Conquest England has been well charted by Pugh,[18] who notes the use of this punishment in cases involving the abuse of legal process and the breach of an oath, the latter recalling the purport of the law of Alfred mentioned earlier. For the most serious form of crime, felony, a term which was applicable to wrongs such as homicide, arson, major theft, etc., the penalty on conviction, as has been seen, was to be death or mutilation either by amputation of a hand or foot, exoculation or castration. The notion of felony incorporated not only a repetition of the old Anglo-Saxon list of unemendable offences (the so-called 'botleas' crimes), it also overlaid them with a feudal significance and an eminently feudal consequence; the convicted felon's land reverting to his feudal lord. Interestingly the legislation of Edward I (1272-1307), which in other areas both marked and sealed the end of the reality of English feudalism, was also to act as an impetus to the significant increase in the use of punitive imprisonment in the later Middle Ages. New offences are created by the statutes of Edward I and his successors and penalties had to be prescribed — in many cases it is imprisonment which is the favoured measure. The statute of Westminster I of 1275, the bail provisions of which have been mentioned earlier, may perhaps be regarded as the first great imprisoning statute. It introduces the penalty for new offences such as the wrongful taking of goods from wrecked ships or the spreading of seditious slanders and regulates its application in a number of other areas.[19] The new statutory applications of punitive imprisonment did not go unnoticed by contemporaries. The archly conservative author of our first book of legal criticism, *The Mirror of Justices*, written around 1290, is highly critical of the imprisoning provisions of this statute.[20] Nevertheless the practice of using penal imprisonment for new statutory offences continues. Although not by any means a purely statutory phenomenon, as witnessed by its development for such offences as petty theft and other forms of indictable trespass which are finding their way into the common law having once been matters of purely local interest, penal imprisonment, the statute and the developed centralised legal system reach maturity at the same time. New offences, of some gravity but outside the list of the ancient, feudally tinged felonies can be introduced and the law, by now confident of its system of gaols can provide an appropriate sanction.

To detail all the various types of offence for which the penalty of imprisonment is laid down by statutory provisions in the years following the statute of Westminster I would be an enormous, and rather tedious, exercise. Moreover it must be stressed that to declare that an offence is punishable under statute by imprisonment tells us nothing about the practical results of that change in the law — the number of prosecutions actually brought and their *de facto* dispositions. To discover such results would prove to be an even more daunting task and one which cannot be attempted here. Nevertheless it is proper to give a few examples of statutory provisions as illustration. In 1300 imprisonment is regarded as an appropriate punishment for breach of the two seminal medieval documents, the Great Charter and the Charter of the Forest, where no remedy had been provided 'by the Common Law'.[21] Official corruption and market offences are frequent precursors to the penalty, while of particular note is the economic and labour legislation following the Black Death of the mid-fourteenth century. Although experts may debate the precise effects of this catastrophe there can be no doubt that the labour shortage which allowed labourers to leave their customary employment and to demand increased payments was the reason for legislation which sought to prevent these activities. Wrong-doers are to be punished by imprisonment or in the stocks, which a statute of 1351 decrees are to be built in every town.[22] Later statutes still further extend the possibilities of imprisonment into other areas so that, for example, by the beginning of the fifteenth century it is laid down as the appropriate penalty for unlawfully playing football or dice.[23]

For felony, however, punitive imprisonment remained throughout the period, in theory at any rate, not applicable, and even when mutilation had given way to the standard execution by hanging no attempt was made to introduce a custodial alternative. In practice, however, many felons did find themselves in gaol in the Middle Ages. The theory that incarceration pending trial may have been seen as a *de facto* punishment in itself has already been alluded to. In this context the administrative instructions issued by Henry III in 1219 should also be noted. In 1215 the Church, doubting both the practical efficacy and the theological rectitude of the ordeal as a means of establishing truth, had withdrawn its support from the procedure. In the ensuing confusion Henry III's government had been obliged to introduce an emergency measure to deal with those suspects who could not be tried since no alternative to the ordeal presented itself. Imprisonment was ordered for those who were accused of grave crimes and suspected of being guilty.[24] Technically the suspect remained unconvicted and the procedure is merely an extension of the remand process. When the trial jury was introduced to fill the gap left by the ordeal its use remained, however, contingent upon the consent of the accused, for he must waive his right to be tried by God in favour of the determination of his fellow men. For those who refused to 'put themselves upon their country' but who were gravely suspect a remand to gaol remained the appropriate measure and, as will be shown later, the provision in the Statute of Westminster I to this effect comes to be understood as a licence for gaolers to torture their unconvicted charges.[25] At this point mention may also be made of those felons who were imprisoned either before or after trial awaiting the readily available royal pardon. Such pardons might be granted as an acknowledgment of the limited nature of the wrongdoer's responsibility for his deed or from more base, financial or military, motives.[26]

A third way in which one responsible for felony might find himself in gaol rather than suffering capital punishment was by the operation of the doctrine of benefit of the clergy.[27] The Church claimed for itself the right to discipline its own members and this right had been maintained despite the dispute between Henry II and Thomas Becket over the Constitutions of Clarendon of 1164. In later years the lay court would itself take a preliminary finding of guilt in cases where clergy was claimed but the individual would thereafter be handed to the Church for trial by that authority and, if convicted, for punishment. The Church would not announce a sentence of death or mutilation and a convicted clerk would be stripped of his orders and imprisoned for life within the bishop's prison. It is clear that as the Middle Ages progress the number of persons making use of the plea of benefit of the clergy is increasing. The test of eligibility for the plea was relaxed from the original requirement that the accused be a clerk in holy orders, to cover all who had taken the tonsure and finally to anyone who was literate. The literacy test was regarded as sufficient proof of clerical status probably by the middle of the fourteenth century and although literacy by that time was not particularly widespread it was steadily increasing towards the end of that century and throughout the next. Evidence of the type of person claiming clergy by the end of the fourteenth century is revealed when the trades of those making the plea are recorded and include even the description 'vaca-bund'.[28] That the ability to read might also be effectively simulated may be gathered from a celebrated case from the time of Edward III where the defendant showed the remarkable capacity to 'read' equally well no matter which way up the bible was presented to him.[29] It would appear then that until the procedure was subjected to the scrutiny of Henry VII the plea of clergy and the prison sentence which attended a consequent finding of guilt were being increasingly used simply as a means of evading the death penalty. Yet the conviction rates of those who appeared before the ecclesiastical courts (as opposed to the preliminary finding by the jury in the lay court) were very low and again practices developed to ensure that considerable prison terms were nevertheless served in appropriate cases. Again we find long remands in custody before purgation, cases suggesting that these might be as long as 14 years, and even the practice of the temporal court handing over the offender with the request or instruction that he should not be allowed to purgation at all.[30]

Acquaintance with the abuses of their position practised by medieval gaolers will illustrate that there were few opportunities for profit which were spurned by them. So it is that we find gaolers in lay prisons implicated in attempts by their charges to take advantage of the clergy system, presumably in return for payment. The man who had 'read' the upside-down bible had in fact been instructed by two boys whom the gaoler had allowed to visit him and Edward III's justices were asked to inquire as to whether gaolers had been providing prisoners with lessons in literacy.[31] Earlier evidence from the reign of Edward I when the tonsure was regarded as a necessary requirement of the condition of clergymen suggests that at least some gaolers were willing to allow tonsures to be given, or even perform the operation themselves, while the prisoner awaited trial in their custody.[32]

In cases of convicted felonious clerics the penalty, as stated earlier, was life imprisonment. This had been laid down for those who had acted otherwise than by accident or in the heat of the moment or who were insane by Archbishop Boniface at a council of the province of Canterbury at Lambeth in May 1261.[33] Secular punitive imprisonment differed in length in accordance with the offence and statutory provisions mention a number of different periods. Anglo-Saxon legislation mentions terms of 40 and 120 days and these sentence lengths recur later. The period of a year and a day is one which is used in a number of areas of medieval law and it is unsurprising that it should have become a popular term for punitive prison sentences. Very common, however, was the sentence of an indefinite period in prison followed by a fine or ransom. 'Fine' in this sense means a payment offered to terminate confinement, to bring to a conclusion the dispute with the king. The combination of the custodial and financial penalty is to be found as early as Aethelstan's legislation but the use of an indefinite term of detention in this context in later years has led to the suggestion that the prison term was at the least merely seen as a mode of ensuring payment of the money — the real penalty contemplated — and at the most as entirely fictitious. Pugh has shown that certainly the incarceration was not in all cases a fiction and had a genuine punitive role.[34]

The possibility of imprisonment of persons in order to bring pressure upon them to do something else, such as pay a sum of money, brings us to a consideration of imprisonment for civil debt, for this is generally categorised as 'coercive' imprisonment in this sense.[35] Whilst this may prove to be a convenient pigeon hole, however, it should not be treated as any more than that. Certainly, as will become apparent, the man imprisoned for civil debt is regarded as a different sort of prisoner from the suspect or convicted criminal and will be kept separately, and certainly the debtors conditions could be, in relative terms, quite comfortable, but a desire to register opprobrium for, and to discourage by extending the threat of confinement to, the debtor should not be overlooked. Insofar as the use of the term 'coercive imprisonment' invites us to ignore such matters it should be resisted.

It will be necessary at this point to hazard some ideas about the origin of the practice of imprisonment for civil debt, for it is even more difficult to explain conceptually than punitive imprisonment. The total of human misery which was produced over the centuries by the basic illogicality of requiring a man to pay off a debt while at the same time placing him in a position which both increases his indebtedness and diminishes his capacity for gaining money, is enormous. The practice of imprisoning debtors is found described as an established system in the *Dialogus de Scaccario* written around 1178,[36] but these are only crown debtors, for whom elements of affront to royal dignity or possible corruption or incompetence in office would seem to demand a severe penalty. An extension in the use of imprisonment for debt did not come about for another century and again it comes in the reign of Edward I. Edward's reign saw a reversal in policy towards the presence of foreign merchants, whose numbers were increasing and whose money was recognised by Edward as an important source of finance for his extensive military campaigns. In April 1266 Edward had been granted control over foreign merchants and neither he, nor his influential Chancellor Robert Burnell, can have been unaware of the merchants' recurrent problem of enforcing their debts. It was to their problems that the first extension of civil imprisonment was directed. The immediate impetus for the Statute of Acton Burnell (generally dated as 1283, ascribed by Powicke to the Michaelmas parliament 1284) and its successor the Statute of Merchants of 1285 may well have been the process of accounting which had been ordered by Edward after a dispute over seized goods with Guy of Dampierre, a Fleming. Under the treaty of Montreuil-sur-Mare (1275) which had ended the dispute the king had enforced his claims to the debt by imprisoning several hostages. The subsequent cases before the auditors took many years to settle and it is possible that the reference of one of them to the royal justices was the spur to the issuing of the Statute of Acton Burnell,[37] which introduced the same penalty for the non payment of registered mercantile debts as had been used under the original treaty. The statute seems to have been a failure and to have needed clarification and amendment by the 1285 enactment. The Statute of Merchants[38] introduced immediate imprisonment for the defaulting debtor where its precursor had used the measure only as a last resort. The same parliament which saw the enactment of Statute of Merchants was also responsible for the Statute of Westminster II[39] which allowed the committal to gaol of one who stood in an accountable relationship — one, that is, who managed another's property — once a balance had been found due by auditors. This again recalls the activity under the Montreiul treaty and may also, as Plucknett suggests, have given legal authority for a mode of disciplining managers which landowners had already shown an inclination to employ extra-legally.

None of the above measures introduced imprisonment generally for the civil debtor, they dealt only with particular types of debt, those registered by merchants or those owed by persons in a position of trust. The more general step was not taken until the next century when in 1352 a terse passage in a statute recited a simple procedural change, extending the account process to matters of debt, which concealed a fundamental step in the history of imprisonment.[40] Again the context of the enactment should be noted. In the wake of the economic upheaval caused by plague it was part of another flurry of economic legislation which saw imprisonment used for a number of economic offences, for debts connected with the Staple and to control the wandering poor.

Philosophies of Crime and Punishment

In the foregoing discussion it has been necessary to consider the reasons behind the introduction of imprisonment into different roles within the legal system. It remains to consider whether there was in the medieval period any overall philosophical aim or justification for the practice, for this is a preoccupation of writers and administrators of later eras. A problem clearly exists in taking the period as a whole for it is, as has been hinted at above, one of momentous social change. The decline in the reality of feudalism, the decline in villeinage, an increasing individualism and secularisation of the later Middle Ages, the social and economic changes of the fourteenth century; all these are factors which must have affected the way in which institutions generally and the institution of imprisonment were regarded.

Some general comments, however, may be justified in our search for medieval criminological and penal theory. It has been suggested that the rationale for pre-trial detention was largely pragmatic, and that for imprisonment for debt is partly coercive but also partly retributive and deterrent. These terms are, of course, those of the modern legal theorist not the medieval one, yet only the terminology is sophisticated — there is no reason to doubt that the concepts behind the terms were familiar in the Middle Ages. Our search for a philosophy behind penal imprisonment leads us in the first place to look for any attempt within the period to discover the origins of criminal behaviour which might have had a bearing on penal philosophy. As to any such criminological speculation writers such as McConville and, to a lesser extent, Bellamy are dismissive, the former remarking, 'even to the church, with its total concern for spiritual life, crime was not a phenomenon requiring explanation : it was an inevitable feature of man's fallen state.'[41] There is an important truth here in the identification of crime and sin, but to the medieval mind sin was something rather more than an unsavoury monolith. The records of both pictorial art (as with the tradition of representation of 'trees' of virtue or vice) and of literature (as exemplified by fourteenth-century texts such as *Ayenbite of Inwyt*) show considerable interest in the cataloguing of the various vices and virtues which could mar or guide human life. From the pulpits of the fourteenth-century preachers the old feudal sin of pride and the new commercial sin of avarice as well as more concrete failings such as drunkenness were inveighed against,[42] while even before that date influential theologians had linked poverty and crime.[43] Nor should we see in this concentration on sin by the Church a tendency in any way to marginalise its importance, particularly in the early Middle Ages. Sin and the theorising about its causes and consequences are a matter for that part of the duality of the medieval state which concerned itself with both the soul and the process of speculation. From that part of the duality which had care of the body, the temporal authority, we have little philosophy on such subjects; that was, quite simply, not its job. To recognise this, however, is not to go so far as to say that medieval man, educated if at all by the Church and, even if not, taking its preaching as regularly as a newspaper, would, if asked about the roots of crime, have responded with blank incomprehension or the unelaborated answer 'Original sin'.

This much said, however, it must be admitted that there is, as McConville asserts,[44] little in the way of a consistent idea that punishment could act as a corrective to vice in the sense of being a reformatory experience. This at any rate would seem to have been true of the secular domain, a fact which is not surprising in view of the above comments. In the thirteenth century there is some evidence of explicit measures which may have been aimed at moral improvement or at the least at expiation for sin but these take the form of exemptions from punishment, pardons being granted on condition that the offender should enter a monastery or go on a pilgrimage to the Holy Land.[45] But in terms of the punishments imposed the correction of vice would seem to have been of little concern to the lay authority. Church services were, as will be seen later, available to some prisoners but the incarceration itself would provide, in fact or in theory, little scope for moral improvement. Solitary confinement, which might (as was certainly believed at a later date) have acted as an aid to contemplation and penance was used only exceptionally in lay prisons. With respect to ecclesiastical and certain monastic imprisonment the penance notion does receive some articulation. In 1444 the Benedictine order laid down that imprisoned monks should be provided with service books.[46] Evidence of the effects of contemplation in a widely illiterate society is, of course, difficult to detect but Boethius, whose *Consolation of Philosophy*, written in prison, was an important medieval text which had been copied in England, had few English equivalents. The papal chaplain Amaury de Montfort, imprisoned by his cousin Edward I at Corfe Castle in 1276, did write treatises on theology there.[47] Other authors who used their time in prison as an opportunity or inspiration to write seem to have been more secular in aim. The legal treatise 'Fleta' of the late thirteenth century purports to have been written in the Fleet prison[48] (although this may be no more than literary artifice) whilst James I of Scotland imprisoned in the fifteenth century found the experience conducive to writing love poems.[49]

If reformation was not seen as a likely or intended consequence of confinement then deterrence and retribution certainly would seem to have so been. Statutes, notably that of Westminster I, the importance of which for purposes of penal policy has already been noted, are sometimes avowedly deterrent in aim while it would seem that, whilst flagrant abuses by the gaoler were to be discouraged, the prisoner was felt to deserve an unpleasant fate for his transgressions.

One other justification for the practice of imprisonment needs to be mentioned here, and it is one which we will see surfacing again at different periods. This is the segregation model based on a contamination theory of antisocial conduct which occasionally surfaces in medieval writing. This theory, that the prisoner is like one who is diseased and therefore should be kept apart from other members of the community, may be seen not only as a concept used to explain imprisonment itself but also as, partially at any rate, the reason behind the segregation between different classes of prisoner within the gaol. The author of the *Mirror of Justices* writes of mortal sin as a kind of leprosy, 'and in order that the innocent may not be tainted with their sins, gaols were ordained in all the counties, so that mortal sinners might be put there to await their judgements'.[50] Similar infection terminology is found in talking of a heretic who had left Leicester gaol after incarceration there in 1385[51] and with regard to disobedient inmates within the regulations of the medieval Chichester hospital.[52]

The Variety and Administration of Prisons[53]

A startling feature, to modern eyes, of the medieval practice of imprisonment is the sheer number of prisons in existence together with the variety of those people who might hold a prison. The county gaols have already been referred to and these were under the control of the sheriffs, the lynchpins of royal administration in the shire, although the actual work of custody of the gaol was delegated to common gaolers. Later as the Crown sought to increase its participation in the conferment of lesser as well as greater government offices the gaoler himself was directly nominated by the Crown, the tenure being conferred, often, for life, a practice not guaranteed to obviate the risks of abuse of position to which the medieval gaoler was prone. The castle building of the Anglo-Norman period often provided a natural base for a gaol in the county town, but the actual place of confinement was unlikely, in the normal run of things, to be within the fabric of the actual castle building itself but would be in huts or cages within the castle yard.

Franchisal prisons also formed part of the medieval system and these too might be housed within castles. A feature of the early English legal system was that it was regarded as a source of revenue for both Crown and private individual alike. The profits of justice had in part financed the military campaigns of Richard I and a chronicler remarked of Edward I that he 'caused justice to be done upon malefactors and . . . gained great treasure by it'.[54]

From Anglo-Saxon times jurisdictional franchises had been granted to individual landowners by the Crown thereby leaving local peacekeeping to a local man who received in return both profit and prestige. Some of these franchises concerned criminal law and the right to jurisdiction over offences conferred, according to the text of '*Bracton*', the right to detain suspects within a gaol.[55] The gaoler would be appointed by the lord of the franchise but the prison was not on that account regarded as being outside the royal system of justice. Indeed from the middle of the thirteenth century the increasing uniformity in the administration of the developed common law was reducing the significance of the franchise gaols, which from this time onwards were delivered by royal justices. Franchise prisons were known as late as the nineteenth century but in reality, save for a few liberties held by ecclesiastics, their heyday had been in the early Middle Ages.

Outside particular jurisdictional franchises the simple fact of feudal lordship bore with it the right to hold a court for the lord's tenants and the right to punish villein tenants for such offences as breach of manorial customs. Details of this area of imprisonment remain obscure and it is possible that confinement was more often in the stocks than in any manorial prison proper although this latter was certainly possible, particularly in the early part of the period. The practice decayed as the social structure which created it, the feudal notion of villeinage, disappeared, this institution being already regarded as an anachronism by the fifteenth century.

Mention has already been made of bishop's prisons, for it is in these that clerks convicted of serious offences were held. Bishops are mentioned as having a role to play in directing the process of imprisonment in Alfred's ninth-century law and it is not until some time after the Conquest that the maturity of both lay and ecclesiastical jurisdictions divided the system of administration of justice. The provincial council at Canterbury in 1261 instructed each bishop to provide one or two prisons within the diocese.[56] Compared with the treatment of felonious clerks the use of bishop's prisons for lesser offences is less clear. They certainly held errant clergymen and heretical preachers, jurisdiction over these classes of miscreant being confirmed by statutes of the fifteenth century,[57] but having in both cases a longer pedigree. A statute of Bishop William Poore for the diocese of Salisbury dating from around 1217 prescribes 'penitence in prison' for clerks who desert their orders,[58] whilst a religious fanatic, a layman, was ordered to be 'immured', presumably in an ecclesiastical prison, by a provincial council at Oxford in 1222.[59] The main stress for the bishops' prisons however came with the imprisonment of Lollards in the late fourteenth and early fifteenth centuries, so much so that in 1428 the bishops were obliged to ask monasteries to receive heretics into their prisons.[60] Interestingly a more common ecclesiastical punishment, one which would seem to have held less terror for wrongdoers as time went on, depended for its ultimate enforcement upon imprisonment but imprisonment directed by the temporal arm. This was excommunication and the procedure employed was known as 'Significavit', under which an excommunicate who refused to make peace with the Church could be gaoled by the sheriff.

In the last paragraph and also in the discussion of the philosophy of imprisonment as the occasion for contrition mention has been made of monastic imprisonment. Prisons within monasteries for the correction of monks who had committed grave offences existed throughout the Middle Ages from at least around the time of the Conquest. A small sunken room, of uncertain date, in the Saxon foundation at Wearmouth may be an early example.[61] The major monastic orders certainly prescribed imprisonment for delinquents and the English Benedictines expressly state in 1343 that there should be a prison in every monastery, and nuns too might be imprisoned.[62] As Pugh points out a monk not only ran the risk of incarceration within his own monastery but might also be transferred to another house; the priory of Earl's Colne was serving as a penitentiary in 1303. Amongst the more celebrated monastic prisoners was Bishop Pecock, who has been desribed as 'the most gifted theologian of fifteenth-century England', who was condemned for heresy in 1457 and spent the rest of his life in Thorney Abbey confined to one room without writing materials.[63]

In most towns provision would be made for the imprisonment of wrongdoers of the locality and even villages might have a lock-up for minor offenders and vagrants. Fourteenth-century legislation in addition stated that all towns should be equipped with stocks, as will be seen later. Prisons were commonly granted in charters to boroughs which would hold their own courts and enforce their own customs. Particular prison accommodation for citizens of the borough might be laid down within the charter to preserve them from the common gaol.[64] As McConville states 'the exact division of labour in the running of the gaols between

the mayor, corporation, town justices and sheriffs varied greatly'
from town to town.[65] London, with its own system of courts and
procedure, is equally well known for its famous municipal prison,
Newgate. In many respects a concentration on London prisons, a
concentration which is tempting for the records are full and
interesting, may mislead for the regulation, indeed even the
population, of the establishments within the city are not typical of
the country as a whole. A few words only will be devoted to the
subject here; further details must be sought elsewhere.[66] Newgate
indeed, which was in existence in the twelfth century, did not
remain simply a large municipal gaol of the sort to be found in
other large towns for it takes a number of important classes of
special prisoners; traitors, prisoners of war and approvers, i.e.
confessed felons seeking to escape execution by accusing others
of complicity in their crimes.

Other London prisons may be equally briefly mentioned.
Ludgate gaol held freemen of the city either on account of
trespass or of debt, and in so doing allowed Newgate to develop
predominantly as a place for containing those accused of serious
crime. Ludgate was opened around 1378 but closed temporarily
on occasions, most notably in 1419 when it was regarded as too
comfortable and its inmates transferred to Newgate where many
died. Another London prison capable of providing a relatively
comfortable confinement (John Paston described it in the
fifteenth century as a 'feyir preson',[67] which is just as well, for he
was himself confined there three times) was the Fleet. This was a
stone building in existence from around 1130 and subsequently
surrounded by a moat. In its mature years the Fleet was
particularly important as a gaol for debtors although its clientele
remained particularly diverse. The Tower of London also
deserves mention for it too served as a place of confinement from
the twelfth century. Although in the thirteenth century it had
been used to hold common suspect felons this side of its work
declined, as that of Newgate grew, and the Tower secured itself a
rather different place in history, as the place of incarceration for
political prisoners, both important individuals, such as the
various kings, English and others, who spent time there, and also
particular groups whose isolation and confinement were important to the Crown, such as religious dissenters and popular
rebels. Other London prisons whose inmates attracted less
celebrity were the two Counters and the Tun.

The Structure and Security of Prisons

By no means all medieval prisons were as impressive as the moated Fleet, the old Roman gatehouse of Newgate or the splendid Tower of London. We have seen that castles were often natural sites for county or franchise gaols but that often the gaol itself would be found within the castle yard rather than within the fabric of the building. Certainly particularly important prisoners would be confined within a castle turret and there is some evidence to indicate that those particularly skilled at prison breach might find themselves actually within the building.[68] As Pugh points out the increasing redundancy of castle buildings as centres of military defence acted as a boost for their use as prisons, although even in areas of the realm which remained militarily insecure castles were used to house felons, as for example at Conwy (Conway) and Chester. Records of account of the Chamberlain of Chester of 1301 describe four separate places of confinement within the castle, a gaol called 'Gowestour' holds a thief, there is a 'Dungun', a 'large new chamber', and a place where Scottish prisoners were held apart.[69]

Structures placed within the castle yard need not have been made of stone. It will be recalled that the Assize of Clarendon had envisaged wooden buildings and the use of wood continued in prison, as of course it did in lay architecture for many years. Indeed although many prisons were purpose built it should be stressed that in early years the 'prison' may be no more than a room set aside for the purpose in another building. The records reveal the pressing of existing buildings into service as accommodation for prisoners particularly within smaller towns. In 1306-7 by the custom of Havering men of the village guarded prisoners who were kept in each of their houses in turn,[70] in Faversham in 1254 thieves were guarded by men of the town who held them in the mill.[71] In 1331-2 the Archbishop of Canterbury was renting a (private) house for use as a prison.[72] The important King's Bench prison presented particular security problems for it was initially itinerant, as was the court it served, and prisoners would be taken from place to place by cart. A statute of 1331 refers to the Marshals of the King's Bench placing prisoners within houses ('mesons') in assigned towns.[73]

It may be gathered from the above that security might be a problem with regard to medieval imprisonment. Certainly in an age when 'housebreaking' meant exactly what it said premises such as those described above would have to be well guarded to prevent escape. Yet not only from such relatively vulnerable gaols but also from the supposedly more secure London prisons such as Newgate, escapes, or attempts at escape, were not infrequent. In 1285, for example, four prisoners escaped onto the roof of Newgate, apparently taking a woman with them as hostage.[74] The most remarkable medieval escaper must surely be Richard son of Nigel, whose case appears in the Curia Regis roll for 1225[75] and whose story displays not only a brilliant imagination but also the material weakness and lack of supervision within even a stone-built prison. Richard, being examined in court after he has made some serious allegations against three others, admits having escaped from Oxford prison, apparently simply by walking out, because, he said, prison was bad for him. He was imprisoned in Northampton gaol where, he said, after a long period in solitary confinement had badly affected him, he believed that the devil had appeared to him in the form of a diseased monk and he had pulled stones out of the wall in order to defend himself with them. It was discovered that he had attempted to break out in three places, removing respectively a bowl full, a wheelbarrow full and a cartload of stones! How his diabolical adversary fared in the encounter we are not told; Richard is drawn and hanged.

It was because of physical weakness in the fabric of prisons that irons were placed on prisoners or the stocks used to provide extra security. It would be idle to pretend that these were invariably effective. Richard son of Nigel, although he had not been in irons at Oxford had, at Northampton, broken the staple of a chain which secured him to a block. In 1220 John Blakeman, removed to a tower in Canterbury after almost escaping from the deepest part of the prison, managed to break out of it notwithstanding three pairs of fetters.[76] Nevertheless the use of irons was a constant feature of medieval imprisonment. The author of *Britton*, writing around 1290, allows them to be used for suspect felons, trespassers in parks and defaulting accountants for which latter category their application had been sanctioned by the 1285 statute.[77] The generic term 'irons' covers a variety of implements attached to various parts of the body. An early manuscript illustration of Boethius produced in the West of England shows the use of a neckchain,[78] whilst a correspondent of the Pastons,

John Perse, claimed to be 'feterid worse than ever I was and manacled in the hands by daye and nyghte'.[79] Gaolers would in certain circumstances take payments for the removal of irons, although reality was soon to become formula and reasonable bargain even sooner to become extortion. In London prison regulations were made on a number of occasions to prevent abuses with regard to the imposition of irons,[80] although as we shall see London was often in advance of the rest of the country in its penal regulations.

Stocks too were in use within prisons as they were outside. It has been seen that stocks were to be erected in all towns by legislation of 1351 in connection with labouring offences and they might still apparently be pressed into service to hold suspect felons. In the fifteenth century we learn from a letter of Margaret Paston that a parson and others who had killed a man had been set in the stocks to await transfer to London for trial.[81] Within the prison stocks were employed both inside and outside the prison building both presumably as a punishment and also as an extra security against escape. The 1301 Chester record shows payment for materials and workmen for the construction of 'four pairs of great wooden stocks' for the 'secure custody' of the prisoners held within the four rooms.[82] Stocks, it should perhaps be observed, were hardly the comfortable pieces of apparatus suggested by their cosy retirement outside village pubs or their place in historical comedy films. We learn in 1384 that prisoners had died from being placed in the stocks in winter time at Salisbury[83] and putrefaction of the feet was a not infrequent occurrence. A case from the time of Henry III shows that a man and a woman, after such confinement, were left with an aggregate of one foot.[84]

Lay prisons were not the only medieval institutions to make use of the stocks. The bishop's prison at Hereford in the fifteenth century contained, *inter alia*, stocks, iron collars, 'armeboltis et neckcheynes'.[85] Hospitals too might use stocks both to discipline their inmates and as a security measure. It was presumably for reasons of restraint that an inventory of 1398 lists the holding within Bethlehem hospital of 'vi cheynes de Iren, com vi Lokkes, Item iiij peir manacles de Iren, ij peir stokkys'.[86]

Escapes from prison nevertheless continued and there were penalties to be exacted from both the escaper and from the keeper of the prison who had allowed the escape. In the laws of

Alfred the escaper is to be returned to gaol, or, if he is not recaptured he is to be banished 'and excommunicated from all the churches of Christ'.[87] Escapes of suspect felons from the king's gaol were in later years treated more harshly and would result in a death sentence being imposed on them. This was not as a result of prison breach being regarded initially as a discrete felony but rather as an expression of guilt of the crime with which the accused was charged, the suspect becoming treated as a manifest criminal. In 1295 a statute established that prison breach in itself was not automatically to result in death but only where the crime for which the suspect is held is a capital one.[88] A statute of 1423, following two instances of traitors escaping, stated that one accused of treason who escaped should be treated as convicted of that offence.[89] Escape from a franchise gaol is not, according to *Britton*, to be treated as a felony, a part perhaps of a late thirteenth century move to run down the importance of franchise gaols as places of confinement for those accused of pleas of the crown.[90] For debtors, by virtue of the 1295 statute, and for clerks convict who broke out of the bishop's prison, by virtue of the clerical refusal to join in judgements of blood, no death penalty could be inflicted. Presumably in such cases, as apparently also was the case occasionally with suspect felons, notwithstanding the above, irons and stocks and a more secure confinement would seem to have combined both an incapacitatory and a punitive function. Certainly the prisoners who broke out of Newgate in 1456 are said to have been 'sore ponysshed with Iryns and ffetyrs'.[91] In a case of a non-felonious escaper of 1292 we find that the time spent in gaol by the prisoner was to count for nothing and he is moved to another gaol to begin the term again.[92]

The person charged wih the duty of custody of the prison, often the sheriff but sometimes the gaoler himself or even an entire community, would be punished for the escape of a prisoner. *Fleta* also suggests that other prisoners within the gaol, even if they were blameless, should be held liable unless they had intended to hinder the escape.[93] From the custodians a money penalty was often extracted, £5 being a common sum although more severe punishment was suggested, perhaps in passages which are more prescriptive than descriptive, by the authors of some treatises for certain types of escape, particularly those in which the gaoler himself was implicated. That gaolers could on occasion be induced to risk a penalty to assist an escape is clear. The fourteenth-century preacher John Bromyard tells of a case in which officials connived at the transposition of names and clothing of two prisoners to ensure the escape of a guilty man.[94] Bishops were more heavily punished for escape of their charges who had, after all, already been convicted. £100 was seen as the appropriate sum in their case. Whilst there is no doubt that such financial penalties were intended to punish errant custodians there is also some evidence to suggest that they were regarded as simply another way of raising money for the Crown from the administration of justice. Escape fines might also be pardoned, not merely in specific instances but also generally as a fiscal privilege towards a class who might be the targets for other drains on their finance imposed by the Crown. A statute of 1380, for example, granted a pardon to the clergy and the commons 'for the great charges which they have had and suffered by the wars and other matter'.[95]

In the case of civil debtors the keeper of the prison was to be liable for the debt if the debtor escaped. This, like imprisonment for debt itself, was a matter regulated by statute. The Statute of Merchants had introduced the possibility that the gaoler might be liable for debts within its compass while the Statute of Westminster II which allowed the imprisonment of accountants provided that sheriffs or gaolers who allowed them out should be liable. In 1377 the Warden of the Fleet was made liable for the debt of anyone whom he allowed out of his custody and he was also to lose his office, though when the liability provision for simple debt was extended to other prisons is unclear.[96] Finally a statute of 1455 allowed executors to claim the sum of £400 from gaolers who allowed the escape of a servant who had taken his master's goods on the death of the master and been imprisoned on that account.[97]

The preceding discussion has used the notion of 'escape' and it will probably be imagined that this entailed a breaking out of confinement. This is, of course, the standard case but there are also a number of cases of persons breaking into a gaol to rescue those confined within it. This might be a purely personal matter, with a prisoner's friend, accomplices or retainers effecting a breach, or it might be more widespread. That gaols were regarded, at least on certain occasions, as symbols of unjust laws is evinced by their status as targets in a number of popular uprisings. The Peasants' Revolt of 1381 saw considerable prison breaking together with the destruction of legal records, another symbol of legal authority. One of the first acts of the rebels was to free an imprisoned villein at Rochester whilst the celebrated preacher John Ball was released from the Archbishop's prison at Canterbury. The London prisons were then attacked and opened and the keeper of the Marshalsea prison, Richard Imworth, was dragged out of sanctuary for execution.[98] Similarly in 1450 Jack Cade's revolt was the occasion for the opening of the King's Bench and Marshalsea prisons and of a riot in Newgate which caused considerable damage and led to the keeper of that prison being dismissed and imprisoned. It may have been in an attempt to ensure that prison breaking should go no further that a fine of £4,000 was declared to be payable by the custodian of three of Cade's men should they escape.[99]

Finance

Under the general heading of finance must be examined the financing of the construction and maintenance of prison buildings, the source of payment to those charged with the running of the gaol and finally the way in which prisoners' food and accommodation was paid for. The inquiry will demand more than a simple recital of facts specifically applicable to the prison system but will entail rather a more general understanding of medieval notions of government, office holding and charity.

We must consider firstly the financing and maintenance of prison buildings. Under the 1166 Assize of Clarendon the finance for the building of the county gaols was to be provided by the Crown and thereafter the cost of repair was generally recovered by the sheriff from the Exchequer although there was occasionally experimentation with other forms of funding such as the imposition of a local rate.[100] Franchises and municipalities generally it would seem had to bear the financial burden of the benefits in terms of income and autonomy which the right to hold their own gaols conferred. Within the realm of construction and repair generally the role of private charity must also be acknowledged and this will be considered shortly.

As to the payment of those charged with the custody of prisoners then anything like a salary was an exception rather than the rule. Rather the gaoler would make his living out of the fees he took from inmates. To the modern reader the notions both of prisoners paying money for their confinement and of gaolers taking their livings directly from it, with all the potential for abuse and extortion thereby entailed, appear much stranger than they would have done to medieval eyes. It was a usual feature of office holding in the Middle Ages that the functionary should reward himself from his office. Abuse and extortion were similarly widespread within the period; the evil sheriff of Nottingham of legend and its successor, television, is representative of a system rather than simply an individual. Certainly the potential for abuse was fully exploited by gaolers, hardly any opportunity for gaining money was spurned. The office might be one which was eagerly sought and letters of 1400 show a campaign being mounted to appoint a particular individual as gaoler of Newgate.[101] The ways in which money might be raised were legion. So we find that individuals are gaoled for no other reason than to extort money from them in the form of fees while bail (the responsibility for making the decision on which long remained with those who had a financial stake in it) was granted or withheld on pecuniary rather than legal grounds. Once inside the prison a number of different fees could be taken; on entrance, for the removal of irons, for better accommodation, for bedding, food, lights and fuel and finally a payment could be taken on release. It is true that there were some attempts at regulation, and it is the municipalities, and in particular London, which led the way. Newgate was subject to regulations on a number of occasions, for example it was laid down in 1393 that lamps and bedding were not to be paid for[102] and ordinances of 1431 and 1460 regulated fees for Newgate, Ludgate and the Counters.[103] In other prisons too regulations had been introduced into the fee system. Scales of fees agreed with the Marshal in 1307 show that prisoners within his custody would pay different fees in accordance with their social status.[104] National regulation was, however, slow in coming. The abuse of the bail process had admittedly attracted legislation from 1275[105] while the 1351 Statute of Labourers had provided rules for the use of the sanction of imprisonment under its provisions. This latter legislation provided that officials should take no fees, either generally or particularly for 'suete' of prison, that is for more comfortable accommodation, from workmen detained under the statute and ten years later monetary penalties are laid down for breach of this requirement.[106] But no general regulation of the fee system was enacted until 1444 when fees are restricted in all prisons, although apparently the Fleet was not affected and the practical consequences of the provision elsewhere may not have been dramatic. This statute, which clearly has as its background a desire to purge all forms of corruption in local government, limits fees payable to sheriffs, bailiffs and gaolers in respect of prisoners arrested or attached, and again the bail issue was tackled.[107]

How then were prisoners to make such payments? That they were obliged to make them is clear and the lucky prisoner would continue to be detained until he had settled the necessary fees even when the original term of imprisonment had expired, whilst the unlucky suspect felon, if he could afford nothing might be given nothing and die in consequence. Some state support for prisoners was known from an early time. Under the Anglo-Saxon legislation of Alfred the prisoner was to be fed by his relatives if he himself had no food, the kinship tie being a focus of much Saxon legal obligation. The law then goes on to provide that if the prisoner has no relative then the king's reeve is to make provision for his sustenance.[108] That this state aid survived for a while after the Conquest is clear and for certain classes of prisoner, notably approvers who were paid and provided with weapons with which to prosecute their trials by battle, it long continued, but from the thirteenth century it is clear that ordinary suspect felons were to support themselves out of their own property. As for debtors the early statutes of Merchants and Acton Burnell had cast an obligation on the creditor to provide the debtor's food for him if he lacked funds but the requirement was not extended beyond these particular forms of debt. Those held within bishops' prisons were, it would appear, sustained by the Church and part of Archbishop Islip's response to the criticism of ecclesiastical confinement in 1352 was to reduce the allowances payable to prisoners.[109]

That medieval prisoners were frequently poor is beyond doubt. Debtors, save for those who made the occasional withdrawal to prison for tactical reasons, were hardly likely to be in a good position to pay for their keep and neither were suspect felons. Pugh found that 87 per cent of the inhabitants of Newgate in the later thirteenth century were 'technically destitute'.[110] Hanawalt's survey doubted Pugh's conclusion and found a higher proportion of more substantial villagers in her group of fourteenth-century suspect felons from outside London.[111] Even if this were typical a stay of any length of time in prison would, given what we have seen about the number of fees to be paid, fees which were often higher for suspect felons than for other classes of prisoner, and given the gaoler's rapacity, have quite quickly diminished the suspect's funds. So prisoners were poor, yet had to pay their fees. It is in this context that private charity was of particular importance.

Alms giving was of immense importance in the Middle Ages and was considered in a very different way than it is today. Charity was a fundamental Christian obligation. Its necessity had been stressed by a decretal of Pope Gregory IX which had been approved by the fourth Lateran Council of 1215.[112] Its objects were typically the poor, the maimed, the growing number of medieval hospitals and the provision of public works. As early as 1248 Henry III had granted money for food for all Newgate prisoners[113] but it would appear to have been in the fourteenth century in particular that the flow of alms specifically to prisons increased significantly, and wills added to the flow of grants by living donors. It may be that this increase is explicable by the social conditions of the fourteenth century. The preaching of the doctrines of good works continued yet a growing anti-clericalism seems to have resulted in a greater secularisation of charity. The fear of death, medieval man's constant pre-occupation and spur to benevolence, must have been further intensified in the century of the Black Death, while the popular medieval parable of Dives and Lazarus would perhaps have a particular immediacy for a growing middle class. Other influences may have been more direct. The preacher John Bromyard promised that in the great reversal of fortunes which would occur on the Day of Judgement those who now lived in comfort would be consigned to an eternal prison house.[114] Prisons too had the attraction for the donor that they would always house large numbers of inmates who would, in theory at any rate, pray for the repose of the donor's soul.

Charity was not unknown to the Crown as the Newgate meal mentioned earlier, the distribution of 'Godspence' to prisoners in the Fleet in 1357[115] and also the occasional release of a prisoner on grounds of poverty demonstrate.[116] But more significant was the charity of the increasing middle classes whose donations and legacies were of considerable importance. The subject-matter of such grants was most often in the form of money for the prisoners' upkeep but on other occasions food or fuel might be provided directly. Some bequests produced marked results. The terms of the will of the celebrated Richard Whittington are not incorporated into the pantomime which commemorates him but his bequest is notable in terms of prison history. Perhaps the immediate cause of the particular legacy was the loss of lives in Newgate after the transfer of Ludgate debtors but its formula is typical of its time, bequests being made for religious purposes, for hospitals for the sick, insane and lepers, the repair of roads and the grant of a sum of money which was used to rebuild Newgate gaol. Another Mayor of London, Stephen Forster, later left money for the rebuilding of Ludgate.[117]

Although post mortem donations were increasing in importance the living too continued to provide casual charity and there was no need for prisoners to wait passively to receive it. Newgate prison allowed inmates to go out soliciting alms although the number was limited to two in the regulations of 1431,[118] while Nottingham gaol was sending out men in 1443 to beg throughout Nottinghamshire and Derbyshire.[119] In the fifteenth century confiscated goods were, on occasion, handed over by some town authorities as elsewhere they were to hospitals.[120] Indeed the two types of institution must have been considerable rivals in the collection of the charity which the structure of the medieval economy and the practical philosophy of the time both required and ensured.

Notes

1. R.B. Pugh, *Imprisonment in Medieval England* (CUP, Cambridge, 1968), p.1, note 4.

2. II Cnut 35; A.J. Robertson, *The Laws of the Kings of England from Edmund to Henry I* (CUP, Cambridge, 1925), p.194.

3. Infra p.5 and note 8.

4. E. De Haas, *Antiquities of Bail* (AMS Press, New York, 1966).

5. XVI *Curia Regis Rolls* (C.R.R.), pp.370-1 (HMSO).

6. Assize of Clarendon 1166. The text is given in W. Stubbs (ed.), *Select Charters and other illustrations of English Constitutional History* (OUP, Oxford, 1905 ed.), p.143. On the authenticity of the text see D. Corner, 'The Texts of Henry II's Assizes' in *Law Making and Law Makers in British History* (Harding (ed.), *Royal Historical Society*, London, 1980), p.7.

7. For a full treatment of the early history of the county gaols see Pugh, *Imprisonment*, Ch. IV.

8. Statute of Westminster I 1275 ch. xv. On the early history of bail generally see De Haas, *Antiquities of Bail* and C.A.F. Meekings in *Crown Pleas of the Wiltshire Eyre, 1249*, Wiltshire Archaeological Society Records vol. XVI (1961), pp.46-51.

9. 4 Edward III, c.ii.

10. B.A. Hanawalt, *Crime and Conflict in English Communities 1300-1348* (Harvard UP, London, 1979), n.39.

11. R.F. Hunnisett, *The Medieval Coroner* (CUP, Cambridge, 1961), pp.130-1. Pugh (*Imprisonment*, p.286) seems to err in taking her to have died in 1378; it was the coroner who had done so.

12. Figures from the late thirteenth century are to be found in Pugh, 'Some Reflections of a Medieval Criminologist', LIX *Proceedings of the British Academy* (1973), p.83. For the fourteenth century see Hanawalt, *Crime and Conflict*, p.54. And see R. Bellamy, *Crime and Public Order in the Later Middle Ages* (Routledge & Kegan Paul, London, 1973), pp.158–61.

13. Hanawalt, *Crime and Conflict*, p.53.

14. Ibid., p.55.

15. Bracton, *De Legibus et Consuetudinibus Angliae* (Thorne Revision and Translation, Harvard UP, Cambridge, Mass., 1968), F.124 (vol. II, pp.349-50); and see Pugh, *Imprisonment*, p.388.

16. Alfred, 1, 2. See F.L. Attenborough, *The Laws of the Earliest English Kings* (CUP, Cambridge, 1922), p.62.
A contrary view as to the antiquity of penal imprisonment is maintained in D. Melossi and M. Pavarini, *The Prison and the Factory* (Macmillan, London, 1981), pp.1-5.

17. VI Athelstan c.12; Attenborough, *Laws*, p.168. C.f. II Aethelstan 1, 3; Attenborough, *Laws*, p.126.

18. Pugh, *Imprisonment*, pp.9-23, 27 et seq.

19. Statute of Westminster I (1275), chs. iv, ix, xii, xiii, xv, xx, xxix, xxxi, xxxiv, xxxvii.

20. *Mirror of Justices* (W.J. Whittaker (ed.), 7 Selden Society Publications (1893), pp.184-9.

21. Articuli Super Cartas (1300) c.1.

22. 25 Edward III stat 2 c.ii.

23. 12 Richard II, c.vi (1388) amended by II Henry IV, c iv (1409-10), c.f. 17 Edward IV, c.iii (1477-78).

24. *Patent Rolls* (1216-25), p.186 (HMSO).

25. Infra, p.47.

26. For the pardon process see Bellamy, *Crime and Public Order*, pp.191-8; and N.D. Hurnard, *The King's Pardon for Homicide before AD 1307* (OUP, Oxford, 1969), passim.

27. The fullest treatment of this process is L.C. Gabel's *Benefit of Clergy in England in the Later Middle Ages* (Octagon Books, New York, 1969).

28. Gabel, *Benefit of Clergy*, p.77.

29. Ibid, p.73.

30. Ibid, pp.104-6, 109-10, where cases are discussed.

31. Supra note 29. For the instruction to the justices see *Liber Assisarum* (1679), p.138, citing 27 Edward III.

32. Gabel, *Benefit of Clergy*, p.64.

33. *Councils and Synods with other documents relating to The English Church*, vol. II, Powicke and Cheney (eds.) (OUP, Oxford, 1964), Part I, p.684.

34. Pugh, *Imprisonment*, pp.15-16.

35. E.g., Pugh, *Imprisonment*, p.5; J. Cohen, 'The History of Imprisonment for Debt and its relation to the Development of Discharge in Bankruptcy',

Journal of Legal History, Vol. 3 (1982), p.155.

36. C. Johnson (ed.) (Nelson, London, 1950), p.21.

37. On the background to the statutes see M. Powicke, *The Thirteenth Century* (OUP, Oxford, 1962), Ch. XIII; James le Roy's Case in H. Jenkinson and B.E.R. Formoy (eds.), *Select Cases in the Exchequer of Pleas*, vol.48, Selden Society (1931), p.18; and T.F.T. Plucknett, *Legislation of Edward I* (OUP, Oxford, 1962), Ch. VI.

38. For the provisions of the statutes see Plucknett, *Legislation*, pp.138-42.

39. 13 Edward I Ch.xi.

40. 25 Edward III stat 5 c.xvii.

41. S. McConville, *A History of English Prison Administration, Vol.1 1750-1877* (Routledge & Kegan Paul, London, 1981), c.f. Bellamy, *Crime and Public Order*, pp.31-2.

42. See generally G.R. Owst, *Literature and Pulpit in Medieval England* (CUP, Cambridge, 1933, reprinted Oxford, 1961), Ch.VI.

43. B. Tierney, *Medieval Poor Law* (University of California Press, Berkeley, 1959), p.11.

44. McConville, *English Prison Administration*, p.4.

45. Hurnard, *King's Pardon*, p.36.

46. Pugh, *Imprisonment*, p.383.

47. L.E. Boyle; 'E Cathene et carcere; The Imprisonment of Amaury de Montfort', J.J.G. Alexander and M.T. Gibson (eds.), *Medieval Learning and Literature: Essays presented to Richard William Hunt* (OUP, Oxford, 1976).

48. *Fleta*, Prologue, H.G. Richardson and G.O. Sayles (eds.), Vol.72, Selden Society (1953), p.3. But see vol. 99 Selden Society p.xxii.

49. A.R. Myers, *England in the Late Middle Ages* (Penguin, Harmondsworth, 1971), p.184.

50. *Mirror of Justices*, Book II, ch.ix, 7 Selden Society, p.52.

51. A.K. McHardy, 'Bishop Buckingham and the Lollards of Lincoln Diocese', p.134, in D. Baker (ed.), *Schism, Heresy and Religious Protest*, Vol. 9, *Studies in Church History* (CUP, Cambridge, 1972).

52. R.B. Clay, *The Medieval Hospitals of England* (Frank Cass, London 1966, reprinted from 1909), p.141-2.

53. For detailed discussion of particular gaols and their administration Pugh, *Imprisonment*, should be consulted.

54. *The French Chronicle of London* (C.J. Aungier (ed.), in vol.28, Camden Society (1844), pp.28-9.

55. *Bracton F.122*, vol.ii, pp.345-6.

56. *Councils and Synods*, vol.II, Part I, p.684.

57. On clergymen I Henry VII, ch.iv (1485); on heresy see 2 Henry IV, ch.xv (1400-1). Note also the letter patent of June 1382, McHardy, 'Bishop Buckingham', p.131, and generally H.G. Richardson, 'Heresy and the Lay Power under Richard II', 51, *English Historical Review* (1936), p.1.

58. *Councils and Synods*, vol.II, part 1, p.93.

59. Ibid., pp.105-6; F.W. Maitland, 'The Deacon and the Jewess; or Apostacy at Common Law', 2, *Law Quarterly Review* (1886), p.153.

60. Myers, *Late Middle Ages*, p.167.

61. D.M. Wilson (ed.), *The Archaeology of Anglo Saxon England* (CUP, Cambridge, 1976), p.234.

62. Pugh, *Imprisonment*, pp.374-83. For an early example of imprisonment of a nun at Watton in Yorkshire in 1150s-1160s see G. Constable, 'Aelred of Rievaulx and the nun of Watton; an episode in the early history of the Gilbertine order', in D. Baker (ed.), *Medieval Women, Studies in Church History, Subsidia* 1, (Blackwell, Oxford, 1978), p.205.

63. Myers, *Late Middle Ages*, pp.167-8.

64. E.g. Bristol (c.1240), Kenfig (1330); M. Bateson (ed.), 'Borough Customs', vol.1, 18, Selden Society (1904), pp.64, 66.

65. McConville, *English Prison Administration*, p.7.

66. M. Bassett, 'The Fleet Prison in the Middle Ages', vol.5, *University of Toronto Law Journal* (1943-4), p.382; 'Newgate Prison in the Middle Ages', vol. 18, *Speculum* (1943), p.233; Bellamy, *Crime and Conflict* gives a summary at pp.168-9, and Pugh, *Imprisonment*, gives much detail in Chs. V and VI.

67. 1472, quoted in Bassett, 'Fleet Prison', p.398, 'The Fleet is a fayir preson, but ye had but smale lyberte therin, for ye must nedys aper when ye were callyd.'

68. E.g. John Blakeman, note 76, infra, Richard son of Nigel, note 75 infra. By a strange irony the treadwheel, later the symbol of useless labour, was used in the construction of many large medieval buildings.

69. Wynnstay, MS 86, National Library of Wales. Printed in *Publications of the Record Society of Lancashire and Cheshire*, vol.92 (1938), p.210.

70. Pugh, *Imprisonment*, p.163-4.

71. *Borough Customs*, p.65.

72 Pugh, *Imprisonment*, p.82. Note the use of church steeples in Scotland; J. Cameron, *Prison and Punishment in Scotland; From the Middle Ages to the Present* (Cannongate, Edinburgh, 1983), p.10.

73. 5 Edward III, ch.8.

74. *Chronicles of Edward I and Edward II*, W. Stubbs (ed.), Rolls Series, vol. 76 (1882), p.93. P.91 of the same volume shows two prisoners escaping from the Tower of London.

75. XII *Curia Regis Rolls*, pp.215-6.

76. VIII *Curia Regis Rolls*, pp.396-7.

77. *Britton*, Book 1, Ch.XII, FM Nichol (ed.) (Clarendon Press, Oxford, 1865), Vol.1, p.44.

78. Oxford, Bodleian Library MS, Auct F.6.5, fol.1.vo Many European variants of this scene exist, an interesting Genoese version being held in Glasgow University Library (MS Hunter, 374, fol. 4ro). For other versions see P. Courcelle, *Histoire Littéraire des Grandes Invasions Germaniques* (Études Augustiniennes, Paris, 1964), plates 37 et seq., though note the erroneous reference to the Glasgow MS.

79. Quoted in Bellamy, *Crime and Public Order*, p.180. Perse claims that he is treated 'worse thanne it weere a dogge', ibid.

80. Pugh, *Imprisonment*, p.179.

81. H.S. Bennett, *The Pastons and their England* (CUP, Cambridge, 1970), p.177.

82. Supra, note 69.

83. B.H. Putnam (ed.), *Proceedings before the Justices of the Peace in the Fourteenth and Fifteenth Centuries, Edward III to Richard III* (Spottiswoode Ballantyne & Co, London, 1938), pp.398-9; Bellamy, *Crime and Conflict*, p.175.

84. J.J. Jusserand, *English Wayfaring Life* (T. Fisher Unwin, London, 1920), p.272. Another man in the case had died in the gaol. The putrefaction of the feet is not in this case (c.f. the case at note 83, supra) directly attributed to the stocks but it is probable that this, or possibly the use of irons, was the cause.

85. Gabel, *Benefit of Clergy*, p.113.

86. Clay, *Medieval Hospitals*, p.33, dated as 1399 in T.F. Graham, *Medieval Minds; Mental Health and the Middle Ages* (Allen & Unwin, London, 1967), p.68.

87. Alfred 1 §6 and §7, Attenborough, *Laws*, p.64.

88. Statute of Breaking Prisons (1295).

89. 2 Henry VI, ch.xxi.

90. *Britton*, Book 1, ch.xii, Nichols (ed.), p.43; and see Pugh, *Imprisonment*, pp.93-6.

91. Bassett, 'Newgate Prison', p.241.

92. Case of Matthew of the Exchequer (1292), *Select Cases in the Exchequer of Pleas*, vol.48, Selden Society (1931), p.141.

93. *Fleta*, Book 1, ch.27 (72 Selden Society, p.68), c.f. *Bracton*, F124, (Thorne, vol. 11, p.350). On the difficult question of who was to bear the liability for the escape see Pugh, *Imprisonment*, pp.248-54.

94. Owst, *Literature and Pulpit*, pp.170-1.

95. 4 Richard II, ch.ii.

96. 1 Richard II, ch.xii.

97. 31 Henry VI, ch.i.

98. M. KcKisack, *The Fourteenth Century* (OUP, Oxford, 1959), pp.408-14.

99. Pugh, *Imprisonment*, pp.223-4; Bassett, 'Newgate Prison', p.241. On the escape fine see Pugh, *Imprisonment*, p.240.

100. Pugh, *Imprisonment*, pp.338-46.

101. M.D. Legge, *Anglo-Norman Letters and Petitions* (Blackwell, Oxford, 1941), pp.80 and 88. The letters, from William Fyncham and Robert Fry, recommend a certain 'G.A.' and those sought to be influenced include Richard Whittington, not then Mayor, for whose subsequent connection with Newgate see infra, note 117.

102. Bassett, 'Newgate Prison', pp.235 et seq.

103. Ibid., pp.239, 242. Regulation had begun in 1346 in Newgate; Pugh, *Imprisonment*, p.170.

104. Pugh, *Imprisonment*, p.171.

105. Supra, note 8.

106. 25 Edward III, stat 2, ch. vi.

107. 23 Henry VI, ch.ix.

108. Alfred 1 §2 and §3; Attenborough, *Laws*, p.62.

109. Pugh, *Imprisonment*, pp.321-2.

110. Pugh, 'Reflections of a Medieval Criminologist', p.100.

111. Hanawalt, *Crime and Conflict*, pp.128-34.

112. G. Jones, *History of the Law of Charity* (CUP, Cambridge, 1969), p.3.

113. Pugh, 'The King's Prisons before 1250', vol.5, *Transactions of the Royal Historical Society*, 5th series, p.15; Pugh, *Imprisonment*, p.319.

114. For Bromyard see Owst, *Literature and Pulpit*, p.293. For the Dives and Lazarus theme in medieval Europe see T.S.R. Boase, *Death in the Middle Ages* (Thames & Hudson, London 1972), pp.28 et seq.

115. Bassett, 'Fleet Prison', p.399.

116. E.g. James le Roy, supra, note 37.

117. For the terms of the will and the career of the man see C.M. Barron, 'Richard Whittington; The Man behind the Myth', in A.E.J. Hollaender and W. Kellaway (eds.), *Studies in London History Presented to P.E. Jones* (Hodder & Stoughton, London, 1969), pp.197 et seq. On Forster see Bassett, 'Newgate Prison', p.242.

118. Bassett, 'Newgate Prison', p.240.

119. Pugh, *Imprisonment*, p.328.

120. Ibid, and c.f. Clay, *Medieval Hospitals*, p.168 and Ch. XIII.

2

THE POPULATION AND CONDITIONS WITHIN PRISONS

The previous chapter has attempted to sketch some of the 'external' factors of medieval imprisonment, its organisation, structures and system of finance. As part of this investigation we have already seen something of the people confined within the prisons for we have identified suspect felons, convicted lesser offenders and debtors among their number. In this chapter some noteworthy categories of prisoner will be considered and then a more detailed investigation of conditions within the medieval prison will be attempted. It is tempting in such an enterprise, and authors on the subject have not always resisted the temptation, to produce a catalogue of grisly tales, 'parchment nasties', to horrify rather than instruct. Yet two things should be borne in mind at all points during an investigation of such material, some of it admittedly rather unpleasant. Firstly, conditions within gaols must, to be fully understood, be judged by the standards of their own time, a time when many people were born in pain and died early and in pain, and their lives and attitudes to those lives were very different from our own. Secondly, it is often the case that the unusual, the atypical, comes down to us in our surviving records leaving the more mundane, paradoxically, less accessible. In an age where many who were confined had neither the ability nor the opportunity to record their experience, and where practice from place to place may have varied widely, it is impossible to piece together an accurate picture of a 'typical' medieval prison. What follows, therefore, must be necessarily incomplete.

Specific Types of Prisoner

One of the earliest legislative enactments concerning imprisonment was, as has been seen, the law of Aethelstan which established that incarceration was to be the fate of the thief aged less than 15 years. The imprisonment of children continued certainly well into the fourteenth century. The royal policy of investigating all crime, coupled with as yet crude methods of procedure to deal with those considered incapable, meant that children accused of crime would find themselves placed in gaol until a pardon had been secured for them, which might be before or after trial. Most of our readily accessible information concerning the imprisonment of children comes from the law of homicide, largely due to the work of Hurnard in this area, but a late case from 1337, unusual in that the remand to gaol seems initially to have been until punishment rather than pardon, concerned a juvenile sheep stealer, Alice Wygodes.[1] Sometimes the children who found themselves in prison seem very young and very innocent indeed. Katherine Passeavant, aged four, was imprisoned in 1249 after accidentally killing another child by knocking it into a vat of hot water by opening a door.[2] Although the granting of the pardon might follow swiftly upon the remand to gaol it was by no means inevitable that action would be so immediate, one reason being the necessity to provide money in return for the exercise of clemency. Alice le Ster who was six when she accidentally knocked a stone over a cliff with fatal consequences had to wait 14 years between her remand to gaol and the granting of her pardon.[3] Details of the treatment of children within the prison are unclear but at least one six-year-old died in custody.[4]

Those who had committed crime whilst suffering from mental disorder might also find themselves facing long periods of incarceration. Although a mixture of charity and superstition argued against the execution of the insane, a pardon, or at least a grant of bail, was necessary before they might be released into the hands of their relatives. For those, and there must have been many, who lacked the funds to secure release or whose families were unwilling to accept the problems of maintaining a disordered and in some cases violent individual the legal formula of a remand pending the exercise of the king's grace gave way to the reality of a life sentence. As Hurnard indicates 'it was probably as much the families' reluctance to receive madmen as the official reluctance to grant them over which led to many lunatics remaining in gaol.'[5] Certainly the result of the imprisonment of the insane (and it must be admitted that it is far from clear exactly what conditions were being so considered within the period under discussion) can hardly have been pleasant either for the individual himself or for other prisoners. Presumably the violent would have been kept in irons, and possibly kept separately, but problems might certainly arise. Richard Pinnok, taken for killing one man in a fit of madness, killed another whilst in a similar condition in Bristol gaol.[6] As the medieval period wore on more places became available for the insane in hospitals, some of which had begun to take on specialist functions in this respect in the fourteenth century after their initial foundation for purposes of general hospitality. The priory of St Mary of Bethlehem, the most famous of such institutions, was designed in 1247 as a general hospital for the poor but came to handle cases of insanity. By the fifteenth century we read of persons being 'detained' within this hospital.[7]

If mental illness could be disruptive to the life of the prison so of course could physical illness. Leprosy, and the diseases which were so diagnosed, were regarded, like insanity, as both a spiritual and a physical affliction and again special institutions developed to cope with sufferers. In general lepers were excluded from the life of the community but nevertheless we learn that in Bristol in 1344 lepers who were found within the city might be imprisoned.[8]

Apart from the young and the ill a more amorphous and disparate category of prisoners may be mentioned, whose numerical significance in terms of medieval imprisonment is far greater than that of the groupings considered above. Strangers to a locality were looked upon with considerable suspicion within the relatively static society of the early Middle Ages and legislation of the thirteenth century allowed town watchmen to imprison overnight strangers who entered their towns.[9] Such caution was perhaps justified for ties of community and lordship, which had to a considerable extent superceded in legal terms the Saxon bond of kinship, were of vital significance within this period. The stranger who was outside his tithing and without a lord at hand to warrant for him stood dangerously beyond these ties. He might be a fugitive villein or, worse, one who had committed felony elsewhere and, having taken sanctuary within a church had been ordered to abjure the realm. The different economic climate of the fourteenth century produced a different type of vagrant but one no less of a problem for the established order of the country. The effects of the Black Death included the creation of a new class of wandering labourers who would leave their villages to go in search of the most profitable employment. For these men too imprisonment was regarded as appropriate. In an attempt to reverse by statute a profound social upheaval legislation of the mid-fourteenth century laid down wage rates and punished offenders with imprisonment and the stocks.[10] Putnam suggests that in fact relatively few were imprisoned for any period of time, although the stocks seem to have been more frequently employed. Similar types of statute to enforce labour regulation and suppress vagabondry continue to be enacted for the remainder of the Middle Ages.[11] It is interesting in this context to note a statute of Henry VII which stated that vagabonds were to be held in the stocks rather than within gaols in order to prevent the expense of delivering them to gaols and also to reduce the loss of life which such incarceration might incur.[12] As will be seen later in this book the problems of vagabondage and the reaction appropriate to it were problems not only of the medieval era but continue to trouble legislators for many years.

Finally there are a number of categories of person whose incarceration, either as individuals or because of their membership of a particular sect or race, merits brief consideration. Within this number may be mentioned prisoners imprisoned as a result of events connected with contemporary political issues who formed always a disparate grouping. The fourteenth century, for example, saw the prisons swollen with the participants in the Peasants' Revolt but it also witnessed the imprisonment within England of four kings; the two English ones, Edward II and Richard II, both dying in confinement, at Berkeley castle and Pontefract castle, respectively.[13] Clearly explanations of such detentions within the period owe less to any general theory or trend than to the vagaries of power politics. The same may be said in respect of the incarceration of prisoners of war, such as those Scots we have seen who were housed in Chester gaol in 1301, which continues throughout the Middle Ages. A cognate class comprises those who by virtue of their nationality are ordered to be detained in gaol as presumed enemy aliens, a procedure used against the Irish in 1413 and 1422 and the Scots in 1491.[14] Within the thirteenth century there had been periodic detentions of Jews who had a particular economic position and legal status, which culminated in the imprisonment of all the Jews in England in 1287 prior to their expulsion from the realm. Templars were imprisoned in England in the early fourteenth century when their condemnation as heretics was under way throughout Europe and we have seen already that the religious dissenters, whose various beliefs are collected under the general title of Lollardy, were later imprisoned in considerable numbers.[15]

Segregation and Overcrowding

Political prisoners were often kept separate from the general mass of the prison population either in separate prisons or separate quarters within the same prison. Often their living conditions were vastly different from those of ordinary suspect felons. Amaury de Montfort, for example, was well served during his detention in Corfe Castle with eight grooms, four valets and only one guard. The expenses of his imprisonment were assessed at the considerable sum of 4s5½d per day.[16] Prisoners of war might also, as we have already noted, be kept apart from others and it remains to be seen how segregation amongst prisoners was carried out more generally, in accordance with social status, the grounds of confinement and the detainee's sex.

It has been observed that certain prisons were reserved for the freemen of particular boroughs, as at Bristol or, of course, Ludgate. Within other prisons then better accommodation might be secured for individual prisoners on account of their status or wealth. Newgate prison after the fifteenth century rebuilding had a number of different chambers, some more pleasant than others.[17] On a more systematic basis was the segregation between debtors and suspect felons for whom the lowest (both physically and in all other senses) part of the prison, the 'pit' or, later, the 'dungeon', was considered appropriate.[18] The prison tower of Edward I's castle at Conwy (Conway) graphically demonstrates the difference in accommodation provided for the two categories of prisoner. The lower chamber, for suspect felons, is accessible only by trapdoor and ventilated only by a very small window high in the wall, whilst the debtors' chamber is entered in conventional manner and has a larger window on the surrounds of which prisoners have carved designs. The reason generally suggested for such segregation was that it was the outcome of contamination theory, but in truth this was probably only part of the reason. The greater moral opprobrium felt towards felons meant, particularly if it is correct to assume that pre-trial detention was considered at times to be punishment enough, that conditions for this group of prisoner would always be particularly unpleasant. Moreover it is possible that from quite early times an empathy was developing between those who framed and administered the laws and the professional class of traders and accountants who formed the earliest group of prisoners for debt.

As to segregation according to sex we have some evidence to suggest that it certainly applied in some gaols but by no means all. The earliest recorded attempt to provide separate accommodation was in York in 1237.[19] In 1293 the Chancellor of Oxford University was urging that the borough gaol should be extended by one floor so that suspect felons, trespassers and women might all be held separately, the segregation of women being declared necessary 'for the avoidance of sin'.[20] The request would appear to have been successful as was that made in 1406 on behalf of female prisoners of Newgate whose existing accommodation was declared to be too small and necessitated their passage through another room in the prison, called 'Bocardo', on their way to the privy.[21] Certainly, however, not all prisons would have such segregation and the sin which the Chancellor of Oxford feared must have been accomplished. Matilda Hereward appears to have been pregnant on every occasion on which the justices of gaol delivery visited her prison over a period of 18 months and her execution was thereby delayed[22] and we have at least one case of a marriage contracted in prison, although whether with another inmate or a visitor is unclear. The presence of women within gaols made them vulnerable to more sinister consequences; William Arnold the gaoler of Newgate was imprisoned for rape of prisoners in his care in 1449 as had an earlier Richmond gaoler, Thomas Porter, been.[23]

Within such broad categories of segregation as did exist, however, living would be communal, a fact which would be less surprising at a time when domestic accommodation knew little concept of privacy. Solitary confinement seems not to have been a general feature of imprisonment although it was used on occasions, most notably for important prisoners of the Crown. But if living was communal it might also on occasion be overcrowded. It is impossible to present an accurate picture of the population of the prisons during the Middle Ages, a population which would differ from time to time and place to place, and those figures which we do have are described by Pugh as 'very puzzling'.[24] Nevertheless we do know of particular occasions when the volume of prisoners severely taxed the resources of the prison even though it cannot be maintained that these instances are indicative of a general condition. So, for example, we know that in February 1306 Warwick gaol was ordered to be delivered 'because it is so full of prisoners that many of them have died and die from day to day', while Newgate in 1341 is described as so 'full of prisoners that they are continually dying of hunger and oppression'.[25]

Starvation and Disease

One of the problems of overcrowding was the pressure, as the last quotation shows, which would be brought to bear upon the gaol's food supply. Food was paid for by the prisoner who purchased it from the gaoler. The gaoler would either buy in goods or produce his own, for we know that Newgate in the fourteenth century was brewing and baking for itself. Alternatively food would be brought into the prison from the outside, either by relatives or friends of the prisoner or as a result of charitable donation. Prison diet then would depend both on the circumstances of the individual prisoner and on external factors which would determine both the amount of food available and the amount of almsgiving which might be expected. Seasons and harvests would of course be important in this latter respect as would the geographical location of the gaol. In 1315 the Commons of Berkshire sought to have the gaol removed from Windsor since robbers interfered with the food supply and the people of the town could not support the prisoners with their alms, 'so that the prisoners frequently die for want of sustenance before judgement is rendered'. As a political gambit to persuade the King to approve the request it is asserted that many forfeited goods which would be taken upon conviction were being lost by such deaths. There is however no need to suppose a more humanitarian motive underlying the request, the drain upon the inhabitants together with an unwelcome accumulation of dangerous men around Windsor would seem to have been the reason for the petition.[26] When famine hit the country as a whole, as it did in 1315-17, its effects within prison might be catastrophic. Apart from the Windsor evidence we learn of the deaths of 71 persons in Maidstone gaol (1316) and of 23 in Northampton castle gaol, the reason given being the lack of food and drink and consequent stomach disorders.[27] The chronicler Johannes de Trokelowe remarks of this period, although with what veracity we do not know, that prisoners were driven to extremes. 'Gaoled thieves', he asserts, 'devoured, half alive, recent arrivals among themselves.'[28]

Plague had arrived with famine in those years and whenever epidemics swept the country thereafter prisons were never immune from their visitations. In addition to these periodic waves of external disease the illnesses generated by the circumstances of confinement themselves must have accounted for many deaths. The medieval diet, deficient in fruit and vegetables and unlikely to be fresh, was, even when abundant, not guaranteed to increase resistance to illness, while the crudity of sanitation, even within those prisons which boasted privies, could not have helped matters. Ventilation, particularly as we have seen from the Conwy evidence within the felon's pit, would be very limited, as much to keep in diseases as to keep out the fresh air. The smoke from the fires which at least some rooms of some prisons maintained would make the atmosphere unpleasant, for chimneys were unknown even in wealthy homes until the fifteenth century. But as the last comment indicates many of these observations are as applicable to the world outside the prisons at this time as within, the problems of the gaol in such respects differed only in degree and not in kind. Indeed London prisoners at least were on occasion troubled by nuisances from the city outside. The moat which had been constructed around the Fleet in the fourteenth century, ten feet wide and deep enough to take a boat laden with a tun of wine, was filled with effluent from various latrines and sewers while butchers used it to deposit cattle entrails, the whole becoming so clogged that it was possible to walk across it. The consequent threat to security and danger to the health of the inmates was a cause of some alarm.[29] Public health measures were the concern of the London council but general legislation was needed in 1388 to deal with those who cast 'annoyances, dung, garbages, entrails and other ordure' into water courses.[30] Another peril of city life beset the inhabitants of Ludgate in 1453-4, for they were removed to

Newgate because of the effects of smoke from a neighbouring fire.[31].

Particular prisons might provide other hazards. It is clear that they could be very cold and also very damp. In 1308 we learn that Richard Sapling's charter of pardon was damaged by water in prison in the winter.[32] That others apart from human company might share the accommodation is shown in the complaint of Richard Lambert in 1315. He states that he has been held in the depths of Wisbech gaol among thieves 'where, by toads and other venomous vermin, he was so inhumanly gnawn that his life was despaired of'. His moribund condition may be no more than standard form but there is no reason to doubt the substance of his complaint.[33] Even the vermin seem to have found the conditions within the Tower of London too much for them. Matthew of the Exchequer complains in 1295 to the King's Council that he had been subjected to a number of enormities while confined there, concluding that he was put in the black cellar on the bare ground where he remained for two years without any kind of fire or light, nor had he anything to drink except from the well of the Tower where the rats drown themselves.[34]

In some prisons attempts were made to improve matters. Newgate was receiving piped water by 1435 or 1436 to supplement the drinking fountain which had been installed in the rebuilding of the prison out of the proceeds of Whittington's will. The prison as then rebuilt was provided with a central hall, and a number of rooms equipped with chimneys and privies where citizens and women were to be kept. Some 'pleasant chambers' were provided for those who could pay for them and a chapel with 'spacious and well lighted recreation rooms' next to it. But there remained the airless basement cells and 'less convenient chambers' for which Newgate remained notorious.[35] London also took the lead in inspecting its gaols, committees being appointed from the middle of the fifteenth century to visit the prisons. Regulations of 1462 sought to ensure the annual visitation of Newgate by two curates and two commoners to investigate the administration of the gaol and hear the complaints of the prisoners. How often the gaol was in fact inspected we do not know, its reputation continued to be most unpleasant and it is possible that inspectors were deterred from entering out of fear that they themselves would contract infection.[36]

Temporary Release and Visitation

Matthew of the Exchequer, whose grim sojourn in the Tower of London was described above, had been transferred there after escaping from the Fleet. An earlier record showed that Matthew, whilst being imprisoned for 'certain falsities' had been discovered spending Christmas at a friend's house 'without leave'.[37] The possibility of spending time outside gaol 'with leave' leads us to one of the more surprising aspects of medieval imprisonment. An early example comes from the reign of John when Jordan de Bianney was allowed out of prison to practise his swordsmanship twice a day on leaving a hostage in his place.[38] The practice of prisoners 'wandering abroad' in return for a payment to the gaoler and without the need for the provision of a hostage becomes well established and is particularly associated with Fleet debtors. Certainly it was known in other prisons, and even on occasion for those accused of crime, but the sight of a man ostensibly confined for debt setting out from the Fleet to spend the day in town accompanied by a warder or 'baston' was a particularly common one. Indeed prisoners held within other establishments would arrange transfers to the Fleet in order to take advantage of the facility. Legislation attempted to curb the practice for some; a statute of 1331 stated that the Marshal, on pain of imprisonment, was to forbid wandering abroad by prisoners in his custody.[39] In 1377, as a result, Pugh suggests, of a case involving someone using his incarceration in the Fleet to protect himself from other legal proceedings whilst treating the prison rather like an hotel, the prohibition was extended to the Warden of the Fleet.[40] He was not to allow debtors out of the gaol until satisfaction had been made to the creditor and the warden himself was to be liable for the debt and was to lose his office should he fail in this duty. The statute seems to have had little effect and the practice continued. A rather different sanction was threatened against the keeper of the king's gaol in Leicester in 1385 as a result of his apparently allowing a heretic, taken as an obdurate excommunicate, to wander round the town 'infecting' others. The keeper was himself threatened with excommunication.[41]

Although it is difficult to discover any regular or consistent pattern of prison visits it is clear that such visits were undertaken from early times. A case from 1220 for example shows a chaplain visiting a gaol to inquire after the fate of his stolen goods and we have already seen that in one case a gaoler allowed boys into a prison so that they might teach a prisoner confined there to read and consequently plead his clergy.[42] It is probable that such visits, even if they had no 'official' status would be granted on an appropriate payment being made to the gaoler, but there is no evidence to suggest that the practice was ever forbidden, save in the cases of specific prohibition for specific prisoners. From the fourteenth century when imprisonment for debt became common much visiting is apparent; we know for example that John Paston's wife Margaret visited him in the Fleet.[43] Fleet prisoners were not, Bellamy asserts, allowed to have food brought in from the outside for this would undermine the warden's monopoly in the provision of sustenance.[44] In all prisons visitations by the clergy were particularly enjoined for this activity formed one of the Works of Mercy established by the Church. As to whether such a duty was regularly performed it is difficult to tell, but certainly in 1250 Robert Grosseteste, the Bishop of Lincoln, who three years later was to be heard complaining about the 'torture' of imprisonment by the secular power, was repeating the worth of such visitation, particularly of the priest's own parishoners, as an important part of pastoral care.[45] Some prisons even had their own chapels; the rebuilt Newgate, as we have seen, was provided with one and we know of one designed for York in 1237.[46] In addition to this importation of religion a prisoner might make use of an exeat, if one could be obtained, to hear mass outside the prison; as had Alan Osmund whilst a prisoner of the King's Bench in 1293.[47]

The Conduct of Gaolers

Gaolers themselves, particularly when facing the prospect of settling a debt should the debtor not return to his prison, would of course only allow the privilege of wandering on receipt of payment. We have seen in the previous chapter that the structure of office holding in the medieval period was a directly contributory cause of much of the hardship inflicted upon prisoners. It was also the case that in a violent age men would find prisoners in their charge an easy target for excesses and although the evidence is clear that brutality by gaolers is seen as unlawful yet in practice both the discovery of it, at a time when death in prison must have been common, was difficult and the prosecution of it rarely likely to be successful. The author of the *Mirror of Justices* at the end of the thirteenth century states quite clearly that it is contrary to law that anyone 'be placed among vermin or putrefaction, or in any horrible or dangerous place, or in the water or in the dark or any other torment; but it is lawful for gaolers to put fetters upon those whom they suspect; but the fetters must not weigh more than twelve ounces.'[48] The author of *Fleta*, writing at about the same time, stresses that prisoners who die in gaol must be examined by coroners before burial, and in the case of gaol break it must be inquired whether there had been ill treatment of the escaper, whether 'a man has been hung by his feet or his nails have been torn off or he has been loaded with irons or such like tortures and in this event the keepers should be treated as homicides.'[49] There are a number of cases of coroners going through the legal process and in one case a Newgate gaoler was condemned to death for killing a prisoner by putting him in excessively heavy and tight irons and sitting on his neck, which broke in consequence. The jury which condemned the gaoler contained other prisoners, a fact which seems perhaps unusual but which is in fact consistent with the early notion of jury trial, namely that jurors were supposed to speak from their own knowledge and should accordingly be drawn from the location of the alleged crime.[50]

Particular instances of individual cruelty must have been many but there is evidence of a rather more general pattern of abuse in some instances. Legislation of 1311, 1326 and 1340 condemns the practice which had obviously become established of gaolers forcing prisoners to become approvers; persons, as we have seen earlier, who will accuse others of complicity in crime.[51] It might be thought that the position of approver, who was in receipt of payment from the Crown and whose prolonged detention might postpone execution and give an increased opportunity to escape or learn to read, would be one which would have no difficulty in attracting volunteers. In fact the offer of personal combat with which the approver was obliged to support his accusation together with the fact that few approvers ultimately seem to have fared well perhaps explains why gaolers were using all means in their power to compel such conversions to the cause of criminal justice. In York castle in the fourteenth century, the means of persuasion extended to the application of devices called 'pirwynkes' to the fingers.[52] The reason for such action by the gaolers is clear for those who were accused by an approver would be lodged within the same gaol as he was, thereby ensuring for the gaoler an increased population and a consequently increased opportunity for the extraction of fees.

For one class of prisoner ill treatment was both permissible and expected, namely the prisoner who refused to plead. It was mentioned in the previous chapter that throughout the Middle Ages the Englishman's right was to be tried by God and not by man and that his express consent was accordingly required if he was to entrust his fate to the decision of a jury. Those who refused to do so provided the legal system with a problem, but one which it was reluctant to overcome by the means which, to much later eyes, seems most obvious, the imposition of jury trial without need of consent. In 1219 it has been seen that suspects were to be held in gaol who could no longer go to the ordeal and it would seem that this treatment, the theoretically correct one for the suspected but unconvicted felon, was retained for those who would not agree to, or could not be tricked into by a judge's eloquence, jury trial. In 1275 the Statute of Westminster I instructed that those gravely suspect were to be placed in 'prison forte et dure' if they refused to plead.[53] This 'strong and hard' prison originally probably indicated no more than a secure place with the usual provision about ironing, and the 'hard' perhaps indicated no more than a restricted diet. As time went on, however, the ironing provisions seem to have received a peculiar interpretation and 'prison forte et dure' becomes 'peine forte et dure'. This is best described by an account from 1322:

> the prisoner shall sit on a cold bare floor dressed only in the thinnest of shirts and pressed with as great a weight of iron as his wretched body can bear. His food shall be a little rotten bread and his drink cloudy and stinking water. The day on which he eats he shall not drink and the day on which he has drunk he shall not taste bread. Only superhuman strength survives this punishment by the fifth and sixth day.[54]

In such a way was the suspect to be persuaded to opt for jury trial. The aim of the process was to prevent the prolonged and wholesale incarceration of the unconvicted with which the system could not cope, even though, as outlined earlier, the notion of imprisonment for grave crime may not at this time have been entirely inimical. The justification for this otherwise impermissible behaviour was that the man who 'stood mute' out of malice had removed himself from the procedures of, and hence also the protection of, the common law. As the outlaw and the man taken in the act of crime had been before him he might be killed legitimately without trial. The practice continued for a long time, not being abolished until 1772.[55]

Conclusion

Of other matters which were to feature large in the later history of imprisonment we know little at this early stage. We come across no reference to work within prisons until the late fifteenth century when small bone objects such as combs are being made by prisoners in Newgate for sale to a neighbouring haberdasher.[56] This would appear to have been the case notwithstanding the fact that work was certainly being carried on within hospitals, in particular those for Jewish converts, within this period.[57] Newgate also made provision in 1421 for its prisoners to exercise within its passages and on its roof but we do not come across the exercise yard proper until 1463 when one is constructed in Ludgate.[58] From Ludgate too comes one of our earliest records of organisation amongst prisoners (apart from the occasional riot) and it is perhaps not surprising that it should emanate from the literate body of London debtors. It is in the form of a petition to Henry IV for leave of five years in which to recover their goods in order to pay off the debts for which they had been imprisoned, whilst from the Fleet in 1357 had come a petition for the distribution of 'Godspence' for the relief of poor prisoners.[59]

There have been problems of generalisation over the last two chapters, problems which are inevitable when describing a time in which there was little central organisation at all and still less of it was effective. Practices vary, as has been pointed out earlier, from time to time and from gaol to gaol and general legislation may signify no more than a sop thrown to a parliament, mere words on a parchment roll. Features within the medieval prison reflect the world outside it. Accommodation within gaols had to be paid for but this was true with inns and hospitals, 'the state' could hardly be expected to provide for its criminal or prodigal element at this time. Certainly there was much suffering within gaol but there was also much suffering outside. 'Vita hominis est bellum super terram', the legend ran, 'the life of man is war upon the earth'. Overt cruelty was clearly regarded as wrong but the system of office holding which promoted it was regarded as natural. Huizinga identified the medieval penal philosophy as one of extremes of ferocity and pity.[60] Both are perhaps to be seen in England's gaols within this period, but pity often remains a commodity which needs to be purchased. Status and wealth are as important inside the prison as they are out, but an age which can sell salvation for the soul in indulgences finds it easy to grant a more pleasant confinement in return for money. Prison isolates its inmates from their environment, to a greater or lesser extent, but it does not change the reality of that environment. Divergence is growing between the debtors, who on occasion might even wander outside the prison and entertain their friends within it, and the suspect felons, whose plight is generally the more wretched. We must see how matters remain, change, and are viewed after the end of the Middle Ages.

Notes

1. *Calendar of Patent Rolls 1334-1338*, p.486 (HMSO).

2. N.D. Hurnard, *The King's Pardon for Homicide before AD 1307* (OUP, Oxford, 1969;, p.viii.

3. Ibid., p.50.

4. Ibid., p.153.

5. Ibid., p.170. Both infants and the insane might be found on occasion pleading clergy. On provision for the insane generally see R.B. Clay, *The Medieval Hospitals of England* (Frank Cass, London, 1966 reprint), Ch. III; T.F. Graham, *Medieval Minds; Mental Health and the Middle Ages* (Allen & Unwin, London 1967); Hanawalt, *Crime and Conflict in English Communities 1300-1348* (Harvard UP, London, 1979), pp.145-50, as well as Ch. VI of Hurnard's work.

6. Hurnard, *King's Pardon*, p.160.

7. Clay, *Medieval Hospitals*, p.33. The reference is in Stephen Forster's will.

8. Ibid., Clay, *Medieval Hospitals*, p.54.

9. For a summary of the legislation see Pugh, *Imprisonment in Medieval England* (CUP, Cambridge, 1968), p.194.

10. 23 Edward III, ch. I; 25 Edward III, stat 2, ch.ii.

11. B.H. Putnam, *The Enforcement of the Statute of Labourers* (Columbia UP, New York, 1908), pp.82-7; Zeigler, *The Black Death* (Penguin, Harmondsworth, 1969), pp.256-7. For other legislation see 31 Edward III, stat 1, ch. vii; 34 Edward III, ch. x; 42 Edward III, ch.vi; 12 Richard II, ch.iii; 7 Henry IV, ch. xviii, et. al.

12. II Henry VII, ch.ii (1495); see also 19 Henry VII, c.xii.

13. In 1327 and 1400, respectively; the others were King David II of Scotland and King John II of France.

14. 1 Henry V, ch. viii; 1 Henry VI, ch. iii; 7 Henry VII, ch. vi.

15. Pugh, *Imprisonment*, p.124, and see also ibid., pp.55-6.

16. L.E. Boyle, 'E Cathena et carcere; The Imprisonment of Amaury de Montfort', in J.J.G. Alexander and M.T. Gibson (eds.), *Medieval Learning and Literature, Essays presented to Richard William Hunt* (OUP, Oxford, 1976), p.385 and n.1.

17. Bassett, 'Newgate Prison in the Middle Ages', vol. 18, *Speculum* (1943), p.233 and p.239.

18. On the terminology see p. xiii supra, and Pugh, *Imprisonment*, pp.355 et seq., where the use of special names for particular rooms — 'Little Ease', 'Bocardo' etc. — is also discussed.

19. Ibid., p.339.

20. *Select Cases in the Court of King's Bench*, G.O. Sayles (ed.), vol. 55, Selden Society (1938), p.153.

21. Bassett, 'Newgate Prison', pp.238-9.

22. Hanawalt, *Crime and Conflict*, p.43.

23. Bassett, 'Newgate Prison', p.241; Bellamy, *Crime and Public Order in England in the Later Middle Ages* (Routledge & Kegan Paul, London, 1973), vol.II, p.177; Hanawalt, *Crime and Conflict*, p.38.

24. Pugh, *Imprisonment*, pp.366-9. Bellamy, *Crime and Public Order*, p.169, gives a figure of between 12 and 100 as an average but provides no support for the estimate.

25. H.R.T. Summerson, 'The Early Development of Peine Forte et Dure', in Ives and Manchester (eds.), *Law, Litigants and the Legal Profession* (Royal Historical Society, London, 1983), p.122.

26. *Calendar of Patent Rolls 1313-17*, p.328.

27. Pugh, *Imprisonment*, p.331; 60 died at Newgate, 28 in Wallingford. For Northampton see Hanawalt, *Crime and Conflict*, p.253.

28. Quoted in Hanawalt, *Crime and Conflict*, pp.251-2.

29. *Public Works in Medieval Law*, vol. II, C.T. Flower (ed.), vol. 40, Selden Society (1923), pp.32 et seq.

30. On the issue generally see Zeigler, *Black Death*, pp.158-61. The Statute is 12 Richard II, ch. xii.

31. Pugh, *Imprisonment*, p.109.

32. Hanawalt, *Crime and Conflict*, p.38.

33. Bellamy, *Crime and Public Order*, p.176.

34. *Select Cases before the King's Council 1243-1482*, L.S. Leadam and J.F. Baldwin (eds.), Vol. 35, Selden Society (1918), pp.15-16.

35. Bassett, 'Newgate Prison', p.239.

36. Ibid, pp.241-2.

37. *Select Cases in the Exchequer of Pleas*, H. Jenkinson and B.E.R. Formoy (eds.), vol. 48, Selden Society (1931), p.141.

38. Jordan was held in Winchester gaol; A.L. Poole, *From Domesday Book to Magna Carta* (OUP, Oxford, 1955), p.396; Pugh, *Imprisonment*, p.335.

39. 5 Edward III, ch.viii.

40. 1 Richard II, c.xii; Pugh, *Imprisonment*, pp.243-4.

41. A.K. McHardy, 'Bishop Buckingham and the Lollards of Lincoln Diocese', in D. Baker (ed.), *Schism, Heresy and Religious Protest*, Vol. 9, *Studies in Church History* (CUP, Cambridge, 1972), p.134.

42. For the chaplain's case see VIII *Curia Regis Rolls*, p.278 (HMSO). For the benefit of clergy ruse see L.C. Gabel, *Benefit of Clergy in the Later Middle Ages* (Octagon Books, New York, 1969 reprint). Hugh of Kirton, a reluctant approver from 1291, makes reference to persons coming to and from the gaol whom Bellamy (*Crime and Public Order*, p.129) takes to include visitors but it is possible that other prisoners alone are meant; *Select Cases in the Court of King's Bench*, vol. ii, p.56.

43. H.S. Bennett, *The Pastons and their England* (CUP, Cambridge, 1970), p.176.

44. Bellamy, *Crime and Public Order*, p.173.

45. For Grosseteste's complaint see *Councils and Synods with other documents relating to the English Church*, Vol. II, F.M. Powicke and C.R. Cheney (eds.) (OUP, Oxford, 1964), Part I, pp.471-2. For his exhortation to visitation, see B. Tierney, *Medieval Poor Law* (University of California Press, Berkeley, 1959), p.101.

46. Supra, note 35, Pugh, *Imprisonment*, p.333.

47. Bellamy, *Crime and Public Order*. Bellamy's example from the complaint of the Commons of Berkshire, whilst very possibly true is a little ambiguous — it may be that the indicted felons are released there on acquittal. For the complaint itself see note 26, supra.

48. *Mirror of Justices*, Book II, ch. ix, W.J. Whittaker (ed.), vol.7, Selden Society (1893), p.52.

49. *Fleta*, Bk 1, ch.27; H.G. Richardson and G.O. Sayles (eds.), vol.72, Selden Society, p.68.

50. Hurnard, *King's Pardon*, p.89.

51. 5 Edward II, Ordinances ch. xxxiv (repealed 15 Edward II, ch.1); 1 Edward III, Stat 1, ch. iii; 14 Edward III, stat 1, ch.x.

52. Hanawalt, *Crime and Conflict*, p.36 cf. Hugh of Kirton's case supra, note 42. On approvers generally see F.C. Hamil, 'The King's Approvers; A Chapter in the History of English Criminal Law', 11, *Speculum* (1936), p.238.

53. Statute of Westminster I, ch.xii. On the provision see Summerson, 'Peine Forte et Dure', pp.116 et seq.

54. Summerson, 'Peine Forte et Dure', p.116.

55. Ibid., p.125.

56. Bassett, 'Newgate Prison', p.245.

57. Clay, *Medieval Hospitals*, p.99.

58. Pugh, *Imprisonment*, p.361.

59. M.D. Legge, *Anglo-Norman Letters and Petitions* (Blackwell, Oxford, 1941), pp.31-2 for Ludgate; M. Bassett, 'The Fleet Prison in the Middle Ages', vol. 5, *University of Toronto Law Journal* (1943-4), p.383 at p.399 on 'Godspence'. This was a deodand paid generally to the poor; Pugh, *Imprisonment*, p.330.

60. J. Huizinga, *The Waning of the Middle Ages* (Penguin ed., Harmondsworth, 1955), p.24.

PART TWO

The Early Modern Period

3
DEVELOPMENTS IN PUNISHMENT

Any consideration of the nature and conditions of imprisonment during the early modern period might at first lead one to suppose that it was a time of little change. In both 1500 and 1750 the majority of those held were either debtors or awaiting criminal trial, and their conditions throughout were generally unpleasant unless they had funds. 'Art thou poor and in prison?' asked Thomas Dekker, 'Then thou art buried before thou art dead'.[1] This was no mere literary exaggeration, for instance the Commons Committee examining conditions in the Marshalsea noted that during the spring between eight and ten prisoners died each day from natural causes.[2] There were some limited attempts at reforming legislation but they were largely ineffective, and this is hardly surprising given the lack of a coherent penal policy, and indeed anything approaching a philosophy of punishment. Thomas More might advocate humanitarian treatment in *Utopia*, but the prevailing views of criminal sanctions two centuries later accorded far more closely with those of the author of *Hanging, Not punishment enough*.

This is not to say that there were no developments during the period under review, and although we should be cautious of any Whiggish view of a steady progression towards a more enlightened and liberal idea of punishment, there were still some important changes in attitudes. These revolved partly around the development of protestant religious views of salvation, and partly relatedly around the realisation of possible economic values in punishment. Although writers agree that imprisonment in the medieval period was largely, although as we have seen not entirely, custodial and coercive in nature, yet by the middle of the eighteenth century there was more recognition that goals of punishment and rehabilitation could be present in the system. Such ideas were closely linked with the extraction of labour from inmates and find their key expression in the establishment of the Bridewell for the vagrant and petty offender. It was realised that those who had transgressed in more serious fashion could also be useful although their removal from society remained a primary consideration. There was, however, scope for service abroad, and as Langbein has noted, both transportation and military service came to provide outlets for penal labour in the seventeenth century. In the new nation states there was a perceptible shift in society's treatment of all types of undesirable, and indeed Foucault has argued that this was the age of the Great Confinement. For the first time the state attempted to remove uneconomic elements from its midst by sending the rogue and vagabond to the Bridewell, whilst the sick and insane were locked in asylums.

Paralleling these changes in the motivation and methods of punishment were measures to ameliorate the lot of the individual prisoner. There was an increasing realisation that wrongdoers were capable of reform, economic factors were not the only ones at play and we should not ignore the work of humanitarian and religious reformers in the civilising process. Humanitarian concerns were always present, at a basic level we can see this in the frequent refusal of juries to convict in cases of felony. There was a widespread realisation of the abuses which were present in the prisons, and indeed they were one reason why prison sentences were so rarely considered as a punishment at this time. Increasingly religious groups and others attempted to fight the worst faults of the system. There were some areas of progress, particularly in the treatment of insolvent debtors, and towards the end of the period there is some slight evidence of increasing attempts to impose some controls on the gaols by those in authority. However, for the most part attempts at improvements achieved little until much later in the eighteenth century, and elements of the unreformed system survived into the Victorian era. Notable failures of reforming groups included the Bray Commission and Oglethorpe's enquiries in the 1720s; like many others they found vested interests hard to fight in a parliament which was dominated by pressure groups. When Howard visited the gaols in the 1770s English practice was far behind that of many other European countries, but changes from his time can often be traced back to the groundwork of an earlier generation.

Although debtors remained the largest numerical group in gaol throughout the period under review and provoked an ever increasing amount of legislation designed to deal with their problems, there are perhaps less significant innovations to be found in their treatment than in that accorded to other groups of inmates. Fuller consideration of debtors will be found in the next chapter but it may be useful to give some further attention to the treatment of criminals and vagrants at this stage, since it was in these areas that new theories and practice came to the fore.

Criminal Sanctions

It would be foolish to suppose that people in early modern England gave much thought to matters of penological principle. Imprisonment was of little account and existed in the main to ensure the presence of a person at trial or to force him into a certain action. As Babington notes 'The only penological principle . . . seems to have been that the criminal should be encouraged to feel a proper sense of repentance for his crime and a stoical resignation regarding his punishment.'[3] This is not to say that there were at this time no changes in types of punishment, and various writers have shown that the sixteenth century saw the introduction of a savage penal code in large areas of Europe. The Carolina in Germany dates from the 1520s, whilst in England a series of harsh penal statutes were introduced in the Marian period. The reasons for this must be sought elsewhere, but procedurally the change was probably assisted by the decline in the old notion of felony as being a feudal matter, and as simply a class of serious crime which was visited by capital punishment.

From the viewpoint of the state the capital sanction was the easiest to impose and the most effective at this early period. There was no widespread rural bureaucracy, at least until the emergence of the Elizabethan JP, to enforce compliance with the criminal law. To a large extent law enforcement rested upon the voluntary, and often unwilling, services of the village constable. Modern criminologists agree that a major deterrent to criminal activity is the certainty of detection; this could not be ensured during the sixteenth century, and the wide range of capital sanctions served instead to enforce the law through terror. A public execution would draw a mass of spectators who would be deterred by example, something which incarceration behind the walls of a prison could not achieve. Also whilst financial sanctions could be used against the nobility, for the mass of landless poor they were useless and little alternative was therefore available to capital punishment.

Although historians since the time of Froude have shown that traditional views of high execution rates need to be regarded with caution, it seems probable that the start of the early modern period saw more executions than the end. This may seem surprising when we consider the increasing number of offences which carried the death penalty especially during the later seventeenth and eighteenth centuries. It seems probable that this increase in the number of capital crimes was a function of the change in the balance of political power after the Restoration, as the newly emergent landed classes sought to protect their property rights against real or imagined threats. They promoted a large number of unconnected measures which sought to cover particular offences that were on occasion already covered by statute. Particular pressure groups could obtain a new act with relative ease, and as a result we find the introduction of a large number of new penal measures, one extreme example the Waltham Black Act[4] adding over 200 capital crimes by itself. This increase in the number of capital offences was paralleled by increasing penalties for other crimes, and for example an Act of 1717 increased the sanction for petty larceny from whipping to transportation.[5]

Yet although the number of capital crimes increased markedly over the period the number of executions showed no such increase, and visions of a vast Tudor and Stuart crime wave need to be viewed with great suspicion. Indeed writers such as Cockburn have shown that there was no dramatic increase in crime.[6] A slow increase in the Elizabethan period tailed off in the seventeenth century although there was something of an increase during the 1620s. There were particular problem areas, and for instance it seems that there were genuine and justified fears of a growth in crime in London in the early eighteenth century, noted among others by Fielding, Defoe and Walpole. However, there have always been fears of an increasing crime rate. As Geoffrey Pearson has shown, hooligans and a juvenile crime wave have been with us for over 200 years. Such beliefs were also to be found in the sixteenth century, and Edward Hext the Somerset JP was much concerned by the 'rapes and theft committed within this county where I serve, and finding they multiply daily to the utter impoverishing of the poor husbandman'.[7]

Although crime rates seem to have changed only slowly, the notions of criminality also changed. To the Elizabethans the main problems were the threat of vagrancy, and perhaps on a wider European scale the developing notion of the criminality of sin. Protestant groups called for severe action against those involved in immoral behaviour, in Switzerland the Calvinists took widespread powers against such practices, whilst Bucer advocated the death penalty for sabbath breaking.[8] During the seventeenth century the concerns of criminal law in this country changed, and we find the increasing use of sanctions against property crime, and attempts to criminalise certain traditional activities of the poorer classes, notably in the new game laws, possibly associated with increasing efforts to enforce wage discipline.

There was probably little significant alteration in the level of criminal activity, although the types of offence might change. Yet for various reasons an increasing number of criminal sanctions resulted in no great increase in the use of the death penalty. Firstly local communities were often ineffectively policed, and villagers were anyway unwilling to take action against transgressors unless they stepped badly out of line. Many actions for theft were dealt with as trespass rather than felonies in order that the perpetrator might escape execution, and indeed Baker suggests that 25 per cent of such actions in the time of Henry VII could have qualified as felonies.[9] If a case did reach court then juries were often unwilling to convict, or if they did undervalued the goods so that capital punishment might be avoided. Offenders might also escape the results of their misdeed by pleading clergy. Despite some attempts at limitation under Henry VII and Henry VIII in the number of clergyable offences in the early part of the period, murder on the highway being added in 1512, piracy in 1536, and stealing from the person privily in 1565, there was at the same time a corresponding increase in the numbers who could so plead, either through enactment or ever increasing literacy, until eventually in 1705[10] the privilege was extended to all without proof. However, there was immediate reaction to this since it was felt that too many offenders were escaping with a whipping (physical punishment served as an alternative to imprisonment in such cases), and there were further attempts to render offences non-clergyable, including for example an act of 1717 which disallowed it for housebreaking.[11]

If an offender was actually adjudged guilty he might still escape the rope through a pardon. The eighteenth century was marked by a growing use of the pardon, and Ignatieff notes that many of those sentenced for 'new' offences were transported rather than executed.[12] Transgressors also relied on their connections with great men, either as their servants or tenants, and asked them to intercede on their behalf. It has been argued that this system helped to increase the power of the gentry as their patronage helped to secure the obedience and docility of the common man. As a result of these various escape routes many of those convicted of felony escaped execution, and Sharpe estimates that 86 per cent of those found guilty of grand larceny in Essex were reprieved.[13]

Theories of Punishment

Although the criminal justice system of the period may seem harsh and illogical to modern humanitarian eyes, it had much to commend it. At a time when justice could not be certain, given the lack of a local bureaucracy, although the system of local JPs was remarkably efficient on a limited scale, it was felt that deterrence had to be severe in order to be effective. Writers at the time said as much, and in the later part of the period we find a large number of pamphlets justifying this doctrine of maximum severity, and indeed calling for a more severe application of penal sanctions. Perhaps the best known of such documents was the anonymous *Hanging, Not punishment enough* of 1701 which advocated severe penalties '[not] that man's blood should be shed, but that it should not'.[14] The terror of example was also advocated by later writers, Ollyffe suggesting that miscreants should be broken on the wheel[15], and were echoed as late as 1785 by William Paley in his *Principles of moral and political philosophy*.[16]

It may be felt that the foregoing strays beyond a history of imprisonment, yet it is important to make the point that imprisonment was little esteemed as a penal sanction at this time. As John Taylor the 'Water Poet' observed, many called 'jaile a magazine of sin, an universitie of villany, an academy of foule blasphemy, a sinke of drunkenesse'.[17] At the same time imprisonment involved no public penalty, and it was also expensive to provide.

However, over the course of the two centuries one may observe an increasing tendency for some authors to argue in favour of a system of punishment which was based on more humanitarian principles, whilst at the same time there was a realisation that 'imprisonment' could be made to serve more economic ends. Perhaps the first significant suggestion that there should be some mitigation in the harsh penal code came from Sir Thomas More. In *Utopia*[18] he notes that despite the large number of executions there are still many robbers about. If there were sufficient livelihood for all then the need for theft would be removed. He suggests that it is morally unjust to take a man's life for theft and also practically foolish not to distinguish between types of crime, 'For simple theft is not so great an offence that it ought to be punished with death'. A system of hard labour would prove more beneficial, with offenders being set upon public works. He did not advocate imprisonment as such, except in cases of robbery with violence, although offenders working in the community would be locked up at night. These views were echoed in remarks by Cardinal Pole reported by Thomas Starkey; rather than execution for every petty theft

> better it were to find some way how the man might be brought to better order and frame . . . I would think it good that the felon should be taken and put in some common work, as to labour in building the walls of cities and towns, or else in some magnificent work of the prince of the realm, which pain should be more grievous to them than death is reputed.[19]

A contrasting traditionalist view is given by Thomas Lupton in *Too good to be true* which imitates the style of Utopia.[20]

Various lawyers in the sixteenth and early seventeenth centuries agreed that frequent use of capital punishment did little to cut the crime rate. Some such as Fortescue thought that if the offender did not fear stern penalties as seemed to be the case then he would certainly not be deterred by milder sanctions.[21] Coke also noted that capital punishments did not deter criminals although he did not propose any alterations in the sanction.[22] Spelman, however, noted that inflation had made lives cheaper over the sixteenth century and proposed that there should be some review of the punishment to take account of this.[23]

Although lawyers generally advocated no great changes in the system other commentators felt that the frequent use of the death penalty was out of all proportion to the need for it. Dekker made reference to the topic in *The Honest Whore*, 'Many lose their lives for scarce as much coin as will hide their palm, which is most cruel',[24] and his views were echoed by the Quaker George Fox, and the Leveller Samuel Chidley who felt that minor property offences in particular should not carry the penalty.[25] During the Commonwealth there was a mass of pamphleteering in favour of reforms in the criminal law and there seemed to be some hope of change. Thus we find Cromwell commenting,

> To hang a man for six and eightpence, and I know not what; to hang for a trifle, and acquit murder is in the ministration of the law through the ill-framing of it. I have known in my experience abominable murders acquitted. And to see men lose their lives for petty matters: this is a thing God will reckon for, And I wish it may not lie upon this nation a day longer than you have an opportunity to give a remedy.[26]

As far as the Levellers were concerned capital punishment should be abolished for all offences except murder, but at the same time they were not in favour of the use of prison as punishment, favouring rather the use of restitution, and forced labour as bondsmen under the supervision of a taskmaster. Such punishments were for example advocated by Chidley and Winstanley; to them prison was only a place for ensuring safe custody before trial.[27] However, the reforming zeal of the period came to nothing and 70 years later we can still find writers such as Sollom Emlyn bewailing the severity of treatment meted out to minor offenders.[28] Nonetheless the idea of hard labour remained popular and commentators like Berkeley felt that it could fill a useful role instead of execution, with some sort of correctional institution for young miscreants.[29]

    Although those calling for a degree of mitigation in the severity of the law met with little success, there was in reality no great increase in executions as a result of the harsher penal code, and a growing proportion of offenders obtained some sort of reprieve. It seems that although relatively little was done in the way of formal legislation there was still an increasing realisation that offenders could be put to the use of the state, perhaps an echo of the views of More and Winstanley, and there is at least some slight development of a concept of rehabilitation.

In these altering ideas of punishment and rehabilitation the prison as yet played little part. To contemporary observers they were rather breeding grounds of vice which were themselves in need of reform. Coke commented 'Few or none are committed to the common gaol . . . but they come out worse than they went in.'[30] Similar views were put forward in the Book of Orders of 1631[31] which suggested that offenders should be sent to the House of Correction (dealt with below) before trial rather than the gaol 'since they may learn honesty by labour, and not live idly and miserably long in prison, whereby they are much worse when they come out than they were when they went in.' The writer of *Hanging, Not punishment enough* also felt that the prison system was in need of reform.

> I have in this paper taken but little notice of the scandalous wickedness and corruption of prisons and none of their keepers . . . They are now known to be the sanctuaries of villains, from whence their emissaries are dispatch'd, and a regular and settled correspondence is said to be fix'd and carried on, through the whole fraternity of rogues in England.

The problem required a treatise of its own and reform by parliament, 'for no less power and wisdom than that of a parliament can regulate and reform them'.[32] He did, however, recommend that gaol delivery should be made more frequent and that suspected felons should be kept in separate cells to increase their punishment and to prevent moral contamination. Other contemporary accounts are full of stories of penal corruption, and although there were attempts at reform, as we shall see later they were almost entirely ineffective.

Transportation and Military Service

However, although the prison as such played little part in the changing penal theories of the time, yet associated measures, in particular transportation and the Bridewell, were of no little significance. This theme has been developed by Langbein in his work *Torture and the Law of Proof,*[33] which suggests that transportation from this country to America and galley service on the Continent were closely linked. Galley service was particularly favoured by states with a Mediterranean seaboard; in the early modern period the sailing vessel had not achieved any great sophistication and was at a disadvantage in areas of relatively calm water. The Ottoman Empire in particular was quick to exploit the manoeuvrability of galleys, and both France and Spain developed similar fleets manned by convicts to counter the threat. The galleys were greatly feared as a punishment in France and there were attempts to stop convicts mutilating themselves to avoid such labour. In this country the idea never really progressed as waters were not suitable, although the statute of 1597 against vagrants mentioned galleys as a penalty,[34] and an attempt was made to create a fleet manned by felons in 1601-2. Sir William Monson still regarded them as a useful deterrent three decades later in his Naval Tracts, 'The terror of galleys will make men avoid sloth and pilfering and apply themselves to labour and pains; it will keep servants and apprentices in awe.' It is noteworthy that he already regards the House of Correction as flawed, a place where 'people are punished or pardoned as they are able to gratify their keeper'.[35]

Although galleys never prospered here, there was, as we have seen, a long tradition of campaigns abroad being serviced by the inmates of prisons who might be pardoned in return for enrolment in the armed forces. Two examples quoted by Griffiths in his *Chronicles of Newgate* will serve to show the practice. In 1589 'certain prisoners shut out from pardon because they are by law bailable beg that the words may be struck out of the order for release, and state that they will gladly enter Her Majesty's Service.'[36] Again in 1619 'The Lord Mayor certifies to the King that certain prisoners in Newgate, whose names and offences are given, are not committed for murder; so they are reprieved as able bodied and fit to do service in foreign parts.'[37] It was pointed out that such men would give excellent service, 'for they would not dare to run away'. Debtors might also be freed to go into the army. An act of 1702 allowed for the release of those with estates amounting to less than £10, but for those under £40, discharge would depend on their willingness 'to serve Her Majesty by sea or land'.[38] An earlier echo of this idea is found in the petition from prisoners in the Fleet asking that they might be freed in order to satisfy their creditors by labour, or 'the king and realm may have use of their bodies for the defence of their country',[39] and for instance Mansfeld's army in the Low Countries in 1624 consisted partly of debtors.

There was also another area in which prisoners could be put to the use of the state in a task which was at first not generally popular, since there was a need to develop the new colonial plantations in America. Transportation of felons on a voluntary basis was mooted in 1611 and the first convicts were sent to Virginia in 1615.[40] Indeed the power to send vagabonds abroad had already been given by an act of 1597-8.[41] Prisoners had their offences pardoned or sentences commuted on the understanding that they would leave the country. A parallel can perhaps be seen with the medieval idea of outlaws being banished from the realm. The new system had the benefit of removing a dangerous threat to society whilst at the same time bringing the state economic and political benefits overseas; estate owners also prospered. Only a few hundred convicts were transported in the period before 1650, but in the reign of Charles II the practice was put on a more regular footing and around 5000 convicts sent to America in the last half of the century.

By the end of the century there was a degree of colonial resistance to any further transportation, and Virginia passed statutes outlawing the practice; however the colonies were overruled by the mother country and transportation was given more legal backing by an act of 1717[42] which made it the stated penalty for certain offences. During the next half century many more miscreants were sent to the Americas under this and other measures. Serious offenders could thus be put to the service of the state in a variety of ways, whilst for the vagabond and minor offender the Bridewell appeared to offer hope of reform.

The origins of the House of Correction

The Elizabethan period was one of great social change. In part this reflected a rapid increase in the population level, estimated by some observers at around 40 per cent during the sixteenth century. At the same time the earlier break up of traditional feudal structures and the introduction of new agricultural techniques encouraged a still greater degree of physical and social mobility. Indeed Weisser has suggested that only 15 per cent of rural families lived in the same villages in 1660 as their ancestors in 1560.[43] The degree of change should not be overstated, agricultural enclosure affected only small sections of the population at this time, predominantly copyholders in the Midland shires. However there were clear indications of the presence of new forces, and most importantly these were evident to contemporary observers. Thus we, find complaints of sheep devouring men and manifestations of peasant unrest, whilst at the same time there were the first small hints of industrialisation and factory production with the establishment of Jack of Newbury's weaving sheds which employed 200 people in the same place.

Enclosure created a growing body of landless labour, and there was an ever present trend towards urbanisation. Wage rates also fell sharply in the second half of the century. As a result many people were forced on to the road and contemporary writers constantly refer to the problem of sturdy beggars whose numbers were apparently ever on the increase. 'Hark hark the dogs do bark, the beggars are coming to town', would have been no mere childish verse to Elizabethan eyes. Modern historians such as A.T. Beier have demonstrated that contemporary fears about vagrancy were partially unfounded.[44] Although the majority of vagrants were single men, and might therefore expect to be viewed with suspicion, they were generally on the move looking for work in the new economic conditions. It is, however, fair to point out as has Pound[45] that a proportion of these vagrants were of dubious character, and other writers have demonstrated that criminal activity was fairly commonplace throughout the lower orders when the opportunity arose. Whatever their nature the increased number of beggars posed a threat to the stability of Tudor society. To the government they represented a challenge to the new political order based on the centralised power of the state, whilst locally the gentry saw their property rights threatened.

Poverty had always been a feature of society, and the medieval religious order had stressed the importance of the relationship between rich and poor. Monastic and other charities had enabled some provision to be made for the needy, although it has been suggested that their indiscriminate relief did little to tackle basic problems. However, to contemporary observers it was apparent that there was some need for measures to deal with the vacuum left by the dissolution of the monastic and other religious foundations, and in the middle of the century we find the consolidation of the system of royal hospitals in London for the various needy elements of society. As far as the poor were concerned Tudor society slowly developed the concepts of two basic orders, the deserving and undeserving poor, and different methods were adopted to deal with them. For the deserving poor, that is the halt and lame, there were traditionally licenses to beg, and there were 1,000 licensed beggars in London in 1517, but later thought suggested that they should be dealt with in hospital and an act of 1535[46] sought to put an end to public begging.

However, it was the growing number of sturdy beggars who represented a threat to the established order. Early provision for such types concentrated on whipping and return to their parish of origin, where they would be a problem for others, but from the 1530s we see the gradual evolution of the idea of enforced labour. It is perhaps no coincidence that the importance of labour was stressed in puritan theology, which also saw indolence at the root of most disorders in society. Thus we find Calvin making the following remarks: 'Let each of us remember that he has been created by God for the purpose of labouring and of being vigorously employed in his work'.[47] He condemns 'indolent and worthless persons who employ themselves in no useful occupation',[48] and also comments 'He therefore, who lives to himself alone, so as to be profitable in no way to the human race, nay more, is a burden to others, giving help to no one, is on good grounds reckoned to be disorderly'.[49] These thoughts were echoed by many English puritan thinkers, one such being William Perkins who described idleness as 'the shop of the Divell', and also commented that 'sloth and negligence in the duties of our callings are a disorder against the comly order which God hath set in the societies of mankind . . . and indeed idleness and sloth are the causes of many damnable sins.'[50]

Such commentators felt that good works in the form of alms provision were an infringement of God's law, and that vagrants should be set to work at all costs. We find an echo of such thoughts in a statute of 1547[51] which directed that vagabonds should be enslaved to those reporting them, for two years, or life if they tried to escape. However, there is no evidence that this statute was ever enforced, and it is to the provision of Bridewell for the correction of vagabonds in London that we should look for the first effective punitive use of labour.

The scheme for the development of Bridewell was in part the

brainchild of one Richard Grafton. He shared the growing belief
that a distinction could be made between the different classes of
pauper, and felt that begging should be forbidden, with some
form of relief being given to the incapable, whilst those who
could should be forced to work. To this end Nicholas Ridley,
Bishop of London, persuaded Edward VI to make available the
little used Royal Palace at Bridewell as a place where a 'house of
occupations' could be provided. Labour could be provided for
the child 'unapt to learning', those who had been sick, 'and unto
this shall be brought the sturdy and idle: and likewise such
prisoners as are quit at the sessions, that there they may be set to
labour'.[52] McConville points out that such a variety of tasks and
inmates shows the confusion of thought behind the experiment,
and suggests that

> Bridewell was also a kind of social lazar house: it kept in limbo
> various petty offenders, and by keeping them apart from society
> in a way which whipping, stocks or pillory did not do, reduced
> for the time of confinement, scandal to the commonwealth and
> subversion of its moral solidarity.[53]

Bridewell received its first inmates at the end of 1556 and for
the next half century it fulfilled a useful function as part of the
city package for dealing with the problems of the poor. A variety
of tasks and trades were carried on there, ranging from the
provision of some apprenticeships for the younger inmates and
children from Christ's Hospital, to a series of hard labouring
tasks for the more recalcitrant offenders, such as the beating of
hemp. Vagrants were generally whipped before being sent to
work and might be set to punitive tasks such as the cleaning of
ditches. However, productive work was available, raw materials
being provided by City merchants, and goods were sold alongside
their own wares so as to remove the problem of competition. In
theory the scheme was to be partly self financed from the profits
of inmate labour, but it seems unlikely that their work was ever
of great value, and for the most part the institution was funded
by a compulsory levy on local inhabitants. This is of some
significance since it enabled a salaried staff to be provided.
Although fees were not entirely absent the keepers did not rely
on them for their livelihood, thus avoiding one of the problems
which was ever present in the gaols. Indeed given the penniless

state of most of the inmates such a self financing system could not have made much headway. It is noteworthy that when the City did attempt to farm out Bridewell to private control for six months in 1602[54] most of the pauper inmates were immediately turned out, and the new owners turned the place into a brothel to make money.

There is considerable evidence that the scheme was successful at least in its early years. Various other towns set up their own Bridewells; some schemes such as that operated in Norwich were openly punitive in intent, others such as Ipswich's catered also for the deserving poor. Indeed the Whitby Bridewell of 1637[55] seems to have been designed entirely for the relief of destitution. An act of 1575-6[56] allowed for the erection of Houses of Correction, as they had become known, in all counties, for the setting to work and punishing of the idle poor and rogues. JPs were to be responsible for the staffing and financing of the institutions. Although such houses were not yet compulsory it is evident that this statute spurred their construction. At the same time although there is some disagreement as to whether it was the only influence it seems likely that the British example encouraged the development of similar institutions abroad, most notably in the case of the Amsterdam Rasphuis (so called from the labour of the inmates rasping hard wood to provide materials for dyes) established in 1596.

Contemporaries quoted approvingly of the results achieved by the Houses of Correction. Perhaps the best known comment comes from Coke, 'Few or none are committed to the common gaol . . . but they come out worse than they went in. And few are committed to the House of Correction or Working House but they come out better'.[57] The Somerset JP Edward Hext made a similar observation.

> I sent divers wandering suspicious persons to the House of Correction, and all in general would beseech me with bitter tears to send them rather to the gaol, and denying it them, some confessed felonies unto me by which they hazarded their lives, to the end they would not be sent to the House of Correction, where they should be enforced to work.[58]

Other commentators such as Perkins felt that Elizabethan pauper legislation was running along the right lines, and of the 1597 Act

which restated the importance of labour and the House of
Correction he said that it was the very law of God and ought
never to be repealed. An Act of 1609[59] made the erection of
Bridewells compulsory in every county, but from this time we
hear less of their value, and slowly during the seventeenth
century their function became indistinguishable from the local
gaols whose faults they inherited. Already in the 1620s Monson
was complaining about the system,[60] whilst by 1751 we find
Fielding commenting about prisoners that 'the most impudent
and flagitious have always been such as have been acquainted
with the discipline of Bridewell,'[61] and noting that magistrates
were unwilling to send offenders to such places for fear of
completing their demoralisation.

At this stage it may be useful to consider the role which various
theorists have ascribed to the House of Correction. To various
Marxist historians the Bridewells at least in their first inception
occupied a key position in the development of imprisonment. To
Melossi and Pavarini[62] it was a system whereby labour could be
conditioned to the development of industrial manufacturing; the
spirit of the feudal peasantry was to be broken by the labour demands of Bridewell. It was not necessarily the most efficient use of
labour but significantly it gave people a taste of wage discipline.
To Weisser the new poor law was a piece of class legislation since it
gave those in power an effective means of dealing with the lower
orders. 'The poor laws of Europe could not ameliorate poverty,
but they could be used as an effective method of social control,
particularly when they were incorporated into the general system
of criminal law.'[63]

Other writers such as Rusche and Kirchheimer and Ignatieff
have also attempted to show that the Bridewell was closely linked
to the needs of the labour market. Rusche and Kirchheimer[64]
suggest that the Bridewells were initially an ideological experiment by the middle class attempting to force a laborious
existence on the lower orders. In the seventeenth century,
however, the fall in population growth forced capitalists to turn
to state assistance in the form of Bridewells which forced labour
into the market. Ignatieff notes these ideas[65] but inverts them
and suggests that incarceration flourished in times of high
unemployment and population growth, when there was a need to
remove labour from the market and put it to the use of the state.
Such theories are highly speculative, and it should be remem-

bered that incarceration rests on many other factors such as the ability of the state to enforce measures which it sees as being theoretically desirable, the contemporary enthusiasm for different types of penal solution, and the varying attitudes present at different times towards prosecution for particular offences. It may be that one should not really attempt to stretch the labour theory beyond Melossi and Pavarini's idea that the Bridewell served to enforce labour discipline, and in this connection one should perhaps note parallels in the Statute of Labourers going back to 1351,[66] and the contemporary Statute of Artificers of 1604[67] which sought to extend state control over the labour force. Certainly the Bridewells were rarely able to provide economically efficient labour and Innes notes that keepers were often to be found seeking reimbursement for the cost of materials which they had provided. Indeed, she suggests that the Bridewell may have done little but provide a package of poor relief at minimal cost to the county authorities, and there were frequent complaints about the expense of such provision.

The idea of relative enthusiasms for different penal sanctions is of some importance and Ignatieff notes four periods when the House of Correction was in vogue. The initial period of growth was at the end of the sixteenth century, then followed the period in the 1690s when there were experiments in Bristol Mint and in Bellar's College of Industry; later periods of enthusiasm came in the 1720s and 1750s.[68] It would, however, generally seem to be the case that the Bridewells lost much of their initial reforming role in the seventeenth century as they underwent some change in function. What went wrong?

At least in part it seems that the problem lay in their loss of a distinctive role. Although the London Bridewell was originally designed for particular groups of pauper, it seems that this clarity of purpose was soon lost. In the later Elizabethan period some religious offenders were sent there, and this practice continued until Thomas Ellwood's time in the middle of the next century.[69] Other political offenders might also be housed there, and certainly from 1591-8 Bridewell was the centre where political offenders were tortured.[70] Then in the seventeenth century JPs took the power to send a growing number of petty offenders to the House of Correction, and Innes points out that assize judges could send defendants there for petty larceny offences after 1615.[71] McConville notes that Bury St Edmunds' Bridewell was receiving non-felonious offenders as early as 1588,[72] whilst the Webbs quote Middlesex where in 1617 the justices tried to ensure that servants, apprentices and other unruly and disorderly persons sent to the Bridewell merely 'to receive correction for the better humbling of them for their duties' should be kept apart from the rogues and criminals housed there.[73] Similarly Dalton's *Countrey Justice* listed five kinds of person who could be sent to the Bridewell, these being, the riotous prodigal person who consumes all in play and drink, the dissolute person, strumpet or pilferer, the slothful person refusing to work, all who wilfully spoil or embezzle their work, and finally the vagabond.[74] As Sharpe has shown a wide range of offenders were sent to the Chelmsford Bridewell during the seventeenth century, as what he terms the more folklorique punishments for misdemeanours fell into disuse.[75] Many misdemeanours were seen as being indicative of an idle and improvident life rather than misdeeds in themselves and were therefore ideally suited to the reformative treatment provided by the Bridewell. Punishment of petty offenders in the House of Correction was regularised by statute in 1719,[76] and from this time the Bridewell could take all types of offenders except felons who were still required to be lodged in the common gaol. With the resultant variety of socially undesirable inmates it is perhaps not surprising that early ideals could not be maintained.

At the same time there were administrative problems. The statute of 1609[77] enjoined that Bridewells should be built close to gaols, and naturally given the desire of county authorities to save money there was a tendency to put both under the same administration. We can therefore note an increasing amount of abuse as justices ceased to make adequate financial provision for the system and merely handed power to the keepers to extract what money they could from fees and the products of inmate labour. Bridewells were never economically cost effective given the quality of labour they dealt with and the unwillingness of county authorities to make sufficient materials available. There was always a desire to reduce the levels of poor relief, and the results of cost cutting experiments in the London Bridewell have already been referred to.

Then one must remember the general problem of inertia. Coke suggests that as JPs became more 'tepidi or trepidi' then beggary began to flourish again,[78] and both Innes and McConville make something of this point. It has been noted elsewhere that different periods concern themselves with different social problems; in penal terms the late sixteenth and early seventeenth century concerns with the poor were replaced with attention to the insolvent debtor, and on a criminal level by the property rights of a newly emergent gentry, and experiments with transportation. Sharpe feels that society became more settled after 1650, and that vagrancy simply ceased to be a major issue; change and decay in the Bridewell may simply have reflected this.

McConville suggests that the erosion in power of the Privy Council may also have been of some importance.[79] It had bolstered the power of the JPs in the sixteenth century, and had also encouraged the Bridewell as a means of social control. However, after the Restoration the Privy Council lost its power whilst the JPs reinforced theirs. This was the period when preeminently sectional interests ruled the country, hence the concern in parliament with capital legislation designed to reinforce property rights, whilst at a local level the wish was to minimise the burden which poor relief and the Bridewells placed on the county. One may notice an increasing tendency merely to pass vagrants on to the next parish. As Ignatieff has shown periods of great social distress in the 1690s and 1720s sparked new concern with the idea of institutions which could enforce labour, reduce the costs of poor relief, and reduce the dangers of petty crime, but he comments 'By the 1750s workhouses had become once more somnolent shelters for the aged, the lunatic, and the orphaned'.[80] However, the ideas of labour discipline which had first been practised in the Bridewell were soon to reappear in the general prison system.

Notes

1. G. Salgado, *Elizabethan Underworld* (Dent, London, 1977), p.169. Dekker provides much useful material on London prisons in his dramatic works. A useful commentary is to be found in P. Shaw, 'The Position of Thomas Dekker in Jacobean Prison Literature', *Publications of the Modern Language Association of America*, vol. 62 (1947), pp.366-91.
2. *Journals of the House of Commons*, vol. 21, p.378.
3. S.McConville, *A History of English Prison Administration*, vol. 1 (Routledge, London, 1981), p.4.
4. 9 George I, ch 22. On the history of the act see E.P. Thompson, *Whigs and Hunters* (Allen Lane, London, 1975).

5. 4 George I, ch.11.

6. 'The Nature and Incidence of Crime in England 1559-1625' in J. Cockburn (ed.) *Crime in England 1550-1800* (Methuen, London, 1977). See also J. Sharpe, *Crime in Early Modern England 1550-1750* (Longmans, London, 1984).

7. R. Tawney and E. Power, *Tudor Economic Documents*, vol. 2 (London, 1924), p.339. An interesting account of the problem generally is given in G. Pearson, *Hooligan, a History of Respectable Fears* (Macmillan, London, 1983).

8. L. Radzinowicz, *A History of English Criminal Law*, vol. 1 (Stevens, London, 1948), p. 262. See also *Complaynt of Roderyck Mors*, EETS (extra series), vol.22 (1874), p.18.

9. E.W. Ives, 'English Law and English Society', *History*, vol. 66 (1981), p.52.

10. M. Ignatieff, *A Just Measure of Pain* (Macmillan, London, 1978), p.18.

11. 4 George I, ch.11.

12. Ignatieff, *Just Measure of Pain*, p.19.

13. J. Sharpe, *Crime in Seventeenth Century England* (CUP, Cambridge, 1983), p.146.

14. Radzinowicz, *History*, vol.1, pp.231-5.

15. G. Ollyffe, *An Essay Humbly Offer'd . . .To Prevent Capital Crimes* (1731). See Radzinowicz, *History*, vol.1, pp.235-8.

16. See also M. Madan, *Thoughts on Executive Justice* (1785). See Radzinowicz, *History*, vol.1, pp.239-59, for a discussion of their ideas.

17. J. Taylor, *All the Works of John Taylor the Water Poet* (1630), p.128. It is only fair to point out that Taylor himself thought gaol, 'a school of vertue is, a house of study and contemplation, a place of discipline and reformation'.

18. T. More, *Utopia*, Book 1 (Penguin, Harmondsworth, 1965), pp.51-2.

19. T. Starkey, *Life and Letters*, EETS (extra series), vol.32, (1927), pp.119-20.

20. An interesting survey of sixteenth-century views of punishment is contained in E. Rose, 'Too Good to be True', in J. Guth (ed.), *Tudor Rule and Revolution* (CUP, Cambridge, 1982), pp.183-200.

21. J. Fortescue, *De Laudibus Legum Angliae* (1616), p.113.

22. E. Coke, *Institutes of the Laws of England*, vol.3 (1797 ed.), p.243.

23. Radzinowicz, *History*, vol. 1, p.265.

24. T. Dekker, *The Honest Whore* (1604), I,i,5.

25. 'A Cry Against a Crying Sin'. See *Harleian Miscellany*, vol.8 (1746), p.457.

26. Radzinowicz, *History*, vol.1, p.264.

27. D. Veall, *The Popular Movement for Law Reform 1640-1660* (OUP, Oxford, 1970), p.132.

28. Radzinowicz, *History*, vol.1, p.266.

29. Ibid., p.263.

30. Coke, *Institutes*, vol.2, p.729.

31. Sharpe, *Crime in Seventeenth Century England*, p.150.

32. Radzinowicz, *History*, vol.1, p.235.

33. J.H. Langbein, *Torture and the Law of Proof* (University of Chicago Press, Chicago, 1977).

34. 39 Elizabeth, ch.4, s.4.

35. A.V. Judges, *The Elizabethan Underworld* (Routledge, London, 1965), p.lxi.

36. A. Griffiths, *The Chronicles of Newgate*, vol. 1 (Chapman, London, 1884), p.93.

37. Ibid., p.106-7.

38. 1 Anne, ch.19; see also 2&3 Anne, ch.10.

39. A. Harris, *The Oeconomy of the Fleete*, Camden Society, n.s. vol. 25 (1879), p.175.

40. W. Holdsworth, *History of English Law*, vol.11 (Methuen, Sweet &

Maxwell, London, 1938), p.570.
41. 39 Elizabeth, ch 4.
42. 4 George I, ch.11.
43. M. Weisser, *Crime and Punishment in Early Modern Europe* (Harvester, Hassocks, 1979), p.52.
44. A.T. Beier, 'Vagrants and the Social Order in Elizabethan England', *Past and Present*, vol. 64 (1974), p.3ff.
45. J. Pound, *Poverty and Vagrancy in Tudor England* (Longmans, London, 1971). See also his reply to Beier in *Past and Present*, vol. 71 (1976), p.126ff.
46. 27 Henry VIII, ch.25.
47. D. Little, *Religion, Order and Law* (Harper & Row, New York, 1969), p.58.
48. Ibid., p.59.
49. Ibid., p.59.
50. Ibid., p.120.
51. 1 Edward VI, ch.3.
52. Tawney and Power, *Tudor Economic Documents*, vol.2, pp.307-8.
53. McConville, *English Prison Administration*, p.30.
54. E. O'Donoghue, *Bridewell Hospital*, vol. 1 (John Lane, London, 1923), pp.187-204.
55. S. Webb, *English Prisons Under Local Government* (Longmans, London, 1922), p.13.
56. 18 Elizabeth, ch.3.
57. Coke, *Institutes*, vol.2, p.729.
58. Tawney and Power, *Tudor Economic Documents*, vol.2, p.340.
59. 7 James I, ch.4.
60. Judges, *Elizabethan Underworld*, p.lxi, and above p.64.
61. H. Fielding, *Inquiry Into the Late Increase of Robbers* (1751), pp.62-3.
62. D. Melossi and M. Pavarini, *The Prison and the Factory* (Macmillan, London, 1980).
63. M. Weisser, *Crime and Punishment*, p.104.
64. G. Rusche and O. Kirchheimer, *Punishment and Social Structure* (Russell & Russell, New York, 1968).
65. Ignatieff, *Just Measure of Pain*, p.12.
66. 25 Edward III, St.1.
67. 1 James I, ch.6.
68. Ignatieff, *Just Measure of Pain*, p.13.
69. T. Ellwood, *History of the life of Thomas Ellwood* (1714).
70. C. Dobb, *Life and Conditions in London Prisons 1553-1643*, unpublished B.Litt. thesis, Oxford (1952), p.117.
71. J. Innes, *English Houses of Correction and Labour Discipline 1600-1780;: A Critical Examination* (unpublished paper at Warwick conference, 1983), p.40.
72. McConville, *English Prison Administration*, p.40.
73. Webb, *English Prisons*, p.16.
74. M. Dalton, *Countrey Justice* (1709 ed.), p.240.
75. Sharpe, *Crime in Seventeenth Century England*, p.149ff.
76. 6 George I, ch.19.
77. 7 James I, ch.4.
78. Coke, *Institutes*, vol.2, p.729.
79. McConville, *English Prison Administration*, p.47.
80. Ignatieff, *Just Measure of Pain*, p.13.

4

THE PRISON SYSTEM

The Prison Population

Various estimates have been given of the size of the prison population in early modern England but as Dobb has pointed out[1] we have almost no records and can therefore produce no certain figures. Nevertheless several contemporaries gave totals for the inmate population in the seventeenth and eighteenth centuries, and from recent work on gaol deliveries we can produce more reliable figures for individual institutions.

Figures for the total gaol population vary greatly and need to be treated with considerable caution. A barrister, William Leach, estimated in 1651 that between 12,000 and 20,000 people were in gaol.[2] Howard calculated prison occupation at 4,084 when he carried out his survey in the 1770s.[3] The first figure is likely to be something of an overestimate, whilst Howard's calculations have been shown to be rather conservative. When we consider individual gaols we can produce totals which are rather more realistic. Work has been done on many of the gaols in London, for which figures are more readily available, and they show for instance that Newgate generally held around 200 prisoners, although on occasion this figure went up to 400. Certainly the prisons in London were larger than those in the provinces. Few of these held as many as 100 inmates, and when Howard toured the country he found that some were empty.

Although figures for the total prison population are difficult to obtain, we do have rather more idea why people were put into prison and how long they could expect to stay there. There were three main categories of prisoner, those held in connection with criminal charges, the majority of whom were awaiting gaol delivery or execution of sentence, those held for political or religious reasons, and debtors. To these should be added the vagabonds incarcerated in the Bridewell, and other undesirables like pauper lunatics who might end up in the gaols for want of other accommodation. Criminals and debtors, however, made up

76

the vast bulk of the prison population at any one time; political prisoners represented a much smaller group even when the Star Chamber was in operation, but had an importance outweighing their numbers.

Those facing criminal charges might not stay in gaol long. Gaol delivery, nominally three times a year, and generally at least annual, ensured that there was a speedy trial. Cases such as that of a murderer awaiting trial in Hull for three years because delivery there was only septennial were fortunately rare, and reforms in Habeas Corpus after 1679[4] helped to overcome some abuses. Convicted felons would be returned to the gaol after trial to await execution of sentence. Even those who had been acquitted might be returned to prison if they were unable to find their discharge fees, a situation which was not remedied until the 1770s.[5] Capital sentences were generally carried out within a few days, although felons might remain in gaol for many months awaiting transportation or a possible pardon. From the medieval period as we have seen a number of offences were actually punishable by a term of imprisonment, although sentences were generally short and rarely exceeded a year. Indeed Ignatieff has noted that only 2.3 per cent of sentences passed at the Old Bailey between 1770 and 1774 involved imprisonment.[6]

However, although imprisonment was not generally available as punishment in cases of felony there is some indication of an increased use of the sanction by Justices of the Peace in the later part of the period, especially in relation to minor game law infringements and cases of vagrancy. The Vagrancy Act of 1744, for instance, gave power to imprison, 'all persons wand'ring abroad and lodging in alehouses, barns and houses, or in the open air, not giving a good account of themselves.'[7] Offenders who had obtained benefit of clergy, or who had been acquitted for lack of evidence, might also face a spell of incarceration, although they were often sent to the Bridewell alongside vagrants since this was felt to have a more reformative influence than the common gaol. Sharpe notes an increasing tendency to use custodial sanctions in preference to what he terms the more folklorique punishments such as the pillory during the later seventeenth century,[8] and it may be that the growing use of the Bridewell for misdemeanants, regularised by statute in 1719,[9] was a reflection of a new reformative zeal on the part of JPs. However, the use of incarceration remained relatively insignificant against more traditional sanctions such as the fine, pillory, or a whipping. Howard noted only 653 petty offenders (15.9 per cent of his total) in confinement at the time of his survey.[10]

In terms of numbers criminal offenders probably represented the largest part of the prison population although at any one time there might be more debtors in gaol. However, the criminal population had a high turnover and few felons were a long-term charge on the community. There were considerable differences between the criminal inmates and debtors who made up the other major section of the prison population; these were widely recognised, and there were sporadic attempts as in an Act of 1670[11] to keep the communities apart. Debtors with means might enjoy conditions which were superficially more favourable than those of the felon. However, they were always subject to the extortions of their gaolers, and their stay in prison could be considerably longer.

The large-scale use of imprisonment for debt developed in the medieval period. Although as has been argued earlier there may have been a punitive element implied in locking debtors away until they could meet the demands of their creditors, such imprisonment has generally been seen as chiefly coercive in nature. Imprisonment could be terminated by the payment of the debt, and incarceration was accompanied by no other punishment of the individual involved. The position was summarised by Mr Justice Page in his charge to the jury during Huggins' trial for the murder of Arne in 1729.

A prisoner for debt is only taken like a distress and kept there until he or his friends can pay his debt for him. Imprisonment is no punishment, it is not taken as part of the debt . . . He [the prisoner] is kept only in such a manner as he may be forthcoming and safe.[12]

We are comparatively well served by descriptions of imprisonment for debt, both through autobiographical accounts such as a valuable one given by Willian Fennor in his *Counter's Commonwealth*,[13] and fictional renderings by Dekker who was in King's Bench from 1613-20 and others. It is worth noting in passing that many playwrights endured such incarceration for short periods which may help to account for such survivals. More recently there have been more critical accounts of the process by Cohen and Innes among others.

It is important to state at the outset that contemporary observers realised the inadequacy of existing legislation to cope with problems of debt, and throughout this period we see the introduction of measures, both designed to ensure that creditors were able to take action against debtors who were seeking to avoid process of the law, and to obtain relief for those insolvent debtors who could not hope to meet their debts whilst in prison. It was perhaps in this area of imprisonment that there was most pressure for, and active reform over the early modern period.

The early modern economy lacked the sophisticated methods of fund raising which are available today, and in particular there were few formal financial institutions. Credit relied upon the ability to find a personal backer, and there was a high degree of risk associated with speculative ventures. In such a situation debt, and debtors, flourished. A creditor could take action against a debtor or his goods, and could obtain the imprisonment of a defaulter at two stages, either before trial if the debtor could not obtain sureties, on mesne process, or after judicial process when he could obtain the imprisonment of the defaulter until the debt was paid. The great strength of the process lay in the threat of imprisonment and Innes has shown that it worked. In 1791 a House of Commons Committee found that of 12,000 writs issued against defaulters in Middlesex and London the year before, only 1,200 committals to prison resulted.[14] Although some of the actions may have failed because the debtor died or fled it seems that the majority must have paid up, which is perhaps unsurprising when one considers the cost and conditions of imprisonment.

Most debtors in prison were there on mesne process, i.e. they were committed before trial because they were unable to find sureties. It seems that most of them attempted to pay their debts which was fortunate for their creditors as they were unlikely to obtain satisfaction if the debtor were imprisoned after judgement. As contemporaries noted 'A prison pays no debts'. It was fairly easy to exploit the debt laws, either to keep out of prison, or paradoxically to seek to go into prison in order to avoid facing one's creditors. A debtor could avoid arrest by 'keeping house', only leaving after dark or on Sundays, or he could flee the country. It was partly in an attempt to meet these problems that

the first Tudor bankruptcy laws were enacted. At the other
extreme those in debt for a large sum might attempt to get
themselves imprisoned, since once inside their creditor could take
no further action to recover his money. At least in the early part
of the period until the 1620s debts were extinguished on death,
and a debtor might seek incarceration to save his estate for his
family. There were many such Politic Debtors, some being in the
Fleet for more than thirty years, and Harris noted that 'rarely
shall be found a poor man, who by accident or visitation hath
been occasioned to come to prison'.[15] Recent work by Veall has
shown that many prisoners had large estates; of 393 prisoners in
the Upper Bench in 1653 only 38 owed less than £100 and the
average debt was £2,500.[16] A similar situation was to be found in
the Fleet. Creditors generally realised that there was little point
in getting poor debtors committed, but although the wealthier
inmates might face heavy fees for their stay in prison they could
live in comparative comfort if they had the means, eventually
forcing their creditor to accept a settlement which was well below
the actual debt. An attempt was made in 1743[17] to control this
abuse by forcing prisoners to declare their estates and make them
over to their creditors, but strangely this and a later measure of
1760[18] were shortly repealed because they were thought to give
too much power to creditors.

Contemporary observers well understood the limitations of
imprisonment for debt. A petition of 1622 from the Fleet said
that it was 'not agreeable to the rule of justice, to thrust all kinds
of debtors into prison together in a heap, without respect
to . . . more or less guilt of fraud or obstinacy',[19] and also noted
that 'in no other country is perpetual imprisonment the
punishment of debt'. Similarly the Levellers gave attention to the
problem in their Large Petition which called for relief for

> all such prisoners for debt as are altogether unable to pay, that
> they may not perish in prison through the hard heartedness of
> their creditors, and that all such who have estates may be
> enforced to make payment accordingly and not shelter
> themselves in prison to defraud their creditors.[20]

From the Elizabethan period there were attempts to provide
relief for the insolvent debtor, with Acts of 1572[21] and 1597[22]
providing for county relief, although they probably had little

effect. The Privy Council established Commissions for Poor Prisoners from 1576 which attempted to mediate between debtor and creditor to obtain a settlement which would allow for the prisoner's release. However the Commission lapsed on Elizabeth's death and was not revived until 1618, and it has been suggested that this may have been because of the doubtful legality of the process.[23] During the Interregnum there was more activity, the £5 Act of 1649[24] allowing for the release of those debtors who had less property. The Act only applied to existing prisoners, although it was extended by further measures in 1650 and 1652, and Veall suggests that about 300 were released from Upper Bench (the Commonwealth name for King's Bench) as a result.[25] Some attention was also given to the condition of those remaining in gaol, and it was stipulated that tables of fees should be displayed and charitable requests correctly channelled.

These measures served as a model for further legislation after the Restoration. The first Act was passed in 1670,[26] although it is at least arguable from the preamble that this was more concerned with the threat of plague and the need to cut overcrowding in gaols, than with the needs of insolvent debtors, who were merely the class of prisoner who could be most readily released. There were several further Acts until 1750, generally small scale and retrospective in their effects, and Innes suggests that they may show how finely tuned the legal process was at the time since they released small numbers of needy debtors without attacking a system which was generally effective.[27] Holdsworth, however, felt that the large number of measures indicated on the contrary that they were not generally effective either in securing the release of prisoners, or controlling the malpractices of gaolers.[28]

Although criminals and debtors made up the majority of the gaol population there were other inmates, and particular mention should be made of religious and political prisoners, especially in the period before the abolition of the prerogative court of the Star Chamber in 1641. Political prisoners were often held in gaol, sometimes under torture, in the hope that they would reveal the names of their accomplices and further details of their offences. It might also be politic to hold people in gaol rather than execute them in order to avoid provoking popular reaction, and some political prisoners were held in limbo for many years before a decision was taken as to their fate. A writ of habeas corpus might have little effect and in 1591 we find a judge commenting

If any person shall be committed by Her Majesty's special commandment or by order from the council-board, or for treason touching Her Majesty's person, any of which causes being generally entered into any court it is good cause for the same court to leave the person committed in custody.[29]

This view was upheld in Darnel's case of 1627 when it was decided that prisoners could be held 'per speciale mandatum' until the Privy Council or King ordered their trial.[30] The gaol was therefore a significant tool in the hands of the Tudor and early Stuart state, removing malcontents from the scene, whilst their eventual execution could serve as a spectacle designed to enhance the authority of the monarch, although unpopular actions could be the occasion for mob action and it was important to break the prisoner's will before this display.

Political prisoners were often held in more restrictive conditions than the ordinary prisoner. They might be fettered to prevent escape, generally only done otherwise for convicted felons or for those with no funds, and their access to outside visitors was often curtailed. It is, however, important to avoid generalisations about such inmates. Dobb mentions the example of Catholic priests who were held in comfort in the Clink for many years,[31] and who were able to carry on their studies with a large collection of books. Similarly priests in Newgate were allowed to say mass by the keeper Simon Houghton in the early part of the seventeenth century.[32] Imprisonment could be used to bring noble families to beggary through the extortionate fees which were charged, an archbishop or duke could be expected to pay £10 simply for admission to the Fleet. Even short sentences would be costly; John Ward was sent to the Fleet in 1593 until 'Sunday next in the morning before prayers',[33] presumably rather as a financial penalty than a short sharp shock. At the same time, curiously, we find that the state, through the Privy Council was still sometimes prepared to pay the fees of certain of its political prisoners, although on occasion they must have been approvers. Obviously gaol served a variety of ends in these cases.

Other members of society who were regarded as undesirable could also face some form of incarceration. The Bridewell acted as a repository for the hordes of vagrants who seemingly represented such a threat to the Tudor state. Similarly those sick in body or mind could be shut away. Bridewell served as one arm of the City of London's attempt to deal with the problem members of society, alongside St Bartholomew's hospital which dealt with the sick, St Thomas which was a home for the aged, and Christ's hospital which cared for orphans. Bethlem had a long history as a hospital for lunatics. There was throughout some confusion of roles between the different institutions. Clay in his work on the prison chaplain notes that the gaol often served as the only repository for the pauper lunatic. Bambridge suggested during the enquiry into the Fleet that he had attempted to arrange for the move of the apparently deranged Arne to Bethlem.[34] The popular confusion of roles is shown by Defoe's *Tour Through the Whole Island of Great Britain* which lists Bethlem as one of the private prisons in the capital as are the other asylums.[35]

It is possible to argue, as Foucault has done in his work on insanity,[36] that the early modern period was the age of the Great Confinement. Society began increasingly to remove undesirables from its midst, criminals could be executed or transported, vagabonds put to work, and the sick confined. He suggests that it is possible to trace a link between physical and mental sickness and wrongdoing from their treatment in the medieval period through to the developing puritan idea of sin. Whether or not his theories are valid it is interesting to note the development of private asylums in eighteenth-century England, since such institutions represented a relatively painless way of removing awkward people who did not conform.[37]

Organisation and Conditions

Although it is possible to classify the gaols of the early modern period both according to their control and the uses to which they were put, it is important to emphasise that there was no clear organisation to the system at this time. Gaols could contain a variety of different types of offender at any time. This was particularly true in the provinces, but even in London, where there was some attempt to classify prisons by function, they could be pressed into different uses when the need arose. The same point may be made with regard to the administration of the system. Although the county gaol and the franchise gaol were under different authority they shared many common features.

The Bridewells were under a different regime at first but become increasingly intertwined with the local gaols.

McConville and others have provided useful surveys of prison administration at this time, and it is not necessary to consider the topic at any length. The common or county gaols were the responsibility of the sheriff from the first, this responsibility being restated by various Acts through the period from 1503-4.[38] They were thus subject to some rudimentary controls, and various attempts were made to regulate such prisons and the practices of their gaolers by statute, generally with limited success in practice. During the early modern period some duties of control passed from the sheriff to the justices, who became responsible for the erection of prison buildings, and later for their inspection. However, these tasks were only carried out erratically both because of the expense and dangers of disease which were attendant upon them; as Howard noted many justices contented themselves by merely examining the outside of the gaols under their care.

Most towns and boroughs also had a gaol or at least a lock-up, either granted under charter or as an *ad hoc* growth. Some, such as those in London, were fairly well administered from the medieval period; others were ignored. Poor though conditions often were in such institutions they were at least subject to more control than the large number of franchise prisons which had grown up over the centuries, either under the control of manorial or ecclesiastical authorities. One of the problems facing prison reform at this time was the need to protect the interests of individuals who controlled them, and many new statutes expressly excluded franchise gaols from their scope. As long as parliament remained the tool of various pressure groups in the early eighteenth century it was unlikely that this situation would change.

Accommodation in gaols could vary greatly. In the provinces prisons were often found in the castles of county towns, but the Webbs note the situation in places such as Reading where three rooms in a public house sufficed.[39] There was rarely any purpose-built accommodation. In London with its greater needs there was some degree of sophistication, John Taylor, 'the Water Poet', noted 18 gaols in the capital in the early seventeenth century,[40] ranging from Newgate which served as the main centre for criminal felons, and the counters, sheriffs' gaols which held minor offenders and some debtors, to the Fleet which acted as the main state prison until the 1640s and thereafter became a centre for debtors along with the King's Bench. Bridewell, as Dekker noted, served the vagabond and bawd. Once again at this period these centres were not purpose-built but merely adaptations of existing structures, although Newgate was rebuilt after the Great Fire. A century later Defoe in his *Tour Through the Whole Island of Great Britain* was able to note 'There are in London more public and private prisons and houses of confinement than in any city in Europe.' He lists 23 public prisons, as well as tolerated prisons, over 100 sponging houses and 15 private asylums.[41]

Although the proliferation of gaols in London allowed for some degree of segregation between different groups of prisoners it is important to realise that divisions were not hard and fast. Some state debtors for instance found their way into Newgate, whilst political prisoners were regularly divided amongst the different institutions to avoid dangers of insurrection. Dobb notes that this happened after the Essex rebellion in the 1590s,[42] and similar precautions were taken after the Jacobite rebellions in the eighteenth century. Prisoners might ask to be sent to a particular gaol in order to pay smaller fees, or in the case of the Fleet to be allowed greater freedom of movement. Thus we find Lord Henry Howard asking that he may be sent to the Fleet in 1572 rather than be kept in close confinement in Lambeth Palace.[43] Prisoners might also be moved between the gaols; Thomas Ellwood the Quaker began his confinement in the Bridewell, he was moved with his fellow prisoners to Newgate and later returned to the Bridewell.[44] Curiously the Quakers were held in such trust that they were allowed to move between the prisons without guard.

There were also changes in the functions of particular prisons in line with changes in penal policy. Mention has already been made of the changed role of the Fleet after the abolition of the Court of Star Chamber when it lost its state prisoners and became increasingly a centre for debtors. Similarly the Bridewells lost their initial role as reformatories for vagabonds as they came increasingly to cater for a wide range of petty offenders.

The problems which are encountered when any attempt is made to classify the prisons of the period are also present when one considers the staffing and conditions of the institutions, and any generalisations on these subjects should be treated with caution. McConville has provided a useful synopsis of the staffing conditions in penal institutions but a few points should be emphasised. Although prison staff were occasionally salaried for the most part they lived on the money which they could make out of their office. Sheriffs controlled the appointment of keepers in the county prisons, but in London and other boroughs the office was controlled by the municipal authorities or the existing office holders. Griffiths points out that in some of the larger gaols the appointment was effectively under royal patronage.[45] In many cases the post of gaoler was bought and sold, and might remain in the same family for generations. The prices which were paid for offices indicate their high value. After the City of London went bankrupt in 1694 the keepership of the gaols was sold for £2500, the bulk of this sum going to the outgoing keeper, although the City took a percentage. In 1708 William Pitt paid £315 for the keepership of Newgate,[46] a third of this sum going to the Corporation, but it proved to be a highly profitable investment since he made £3000 from Jacobite prisoners alone less than ten years later. Subordinate posts were also purchased and McConville notes that even the menial post of porter was leased for £20 in the mid-sixteenth century.[47]

Gaolers were subject to some rudimentary control from state or local authority. It would seem that the major threat to the office came from allowing captives to escape; for instance Richard Johnson was dismissed from Newgate in 1641 for this reason,[48] and various other keepers in the seventeenth century suffered the same fate. However, dismissal was not inevitable and Fell managed to keep his position after escapes in 1696 from the Fleet. Various Acts were passed through the period from as early as 1503-4[49] in a bid to prevent escapes, and sheriffs were made liable if captives did disappear. However, such measures were by no means effective and the parliamentary enquiry into the Fleet in the 1720s showed that gaolers were in the habit of selling the right to escape to those debtors who could afford it. Bambridge even provided a special door from the Fleet for such prisoners.[50]

Other faults of gaolers excited less attention, although keepers in Newgate lost their position in 1595 and 1636 for living outside the prison.[51] There were frequent petitions from prisoners to Parliament against the extortions of their keepers but these seem to have been regarded as a matter of course, and although there was general rejoicing when Lenthall lost his post in the Upper

Bench in 1653 for corruption,[52] it was extremely rare for cases of maltreatment such as those practised by Huggins and Bambridge to become public. Society expected little of its gaolers; the *Gentleman's Magazine* for July 1767 described them as 'low bred, mercenary and oppressive, barbarous fellows who think of nothing but enriching themselves by the most cruel extortion, and who have less regard for the life of a poor prisoner than for the life of a brute.'[53] Such men might excite the interest of polite society in the same way as the 'thief taker' Jonathan Wild, but they were generally of dubious moral worth, and rarely moved by humanitarian motives toward their charges.

The gaoler was at the top of the prison hierarchy, and although he was normally supposed to live in the prison, most of the day-to-day routine was in the hands of subordinate turnkeys and porters. Such staff were often supposed to be provided from the keeper's income, although we rarely find that this was the practice, and there were often complaints from the gaolers about the payments which they actually had to make.

It is possible to find some faint stirring of humanitarian concern in the staffing of London prisons during the period. For instance a clergyman started to visit Newgate in 1544,[54] and his work is mentioned by Luke Hutton later in the century.[55] A permanent appointment of a chaplain or ordinary was made from 1620, although in the eighteenth century we find that he relied on the sale of 'dying confessions' of felons for a large part of his income.[56] At the end of the seventeenth century a surgeon from St Bartholomew's hospital started to attend the gaol;[57] before this time no provision had been made for the health of inmates. Attempts were also made to provide for regular inspection of Newgate by a board of visitors. In 1681 it was determined that prison visitors were to be elected annually to inspect the gaol, hear complaints and see whether the rules were being observed.[58] McConville suggests that some of these reforms may be traced to the adherence of city authorities to puritan doctrines, although it should be noted that conditions in London were often better than those elsewhere and indeed some of the innovations may be traced back as far as the fifteenth century. It seems that the experience of the Bridewell also had a part to play in encouraging better conditions. The London Bridewell had at the first provided for salaries to be paid to its staff, and enjoyed the services of a surgeon long before Newgate. However, although revelations of the scandals involving Huggins and Bambridge prompted calls for stricter controls of gaolers and abuses such as sales of offices, reforms in the 1730s were generally ineffective.

Most abuses in the early modern gaol were related to finance. Prisons were for the most part self financing, which may appear strange but it must be remembered that many of them were under private control, whilst those in the 'public sector' were still entrusted to gaolers who relied on them for their income. As McConville has pointed out, although there were a mass of petty officials in the Tudor state most of them received no salary. Tasks such as that of the village constable were carried out in rotation. The state simply did not have the means to pay for such services and it was regarded as quite normal that they should be run for profit with all the inherent abuses which this entailed. Contemporaries were well aware of the problems; James Whiston in *England's Calamities Discovered* (1696) noted 'It is by this means that purchased cruelty grows bold, and plumes itself in its extortion . . . gaolers excuse their brutality and unreasonable exactions, in alleging that they have no other way to make up their purchase money.'[59]

Fees rested on local custom, generally ratified by the justices and might vary from gaol to gaol. They were payable on admission and discharge and at all stages in between. Thus a yeoman might expect to pay 13/4 for admission to the Fleet, those of greater means paid more, whilst a poor man paid nothing.[60] Discharge rates were lower but all had to pay, hence the problem of poor men acquitted at trial still languishing in prison because they could not find their fees. Attempts by the London authorities to get all those acquitted at the Old Bailey discharged without fees were ineffective. Accommodation in the gaol was also related to one's income. William Fennor recounted how he was admitted to the Master's side,[61] the best accommodation in the counter, on payment of a series of fees to gaolers. Unfortunately his discharge did not come as quickly as he had hoped and he was forced to transfer to the cheaper Knight's Ward when funds ran low. Again fees were demanded, and when he refused to pay he was given a room unpleasantly close to the privy. Those who could not afford the tolerable accommodation in the Master's or Knight's Ward were in dire straits, and might expect to be lodged in apartments such as the aptly named Hole. The scale of fees for better accommodation was often exorbitant,

The History of the Press Yard published in 1717 noted that the fee for a better lodging might be 20 guineas in addition to a further weekly rent of 11/-.[62]

In many ways the regime within prisons remained similar to that of the medieval period. All aspects of daily life needed money, irons could be lightened or evaded for a fee, food or drink could be purchased, although this might be of inferior quality and Mynshul noted that his gaoler was begging bullocks' liver for his dog and then selling it to prisoners.[63] One of the more significant riots in this period in the King's Bench in 1620 was caused when the gaoler Sir George Reinell stopped up a window through which poor prisoners obtained charity and food from outside and forced them to purchase his costlier fare.[64] (Riots were not unknown at this time and there were also significant eruptions in the Fleet in 1619 and Marshalsea in 1639.[65]) Charitable donations were of importance if one did not have family or friends to support an expensive sojourn in prison. Alms baskets were hung outside the gaol, or one of the inmates might be sent round the town to beg money and food, such a character being represented by Gatherscrap in John Cooke's *Greene's Tu Quoque*.[66] We find various charitable bequests to the inmates of London prisons; for instance Stow mentions one Ralph Rokeley who left £100 for each of the five main gaols in the capital.[67] Such action was traditionally encouraged by the Church, and perhaps surprisingly survived sixteenth-century attacks on the value of good works perhaps, as an insurance policy by merchants in an era of limited credit. However, the importance of such relief should not be overstated, and it has been calculated that the legacies for Newgate amounted to £52 a year, about 1d per inmate per week.[68] Poor debtors appear to have aroused more sympathy than other groups both from individual bequests and later from the work of organised groups such as the Thatched House Society.

There was some limited recognition of the need for the state to make provision for prisoners, and certain groups such as approvers had their fees paid out of the public purse. A statute of 1572[69] allowed for the maintenance of felons in county gaols, although in practice the funds raised were only sufficient to provide bread for convicted felons awaiting capital punishment. Pugh suggests that this Act had a forerunner in the Gaols Act of 1531[70] which enabled JPs to distribute any excess funds which they had raised for the construction of prisons as alms for the inmates. However, these measures and those designed to ensure that creditors paid for the upkeep of debtors in gaol were rarely effective.

Perhaps unsurprisingly fees were one of the major sources of disagreement in the prison system. Gaolers were keen to exploit their position to the full and the condition of poor prisoners was pitiable. The House of Commons enquiry of 1729 noted that gaolers not only encouraged riot and drunkenness, 'but also prevent the needy prisoner from being supplied by his friends with the mere necessaries of life in order to increase an exorbitant gain to their tenants.'[71] Attempts were made to justify the system, most notably by one of the gaolers, Harris, in his *Oeconomy of the Fleet* which attempted to show that exactions in the prison were reasonable. There were also attempts in Parliament to curb the worst excesses of the fee system. Various Acts stipulated that tables of fees and legacies should be displayed in all gaols. Similarly Acts of 1670 and 1728[72] noted that prisoners should be able to send for food from outside the prison if they wished and were not to be carried off to alehouses without their consent. This probably represented an attempt to curb the development of sponging houses run by gaolers,[73] but it is doubtful whether it had much effect, and there were still over 100 such establishments in London in the 1740s. Similarly when Howard toured the gaols in the 1770s he was able to find many in which fees were not displayed.

The fees exacted by gaolers were not the only financial burden of imprisonment since they had a parallel in the garnish or chummage exacted by prisoners. John Hall noted that after the turnkeys had extracted money from the prisoner,

> then they turned him out to the convicts, who hover about him (like so many crows about a piece of carrion) for garnish, which is six shillings and eight pence, which they from an old custom, claim by prescription, time out of mind, for entering in the society, otherwise they strip the poor wretch, if he has not the wherewithal to pay it.[74]

This practice was known as letting the black dog walk. Other contemporary accounts such as that supplied by Fennor note the same custom and it seems to have received at least some official sanction since in the Marshalsea there was a table of garnish fees demanded by the prisoners on display, whilst in Richmond garnish was officially sanctioned by JPs in a table of fees approved in 1671.[75]

Little attempt was made to regulate the day-to-day life of prisoners at this time, partly because imprisonment was seen as fulfilling only a very limited function, and also because of the need to provide prison staff with access to an income. For those with funds most things were possible. Food could often be purchased from outside the gaol whilst beer and spirits were available through the prison tap run by the gaoler. The tap served as one of the main sources of the gaoler's income and as a major escape route for the inmates. Prices were often high and the enquiry into the Marshalsea noted that the necessitous prisoner 'is obliged to pay three pence per quart for worse beer, than he can buy out of the prison for two pence halfpenny'.[76] Nevertheless attempts to control the widespread amount of drunkenness amongst prisoners met with little success and prohibition of spirit sales was not achieved until the Gin Act of 1751[77] was passed, whilst beer sales were not curbed until the start of the nineteenth century.

Prisoners were with few exceptions allowed to wander freely within the prison and could spend the day in such idle pursuits as they wished. Accounts by Fennor and others show days given over to drink and gambling, and Mandeville's comments on Newgate are particularly noteworthy.

> The licentiousness of the place is abominable, and there are no low jests so filthy, no maxims so destructive to good manners, or expressions so vile and prophane, but what are utter'd there with applause, and repeated with impunity. They eat and drink what they can purchase, everybody has admittance to them, and they are debarr'd from nothing but going out. Their most serious hours they spend in mock tryals, and instructing one another in cross questions, to confound witnesses; and all the strategies and evasions that can be of service, to elude the charge that shall be made against them.[78]

There were some attempts to keep men and women apart, and Newgate in particular had separate wards for male and female prisoners, but in reality segregation was not possible. Gaolers were always happy to allow prostitutes in for a fee (in the Press Yard in 1717 the fee was 1/- a night[79]), and might keep separate rooms available for their use. Attempts were also made to keep different categories of prisoner apart again with only limited success.

It should not be supposed that prisoners were without exception given over to idleness and vice. Debtors were often accompanied by their families in prison, and some men carried on their trades. Prisoners in Coventry were allowed to engage in trade in 1515 so long as they gave a percentage of the profits to the gaoler,[80] whilst a much later fictional record is given by Thackeray in *Pendennis*.[81] Debtors might indeed be able to lead a life which was to all intents normal, and Harris notes that Sir Francis Englefield received up to 60 visitors daily in the Fleet.[82] Many prisoners obtained permission to live outside the King's Bench prison in nearby streets, an area known as the Rules. The House of Commons Committee enquiring into the prison noted that 'the prisoners make large presents to the Marshal for the liberty of these Rules; and being under his protection and in his favour, may take house or lodging within the rules and live in a very easy manner.'[83] Those inside prison could often obtain release for a day or more in return for payment; Thomas Dumay was released to go on a voyage to France,[84] whilst in 1632 there were complaints of a debtor being seen in the streets of London in a coach drawn by four horses, although the Privy Council subsequently censured the warden of the Fleet for allowing this to happen. Harris employed about 200 men in the Fleet simply to attend on those with leave of absence,[85] which shows that the practice was widespread.

Life within prison was therefore comparatively free for many prisoners. Certain inmates, such as convicted felons and political offenders, might be closely confined, but those with money suffered no real constraints. Conditions for the poor prisoner were however much harder. He was confined in the worst accommodation, and for the most part relied on garnish or the charity of others for his survival. Henry Brinkelow's *Complaynt of Roderyck Mors* noted 'I see also a pitiful abuse for prisoners. O Lord God, their lodging is too bad for hogs, and as for their meat it is evil enough for dogs, and yet, the Lord knoweth, they have not enough thereof.'[86] A century and a half later Hall described Lower Ward prisoners as lying 'upon ragged blankets, amidst unutterable filth, trampling on the floor, the lice crackling under their feet make such a noise as walking on shells which are strew'd over garden walks.'[87] Poor debtors were rarely maintained by their creditors, and the county bread allowance for felons was not reliable. Attention was given to their needs by an Act of 1666 which noted 'whereas there is not yet any sufficient provision made for the relief and setting on work of poor and needy persons committed to the common goal [sic] for felony and other misdemeanours who may thus perish before their tryall, and the poor thus living idly and unemployed become debauched',[88] and gave JPs the power to levy a rate to provide a stock of material to give employment and relief to such people. Given the expense of such action there is little evidence that the statute was acted upon. There were, however, a number of charitable bequests to poor prisoners, whilst garnish extracted from new arrivals also helped to overcome the problems of want. It is worth noting in passing that in some prisons such as King's Bench these informal extortions were legalised by a 'court' of prisoners who were effectively responsible for much of the day-to-day running of the gaol. A similar situation existed in Newgate, where from the end of the seventeenth century the inmates elected a steward and wardsmen from among their numbers to deal with daily problems and the distribution of charitable donations. The poor prisoner, however, faced a miserable ordeal, and his problems were increased by the insanitary and crowded conditions which he was forced to endure, and the ever present threat of gaol fever.

Gaol fever or typhus was endemic to the prisons of early modern England. As McConville has noted, 'The unregulated, frequently packed, assemblage of unwashed, verminous, often starving and diseased prisoners in ill ventilated and badly sewered rooms, was a spontaneous breeding ground of typhus'.[89] Indeed, if Howard is to be believed the situation was much worse in this country than in most of Europe. Dr Johnson estimated in 1759 that one in four of the prison population died every year from fever or other causes,[90] and support for his claim is to be found in the parliamentary report on the Marshalsea in 1729, which noted that between 8 and 10 prisoners died every day at the end of winter from the effects of want and fever.[91] Clearly disease was as effective as the rope in carrying off society's undesirables.

It would be tedious to enumerate the numerous contemporary

accounts of the filth and stench in the prisons, and we can perhaps get a sufficient idea of the conditions from the comment made by Geoffrey Mynshul on the King's Bench prison in 1618, 'As to health, it hath more diseases predominant in it than the pest house in the plague time and stinks more than the Lord Mayor's dog house or Paris Garden in August.'[92] There were frequent outbreaks of fever in the gaols. A petition from the Queen's Bench prison in Southwark in 1579 refers to nearly 100 inmates dying from fever in the previous six years, with many others sick, whilst there was another large outbreak in the same gaol in 1650.

Such conditions were taken as a matter of course. Attempts might be made to overcome the worst of the smell by strewing herbs, but it was only to be expected that disease would be rife when large numbers were herded together in insanitary conditions. We find many accounts of fever in ships and workhouses which can be traced to the same cause. In line with the doctrine of maximum severity in punishment such conditions might be seen as necessary for the protection of society. Thus we find Wedderburn in the 1790s suggesting that 'in the case of debtors, squalor carceris, was a proper means of compelling them to do justice to their creditors',[93] a fair point when one considers the evasions of politic debtors. Similarly Nield considered that the prisoner 'has abandoned the protection of the laws. Leave him to his doom of misery; Let him rot in the vapours of a dungeon.'[94]

Nevertheless there were problems inherent in this policy of malign neglect. As McConville has noted even gaolers were unwilling to go into certain parts of the prisons. It also seems likely that many of the early moves towards regular prison inspection foundered because outsiders were unwilling to risk contamination. However, there were times when it could not be avoided; in York prison it was said that, 'the very walls are covered with lice in the room over which the grand jury sit'.[95] The assizes posed their own special problem, since when the prisoners appeared in court they might spread disease to judge and jury. This happened in the Cambridge Black assizes of 1522, Oxford in 1577, Exeter in 1586, and perhaps most notably in the Old Bailey in 1750 when two judges died.

Francis Bacon gave the matter some attention in his Natural History:

The most pernicious infection next the plague, is the smell of
the gaol, when the prisoners have been long and close and
nastily kept: whereof we have had in our time experience twice
or thrice; when both the judges that sat upon the gaol and
numbers of those that attended the business or were present,
sickened upon it and died. Therefore it were good wisdom,
that in such cases the gaol were aired before they be brought
forth.[96]

The court at the Old Bailey was erected in 1539 in a bid to
overcome the problems of gaol fever emanating from nearby
Newgate, and after the deaths at the court in 1750 some further
attention was given to the ventilation in the prison. It seems that
as in other gaols windows had been blocked up to avoid tax, and
in 1749 attempts had been made to provide increased ventilation
through the roof. Now a windmill was provided on the roof to
dispel noxious smells, though it is recorded that several of the
workmen installing the new apparatus caught fever themselves.
Interestingly Pugh notes that this particular reform had already
been tried as early as 1535.

Improvements at Newgate were largely a response to the threat
of fever and disease outside the prison, and it is arguable that
some of the other attempts at reform in the seventeenth and
eighteenth century were not necessarily aimed at prison inmates,
but were rather concerned to protect society at large. An Act of
1666 noted that judge and jury often caught disease from
prisoners, and enabled sheriffs to provide safe places for the
reception of sick inmates. Then four years after the great plague
we find one of the earliest attempts to resolve the problem of the
impecunious debtor in gaol. It was obviously illogical for a man
who could not afford to pay his debts to be lodged in gaol where
he could not work to pay them off, but when we consider the
preamble to the statute it seems that other factors may have
prompted this reform. Having set out the unhappy conditions of
these prisoners, it goes on to state that they 'become, without
advantage to any, a charge and burden to the kingdom, and by
noisomness (inseparably incident to extreme poverty) may
become the occasion of pestilence and contagious diseases, to the
great prejudice of the kingdom.'[97]

It is at least arguable that the concern here was to try and
empty the gaols of those who represented least risk to society, so

that a larger danger in the form of renewed outbreaks of disease could be avoided. It is noteworthy that an earlier attempt to deal with the problems of impoverished debtors in the period of the Commonwealth coincided with an outbreak of gaol fever in the Upper Bench prison,[98] whilst this and later statutes referred to those already in gaol rather than all poor debtors. It seems at this stage of prison development that although individuals might wish to see reforms, for the most part the problems of gaol fever did not cause concern. Indeed in line with the doctrine of maximum severity such conditions might seem a necessary part of prison life. It was only when such conditions threatened to break out of the gaols that public concern was aroused.

Gaol Reforms

It is generally agreed that the early modern period was a dark age in the history of imprisonment, yet there were some significant developments in penal practice. Although the theories of humanitarian reformers made little apparent headway against the contemporary orthodoxy of maximum severity in punishment, in practice the harsh penal code was considerably tempered in its operation. A growing percentage of pardons released a significant number of felons for service overseas either in the forces or the new colonies. At the same time new methods of treatment for vagabonds paved the way for the introduction of physical labour and ideas of rehabilitation into penal policy.

When considering conditions within the gaols and the prison regime it is however less easy to see any clear developments over the period. Contemporaries such as Coke painted an invariably gloomy view of the situation, and attempts at reform were generally still born or fell in the face of gaolers' vested interests. However, although new ideas were rarely successful it is possible to suggest that many of the seeds of later reform were in fact planted at this time.

There were some significant changes within the field of prison administration, and these are most evident in the gradual transfer of responsibility for the common gaol from the sheriff to the justice of the peace. Clay and others have commented on the overlap of responsibility between the two groups. The sheriff was traditionally responsible for the keeping of the gaol and the safe custody of prisoners. An Act of 1503-4[99] had confirmed his position and later Acts reiterated his rights and responsibility for the prevention of escapes. However, justices came increasingly to have control over the building of prisons. An Act of 1531[100] gave them the duty of surveying counties to decide upon a site for a gaol, and then to set a rate which would provide funds for its erection. Progressive extensions of the Act kept it in force until 1582-3, although Coke suggests that it may have been rarely enforced.[101] The relative powers of justices and sheriffs were vague throughout the seventeenth century since the latter group remained responsible for the maintenance of the fabric, and Pugh suggests that the ruinous condition of many prisons at this time may have been due to this confusion.[102] However, at the end of the century new temporary powers were given to JPs to construct and repair gaols, and these were finally made permanent in 1719.[103] Justices also began to acquire some powers within the prison during the seventeenth century, notably by an Act of 1666[104] concerning poor prisoners which ordered them to ensure that fees were reasonable and displayed within the gaol. These powers were reinforced by an Act of 1728.[105]

To some extent this extension in the role of the justices may have been related to their interest in the supervision of the Bridewell, which was slowly becoming integrated with the prison system. They were given the power to inspect Bridewells in 1744,[106] although they did not finally gain the power of inspection over gaols until 1784.[107] On a broader scale their new power may be seen as a logical result of the policy which made them the key figures in local bureaucracy with a major degree of control over the dispersal of county funds.

It should, however, be stressed once again that the financial involvement of state and county in the prison system was extremely limited at this time. Although JPs gained the power to build prisons by a series of temporary Acts, and finally by a permanent statute in 1719,[108] in reality they did very little because of their desire to save funds. Cumbersome procedures might also inhibit action. The Act of 1711[109] on the subject, for example, stressed that the Quarter Sessions could act only after the inadequacy of a local gaol had been presented by a Grand Jury, and as usual the interests of local gaolers were to be protected. Little other provision for the gaol and its inmates was made from the public purse. The Act of 1572[110] allowed justices to levy a sum of up to 6d a week from each parish to provide prisoners with bread twice a day, but in reality the practice varied widely from gaol to gaol and generally only enough money was raised to feed convicted felons who had forfeited their property. Similarly the Poor Prisoners Act of 1666[111] allowed the justice to levy a further 6d a week for the provision of materials to set prisoners to work, the profits of such action being devoted to their relief, but there is little evidence that anything was ever done. The limitations of public expenditure can be seen from the fact that prisoners were even expected to pay for their transport to gaol under a statute of 1605.[112] Slightly greater provision was made in some boroughs and Bridewells, but on the whole such lack of involvement was in line with public policy.

The prevalent view was explained by Montague in 1550 in Dive v Manningham.[113]

If one be in execution he ought to live on his own: and neither the Plaintiff nor the Sheriff is bound to give him meat or drink, no more than if one distrains cattle and puts them in a pound, for the owner is responsible for feeding them, and not he that distrained on them. No more is the Sheriff bound to give meat to the prisoners, but he ought to live on his own goods . . . for before attainder the goods are his own . . . and if he has no goods he shall live on the charity of others, and if others will give him nothing then let him die in the name of God if he will . . . for his own presumption and ill-behaviour brought him to that imprisonment.

Financial constraints rendered any reforms nugatory in an age when the gaols and all other offices were run for private profit. Those few attempts to reform conditions which conflicted with the interests of prison staff, as in the attempt to reduce overcrowding in the Fleet in 1701, were invariably unsuccessful. Gaolers might be subject to discipline if they allowed prisoners to escape but there were few other controls over them, and even the revelations of abuses practised by Huggins and Bambridge in the Fleet failed to provoke any effective action in the face of judicial and parliamentary connivance. Sheehan argues that there was in fact something of a turning point in the 1730s[114] after the end of William Pitt's keepership of Newgate, a period which had been particularly riddled with abuses. However, although it is true that the City authorities regained their control of London gaols in 1734, and there were at the same time attempts to forbid the sale of offices, there is little evidence of any real advance at this time. An ineffectual attempt to control such sales had already been made in 1716[115] but effective reforms belong to a later period. Although slight progress was made in the provision of religious and medical care at Bridewell and Newgate in London, it was not as Clay suggests until the sale of offices was controlled and salaries introduced for all prison staff that any improvement could be hoped for in the treatment of prisoners.[116]

It was well remarked at this time that gaolers purchasing their office would deal harshly with pitiful prisoners. The plight of such inmates was generally realised and there were attempts by legislation and charitable acts to provide for them. However it is arguable that self interest rather than philanthropy was the major motivation of these concerns. In an era of risky credit any merchant could end in gaol, and once there, was not to be suffered as a drain on the public purse or to increase the risk of gaol fever.

The threat of gaol fever which brought the problems of the gaol into the outside world was one of the few abuses to provoke reform, both by attention to the overcrowding in the institutions, and their ventilation. Otherwise little was done. It took two centuries from 1443-1681 before inspection of Newgate was regularly provided; as Humphrey Gyffard, keeper of the Poultry Counter, noted in 1670, the gaols were 'so stifled up and subject to annoyances, infection, contagion, sickness and disease'[117] that justices and others were only concerned to keep away from the places, even gaolers were unwilling to go into certain wards. Attempts to provide for the segregation of different categories of prisoners and the sexes were largely ineffective. The Bray committee recommended in 1702 that 'provision be made to keep every prisoner in distinct cells', and proposed an act to this end in 1710 at least for condemned felons.[118] On the Continent Clement XI built a House of Correction at San Michele on cellular principles in 1703.[119] Ecclesiastical punishment from the medieval period had traditionally centred around ideas of solitude and repentance, but it was another hundred years before such ideas were to come into fashion in this country.

Religious groups became increasingly active in agitating for prison reform in the later part of the period. Dobb argues that many of the reforms in London gaols in the first part of the seventeenth century can be related to the action of puritan City authorities, and puritan attitudes to work found an outlet in the Bridewell.[120] The Quakers also concerned themselves with penal affairs. George Fox was complaining about prison hygiene in the 1650s, and urged that none should be appointed as keepers of prisons, 'but such as fear God and hate covetousness, gaming and drunkenness'.[121] At the end of the century the newly formed SPCK founded a committee under Dr Thomas Bray to investigate conditions in Newgate and the Marshalsea at the instigation of Bishop Compton. Their report in 1702 was not published but revealed a host of abuses and made various proposals for reform. Shute and Bray recommended that there should be legislation to enable keepers to be dismissed for misconduct and to prevent the sale of offices. As well as segregation they recommended the classification of inmates. Young offenders would be kept away from hardened criminals who were to be set on hard labour. Curiously they also recommended that the names of those with a good prison record should be advertised in the hope that this would encourage people to give them employment.[122] Although their report came to nothing the group continued to press for reform. Bray later preached to the Society for the Reformation of Manners, which was also active in the field, and in the 1720s he developed links with Oglethorpe. In 1727 he was involved in relief work in Whitechapel gaol[123] and sent missioners to preach to the inmates. Similar work was done by the Wesleys who began to visit Newgate in 1739.[124].

There were also occasional attempts at reform in the prison system from groups and individuals in Parliament. For instance a House of Commons Committee under Pocklington brought various abuses in the Fleet to light in 1696[125] and there was a further report on the King's Bench and Fleet in 1699,[126] however with little effect. Holdsworth remarks that there were numerous petitions and complaints from prisoners laid before Parliament, but they seem to have been regarded as a matter of form and little action was normally taken about them.[127] Whiston notes that other groups were petitioned,

How often have the suffering prisoners remonstrated against all this cruelty, and petitioned the magistracy for a redress of their grievances . . . but all their prayers have either never been heard, or never minded. For the Magistracy is deaf to such a work of reformation, by reason his own interest is concerned in the matter.

Perhaps the most significant attempts at reform came at the end of the 1720s with Oglethorpe's investigation of conditions in the Fleet and Marshalsea, provoked by treatment of his friend Robert Castell in the Fleet. Widespread abuses were revealed in a report by a Select Committee of Inquiry,[128] statutes were not being observed, warders were found to be conniving at the escape of prisoners, and were maltreating many of their inmates, as well as subjecting them to heavy fees. Criminal proceedings were recommended against the staff, and the gaolers Huggins and Barnes indicted for the murder of Edward Arne. Judicial connivance by Page and Raymond ensured Huggins' acquittal[129] while Barnes fled, and a later trial of Bambridge also failed.

Although the report of a parallel House of Lords Committee into the problems of impoverished debtors provoked some legislation to deal with their conditions, attempts by Oglethorpe and a fellow MP Hay to deal with major abuses achieved little. Hay led a committee investigating the effects of the Poor Laws in 1735[130] which proposed the reform of local gaols and Bridewells, and he promoted various bills to build new gaols and ensure their supervision by inspectors appointed by the Lord Chancellor. However, as Clay notes, 'The commons disembowelled the bill of all that was important, and the Lords rejected the residue.'[131] A further report on conditions in the King's Bench was prepared by Oglethorpe and Calvert in the 1750s, again with little result.

It is difficult to resist the conclusion that although there was a widespread realisation of prison abuses, the will to tackle them was lacking, and this remained the case throughout the eighteenth century. There was at this time only a limited function for the state, and interference with gaolers' activities was seen as being wrong in principle and expensive in practice. As the House of Lords commented when refusing to pass a bill to reduce overcrowding in the King's Bench prison, any diminution in the number of inmates would lead to a situation where 'the profits thereby accruing will not be a proportional recompense to the officers to attend the courts, so that the King's four courts at Westminster will be without prisoners and without officers to assist them.'[132] Pressure groups and individuals might propose reforms, but financial realities made it impossible for them to generate effective support for change, and as a result abuse thrived. Lest it be felt that this presents a wholly dismal view of the prison system at this time we should perhaps close the survey by quoting Ives: 'If gaols were hotbeds of infection and cesspits of corruption, at least they were not the ghastly whited sepulchres which were built in the 19th century.'[133]

Notes

1. C. Dobb, *Life and Conditions in London Prisons 1553-1643*, unpublished B.Litt. thesis, Oxford, (1952), p.2.
2. D. Veall, *The Popular Movement for Law Reform 1640-1660* (OUP, Oxford, 1970), p.13.
3. J. Howard, *State of the Prisons* (Professional Books, Abingdon, 1977), p.35.
4. 31 Charles II, ch.2; see J. Clay, *The Prison Chaplain* (Macmillan, Cambridge, 1861), p.18.
5. 14 George III, ch.20.
6. M. Ignatieff, *A Just Measure of Pain* (Macmillan, London, 1978), p.15.
7. 17 George II, ch.5.
8. J. Sharpe, *Crime in Seventeenth Century England* (CUP, Cambridge, 1983), p.149.
9. 6 George I, ch.19.
10. Howard, *State of the Prisons*, p.35.
11. 22 & 23 Charles II, ch.20.
12. 17 *State Trials*, p.309ff.
13. W. Fennor, *The Counter's Commonwealth*, reprinted in A.V. Judges, *The Elizabethan Underworld* (Routledge, London, 1965), p.423ff.
14. J. Innes, 'The King's Bench Prison in the Later Eighteenth Century', in J. Brewer (ed.) *An Ungovernable People* (Hutchinson, London, 1980), p.254. See also *Journals of the House of Commons*, vol.47, p.640ff.
15. A Harris, *The Oeconomy of the Fleete*, Camden Society n.s., vol. 25 (1879), p.27.
16. Veall, *Popular Movement for Law Reform*, p.17.
17. 16 George II, ch.17.
18. 1 George III, ch.17.
19. J. Cohen, 'The History of Imprisonment for Debt', *Journal of Legal History*, vol.3 (1982), p.157.
20. Veall, *Popular Movement for Law Reform*, p.146.
21. 14 Elizabeth, ch.5.
22. 39 Elizabeth, ch.3, s.13.
23. J. Dawson, 'The Privy Council and Private Law in the Tudor and Stuart Periods', *Michigan Law Review*, vol.48, (1950), p.416. See also P. Shaw, *PMLA*, vol.62 (1947), pp.366-91.
24. An act for the discharging from imprisonment poor prisoners unable to satisfy their creditors, 21 December 1649. C. Firth and R. Rait, *Acts and Ordinances of the Interregnum*, vol.2, p.321.
25. Veall, *Popular Movement for Law Reform*, p.150.
26. 22 & 23 Charles, ch.20.

27. Innes, in Brewer *An Ungovernable People*, p.260.

28. W. Holdsworth, *History of English Law*, vol. 8 (Methuen, Sweet & Maxwell, London, 1925), p.236.

29. G.W. Prothero, *Select Statutes*, 4 ed. (OUP, Oxford, 1913), pp.547-8.

30. 3 *State Trials*, p.1.

31. C. Dobb, 'London's Prisons', in A. Nicoll (ed.), *Shakespeare in His Own Age* (CUP, Cambridge, 1965), p.90.

32. A. Griffiths, *The Chronicles of Newgate*, vol.1 (Chapman, London, 1884), p.99.

33. Dobb, *Life and Conditions*, p.14.

34. D. Thomas, *State Trials*, vol.2 (Routledge, London, 1972), p.119.

35. D. Defoe, *Tour Through the Whole Island of Great Britain*, vol.2 (1742 ed.), p.137.

36. M. Foucault, *Madness and Civilisation* (Tavistock, London, 1967).

37. A summary of Foucault's arguments is given in H. Erik Midelfort, 'Madness and Civilisation in Early Modern Europe', in B. Malament (ed.), *After the Reformation* (Manchester University Press, Manchester, 1980), pp.247-65.

38. 19 Henry VII, ch.10.

39. Howard, *State of the Prisons*, p.300.

40. J. Taylor, *All the Works of John Taylor the Water Poet* (1630), p.128.

41. Defoe, *Tour Through Great Britain*, p.137.

42. Dobb, *Life and Conditions*, p.82.

43. Harris, *Oeconomy of the Fleete*, p.xii.

44. T. Ellwood, *The History of the Life of Thomas Ellwood* (1714), p.128ff.

45. A Griffiths, *Chronicles of Newgate*, vol.1, p.50.

46. D. Rumbelow, *The Triple Tree* (Harrap, London, 1982), p.20. Whiston noted that the post went for £3500 in the 1690s, *Harleian Miscellany*, vol.6 (1745), p.335.

47. McConville, *English Prison Administration*, p.12.

48. Dobb, *London's Prisons*, p.94.

49. 19 Henry VII, ch.10.

50. *Journals of the House of Commons*, vol.21, p.277.

51. Dobb, *London's Prisons*, p.93.

52. Veall, *Popular Movement for Law Reform*, p.144.

53. S. Webb, *English Prisons Under Local Government* (Longmans, London, 1922), p.18; *Gentleman's Magazine* (1767), p.340.

54. McConville, *English Prison Administration*, p.14.

55. L. Hutton, 'Black Dog of Newgate', reprinted in A.V. Judges, *The Elizabethan Underworld* (Routledge, London, 1965), p.247ff.

56. P. Linebaugh, 'The Ordinary of Newgate and his Account', in J. Cockburn (ed.) *Crime in England 1550-1800* (Methuen, London, 1977), pp.246-69.

57. McConville, *English Prison Administration*, p.15.

58. Ibid., p.18.

59. *Harleian Miscellany*, vol.6 (1745), p.336.

60. McConville, *English Prison Administration*, p.9.

61. W. Fennor, in Judges, *Elizabethan Underworld*, p.430ff.

62. Rumbelow, *Triple Tree*, p.29.

63. G. Mynshul, *Essays and Character of a Prison* (1618), pp.38-9.

64. Harris, *Oeconomy of the Fleete*, p.170.

65. Ibid., p.xx and p.43.

66. Dobb, *London's Prisons*, p.98.

67. J. Stow, *Survey of London* (1603), p.392.

68. B. Kirkman Gray, *History of English Philanthropy* (Cass, London, 1967), p.182.

69. 14 Elizabeth, ch.5.

70. 23 Henry VIII, ch.2.

71. *Journals of the House of Commons*, vol.21, p.377.

72. 22 & 23 Charles II, ch.20 and 2 George II, ch.22.

73. Some illustrative material is to be found in W.M. Thackeray, *Vanity Fair* (1847), ch.53.

74. Rumbelow, *Triple Tree*, p.81.

75. Webb, *English Prisons*, p.25.

76. *Journals of the House of Commons*, vol.21, p.377.

77. 24 George II, ch.40, s.13.

78. Rumbelow, *Triple Tree*, p.66.

79. Ibid., p.29.

80. R.B. Pugh, *Imprisonment in Medieval England* (CUP, Cambridge, 1968), p.330.

81. W.M. Thackeray, *The History of Pendennis* (1850), ch.32. There are many literary accounts by Fielding and others.

82. Harris, *Oeconomy of the Fleete*, p.xiii.

83. Holdsworth, *History of English Law*, vol.11, p.600.

84. *Journals of the House of Commons*, vol.21, p.275.

85. Harris, *Oeconomy of the Fleete*, p.viii.

86. H. Brinklow, *Complaynt of Roderyck Mors*, EETS extra series, vol.22 (1874), p.27.

87. Rumbelow, *Triple Tree*, p.82.

88. 18 & 19 Charles II, ch.9.

89. McConville, *English Prison Administration*, p.90.

90. Webb, *English Prisons*, p.21.

91. *Journals of the House of Commons*, vol.21, p.378.

92. C. Creighton, *History of Epidemics in Britain* (Cass, London, 1965), p.539.

93. McConville, *English Prison Administration*, p.61.

94. Ibid., p.62.

95. Holdsworth, *History of English Law*, vol.10, p.182.

96. Creighton, *History of Epidemics*, p.383. It was also suggested that vinegar should be sprinkled in all the rooms, *Gentleman's Magazine* (1767), p.340.

97. 22 & 23 Charles II, ch.20.

98. Veall, *Popular Movement for Law Reform*, pp.149-50.

99. 19 Henry VII, ch.10.

100. 23 Henry VIII, ch.2.

101. Coke, *Institutes*, vol.2, p.705.

102. Pugh, *Imprisonment in Medieval England*, p.346.

103. 11 William III, ch.19, finally made permanent by 6 George I, ch.19.

104. 18 & 19 Charles II, ch.9.

105. 2 George II, ch.22.

106. 17 George II, ch.5.

107. 24 George III, sess. 2, ch.54.

108. 6 George I, ch.19.

109. 10 Anne, ch.14.

110. 14 Elizabeth, ch.5.

111. 18 & 19 Charles II, ch.9.

112. 3 James I, ch.10.

113. *English Reports*, vol.75, p.96.

114. W. Sheehan, *The London Prison System 1666-1795*, unpublished Ph.D., University of Maryland, 1975, p.386.

115. 3 George I, ch.15, s.10.

116. Clay, *Prison Chaplain*, p.33.
117. Sheehan, *London Prison System*. See also Clay, p.16.
118. Clay, *Prison Chaplain*, p.27.
119. G. Ives, *A History of Penal Methods* (Stanley Paul, London, 1914), p.85.
120. Dobb, *London's Prisons*, p.98.
121. Veall, *Popular Movement for Law Reform*, p.144.
122. Kirkman Gray, *History of English Philanthropy*, pp.174-5.
123. Ibid., p.175.
124. McConville, *English Prison Administration*, p.74.
125. *Journals of the House of Commons*, vol.11, p.641ff and p.675.
126. *Journals of the House of Commons*, vol.12, p.684.
127. *Harleian Miscellany*, vol.6 (1745), p.335.
128. *Journals of the House of Commons*, vol.21, p.274ff, p.376, p.513.
129. *State Trials*, vol.17, p.309.
130. Webb, *English Prisons*, p.27.
131. Clay, *Prison Chaplain*, p.34.
132. *Journals of the House of Commons*, vol.13, p.542.
133. Ives, *History of Penal Methods*, p.21.

PART THREE

The Period 1750 to 1877

5
THE REDISCOVERY OF
THE PRISON

Beccaria and Reform

The principal text of the movement for the reform of the penal codes of Europe in the eighteenth century was a little book by Cesare Beccaria. Beccaria was born in Milan in 1738 and died there in 1794. His book, *Dei Delitti e delle Pene*, published in 1764, was an attack on the widespread use of the death penalty. Capital punishment he regarded as being inefficient since its cruelty tended rather to corrupt the people than to prevent crime. Punishment, he argued, should deter and should, therefore, be designed to create an impression on the people, it should not be a torment to the criminal beyond what was needed for the purposes of general deterrence. The book immediately met with acclaim throughout Europe — Voltaire wrote an appreciative commentary in 1766. It was first published in Britain in 1767 as *On Crimes and Punishments*. The popularity of the book can be ascribed both to the style and passion with which he wrote his book, and to the time at which it was written. He caught the mood of a Europe whose rulers and people were turning away from the excesses of the penal codes which prevailed at the time.[1]

In Britain his most notable follower was William Eden, whose book *Principles of Penal Law* was published in 1771. Eden symbolised the social heights to which Beccarian ideals, chief amongst which was an opposition to the blanket use of the death penalty, had penetrated. Eden (1745-1814) came from a distinguished family, was a lawyer, became an Under-Secretary of State in 1772 — the year after his book was published — as well as an MP; he also performed various diplomatic duties, and eventually became a peer, Lord Auckland. Like Beccaria, Eden regarded a criminal justice system based on capital punishment as ineffective for dealing with crime, and he also subscribed to the idea that the public spectacle of an execution had lost most of its effect. Eden proposed that some form of continuous public punishment be substituted, so that the wages of crime could be permanently displayed to the public and thereby act as a continuing deterrent to those who might be tempted into crime: the convict was to act as a source of instruction. Eden considered that imprisonment and transportation were of little value because of their lack of public spectacle.

Eden's ideas were never implemented by legislation. The normal reason adduced for this was that the public exposure of convicts working was something too closely akin to slavery for Britain. It was also felt that one of the causes of crime was indeed the stigma of punishment: a felon who had worked in full view of the public would find lawful employment difficult to obtain on release and would inevitably be forced back to crime. There was also the view that the general public, used to getting rid of its felons, either through execution or transportation, would react unfavourably to the spectre of such convicts being in their midst. But perhaps the most telling consideration was that such a punishment as Eden proposed would require permanent administration by central government, something for which it was hardly adapted, and something to which the local justices, ever jealous of their own powers, would be opposed.[2]

So it was that Beccaria's influence in England through Eden was more in the area of theory than practice: they placed the issue of penal reform firmly on the political agenda, a position it has maintained ever since. Punishment became a topic which required a programme of rationally explicable aims and principles: arguments for and against capital punishment had to be carefully reasoned.[3]

It was largely a coincidence of circumstances that actually led to a change in the system of punishment. By the 1770s there was growing dissatisfaction with capital punishment and transportation. Transportation was coming to be regarded as ineffective not only because it lacked the element of public spectacle, but also because many felt that criminals did not fear transportation — indeed, it was widely believed that people committed crimes in order to be transported. It was also argued that the severity of transportation as a punishment depended not on the crime committed but on the convict's accomplishments; if suited to the life then he or she might even regard transportation as a boon. However, the Beauchamp committee of 1785, whilst recognising its defects, favoured transportation claiming that it tended to reform criminals, that it was beneficial to the colonies in its provision of a workforce, and that it was inexpensive, but most importantly, there was no viable alternative way of dealing with the majority of felons.[4]

Of more immediate importance than these theoretical considerations was the American War of Independence which began in 1776 and left the government with nowhere to send those sentenced to transportation — although, despite the general belief to the contrary, some convicts were apparently landed on the North American continent even after 1776, and indeed the Beauchamp committee were hoping, as late as 1785, that there might be a resumption of transportation. Transportation to Africa was considered, but rejected.[5] Whilst the government was dithering, people were being sentenced. They were sent to local prisons; in 1785 it was recorded that a felon called Lowe had been in Presteigne County Gaol for seven years.[6] Other convicts were sent to live in ships, called the hulks, moored at naval dockyards where the prisoners were set to work in the dockyards or dredging rivers.[7] This was an important moment in the history of penal administration. Previously the central government had only taken part in penal administration through transportation, now it was involved in the administration of large prisons in this country. The hulks to some extent enabled the issue of prisons to become a governmental one.

Philanthropy

In the 1770s and 1780s, there was also an important philanthropic movement, which had, as well as 'humanitarian' aims — humanitarian, that is, according to the philanthropist's definition of the word — political and religious elements. It was a response, in part, to the loss of America, the growth in crime and the rise in the poor rates without a concomitant fall in poverty, all of which were regarded by many as merely symptoms of a deeper malaise, namely a decline in morals and the bankrupt nature of old, gentry values. The philanthropists did much that might be regarded as alleviating the worst excesses of the eighteenth century, but inevitably the poor, be they simply paupers or also prisoners, had to pay the price, since helping the poor was insufficient unless that action resulted in the reinforcement of social bonds and the inculcation of certain values, both of which were believed vital in a period of upheaval due to industrialisation, an increasing population and a more mobile poor.

Philanthropy was not simply a humanitarian or even a religious act, it was also political. It was a response to a social crisis which typically surfaced in the form of crime or poverty. Furthermore, philanthropy involved an inherent criticism of the state for its failure to attack crime and poverty effectively. As Ignatieff puts it,

> Philanthropy is not simply a vocation, a moral choice; it is also an act of authority that creates a linkage of dependency and obligation between rich and poor. Of necessity, therefore, it is a political act, embarked upon not merely to fulfill personal needs, but also to address the needs of those who rule, and those who are ruled.[8]

In part, philanthropy was a prod to the state to assume more effective control through the legitimation of the criminal law, for once the poor had accepted the law as fully legitimate then they would tend to discipline themselves and the need for coercion would recede. The implication was that for such legitimation to be achieved there was a need for a new system of values and new pedagogical machinery for inculcating those values.

John Howard

John Howard was typical of the late eighteenth century ideal of a true philanthropist. Born in 1727, he was a wealthy country gentleman who, on being appointed to be High Sheriff for Bedfordshire in 1773 at the age of 47, was horrified to find the conditions in which prisoners lived, these abuses seeming to be encouraged by the gaoler's reliance for income upon fees charged to the prisoners. This fee system often meant that a person who had been acquitted by a court was not immediately released because he or she was unable to pay the fees owed to the gaoler. So it was that Howard's long travels cataloguing prisons in Britain and abroad began.[9]

John Howard's interest in prison reform was motivated by the search for a vocation by which he could salve his conscience. Weighed down as it was by the life of idleness to which his wealth had brought him Howard was obsessed by the idea that he was grappling with the forces of darkness: bringing the light of philanthropy into the darkness of the dungeon. For him the Fall meant that all people were sinners, so that criminals merely symbolised the sins of all; their punishment was a reminder of the punishment that awaited all in the hereafter. God had shown that the battle against evil must be fought upon earth by sacrificing his son, and Howard's efforts in seeking both to comfort and to reform those who had broken secular laws was in this way a furthering of God's purpose. The famous painting of Howard visiting prisoners reminds the viewer of countless similar paintings of Christ, and the analogy could be carried on into the manner of his death, occurring as it did whilst in Russia inquiring into the conditions of the poor in 1790.[10]

Howard gave the developing bourgeoisie a perfect hero. He stressed the bourgeois values of authoritarianism, self-reliance, frugality, the rejection of luxury, and an obsession with inquiry and measurement, and, through his quasi-saintly character, he gave these values a rightness and a righteousness. The contrast between Howard and the typical travelling aristocrat, which Burke brought out in a speech given in Bristol in 1781, is the same contrast which the bourgeoisie saw between their humanitarianism, hard and unselfish work and their empiricism, and the luxury and laxity of the ruling gentry.

> He visited all Europe, not to survey the sumptuousness of palaces, or the stateliness of temples; nor to make accurate measurements of the remains of ancient grandeur; nor to form a scale of the curiosity of modern art; nor to collect medals, or collate manuscripts — but to dive into the depths of dungeons, to plunge into the infection of hospitals, to survey the mansions of sorrow and pain, to take the guage and dimensions of misery and depression, and contempt; to remember the forgotten, to attend to the neglected, to visit the forsaken, and compare and collate the distressed men in all countries . . .[11]

For the bourgeoisie, the corrupt prison was a symbol of the corrupt nature of the old ruling class, and Howard a symbol of a new, caring, frugal, disciplined society of the bourgeoisie.

Principally through the work of Howard, imprisonment became a serious candidate as a replacement for execution and transportation. Even after transportation had been resumed in 1787 — this time to Australia — its unsuitability for minor offenders, the need for a place in which to hold those awaiting transportation in which neither their health nor their morals would be adversely affected, and the general criticism of transportation meant that the prison did not lose its attraction.

The major objection to imprisonment had always been that it was a place where the hardened felons were mixed with, and consequently passed on vicious habits to, the first offenders and those merely awaiting trial. Also, the unhealthy state of prisons meant that there was an excellent chance that a term of imprisonment would turn out to be a death sentence. Furthermore, the administration of the prisons was rife with corruption: the gaolers lived off the fees they extracted from prisoners; in many prisons the inmates were left to run their own affairs by virtue of the payments made to the officers and because employing staff to control the prisoners would cost the gaolers money. As such imprisonment was hardly regarded as a suitable form of punishment. Yet it was the very corrupt nature of the prison that made it a target for the philanthropist and a virgin medium through which the bourgeoisie could imprint its own value-system.

The abuses which Howard pointed out had long been recognised, but it was he who, in his book *The State of the Prisons* (1777),[12] really caught the popular imagination. Rather like Beccaria, the book came at the right time, but he also provided an argument based not on anecdote and impression, as had been the case with previous works on prisons, rather he amassed a wealth of convincing detail which overwhelms the reader not with passion but with sheer volume. Whilst Bentham was to a large extent correct when he referred to the book as 'a rich fund of materials; but a quarry is not a house',[13] Howard's great importance in the field of penology lay in his indication of the possibilities of imprisonment rather than in realising those possibilities.

Broadly speaking the problems which Howard saw in his visits to prisons were chiefly ones of administration, and, therefore, the solutions, for him, lay mainly in the reform of that administration. There were too many prisons, many with no prisoners;

gaolers had to make a profit from the prisoners and this led either
to cruelty or to laxness, those who could pay could have almost
anything they desired, those who could not pay might suffer
appalling deprivations. It was profit which tended to dictate the
organisation and the discipline of the prison.[14]

This state of affairs was allowed to continue for several
reasons. The gaoler's job, like so many others in the eighteenth
century, was often similar to a piece of property: it was
something which the gaoler or an ancestor had paid for, and,
therefore, he or she had the right to exploit it free from
interference. Then again, the local justices, who, with the sheriff,
had responsibility for the prisons, were generally unwilling to
spend the ratepayers' money on improving the prison, and
because of this the justices felt unable to interfere in the running
of the prison, since interference might have involved expenditure. In any case, the justices seem not to have been unduly
concerned until the matter was brought to public notice both by
Howard and by the risk of gaol fever. Finally, it was part of the
contemporary view that those in prison should suffer: the prisons
should be places of terror. According to the prison reformer,
Neild, the typical argument was that since the prison was

provided for the Miscreant, and for the Miscreant alone: who,
having opposed the *ordinances*, has abandoned the *protection
of the Laws*. Leave him to his doom of misery: Let him rot in
the vapours of a dungeon; and drag his unwieldy chain, at the
mercy of his Keeper.[15]

A crucial part of Howard's criticism was that bad gaol
conditions led to gaol fever. It was not so much the danger of
prisoners succumbing to the fever that worried the justices, but
rather the desire to prevent the spread of the fever to the people
who lived in the areas around prisons and to those in the courts
in which prisoners were tried. The assize judges almost certainly
urged measures to be taken against gaol fever. Indeed an
outbreak of the fever which killed some of the judges at the Old
Bailey in 1750 led to urgent consideration of alterations to
Newgate prison, and it may have been this incident that lay
behind the order to the Shrewsbury gaoler in 1752 to 'take care
that prisoners have clean straw every week and soap for washing
their linen'. In evidence to the House of Commons Committee on

the Gaols in 1774, Dr Fothergill and Surgeon Potts recommended that clean clothes be provided for the prisoners before they appeared in court 'as a preservative to the Courts of Judicature'. Howard argued that gaol fever might be eradicated in a properly reformed prison, and medical evidence supported this view.[16]

However, although Howard's main line of attack was perhaps deliberately and wisely one which would appeal to the justices' self interest, it was not his only objective. He also pointed out the great possibilities for the moral improvement of the prisoners. The jump from body to mind was, in the eighteenth century, no jump at all. Sickness of the body indicated sickness of the mind, and vice versa, to cure one resort might need to be had to the other: measures taken to prevent the spread, and eventually achieve the eradication of, gaol fever, would at the same time prevent the spread of immorality. So his suggestions were double-edged: in order to stop the spread of gaol fever, Howard suggested that the prisoners be split up into classes, and if each of those classes contained prisoners of equal immorality, then this arrangement would also prevent the spread of vice from hardened criminals to those in prison for the first time.[17]

Finally, implicit within Howard's work was the view that prisons had been neglected by the justices who were responsible for them, and that if they were ever to be properly administered then not only must they be removed from the private control of the gaoler, but they must also be subjected to proper inspection.

The New Prisons

By popularising the notion of the prison as a positive institution, Howard had indicated that a viable alternative to the death penalty and transportation existed. Before his book was published he appeared before a committee of the House of Commons in 1774 where he criticised the Sussex prisons. This criticism led the Duke of Richmond, one of the Sussex justices, to build a new house of correction at Horsham in 1775, in order to improve both health and morals through classification and restrictions on the staff-prisoner relationship.[18] More generally, the 1774 committee led to two Acts, both bearing Howard's imprint: the Discharged Prisoners' Act 1774 (14 Geo. III, c. 20) was for the payment of the fees of prisoners who were acquitted at their trials; and the Health of Prisoners' Act 1774 (14 Geo. III, c. 59) required prisons to be ventilated, regularly cleaned, provided with sick rooms, baths and a surgeon, and it prohibited, wherever practicable, underground cells — the symbolic dungeons.

Then in 1779 came the Penitentiary Act (19 Geo. III, c. 74). This was the work of Howard, Sir William Blackstone, the High Court judge and author of *Commentaries on the Laws of England*, and Eden, who had now been converted to the possibilities of prisons. (Blackstone was to complain later that the Act did not resemble the original plan drawn up in 1776.[19])

In section 5 of the Act an implicit criticism of transportation is followed by principles which were to influence the debate on prison discipline for the next 70 years:

And whereas, if many Offenders, convicted of Crimes for which Transportation hath been usually inflicted, were ordered to solitary Imprisonment, accompanied by well regulated labour, and religious Instruction, it might be the means, under Providence, not only of deterring others from the Commission of the like Crimes, but also of reforming the Individuals, and inuring them to Habits of Industry.

Two penitentiary houses were to be erected. They were to be administered by a committee of supervisors. The prison officers were to be salaried, although section 18 expressed the hope that the salaries of the governors and the taskmasters would be taken from the profits of the prisoners' labour so that 'it may become the Interest, as well as Duty of each Governor and Task Master to see that all Persons under his and their Custody and Direction be regularly and profitably employed.'

Courts could, instead of sentencing a person to transportation, sentence them to imprisonment at hard labour in one of the penitentiaries (section 24).[20] The labour to be performed was to be

of the hardest and most servile Kind, in which Drudgery is chiefly required . . . such as treading in a Wheel, or drawing in a Capstern, for turning a Mill or other Machine or Engine, sawing Stone, polishing Marble, beating Hemp, rasping Logwood, chopping Rags, making Cordage . . .

This labour might be made less severe in order to suit a weaker convict (section 32). The prisoners, if the nature of their work allowed it, were to work alone. Separate sleeping cells were to be provided which would be warmed (section 33). Uniforms were to be provided 'as well to humiliate the Wearers as to facilitate Discovery in case of Escapes'.

The prisoners were to have only the prison diet (section 35), and they were to be divided into three classes. A prisoner was to enter in the first class which was the most severe, then progress through the second and third classes, each of which was less severe than the one before (sections 38-39). This enabled not only rewards for good behaviour, but also punishments, in the form of being moved into a lower class (section 47). The committee was also empowered to reward those who were 'the most diligent and meritorious' with a payment out of the profits of their own labour (section 45), although exactly how profitable production could be achieved within the restricted possibilities of the work prescribed was not clear. Those prisoners who showed 'extraordinary Diligence or Merit' could be recommended to the assize judges by the committee for remission of their sentence (section 49).

The Act was well received; even before it became law, Dr William Smith, a long-time proponent of penal reform, saw in it great possibilities, since the rigid regime of the Act would 'convey as ignominious and horrid an idea as possible where no eye should pity — no hand relieve — no sympathising friend have it in their power to make the criminals state less wretched.'[21] The Penitentiary Act, then, provided the next step on from Howard's book. It put forward the notion that the prison might be more than simply a morally and physically healthy place of incarceration, that it might be used in a positive fashion to change the prisoner and to act as a general deterrent.

The project never got off the ground, however. Those appointed as commissioners — Howard, Fothergill and the treasurer of the Foundling Hospital, George Whately — could not agree on a suitable site. Howard resigned and Fothergill died, so Whately was joined by three new commissioners, but although they agreed on a site and a plan, no prison was actually built. The government itself was reluctant to get involved in long-term financial and administrative commitments. The hulks, which with hindsight did involve long-term central government commitment, were acceptable because of the belief that they were simply a short-term expedient. In truth, it seems that the government wished to return to the use of transportation, and in 1784 a new Transportation Act was passed (24 Geo. III, session 2, c. 56) despite the lack of a settlement to which convicts might be transported.[22]

In spite of this setback and despite reluctance not simply at central government level, but also in the counties to spend money, the idea of a reformed prison was still very much alive at the beginning of the 1780s. Jonas Hanway, the social reformer best known for his invention of the umbrella, had gained much support for his proposal, originally made in 1776, that a combination of solitary imprisonment, labour and religion be used in prisons.[23] The Gilbert Acts of 1782 (22 Geo. III, c. 64) and 1784 (24 Geo. III, c. 55) used the new theories, and also showed evidence of the increasing importance given to labour discipline within institutions.

Gilbert's plans for poor relief were based on outwork being provided for those who were willing and able to work; only the impotent poor were to placed in workhouses. Those who were able-bodied, but who refused to work were to be imprisoned in houses of correction. In essence the Acts allowed for improved administration coupled with independent supervision of the houses of correction. In detail they provided for the appointment by the quarter sessions of an inspector of the houses of correction, they forbade the sale by the keeper of alcohol, they divided the inmates into classes, prisoners were to be put to work, there was provision for the appointment of a chaplain, and the keeper was to receive a salary plus a share of any profits derived from the work of the inmates. The Acts were merely permissive, they required positive adoption by the counties, and so did not have a great effect on actual practice. However, the Duke of Richmond, who had been behind the building of Horsham gaol in 1775, managed to cajole his fellow Sussex justices into using the Gilbert Acts to build a new house of correction at Petworth. This was completed in 1789 and featured separate cells, separate exercise yards and separation in the chapel by means of stalls. The Acts were also the basis for Southwell house of correction which drew much attention from the Holford Committee in 1810, as will be seen later.[24]

From 1785, there was a spate of local Prison Acts under which particular areas acquired powers to build new prisons. The usual explanation for this is the loss of America in 1776 as a penal colony, the work of Howard and the Penitentiary Act. Although these had an effect on the form which the new prisons took and no doubt awoke justices to the possibilities which prisons offered, they do not explain why there was a gap of six to nine years between these events and the sudden burst of prison building. The explanation lies in crime and more importantly contemporary perceptions of crime. What people imagined the levels of crime to have been, was of greater significance in penal reform than the real quantity of crime committed. Since this doubtless had an influence on actual indictment levels, it is for their indication of these perceptions of crime that indictment levels are of interest.

Douglas Hay has recently shown that a rise in indictment levels coincided with demobilisation following a war, with a rise in prices and with an increase in destitution.

> The greatest pressure on the poor could be expected when dearth and the disaster of demobilization coincided. Such a year was 1783, when 20 per cent of the population was destitute . . . , and when the second-largest army and navy of the century was paid off. That year saw the greatest percentage increase in indictments for theft in both Staffordshire and the counties of the Home Circuit.

During wars prosecutions tended to decline, partly because the fear of crime declined as those on the lowest rungs of society's ladder went into the forces, and partly because impressment was used instead of prosecution. So there was no acute crisis in the prisons between 1776-83, and hence no need for action.

After that time it was not simply an increase in crime — indeed this is difficult to guage, certainly it is not possible to assume that an increase in indictments indicated an increase in crime — but also a moral panic in expectation of such an increase in crime. The Gloucestershire county justices issued a notice in 1786,

> . . . felonies and other heinous crimes and offences, have lately very much increased within this county, and it is apprehended that the greater part thereof, are chiefly committed by some of the uncommon number of vagrants, and other idle and

disorderly persons wandering up and down the said county, or pretending to be passing through the same.

People expected that a dearth would lead to more crime and to crime being committed by people who did not normally commit crime, and that demobilisation would lead to gangs of vagrants. The end of the war also meant that the easy disposition of suspected criminals and vagrants without trial through impressment into the forces was no longer a possibility. The prisons were filling up because there was nowhere to send those sentenced to transportation. These fears and pressures were translated into criminal statistics by their influence on the prosecutors, juries and judges: prosecution and conviction were now more likely on the basis that it is fear of crime that motivates people to do something about real crime. The state responded by announcing in 1782 that in future those convicted of the capital offences of housebreaking and burglary could not expect a pardon — a measure which was rescinded in 1783 — and in 1784-5 unemployed seamen were put into the fishing industry.[25]

There was also encouragement at this time from Parliament to use the criminal justice system through measures allowing costs to prosecutors and witnesses. Furthermore, there was the growth in associations which funded prosecutions by members. The real effect that such measures had is less important than the way in which they indicate an adjustment in the attitudes to the criminal law values. The criminal law was increasingly to be regarded not as an instrument built around spectacular, but rare interventions in the lives of the poor, epitomised by the assizes and the gallows, but as a regular means of social control to which people were being encouraged to resort.

As the eighteenth century wore on so capital punishment, and eventually in the nineteenth century capital offences themselves, became less common. Summary offences were increased, reformed prisons were built, and a modern police force established. There was an assault upon what the poor regarded as their traditional rights: so that, to take two examples, the collecting of waste materials left over after manufacturing was increasingly criminalised, as was the gathering of fallen wood for fuel. These trends when added to the poor law meant an increasing criminalisation of the poor, or more accurately, the easier accessibility of authority to the poor. In essence, there was a change in the role of the criminal justice system. The poor became more mobile due to enclosures, higher population and alterations in employment practices — the discarding of long-term and live-in employment contracts — as also the urban poor outgrew an antiquated system of local government. So it was that the state was drawn more and more into social control which had previously been largely the concern of the rural gentry and of employers. The discipline of labour had to be reinforced by a more detailed and effective criminal justice system. Gradually, there was a shift from a system in which, on the whole, only major offenders or vagrants appeared before the courts, and minor offenders were treated on an *ad hoc* basis by the victims of crime, by employers, or by social superiors.[26]

Gloucester Penitentiary

Although Parliament had made its first excursions into penology, prison reform was very much a matter for individual zeal, so that despite new building in the 1780s much remained the same. However, precedents had been set for intervention, nationally and locally, to alter prisons and prison discipline. Furthermore, there had been established the possibility of a prison regime which affected a change in individual criminals and deterred the poor from entering crime.[27]

The most influential of the new local prisons built in this first period of building was Gloucester Penitentiary. It was, once again, the inspiration of one person, Sir George Onesiphorous Paul (1746-1820), who was the son of a cloth manufacturer. Like Howard, it was when he became High Sheriff of Gloucestershire that he took an interest in the county's prisons. Unlike Howard, he actually managed to build a prison.[28] The prison was begun in 1785 and completed in 1789. It drew praise from Howard and a visit from George III.[29]

Whilst Paul believed that it was possible to achieve an inner change in prisoners, he was aware of the possible criticism that reformed prisons by losing their disgusting features also lost their deterrent nature, so he emphasised that this prison was to act as a terror. However, this was meant to be terror in a sense which followed the Penitentiary Act, that was, without endangering physical health. Instead, there was terror of a more psychological kind: humiliation, enforced solitude. As with all post-Howard prisons, health was an important consideration, because of the concern for the physical well-being of the prisoners, and because of the assumed relationship between physical and moral 'health', and also as a deterrent, for hygiene involved humiliation. Kidd Wake, who was imprisoned for five years in 1795 for shouting 'No war' at George III, wrote of his reception at Gloucester Penitentiary in May 1796,

Next morning I was taken to the bath; and, being stripped of all my clothes, compelled to put on the parti-coloured dress of convicted felons. My head was shaved; an iron ring put around my leg; and I was shut into a solitary cell . . .[30]

Although solitary confinement at Gloucester was not total — association being allowed for exercise, work and chapel — it was the principal tool of the penitentiary's discipline. It was regarded by Paul as a terror to the wicked, who, in solitary confinement, would be forced to face up to their own wickedness, and an act of kindness to the less wicked, who would not be polluted by the more vicious inmates and who would have little to fear from their own past deeds. Solitary confinement would stop the spread of fever and of immorality. It would also destroy the mutual support of the inmate subculture. The prisoners would be within the absolute power of the prison staff, so that the work of religious reformation might go ahead undistracted. The governor and the chaplain worked in concert to legitimate the punishment by persuading the prisoner to acknowledge guilt and to accept the sentence as just, and then to achieve a conversion into a Christian citizen, that is, loyal, obedient, self-disciplined and hard-working.[31] To Kidd Wake this regime was extremely cruel:

Five years confinement, even in common gaols, must surely be a very severe suffering; but if Judges or Juries would only reflect seriously on the horrors of solitary imprisonment, under penitentiary discipline! if they would allow their minds to dwell a little on what it is to be locked up, winter after winter, for sixteen hours out of the twenty-four, in a small brick cell — without company — without fire — without light — without employment — and scarcely to see a face but those of criminals or turnkeys.

It is a calamity beyond description, more easily to be conceived than explained!!![32]

Work had an important·role to play in Gloucester Penitentiary. It was subordinated to the aims of the prison rather than to consideration of profit, so the prison was not a factory, rather its aim was to teach a love of work in the abstract, and to demonstrate that the only means of living for the propertyless was through work. Prisoners were given work as a relief from solitary confinement, so its withdrawal was designed to be regarded as a punishment. Kidd Wake described the work as a drudgery, but suited to the individual prisoner's strength and, therefore, 'rather an amusement than a burthen'.[33] Work was not part of the terror, it was part of the reformation.

Prisons in the Napoleonic Period

The first wave of prison building ended in the 1790s. In the main, despite a number of interesting experiments, the majority of local prisons had not been affected; indeed in some it was merely a matter of maintaining the minimum standard of safe custody. At Presteigne County Gaol, men were employed in 1788 'to secure the Gaol so as to prevent if possible the Prisoners from Escaping'. When the Radnorshire Quarter Sessions decided in 1790 that the county required a house of correction, instead of a purpose-built institution, the justices simply converted a house which they had bought for 130 guineas. One aspect of the new prisons which did appeal to the justices in Radnorshire was that of the profits made by prison labour at Dorchester Penitentiary; they ordered an account of these to be hung up in the County Gaol, although, predictably, that was as far as their reforming zeal took them.[34]

In fact, faith in institutions was waning. The factory was under attack for suborning everything to profit; the workhouse had failed to reduce the poor rates and was being replaced by outdoor relief.[35] This pessimism was intermingled, after the French Revolution, with a fear of the working class who were increasingly class conscious and increasingly radical. They seemed to have outstripped the existing methods of social control, and provided a threat to the hegemony of the aristocrats.

The government reacted with a moratorium on reform and a resort to crude repression which revealed the underbelly of paternalism. There followed the political trials of the 1790s; the introduction of capital punishment for machine-breaking in 1812 (52 Geo. III, c. 16); the events at Peterloo in 1819; the 'Six Acts'.[36] The fear of radicalism tended to throw the gentry and the rising bourgeoisie into common cause against the poor who were regarded as 'potential Jacobins . . . ready to prey on the property of their richer neighbours'.[37]

Crime appeared to be still increasing, especially in the depression after 1815. One woman writing to a friend in 1816 commented

> Nothing is talked of in England but distress no end of the Bankrupts — no body has any money — riots in every Mercantile Town — all the Miners and North country Work men out of employ — in short sad work and above all a universal discontent . . .[38]

Although Lord Castlereagh assured Parliament in 1819 that the rise in crime was only temporary, his willingness to hold an inquiry into the state of the criminal law and its administration was, perhaps, a more clear indication of his real view.[39] Increasing crime was regarded as a symptom of the wider political alienation of which radical working-class politics was another expression, so crime became an important problem for the state. Social control became crucial not simply for the furtherance of the economic interests of the capitalists, but also the maintenance of the existing political order.

On the other hand, the reformed prisons came under heavy attack following the imprisonment of radicals in the 1790s. Many radicals were put in Gloucester Penitentiary. Initially they requested separation from ordinary criminals as an acknowledgement of their political status, but later they claimed that solitary confinement was being used as a punishment. Radicals and Nore mutineers confined in Coldbath Fields House of Correction in 1798 protested at solitary confinement in particular and the prison's conditions in general. Built in 1794 with the intention of following the Gloucester model, it quickly cast off the penitentiary discipline largely because of the avarice of the keeper, a man called Aris, who, being left to his own devices, had

introduced extortion, dietary cuts and overcrowding; in addition
disease was rife. There followed a long campaign against this
prison in particular and against penitentiary discipline in general.
It was a rod with which Fox and Sheridan, opposition MPs, could
beat the government.

Although the lines of the debate are rather blurred, Ignatieff
claims that it was largely between anti-Jacobins, who supported
the prison, and radicals, who, although not necessarily Jacobins,
opposed it. Committees of Inquiry were held without much
effect. Then in 1802 Burdett, in a piece of blatant political
opportunism, used the issue in his battle for the Westminster seat
in the House of Commons. His opponent was William Main-
wairing, the chairman of the Middlesex bench in whose area
Coldbath Fields was situated. Once the election was over and
Burdett had won, he simply forgot about the prison. Others took
up the cudgels, however, and more inquiries followed. The
campaign's importance was not in its effect on Coldbath Fields,
but rather its effect on popular opinion which turned decidedly
against solitary confinement. This seems to have been an
important factor in slowing the spread of penitentiary discipline
in England and Wales. It also had an important effect on that
discipline when introduced. Hence in the first national penitentiary, Millbank, prisoners were only put in solitary confinement
for a limited period or for a breach of disciplinary regulations,
and during the nineteenth century reformers, such as Crawford
and Russell, who favoured solitary confinement had to dress it up
as in some way different and had to attach a new label to it — the
separate system.[40]

Bentham and the Panopticon

Whilst reform slowed down considerably during the period of the
French Wars and for a few years after them, it is not true to say
that all reform stopped, for these were the years when the
famous utilitarian philosopher, Jeremy Bentham (1748-1832),
was at the height of his powers and he had turned his energies to
prisons. He drafted a plan for a prison which he called the
Panopticon in 1787, revising it in 1791.[41] This plan became an
obsession with him. Some writers have found this an inexplicable
part of his life, but the obsession was clearly because he saw his

utilitarian philosophy as essentially practical, and in his plan for a prison he felt he had translated that philosophical system into a blueprint for a society.

For him the objective of any system of punishment was the prevention of crime, and the best method of achieving this was through example. The reformation of the offender was a subordinate objective simply because there were fewer actual criminals than there were potential criminals.[42] He enunciated certain principles which should guide any punishment. These were: the rule of lenity, that is, no prisoner was to be subjected to suffering which was prejudicial to his or her health; the rule of severity, which was in effect the principle of lesser-eligibility that became a central theme in the Poor Law Report of 1834,[43] this was that no prisoner should enjoy a better lifestyle than that of the poorest of free persons; finally, the rule of economy, that the institution should be run as cheaply as was possible having regard to the overriding considerations of the first two rules.[44]

Although Bentham wished punishment to provide an example by which potential offenders would be deterred, and so his thoughts were close to those of Beccaria, he reached a different conclusion as to how this might be achieved. He rejected the idea of public punishment, such as the convict gang,[45] adopting instead a prison which the public would be encouraged to visit in order to view the convicts. He saw the prison as rather like a theatre and the prisoners as actors creating a dramatic effect rather than portraying their real situation: the aim was to play on the imagination and allow it to construct the terror. In 1791 he wrote, 'In a well-composed committee of penal law, I know not of a more essential personage than the manager of a theatre.'[46] In order to increase the effect and at the same time prevent the prisoners from being recognised, which might have the effect of stigmatising them on release, Bentham proposed the use of masks. Bentham, then, was very much a transitional figure in penology. For whilst he proposed a highly sophisticated form of prison, he also subscribed to the view that punishment to be effective had to make use of theatre, so bridging the gap between the theatrical spectacle of the public execution and the hidden punishment of the prisoners in Pentonville prison.

The internal organisation of Bentham's prison was to be guided by the need to prevent the prisoners from not conforming to the discipline of the prison. This was to be achieved by a system of inspection which prevented the convict from knowing when he or she was being watched. Bentham sought 'to make them not only *suspect*, but be assured, that whatever they do is known even though that should not be the case.'[47] For Howard, a system of inspection had been crucial. The difference was that whilst Howard's system was to work from the outside through visits by inspectors, Bentham's was to work principally from within the prison. The design of the building aimed to allow the governor to see the whole of the prison without being seen, so that neither prisoners nor staff could be sure if they were being watched or not. They would, therefore, Bentham surmised, be forced to act at all times on the assumption that they were being watched: they would police themselves. This idea dictated the plan of the building and also its name, the Panopticon. Quite simply, the cells were arranged in a circle facing in towards an unlit central tower in which the governor lived.

In addition, the duties of caring for the prisoners and of disciplining them were to be combined with the self-interest of the gaoler who was to earn his living entirely out of the profits of the prisoners' labour: in other words, the main guarantee that the prison would be well run, and the prisoners kept healthy and put to work was self-interest. As a final safeguard, the visitors to the prison would be a check upon the governor.

The observation which the Panopticon allowed meant the governor could more easily measure a prisoner's behavioural reformation, although Bentham regarded the best measurement to be the quantity of work which a prisoner did: '. . . I must confess I know of no test of reformation so plain or so sure as the improved quantity and value of their work.'[48] Work, then, was an essential part of the Panopticon; it both ensured that the governor ran the prison properly and it was a measure of a prisoner's reformation.

Bentham's main concern was to change habits not to seek an internal change of character. At one point he writes that a person's thoughts are a matter for God, and although he does express the hope that the Panopticon might achieve an inner reformation, it is clear that this was not crucial. He wished to turn the prisoner into a self-disciplined worker by showing him or her that work was a pleasure, hence prison work was not to be a curse, or part of a discipline which aimed to achieve an internal reformation; it was to be rewarded, it was to be 'a cordial', a pleasure not a burden. This fitted in with his view that people did things according to their calculation of the likely pleasure as against the likely pain involved. If an act, such as prison work, was a pleasure then prisoners would be glad to do it, and would then associate work with pleasure. It was on this basis that he criticised the Hard Labour Bill — later the Penitentiary Act of 1779 — since it included labour as part of the punishment.[49]

However, work, and profitable work at that, became such an important part of his later revisions of the Panopticon that it caused him to alter one of the main features of the original design. In the original plan he had laid emphasis on the need for solitary cells which would prevent contact with other prisoners and which would put the prisoner entirely under the control of the prison staff. To increase the profitability of the prison work, Bentham's revised plan of 1791 insisted on cells containing two, three or four morally compatible prisoners, although he did not regard the question of moral contamination as such a large problem since it was his view that most crime was caused by drunkenness which was a vice that could not be passed on inside a temperate prison. Solitary confinement was now only for breaking the spirit of new prisoners or for punishing refractory ones. Anyway, he argued, to use solitary confinement for all prisoners was to remove the best mode of punishing for disciplinary offences. Furthermore, it was expensive; it prevented socialisation, so crucial if a prisoner was to make a successful return to society; it could be made very cruel; it could lead to gloom and despondency.

At first the government accepted Bentham's scheme and took steps to implement it, but the expense of running both the Panopticon and the new colony in New South Wales led to the former being dropped, although it was not finally discarded until the Holford Committee of 1810. The Committee regarded the Panopticon as badly defective. The idea of contracting out the prison to a gaoler with a very wide discretion was too readily associated with the old system where the gaoler depended on the prisoners for his or her income — even though in that case the income was from fees rather than work. Also, since the gaoler depended on the prisoners' productivity for a living, the objection was that work would take priority and the prison would be turned into a factory, and to a large extent Bentham's revisions bore this out. The Committee disagreed with Bentham's view that this would actually be beneficial in the long run. The desire to re-establish the legitimacy of the penal system meant that it could not afford to be tainted with commercialism, nor could commercialism be squared with assertions of philanthropy, humanitarianism and simple deterrence.[50]

The Panopticon was, however, an important influence on prison design. It has been commonly asserted that this influence lay in architecture. Cooper, for instance, has recently asserted that the major problem of inspection had been solved not by the early prison architect and friend of John Howard, William Blackburn, when he invented the radial plan — that is, where rows of cells radiate out from a central tower rather in the manner of spokes in a wheel — for although that was an important breakthrough, it was, according to Cooper, Bentham who 'was completely successful in solving the problem'. Although in theory Bentham seemed to have solved the inspection problem, since his governor need not walk up and down corridors in order to see the prisoners, in practical terms there were believed to be essential defects in this basic idea. William Crawford, a member of the Society for the Improvement of Prison Discipline and later a government prison inspector, wrote that Bentham's plan could only work in a small prison, for if the prison were large then the prisoners would be too far away from the central tower for the governor satisfactorily to observe them; furthermore, the outer wall would be obscured from the central tower which would facilitate escapes. Crawford favoured the radial plan and indeed this was the most influential design in modern prison building.[51] It was, therefore, not so much in a particular style of prison building that the Panopticon was influential, it was rather that it clarified the major points of the debate on prisons, and that it set a standard for the detail which would, in future, be required in their design.

In 1810 Sir Samuel Romilly moved for the execution of the Penitentiary Act of 1779. In pursuing his campaign to reduce the number of capital offences, Romilly clearly recognised that a satisfactory alternative was required. Since neither transportation nor the existing prison system could be regarded as viable alternatives because of the criticisms levelled at both, he supported the penitentiary prison. Although he was a friend of Bentham's, he did not support the Panopticon, and this may indicate its lack of general support. The Penitentiary Act, on the other hand, had an impressive pedigree. Being the product not of a controversial figure like Bentham, but rather of elements of the establishment, of religion, of philanthropy and of the rising bourgeoisie, it could rely on wider support than the Panopticon. However, Romilly's motion was defeated. Instead, and against Romilly's wishes since he saw it as merely a delaying tactic by the government, a committee was set up to look into the matter.[52]

The First National Penitentiary

The committee[53] was set up under the chairmanship of George Holford, MP, and included avid supporters of penitentiary discipline, such as Romilly, Wilberforce, who had defended Coldbath Fields House of Correction when its disciplinary system had come under attack a few years previously, and William Morton Pitt, who had instigated the building of a penitentiary at Dorchester in 1785. It was a sign of the increasing acceptance of imprisonment for serious offences that the Holford Committee in conducting its inquiry did not question its desirability, but merely sought to make a choice between the different types of discipline. They had before them the example of various plans and local experiments.

Chief amongst the plans was, of course, Bentham's Panopticon. However, Holford was antagonistic to Bentham's plan even before the committee had heard his evidence. It seems a reasonable assumption that the committee was to some extent set up to reject Bentham's plan without embarassing the government. In the end the committee did reject the Panopticon, but it felt that the government should compensate Bentham. The local experiments could be divided into two: those which sought an internal change of character, in which religion played a crucial part in the 'treatment', such as Gloucester Penitentiary; and those which merely sought a behavioural change, such as at Southwell House of Correction. Rev. Thomas Becher, a visiting justice to Southwell, had been behind the disciplinary system instituted there. Since it was a house of correction, inmates tended to serve only relatively short sentences, usually a matter of weeks; because of this the discipline aimed to achieve a change in habits. To try to achieve this prisoners were given incentives to work since habits of idleness were commonly believed to be at

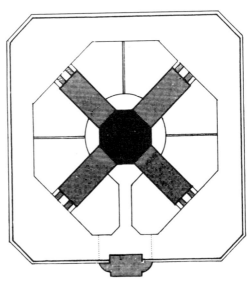

Figure 5.1: Plan of Ipswich County Gaol William Blackburn, 1786.

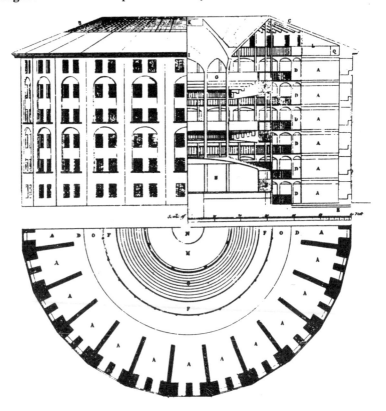

Figure 5.2: The Panopticon Jeremy Bentham, 1787—91.

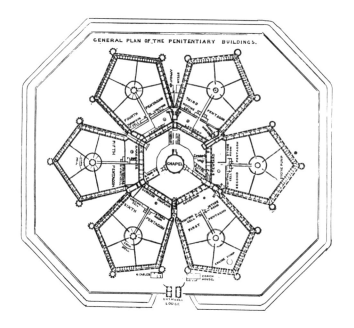

Figure 5.3: Plan of Millbank Penitentiary

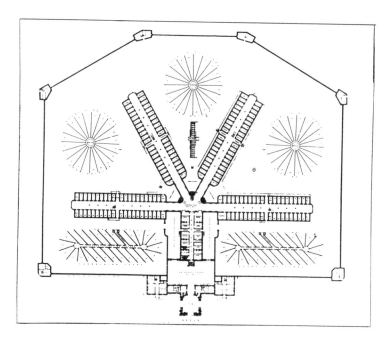

Figure 5.4: Plan of Pentonville Prison Joshua Jebb, 1842.

the bottom of most crime. Prisoners worked in association and received a share of the profits made from their labour.

The Holford Committee came out in favour of a system of internal reformation of the prisoners by means of an initial period of solitary confinement, religious instruction and work, after the model of Gloucester Penitentiary, followed by work in association, after Southwell. The management of the prison was to be given to a committee, after the models of the Penitentiary Act and Southwell House of Correction rather than that of Gloucester where the governor had relative autonomy. The government accepted the proposals and construction of the new prison, to be called Millbank, began beside the River Thames in London.

The government's decision to build Millbank meant that it had accepted a permanent role in prison administration and prison building within this country. This carried with it inevitably large financial implications and the need for a bureaucracy, and these in their turn meant that an official penology decided upon by government officials was also inevitable.

The Millbank Penitentiary was opened in 1816. Its inmates were selected from those who were most likely to be reformed. However, it was massively expensive both to build — around half a million pounds — and to run. Furthermore, the complexity of the construction with its seemingly endless corridors made it impossible to maintain easy observation.

For the first half of their sentences prisoners were placed in the First Class which was run according to the separate system. However, separation was not total, for, with the exception of the first five days, communication of a limited kind was allowed with other prisoners, and both the school and the chapel were attended in association with other prisoners. The Second Class was based on the association of prisoners at work.[54]

Fry, Newgate and Sydney Smith's Critique of Reform

Although Millbank was large, capable of holding up to 1,000 prisoners, it was still necessary to use the old prisons. Some prisoners were not suitable for penitentiary discipline because of their status as debtors. This led to the maintenance of the old prisons, such as the Fleet, and the old problems. William Hardwick, a prisoner in the Fleet in 1825, wrote that 'the Fleet is

so full we are crowded five or six in the Rooms to sleep . . .'[55]
Other prisons were also retained despite mounting criticism, both
from the reformers who regarded them as inhumane and from
the conservatives who regarded them as too comfortable. For
instance, Newgate was described by the Benthamite, Basil
Montagu, as 'of all places the most horrid' being suitable for
preserving neither health nor morals. Whereas the opposite view
was summed up by the fictional hero of *The Disabled Sailor*, a
humorous penny tract issued in the early years of the nineteenth
century, when he recalled that Newgate was 'as agreeable a place
as ever I was in, in all my life. I had my belly-full to eat and
drink, and did no work at all.'[56]

It was on Newgate that Elizabeth Fry, daughter of wealthy
Quaker parents, decided to concentrate her efforts in 1816. She
was very much in the mould of John Howard, having a burning
missionary zeal born out of the guilt of idle luxury. She too
sought to fight evil on earth, and the clearest, as well as the most
accessible, symbols of human evil were prisoners. In them she
saw her earlier self, people who had lost their way through failing
to adhere to the dictates of conscience. Her method was based
not so much upon systems of discipline or prison design, but on
the awakening of conscience through self-discipline brought
about by persuasion: she sought 'to win Souls to Christ'.

Fry formed a Ladies Committee for the purpose of visiting the
women prisoners in Newgate. Fry offered hope to the ruling
classes in her apparent success in restoring discipline amongst
these notoriously unruly women. However, her approach relied
very much on individual effort and zeal. The penitentiary, on the
other hand, sought to minimise the need for the guiding hand by
turning prison discipline into an automatic mechanism. Millbank
signalled the era of such prisons, Fry was from an earlier time.
But she did provide the bourgeoisie with another symbol of their
humanitarianism and philanthropy, and she drew influential
acquaintances into the prison debate, people who formed the
backbone of the Society for the Improvement of Prison
Discipline which was founded in 1817 from an amalgam of
Quakers and utilitarians, and became a prime mover in
nineteenth-century prison reform. Amongst these people was
William Crawford, secretary of the society and later a prison
inspector.[57]

At the same time as Fry was carrying out her early work and

the Millbank was receiving its first prisoners, the first wave of new prisons, built chiefly in the 1780s, was faltering. Petworth House of Correction had to give up the separate system in 1816 due to overcrowding caused by the post-war rise in crime and to Parliamentary criticism. At Gloucester the separate system also collapsed because of overcrowding, and the prison suffered further blows through Paul's retirement in 1818 and the mechanisation of the wool industry which reduced the demand for the prisoners' labour.[58]

In the 1820s, there was a growing criticism of the new prisons, or, more accurately, a more vociferous expression of views which had always been held. The best-known criticism is in the Rev. Sydney Smith's articles in the *Edinburgh Review* in 1821 and 1822. Sydney Smith (1771-1845) was canon of St Paul's; however, he had originally wanted to be a lawyer and maintained a lifelong interest in legal issues. He was one of the founders of the *Edinburgh Review*.

Smith attacked both the unreformed county prisons and the new penitentiaries. Of the former he wrote,

There are, in every county in England, large public schools maintained at the expense of the county, for the encouragement of profligacy and vice, and for providing a proper succession of housebreakers, profligates, and thieves. They are schools, too conducted without the smallest degree of partiality or favour; there being no man (however mean his birth, or obscure his situation) who may not easily procure admission to them. The moment any young person evinces the slightest propensity of these pursuits, he is provided with food, clothing, and lodging, and put to his studies under the most accomplished thieves and cut-throats the county can supply. There is not, to be sure, a formal arrangement of lectures, after the manner of our Universities; but the petty larcenous stripling, being left destitute of every species of employment, and locked up with accomplished villains as idle as himself, listens to their pleasant narrative of successful crimes, and pants for the hour of freedom, that he may begin the same bold and interesting career.

Smith attacked those who allowed abuses in prisons to continue, and criticised those in local government who defended such abuses for fear that their reform might lead to other, more far-reaching reforms. On the subject of the new prisons, however, he had some scathing criticisms. In the first place he doubted the claims made of prisoners who had been reformed by such prisons. Anyway, he argued, people were imprisoned, *'principally* for a warning to others, partly for their own good', and he therefore rejected the idea that the first aim was to reform the criminal. He also felt it wrongheaded to discuss the success of a prison on the basis of recidivism; for him success should be measured by the effect of the prison on crime as a whole. He desired punishment, and on this ground criticised prisons which he regarded as no better than factories, such as Bury gaol and Preston House of Correction, where prisoners, he said, came out educated and with money in their pockets: these prisons provided no source of terror.

> we would banish all the looms of Preston jails, and substitute nothing but the tread-wheel, or the capstan, or some species of labour where the labourer could not see the results of his toil, — where it was as monotonous, irksome, and dull as possible, — pulling and pushing, instead of reading and writing, — no share of the profits — not a single shilling. There should be no tea and sugar, no assemblage of female felons round the washing-tub, — no work but what was tedious, unusual, and unfeminine. Man, woman, boy and girl, should all leave the jails unimpaired indeed in health, but heartily wearied of their residence; and taught by sad experience to consider it as the greatest misfortune of their lives to return to it. We have the strongest belief that the present lenity of jails, the education carried on there — the cheerful assemblage of workmen — the indulgence in diet — the shares of earnings enjoyed by prisoners, are one great cause of the astonishingly rapid increase of commitments.

He accepted that it was impossible not to make a prison more eligible than the home of the free labourer: cleaner, warmer, larger, better ventilated. Therefore, other things must be used to make the prison disagreeable. The first of these was diet, which Smith felt should be set by the judges as part of the punishment. The next was 'as much solitary confinement as would not injure men's minds' — he favoured a period of three months in darkness followed by ordinary solitude. On the length of sentence he favoured punishment which was 'sharp and short'. In addition he felt moral and religious instruction to be valuable, but rejected Fry's methods which extended to general education, not available to poor labourers, and to profitable work, since both reduced the terror of prison. He advocated prisons that whilst they did no harm to mind nor body were 'engines of punishment, and objects of terror'.

> A return to prison should be contemplated with horror — horror, not excited by the ancient filth, disease, and extortion of jails; but by calm, well-regulated, well-watched austerity — by the gloom and sadness wisely and intentionally thrown over such an abode.[59]

Smith, then, was not against the new prisons *per se*, he merely opposed what he saw as their failure to deter potential criminals, and, in view of the rapid increase in crime, he found that many agreed with him. The Society for the Improvement of Prison Discipline advocated the treadwheel in 1818, and within six years it had been adopted by 26 counties. In its nineteenth-century form, the treadwheel derived from a design by the builder Cubitt, whose firm survives to this day. However, the treadwheel was not only a response to the criticism of productive labour, such as that made by Sydney Smith, it was also a result of the reduction in demand for prison labour due both to increasing mechanisation of manufacturing and to the trade depression which followed the end of the Napoleonic Wars in 1815.

There were also accusations that Millbank was too soft. George Holford, now on the management committee of the prison, sprang to its defence in a series of pamphlets in which he protested that prisoners were not cossetted.[60] However, the criticisms reached their mark for in 1822-3 the diet at Millbank was cut. The outbreak of scurvy which followed led to several deaths and consequently to an official inquiry. The inquiry linked the deaths to the poor diet, a link which had been made since at least the end of the eighteenth century, but despite this local prisons continued to use diet as a method of punishment into the 1840s.[61]

The requirement that prisons be 'engines of punishment, and objects of terror' had been a constant theme right from Howard's time, but its importance during the period after 1815 reflected the reaction to an apparently relentless increase in crime and poverty.[62] In future deterrence was to be regarded as crucial: projects of reformation of prisoners were required to be justified also in terms of punishment. Penitentiary discipline was, therefore, shown to deter as well as to reform; for instance, solitary confinement promised not only the conversion of a convict into a Christian, but also, through the strict discipline that the attainment of this transformation was supposed to require, it was a terrifying deterrent. It was within this context that William Crawford and Rev. Whitworth Russell devised their plans for prison discipline which were to find material form in Pentonville prison.

Notes

1. L. Radzinowicz, *A History of English Criminal Law and its Administration from 1750*, 4 volumes (London, 1948-68), I, pp. 277-300; S. McConville, *A History of English Prison Administration: Volume I 1750-1877* (London, 1981), pp. 80-4.

2. Radzinowicz, *History of English Criminal Law*, vol. I, pp. 301-13.

3. See generally, ibid., passim.

4. Ibid., pp.31-2; Beauchamp Committee (1785), *Journals of the House of Commons*, vol. 40, pp. 954-60, 9 May 1785, pp. 1160-4, 28 July 1785; Sir Samuel Romilly, *Parliamentary Debates*, vol. 17, cols. 325-8, 5 June 1810; Dr W. Smith, *Mild Punishments Sound Policy: or Observations on the Laws relative to Debtors and Felons, With an Account of the Frauds practised by Swindlers, Sharpers, and others* (2nd edition) (London, 1778), pp. 35-6; J. Howard, *An Account of the Principal Lazarettos in Europe; with various papers relative to the Plague: together with further observations on some Foreign Prisons and Hospitals; and additional remarks on the present state of those in Great Britain and Ireland* (Warrington, 1789), p. 220n.

5. Beauchamp Committee; A.G.L. Shaw, *Convicts and the Colonies: A Study of Penal Transportation from Great Britain and Ireland to Australia and other parts of the British Empire* (London, 1966), pp.45-8. On transportation generally, especially post-1787, see also, L.L. Robson, *The Convict Settlers of Australia: An Enquiry into the Origin and Character of the Convicts transported to New South Wales and Van Diemen's Land 1787-1852* (Melbourne, 1970); G. Rudé, *Protest and Punishment: The Story of the Social and Political Protestors transported to Australia 1788-1868* (Oxford, 1978).

6. National Library of Wales, Manuscripts Department (NLW), Radnorshire Quarter Sessions (RQS), Order Book 1, 6 April 1785.

7. 16 Geo. III, c. 43 (1776); G. Holford, *Statements and Observations concerning the Hulks* (London, 1826); W. Branch-Johnson, *The English Prison Hulks* (London, 1957); McConville, *A History of English Prison Administration*, pp.105-7.

8. M. Ignatieff, *A Just Measure of Pain* (London, 1978), p. 153, also pp. 210-15; McConville, *A History of English Prison Administration*, chapter 4.

9. D.L. Howard, *John Howard: Prison Reformer* (London, 1958); M. Ramsay, 'John Howard and the Discovery of the Prison', *The Howard Journal of Penology & Crime Prevention*, vol. XVI, no. 2 (1977), pp. 1-16; McConville, *A History of English Prison Administration*, pp. 84-8; Ignatieff, *Just Measure of Pain*, pp. 47-59; *The London Evening Post*, 3 March 1774.

10. Howard, *John Howard: Prison Reformer*, pp. 159-63.

11. Ibid., p. 42.

12. J. Howard, *The State of the Prisons in England and Wales, with Preliminary Observations, and an account of some Foreign Prisons* (Warrington, 1777); for earlier views see, for example, T.H., *A Glimpse of Hell: Or a Short Description, of The Common Side of Newgate* (London, 1705); Dr William Smith, *State of the Gaols in London, Westminster, and Borough of Southwark* (London, 1776).

13. J. Bentham, 'Panopticon; or The Inspection-House: containing the idea of a new principle of construction applicable to any sort of establishment, in which persons of any description are to be kept under inspection', in J. Bowring (ed.), *The Works of Jeremy Bentham* (reprint), 11 volumes (New York, 1962), IV, pp. 37-172 at p. 121.

14. Ignatieff, *Just Measure of Pain*, pp. 29-38.

15. McConville, *A History of English Prison Administration*, p. 62.

16. Ignatieff, *Just Measure of Pain*, p. 45; Anon., *Shrewsbury Prison — 1500-1877*, mimeograph, Shrewsbury, n.d., p. 2; *London Evening Post*, 3 March 1774; J.C. Lettsom, *Hints respecting the prison of Newgate* (London, 1794); J. Mason Good, *A Dissertation on the Diseases of Prisons and Poor Houses* (London, 1795). On gaol fever generally, see C. Creighton, *A History of Epidemics in Britain* (1894), 2 volumes (London, 1965), II, pp. 88-102. Creighton puts much of the blame for this disease — a form of typhus — down to the window tax which gaolers had to pay. In 1767 *The Gentleman's Magazine* blamed gaol fever on 'the horrid neglects of gaolers, and even of the sheriffs and magistrates whose office it is to compel gaolers . . . to do their duty'. *The Gentleman's Magazine*, vol. 37 (1767), p. 340.

17. Ignatieff, *Just Measure of Pain*, pp. 59-69.

18. McConville, *A History of Prison Administration*, pp. 89-92.

19. Sir. W. Blackstone, *Commentaries on the Laws of England* (ed. A. Ryland), 4 volumes (London, 1829), IV, pp. 371-2; McConville, ibid., pp. 107-8.

20. Section 24 prescribed periods of imprisonment which were much shorter than the periods for which the offender would have been transported: for instance, where the offence carried a sentence of 14 years' transportation, the equivalent period in the penitentiary was not less than two and not more than seven years.

21. Dr W. Smith, *Mild Punishments Sound Policy*, p. 103; also pp. 104-5 for Dr Smith's provisos to this statement.

22. Bunbury Committee, *Journals of the House of Commons*, vol. 39, pp. 1040-6, 22 March 1784; Ignatieff, *Just Measure of Pain*, pp. 93-6; McConville, *A History of English Prison Administration*, pp. 107-9.

23. J. Hanway, *Solitude in imprisonment* (London, 1776); J. Dornford, *Nine Letters to the Right Honourable the Lord Mayor and Aldermen of the City of London, on the State of the Prisons and Prisoners with their Jurisdiction* (London [1786]).

24. McConville, *A History of English Prison Administration*, pp. 92-5.

25. R. Evans, *The fabrication of virtue: English prison architecture 1750-1840* (Cambridge, 1982), pp. 135-87; D. Hay, 'War, Dearth and Theft in the Eighteenth Century: The Record of the English Courts', *Past and Present*, 95 (May 1982), pp. 117-60; J.M. Beattie, 'The Pattern of Crime in England 1660-1800', *Past and Present*, no. 62 (1974), pp. 47-95; NLW, RQS, Order Book 2,

inside front cover.

26. D. Hay, 'Property, Authority and the Criminal Law', in D. Hay, P. Linebaugh, J.G. Rule, E.P. Thompson, C. Winslow, *Albion's Fatal Tree: Crime and Society in Eighteenth-Century England* (Harmondsworth, 1977); A. Redford, *Labour Migration in England 1800-1850* (3rd. edition) (Manchester, 1976); Ignatieff, *Just Measure of Pain*, pp. 153-63; E.J. Hobsbawm and G. Rudé, *Captain Swing* (Harmondsworth, 1973); Radzinowicz, *A History of English Criminal Law*, vol. I; R. Samuel, 'Industrial Crime in the 19th Century', *Society for the Study of Labour History*, Bulletin 25 (Autumn 1972), pp. 7-8; R.W. Bushaway, 'Ceremony, Custom and Ritual: Some Observations on Social Conflict in the Rural Community, 1750-1850', in W. Minchinton (ed.), *Reactions to Social and Economic Change 1750-1939* (Exeter, 1979), pp. 9-29.

27. In addition to local Acts, there were general powers to build and to repair gaols and houses of correction in two Acts of 1784: 24 Geo. III, sess. 2, c. 54 and c. 55. On the lack of change in local prisons as a whole see below.

28. Ignatieff, *Just Measure of Pain*, pp. 98-109; McConville, *A History of English Prison Administration*, pp. 98-104.

29. Howard (1789), *An Account of the Principal Lazarettos*, pp. 177-8; J.R.S. Whiting, *Prison Reform in Gloucestershire 1776-1820* (London, 1975).

30. Kidd Wake, *The Case of Kidd Wake. Being a Narrative of His Suffering, during five years confinement !!! In Gloucester Penitentiary House: for Hooting, Hissing, and Calling Out No War! As His Majesty was Passing in State to the House of Peers, on the 29th December, 1795* (London [1801]), p. 9.

31. Ignatieff, *Just Measure of Pain*, p. 78; M. Foucault, *Discipline and Punish: The Birth of the Prison* (London, 1977), pp. 236-7.

32. Wake, *The Case of Kidd Wake*, pp. 17-18.

33. Ibid., pp. 10-11.

34. NLW, RQS, Order Book 1, 8 Oct. 1788; Order Book 2, 14 July 1790, passim; Order Book 2, 11 July 1792. On Dorchester penitentiary, Evans, *The Fabrication of Virtue*, p. 132.

35. Ignatieff, *Just Measure of Pain*, pp. 114-20.

36. E.P. Thompson, *The Making of the English Working Class* (Harmondsworth, 1980); C. Emsley, *British Society and the French Wars 1793-1815* (London, 1979); C. Emsley, 'An Aspect of Pitt's Terror: prosecutions for sedition during the 1790s', *Social History*, vol. 6 (1981), pp. 155-84; S. Bamford, *Passages in the Life of a Radical* (Oxford, 1984).

37. Sir George Nicholls, a leading proponent of the 'New' Poor Law of 1834, quoted in D. Melossi and M. Pavarini, *The Prison and the Factory: Origins of the Penitentiary System* (London, 1981), p. 38.

38. Letter from Lady Louisa Hervey to Mrs L. Lloyd, 3 July [1816], NLW, Aston Hall Correspondence 3364. See also letters from Louisa Kenyon to Mr Lloyd, 25 March 1816 to 9 December 1816, NLW, Aston Hall Correspondence 583-5 and 649; letter from G.N.K. Lloyd to Mr Lloyd, 28 Oct. 1816, NLW, Aston Hall Correspondence 648.

39. *Parliamentary Debates*, XXXIX, cols. 744-50.

40. Ignatieff, *Just Measure of Pain*, pp. 120-42.

41. Bentham, 'Panopticon'; Evans, *The Fabrication of Virtue*, pp. 195-235; M. Foucault, 'The Eye of Power', in C. Gordon (ed.), *Power/Knowledge: Selected Interviews and Other Writings 1972-1977, Michel Foucault* (Brighton, 1980), pp. 146-65; Ignatieff, *Just Measure of Pain*, pp. 109-113.

42. Bentham, 'Panopticon', p. 79n, also p. 122.

43. *Report from His Majesty's Commissioners on the Administration and Practical Operation of the Poor Laws*, Parliamentary Papers, 1834 (44), vol. XXVII.

44. Bentham, 'Panopticon', pp. 122-5.

45. J. Bentham, 'Panopticon versus New South Wales: or, The Panopticon Penitentiary System, and The Penal Colonization System, compared. In a Letter addressed to the Right Honourable Lord Pelham', in Bowring *Works*, IV, pp. 173-248, at pp. 211-13.

46. Bentham, 'Panopticon', p. 72n.

47. Ibid., p. 66.

48. Ibid., p. 50 and p. 73.

49. Ibid., passim; J. Bentham, 'A View of the Hard Labour Bill', in Bowring, *Works*, IV, pp. 1-35, at pp. 12-13.

50. McConville, *A History of English Prison Administration*, pp. 113-34, especially pp. 132-4; Ignatieff, *Just Measure of Pain*, pp. 109-13.

51. R.A. Cooper, 'Jeremy Bentham, Elizabeth Fry, and English Prison Reform', *Journal of the History of Ideas* (1981), pp. 675-90, at p. 679; *Report of William Crawford, Esq., of the Penitentiaries on the United States, addressed to His Majesty's Principal Secretary of State for the Home Department*, Parliamentary Papers, 1834 (593), vol. XVI, p. 9n.; Evans, *The Fabrication of Virtue*, p. 228.

52. William Peter (ed.), *The Speeches of Sir Samuel Romilly in the House of Commons*, 2 volumes (London, 1820), I, pp. 247-54. On Romilly's campaign against the death penalty for certain offences, see Radzinowicz, *A History of English Criminal Law*, vol. I, pp. 318-36, 497-525.

53. McConville, *A History of English Prison Administration*, pp. 113-34.

54. *Select Committee on the Laws relating to Penitentiary-houses*, First and Second Reports, Parliamentary Papers, 1810-11 (199, 217), vol. III; McConville, *A History of English Prison Administration*, pp. 135-44.

55. Letter from William Hardwicke to Charles Tyler, 25 Dec. 1825, NLW, Twiston Davies Mss. 914.

56. *Report from the Select Committee on the State of the Gaols, &c.*, Parliamentary Papers, 1819 (579), vol. VII, p. 4; B. Montagu, *An Inquiry into the Aspersions upon the late Ordinary of Newgate, with Some Observations upon Newgate and upon the Punishment of Death* (London, 1815), pp. 4-6; Anon., *The Disabled Sailor* (London [1800?]), p. 5.

57. Cooper, 'Jeremy Bentham, Elizabeth Fry, and English Prison Reform'; *Select Committee of the House of Lords appointed to inquire into The Present State of the several Gaols and Houses of Correction in England and Wales*, First Report, Parliamentary Papers, 1835 (438), vol. XI, p. 4.

58. McConville, *A History of English Prison Administration*, p. 95 and p. 225; *Report of William Crawford*, p.29; Ignatieff, *Just Measure of Pain*, pp. 105-7.

59. Rev. S. Smith, *The Works of the Rev. Sydney Smith* (new edn.) (London, 1869), pp. 373-85, 400-15.

60. For example, G. Holford, *A Short Vindication of the General Penitentiary at Millbank, From the Censures contained in 'a Letter addressed by C.C. Western, Esq. to the Lord Lieutenant and Magistrates of the County of Essex'* (London, 1825); G. Holford, *The Convict's Complaint in 1815, and the Thanks of the Convict in 1825; or, sketches in verse of A Hulk in the former year, and of the Millbank Penitentiary in the latter* (London, 1825).

61. *Report of the Physicians On the State of the General Penitentiary at Millbank*, Parliamentary Papers, 1823 (256), vol. V; McConville, *A History of English Prison Administration*, pp. 144-6; Ignatieff, *op. cit.*, pp. 175-9; Lettsom, *Hints*; Mason Good, *A Dissertation*.

62. Ignatieff, *Just Measure of Pain*, pp. 177-87.

6

REFORMATION OR PUNISHMENT?

Crawford, Russell and Religious Reformation

The penology debate in the nineteenth century, then, did not seek to challenge the need for the prison, but rather centred on the type of discipline and its particular goals: should emphasis be laid on reformation of the individual prisoner, or on a generally deterrent effect which might reduce crime? Was it possible to combine these two objectives? There was the problem of how to deal with those who had not been convicted, but were merely awaiting trial and of those who were imprisoned for debt. But the difficulties lay not only at a theoretical level, there was the resistance, or simple disinterest, of local justices, local gaolers and local ratepayers to new ideas, especially since such ideas generally involved an increase in expenditure.

Although there had been general legislation before — for instance, the Gaol Fees Abolition Act 1815 — the Gaol Act 1823 (4 Geo. IV, c. 64) sponsored by Peel, the Secretary of State, was the first comprehensive statement of principle from central government to be applied to local prisons. It followed the apparent increase in crime and poverty, and was part of Peel's reform of the criminal law. More specifically, there had been pressure from the Society for the Improvement of Prison Discipline for local reforms and a greater uniformity of prison discipline. There had also been a report on prisons from a select committee in 1822 which stated that prisons should be managed according to the familiar principles of 'terror and . . . real punishment . . .' but 'at the same time that the exercise of all unnecessary severity is restrained by wholesome regulations', and that the prisoners 'do not, by the effect of that sentence, become worse members of society, or more hardened offenders.'[1]

The Gaol Act 1823 sought to achieve a measure of uniformity of practice (section 10), but more than that it sought to impose some of the penological ideas initially established in the late eighteenth century and endorsed in the Millbank prison. The preamble stated that prisons should

> not only provide for the safe Custody, but shall also tend more effectually to preserve the Health and to improve the Morals of the Prisoners confined therein, and shall insure the proper Measure of Punishment to convicted Offenders.

These aims were to be achieved by 'due Classification, Inspection, regular Labour and Employment, and Religious and Moral Instruction'. However, for reasons which are not given, the Act did not apply to all prisons. Furthermore, its rather vague drafting meant that its provisions were open to local interpretation: for instance, section 10 required facilities for hard labour to be made available at each prison, but it did not specify what these facilities had to be.

On the other hand, the Act did abolish the use of alcohol in prisons (section 10). It also imposed health requirements: cleaning, medical facilities (section 10) and the appointment of a surgeon (section 33). The visiting justices were required to inspect their prisons at least three times a quarter (section 16). A chaplain was obligatory (section 28) and his duties reflected the new mood, for in addition to holding divine service, he was to visit and instruct prisoners, and he was to inform the visiting justices of 'any Abuse or Impropriety which may have come to his Knowledge' (section 30). If a new prison was to be built it had to provide for classification of the prisoners: males and females were to be separated and then divided into five classes (section 10). A separate sleeping cell was to be assigned to each prisoner 'if possible'. There was to be no solitary confinement, except at night or for the purpose of punishing those who broke prison rules; indeed the amending Act of 1824 sought to prevent accidental solitary confinement, if there was only one prisoner in a particular class then with his or her agreement and the justices' consent the prisoner could be transferred into another class (5 Geo. IV, c. 85, section 13). Finally, under section 24 an annual report on the state of each prison covered by the Act had to be made to the Secretary of State.

The Gaol Act lacked effective sanctions and its provisions seem to have been widely ignored;[2] even so it provided an important precedent for government intervention in local prisons.

More direct intervention was justified on the basis of the fiscal assistance given by central government to the prisons which only really began in the 1830s. Furthermore, in the factory inspectorate there was a model for the method of intervention.

In 1833 a select committee on agriculture pointed out that recent legislation on, amongst other things, prisons and the payment of prosecution costs, had put an increased burden upon county rates and, hence, upon farmers, yet those who spent these funds were not accountable. Then in 1835 a massive inquiry into municipal corporations criticised the poor state of borough gaols.[3]

In 1835 a House of Lords committee urged the need for greater uniformity in prison discipline. Two of their main suggestions were instantly enacted in the Prisons Act 1835 (5 & 6 Will. IV, c. 38). The first was that all prisons' rules and diets should be referred to the Secretary of State for approval rather than to the assize judges as had been the practice in the past — this became sections 2 and 5. Second, was the appointment of government inspectors to visit prisons and make reports to the Secretary of State; they would supplement and add a national perspective to the visits by the visiting justices (section 7).

Initially five inspectors were appointed, two of whom were William Crawford, who had just completed an exhaustive report of prisons in the USA, and Reverend Whitworth Russell, the chaplain of Millbank and a nephew of the Home Secretary, Lord John Russell. They remained inspectors for the important Home Division until their deaths in 1847. Whilst Crawford seems to have made a favourable impression even on his opponents — Chesterton, the governor of Cold Bath Fields House of Correction, called him 'an honest advocate' — Russell seems to have been a more unpleasant character, Chesterton finding him 'dogmatical and arbitrary to the last degree. He was singularly indifferent to the feelings of others . . .'

The Act did not authorise the inspectors to order changes in the local prisons; on the other hand, it created a small corps of prison experts who had access to the prisons, the Secretary of State and Parliament and whose reports could, therefore, create public embarrassment. It seems that to a large extent the local justices followed the advice of the inspectors, although they would sometimes assert their independence. An extreme example of this was the case of William George, governor of Caernarvon

County Gaol, who was the subject of an inquiry by the prison inspector, Whitworth Russell, in 1843. George was charged with drunkenness and various abuses. Russell recommended that he be dismissed, a view which the Secretary of State supported, but which the justices chose to ignore. It was undoubtedly a source of great embarrassment to them when similar charges were brought in 1848 and a second inquiry set up under the inspector Frederic Hill. This time George was speedily dismissed before the inquiry began.[4]

Despite the appointment of the inspectors, reform of local prisons was, at it had always been, notoriously slow. Things were not helped by the disagreement amongst the inspectors as to the best form of prison discipline. It was in the government administered prisons that the inspectors were best able to realise their ideas, and these gradually increased in number during the nineteenth century.

The Gaol Act idea — following on Howard's suggestion — of classification with work but no silence or separation beyond the separate night cells, was basically a negative approach in that it merely sought to prevent moral contamination, it did not seek to reform the prisoner. There were two other basic types of prison discipline which did seek reformation: the separate system and the silent system, respectively represented by the American prisons at Philadelphia and at Auburn. The difference between them might be categorised as the difference between a religious and a capitalist conversion. Although, in practice, the means of conversion differed the aim was in both cases to produce a worker-citizen — loyal, self-disciplined, independent yet reliant on wage labour, hard working. Both sought the obliteration of the individual with individual aspirations, and his or her replacement by the individual who was one of a mass of identical individuals moulded not in the image of the bourgeoisie, but in the image which the bourgeoisie had of the 'worker-citizen'. The prison was to be a model of bourgeois egalitarianism, with each prisoner being treated equally, none being allowed to exempt themselves through wealth from the rigours of imprisonment. The principal difference, then, lay only in the way each of these systems — the separate and the silent — sought to achieve this aim: one, the separate system, through an internalisation of a particular set of values; the other, the silent system, through a behavioural change.

At Auburn, where the silent system was operated, there was a microcosm of the ideal bourgeois productive unit with its socialisation restricted to vertical relationships — prisoner-warder (employer-worker), never prisoner-prisoner (worker-worker) since silence was rigorously enforced — and thereby seeking to break up prisoner (worker) sub-cultures (trade unions). Pavarini recently described this system as one where the prisoners are 'no longer just "disciplined in abstraction" (as in Philadelphia prison), but perfectly "synchronised" in collective, dissociative activity'. Solitary confinement was only used to break the prisoner's spirit on his or her first arrival, or as a disciplinary measure; it was not a part of the discipline itself since this was based on socialisation and productive work motivated by rewards (remission or wages). The individual was one of a productive mass, but at the same time, through the operation of the silent system, was on his or her own.[5]

Crawford, in his massive survey of American prisons (1834), criticised the silent system. Prisoners managed to communicate in signs and whispers, and this reduced the terrors of imprisonment and undermined the deterrent effect. The officers in such a prison had too much discretion and this could lead to both a lack of uniformity of practice and to abuses. Furthermore, the punishments required to maintain silence might lead to a temporary obedience, but in the long term would not change the prisoner and would probably create a feeling of bitterness leading to a hardening of his or her vices.[6]

Crawford, on the other hand, praised the Philadelphia system. Solitary confinement was the very essence of the disciplinary technique here. The prison was the translation into penological practice of the religious beliefs of the Quakers. According to the Quaker writer Fox, 'Every man . . . is illuminated by the divine light and I have seen it shine through every man.' To achieve this illumination a person had to be quiet, hence the format of Quaker meetings — long periods of silence with no ritual, punctuated by occasional declarations by those present.

The Quakers regarded prisoners merely as people who had never listened to the Inner Light. The solution seemed obvious: lock criminals up in separate cells and they could not ignore the Inner Light. They would then recognise past sins. This view was widely accepted. The Hanoverian royal physician, Zimmerman, had argued in a pamphlet published here in 1795, 'Solitude restores every thing to its proper place', for whilst the world weakened the soul, solitude led to self-scrutiny, virtue and religion. But Crawford regarded solitary confinement as insufficient to achieve these aims. In his 1834 report, he remarked of solitude in the Eastern Penitentiary in Philadelphia: 'The mind becomes open to the best impressions and prepared for the reception of those truths and consolations which Christianity can alone impart.' Religious instruction was, therefore, the other essential feature of a prison.[7]

This solitude was also regarded as providing an excellent means for deterring those criminals at large from committing further crimes, since it was believed that past vices were such a terror to criminals that they were frightened to face them. Furthermore, prisoners under the separate system would not be angry or feel vindictive as they would under the silent system, since architecture rather than constant punishment was used to enforce the discipline. This system guaranteed that prisoners would not be recognised on release by former inmates and so would not run the risk of blackmail. Finally, even if the separate system did not reform the prisoner, it at least prevented him or her from getting any worse.[8]

Work was an essential feature of the separate system, but it was always subsidiary to the requirements of solitary confinement. Crawford criticised the emphasis placed on productive prison labour and on the training of prisoners in work skills: 'It is one thing to render a convict a skilful mechanic, and another to induce him to become an honest man . . .' And elsewhere, he wrote, in the spirit of Sydney Smith, 'It should never be forgotten that a gaol is not a school for the instruction of artisans, but a place of punishment.' Work was a comfort to prevent insanity through prolonged dwelling on past sins; it would come to be regarded by the prisoners as a privilege and a pleasure, and inevitably it would become an internalised part of the convict's values. It was, therefore, work, not a particular kind of work or work of a productive nature, that was important.[9]

The distinction between the methods of the silent system and the separate system can most easily be discerned in their differing attitudes to the role that work had within the prison. Unlike those prisons which used a system based on productive labour where reformation might be measured in capitalist terms, that is, according to the amount or value of work produced by an

Plate 1. Boethius in prison

From a twelfth-century West of England manuscript (Bodleian MS. Auct. F.6.5. fol 1ᵛ), by permission of the Bodleian Library, Oxford.

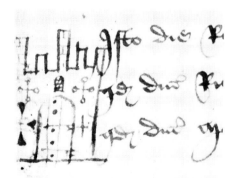

Plate 2. Sketch of Newgate Gaol in the fifteenth century

From the City of London Journals (Journal 4, fol 79b), by permission of the Corporation of London Records Office.

Accurate representations of Medieval gaols are rare. A scribe has drawn the Newgate gatehouse next to an entry from June 1445, which records one Richard Alton's committal to prison.

Plate 3. 'The Representations', 1728: conditions in the Marshalsea Prison

From the Report to the House of Commons, by permission of the Trustees of the British Library.

Plate 4. Portrait of Howard visiting a prison

Plate 5. Prisoners exercising at Pentonville Prison
Engraving from Mayhew and Binney's *Criminal Prisons of London*, 1862.

Plate 6.   Interior of the Surrey House of Correction, Wandsworth
Engraving from Mayhew and Binney's *Criminal Prisons of London*, 1862.

Plate 7. Treadwheel at Pentonville Prison, c. 1890
By permission of the Hertfordshire Constabulary.

Plate 8. Prisoners working on land reclamation on Dartmoor, early 1890s
By permission of the Hertfordshire Constabulary.

Plate 9. Children shoe-shining at Upton House Industrial School, London, at the turn of the century
By permission of the Greater London Council Photograph Library.

Plate 10. Prisoner working a hand crank at Wormwood Scrubs Prison, late nineteenth century
By permission of the Hertfordshire Constabulary.

Plate 11. Contrasting architectural styles: entrances to Dartmoor, Manchester (Strangeways) and Coldingley Prisons
From the report on the Work of the Prison Department (HMSO, 1977).

Plate 12. Sir Alexander Paterson

From S.K. Ruck (ed.), *Paterson on Prisons* (Frederick Muller, 1951).

individual prisoner, the separate system measured reformation of the prisoner in terms of religion and typically this took the form of seeing how much of the Bible a particular prisoner had learnt by rote.[10] Hence, also the rejection of incentives under the separate system, for whereas the behaviourists merely sought to improve habits, the proponents of the separate system sought a change of the internalised values and, therefore, wished to avoid the hypocrisy which might be encouraged by incentives.[11]

Crawford and Russell adopted the separate system on the ground that it led, they believed, to religious reformation which was the only genuine and permanent sort. However, in his 1834 report Crawford admitted that it was impracticable, at that time, to expect every local prison to be converted to the separate system because of the expense, so although it should be used wherever possible, as a second-best separation with work in silent association was acceptable, but he still emphasised the need for religion. A system based on the Gaol Act idea of classification without silence he rejected. He also dismissed the idea of subordinating the prison to profitable labour, both because it rarely produced a profit and because religious reformation was more important.[12] Since Crawford and Russell's notion of the purpose of imprisonment was unconnected with ideas of retribution, they were freed from limitations on the length of a punishment which might be imposed by any requirement of proportioning it to the offence. Whilst this legitimised lengthy sentences, some believed that the separate system might work so rapidly that sentences would actually be shortened.[13]

Religion had been of a low priority in the eighteenth century (see below), but in the new penitentiaries it had been given an important part to play, the chaplain no longer simply comforted the felon awaiting execution. In the Gloucester Penitentiary the chaplain was involved in the system of prison discipline. First, he sought to legitimise the punishment, persuading the prisoner to admit guilt for the crime and to accept the justice of the sentence. Second, and linked to the first function, the chaplain tried to persuade the prisoner to submit to the prison discipline: since reformation amounted to an acceptance of certain dominant values — work, quiet submission to authority, self-discipline — so religious conversion was defined in alignment with this objective. Third, the chaplain acted as a check on the actions of the governor and the staff. Crawford and Russell sought to enlarge the chaplain's role in line with their emphasis on the objective of religious reformation.[14]

In 1835 the Lords Committee adopted the separate system, although an examination of the evidence presented to the committee gives little clear support for it as a means of reformation: those prisons where it was in operation generally based their assessment of its success on whether or not a prisoner was recommitted to *that* prison ignoring the possibility of imprisonment elsewhere; others simply expressed opinions based on no evidence; some prisons actually denied that the system provided any beneficial effect at all, or they felt unable to guage any possible effect. The committee recommended the national adoption of a separate system which combined solitary confinement with religion and work, although they also urged the mitigation of the rigours of such a system by allowing silent association in chapel and at work.[15]

The Prison Act 1839 (2 & 3 Vic., c. 56) bears the imprint of Crawford and Russell. Although the Act fell short of actually directing the local prisons to adopt a particular form of prison discipline, the possibilities for intervention were increased as were measures which sought to restrict the discretion of the justices. Furthermore, the Act showed a distinct change in central policy from that laid out in the 1823 Act. Classification was continued by the Act, and extended to prisons not within the 1823 Act (section 5); however, this fits in with Crawford's acceptance in 1834 that the implementation of the separate system was unrealistic in some local prisons since it would involve large expenditure on new buildings. But section 2 allows separate confinement, and section 3 states

> . . . That, in order to prevent the Contamination arising from the Association of Prisoners in any Prison in which Rules for the Individual Separation of Prisoners shall be in force, any Prisoner may be separately confined during the Whole or any Part of the Period of his or her Imprisonment . . .

In that separate confinement there was to be 'Moral and Religious Instruction' (section 4). Association of prisoners was positively discouraged by the financial implications of section 6 which prohibited the use of prisoners in the administration of prison discipline. This meant that an increase in staff to supervise prisoners would be required unless a prison was converted to the separate system. Crawford and Russell's hand can also be seen both in the repeal of the provision in the 1823 Act which had provided for payments to prisoners for prison work (section 8), and in the obligation on all prisons to have chaplains (section 15). All separate cells had to be certified by the inspectors (section 4). In addition, plans for new prisons were to be approved by the Secretary of State (section 12), a provision which led to the creation of the office of Surveyor-General of Prisons in 1839 and increased centralised knowledge, power and inspection.

Under the influence of Crawford and Russell, the role of the chaplain in the discpline at Millbank had increased. By the late 1830s religious reformation was serving as the guiding objective of penal discipline in Millbank; other matters were subordinated to it. Hence there was a greater emphasis on the separate system with its hope of internal reformation, and a consequent move away from association and the behaviourist approach. In 1836 this was combined with the removal of incentives to prisoners which Crawford and Russell regarded as encouraging hypocrisy rather than genuine reformation. Inevitably this led to a conflict with the governor of Millbank whose function had degenerated into that of an administrator. In 1837 the governor, Captain Chapman, resigned, and the opportunity was taken to appoint a chaplain-governor, Rev Daniel Nihill.

However, the new discipline did not last long. In 1842 the severity of the regime was relaxed following a Parliamentary inquiry which had found that lengthy periods of solitary confinement were causing insanity amongst the prisoners. Then in 1843 the prison was turned into a depot where prisoners were assessed and then sent elsewhere. This seems to have been due, in part, to the demoralising effect of the Parliamentary inquiry and, in part, to doubts as to Millbank's success in reforming prisoners.[16]

Russell and Crawford did not, however, regard this failure at Millbank as in anyway a reflection on their ideas. For them Millbank had failed because it was not purpose built around the concept of religious reformation. Indeed the way was clear for their ideas to be fully realised in the new government penitentiary which was under construction at Pentonville. Their determination to achieve their aims can be grasped from the evidence to the Grey Committee in 1850 of Sir Joshua Jebb who, as the

Surveyor-General of Prisons, was responsible for the design:

> When Lord John Russell determined upon erecting Pentonville
> Prison, I was requested by the then inspectors of prisons, Mr.
> Crawford and Mr. Russell, who had brought the subject of
> separate confinement forward, to allow them to be associated
> with me in the consideration of the plans, and they urged this
> reason: they said, 'We do not wish to control your professional
> opinion; but if you erect a prison which we do not consider to
> be adapted for the enforcement of the system which we
> advocate, we will not certify the cells, and the prison will be
> useless.'[17]

Pentonville was completed in 1842 and represented the high
point of the attempt to build a disciplinary system into an
institution. Robin Evans, the historian of prison architecture, has
called Pentonville the 'most comprehensive expression' of
Victorian penal institutions; according to Ignatieff it 'represented
the culmination of three generations of thinking and experimentation with penitentiary routine'.[18]

Pentonville was built on a radial plan with four wings and cells
on each side of these wings. The cell doors could be seen from a
central point in the prison. Each cell was designed to provide for
all the requirements of its solitary inmate. Prisoners did leave
their cells for exercise and for chapel, but elaborate arrangements
were made to keep the prisoners completely separate: each
prisoner had a box in chapel and a solitary exercise yard. The
prison was remarkably quiet due to the use of heavy duty bricks;
indeed this desire for silence was carried so far as to include
making the warders wear felt overshoes. The warders, themselves, were kept to a strict discipline by means of clocks
positioned around the prison with levers which had to be pressed
down at set times, so forcing them to patrol the prison.

Here, then, was a machine which to as large an extent as
possible would operate independently of the wills of both staff
and prisoners, the main exception being the chaplain whose job it
was to use the raw material which the prison machine had
produced — the softened, impressionable human being — and
from that create a Christian citizen.[19]

Since all new plans for prisons had, after 1839, to be approved
by Jebb, the Home Officer advisor (later the Surveyor-General of

Prisons), he was able to impose the Pentonville model. By 1850 its influence could be seen in 50 prisons. It signalled, then, what Evans has called, a 'second, more comprehensive and uniform rebuilding of the English prison system'.[20]

However, whatever the initial hopes of Crawford and Russell, the worry over the mental effects meant that prisoners were only kept in prison for 18 months; they were then transported. Soon even this was found to lead to insanity, so the period of confinement was reduced first to twelve months and later to nine months. Paradoxically, as well as criticism based on the cases of insanity, there was also a belief that Pentonville was not sufficiently punitive, and an impression that it was not preventing recidivism. As Evans put it, the critics believed Pentonville 'was at once too well-appointed to deter, and too dreadful to reform'.[21]

It was not surprising that this criticism provoked a response from the chaplains whose power base within their prisons rested on the acceptance of the probability of religious reformation through the separate system. Clay, chaplain at Preston, and Field, chaplain at Reading, claimed that the recidivism was not a fault of the system, it was due either to the character of the prisoner — too feeble to make an impression upon, or too hardened — or to the lack of employment for prisoners on their discharge forcing them into crime in order to live. But even Crawford had doubts about the effectiveness of his ideas. In 1845 he was very downhearted at the increasing numbers of convicts and the apparent failures of attempts at reformation at Pentonville and at the juvenile penitentiary which had been opened in 1838. On top of all this came the deaths in 1847 of both Crawford and Russell, events which removed the principal supports for a system based around the objective of reformation: Crawford collapsed during a meeting in Pentonville prison and Russell committed suicide in Millbank.[22]

Their deaths created a void within the ranks of the inspectors. Admittedly, there had been disagreement between the inspectors since their inception, but Crawford and Russell had generated such a degree of authority that such disagreements were rather obscured. By 1850 the Duke of Richmond was saying that there was no agreement amongst the prison inspectors as to the best form of discipline; this naturally weakened the likelihood of any single system being adopted throughout England and Wales let alone the controversial one proposed by Crawford and Russell. The role of religion declined — although, as will be seen later, it is clear that whatever happened in the penitentiaries, religion never had more than a secondary role in most of the local prisons. Many now accepted the limitations of a single approach being applied to such a diverse group of individuals as convicts. In 1849 David Price, the chaplain at Brecon County Gaol, remarked that the prison did not have an equal effect on all prisoners, 'for they form a very heterogeneous mass of different views, habits, manners, dispositions, and connections . . .' For Price the role of religion was that it might help to alter the conduct of some of the prisoners and 'teach more effectually their duties towards God and Man'. The failure of Pentonville marked the failure of religious reformation and also the failure of penal architecture.[23]

Jebb and the End of Transportation

In contrast to those arch theorists, Crawford and Russell, Jebb was a pragmatist. He was the very epitome of a core of professional administrators that grew up in the middle third of the nineteenth century. A former Royal Engineer, he advised Crawford and Russell on prison construction before being appointed advisor to the Home Office on prison building in 1839; he was already involved in administration having been appointed a visitor to Parkhurst Juvenile Prison earlier in the same year. He became a commissioner of Pentonville prison in 1842. Then in 1844 he became Inspector-General of Military Prisons and was appointed to the newly created post of Surveyor-General of Prisons.

In 1847 Jebb was able to step into the gap left by the deaths of Crawford and Russell. He was the most experienced person in prison administration and so, in 1850, he was made head of a new Directorate of Convict Prisons which had been created to oversee the administration of the increasing area of government involvement in prisons. The inspection system declined, so that in 1863 the Carnarvon Committee reported that instead of five inspectors there were only two for the whole of England, Scotland and Wales, which inevitably meant that inspections were infrequent, and made the possibility of a uniform prison discipline being achieved through the inspectors a very slim hope.[24]

Although he consistently paid lip-service to the separate system, Jebb placed less reliance on internal reformation and more on the possibilities of a military discipline designed to produce outward conformity and obedience, both of which were measured in terms of work. He argued that since prison sentences were generally short there was little realistic chance of achieving internal reformation. For him the principal advantage of the separate system seems to have lain in its essentially negative ability to prevent the dissemination of vice. In 1847 he wrote

> the separation of one prisoner from another is indispensable as the basis of any sound system. It would appear, however, that, even should the construction of a prison admit of such separation, the means will still be required for varying the administration of the discipline to suit the varying circumstances under which it must of necessity be applied.

Hence, he watered down the separate system by removing what he regarded as its absurdities, such as separation in chapel and the wearing of masks whilst exercising (this he called, 'a theory presed beyond its practical usefulness'), and in its place he developed the public works prison where convicts worked in association, and which used the incentives of the progressive stage system and remission. He saw these prisons as combining deterrence and a more clearly punitive element, namely hard labour. Transportation was being wound down and the public works prisons were to be its replacement. Pentonville, like Millbank before it, became a depot for initial disciplining and assessment of convicts in 1849.[25]

The need for more government prisons in England and Wales was spurred by the winding down both of transportation and of the hulks. The transportation of convicts to Australia and to Van Diemen's Land (later to be renamed Tasmania) had been under criticism for a long time (see above). In 1837-8 the Molesworth Committee had recommended the abolition of transportation believing it to be unequal in its effect, to have no terror for criminals and to be expensive. The last criticism represented a radical change from the situation a few years previously when Bentham wrote that the only reason for not building penitentiaries was the belief that transportation was cheaper: '. . . it is the mere dread of extravagance that has *driven* your thrifty minister from the penitentiary-house plan — not the love of transportation that has *seduced* him from it.'[26]

This early policy had created a lack of home facilities which in turn had led to the continuation of transportation. The only facilities at home were cells rented by the government in local prisons and the hulks. In spite of the heavy criticism that had been levelled at them since Howard's day, the hulks accounted for 70 per cent of the felons imprisoned in England and Wales. After 1843 the numbers in the hulks did drop owing to the opening of Pentonville and the expansion of Parkhurst, so that by 1847 only a little over 30 per cent were in the hulks.

Inquiries into the hulks in 1847 and 1850 reported that control of prisoners was almost impossible, and immorality and disease were rife. Attempts to tighten the discipline largely failed. Then in 1850 the newly created Directorate of Convict Prisons joined in the criticism of the hulks. The hulks were doomed: the last English one going out of service in 1857, although hulks in Bermuda and Gibraltar, where the demand for convict labour outweighed other considerations, continued until Bermuda divested itself of its British convicts in 1875 and used the hulks for its own criminals.[27]

For Jebb the public works prisons were an ideal replacement for both the hulks and transportation, and in 1848 a public works prison at Portland was opened. Convicts were to be kept under the separate system for an initial period, but for the major part of their sentence they were to work in association with other convicts. Labour had displaced religious reformation as the governing factor in penal discipline, and this raised a problem of control. These prisons had large areas of open spaces which allowed prisoners to gather together and which were, therefore, held partly to blame for riots in the 1860s, leading to the inevitable change in policy: 'The evils attendant on the massing together of such large bodies of convicts . . . having become evident, we have taken steps . . . for sub-dividing them so as to effect complete separation . . .'[28]

As home facilities improved so the government were more willing to respond to pressure from the colonies to end transportation — only Western Australia responded favourably to a circular on transportation. In 1853 the Penal Servitude Act

(16 & 17 Vic., c. 99) confirmed a practice which had begun in the hulks and had been continued both there and in the new public works prisons, of not transporting some of the convicts. Under this Act sentences of transportation for less than 14 years were no longer to be imposed; anyone who before the Act might have been given a sentence of less than 14 years transportation was to be dealt with at home (section 1). The courts were given the discretion to sentence to penal servitude anyone who might, but for the Act, have been sentenced to less than 14 years transportation (section 2). Those who could be sentenced to 14 years or more transportation might still be transported; however the court were now given the discretion to sentence them to penal servitude instead (section 3). The terms of penal servitude were less than the terms of transportation for which they were substituted, with the exception of transportation for life (section 4), presumably because transportation was regarded as a less severe punishment. Those sentenced to penal servitude were to be used on public works (section 6). All convicts might be released early on licence or ticket-of-leave, as it was known (sections 9 to 11).

The remission provisions did apply to those sentenced to penal servitude, but the policy was that, with rare exceptions, tickets-of-leave were only to be given to those sentenced to transportation, many of whom were still not being actually transported. The reason for this discrimination was the fear of adverse public reaction if those sentenced to penal servitude whose sentences were already shorter than the old transportation terms had their punishment reduced further. This led to much ill feeling and disorder in the public works prisons, leading, in 1857, to the end of the distinction between sentences of transportation and penal servitude, which had the effect of extending remission provisions to all convicts (20 & 21 Vic., c. 3). This Act abolished transportation; however, the Home Office retained the power to order convicts to be transported, and it was not until 1867 that the system formally ended.[29]

The Prison Acts of 1865 and 1877

In 1863 a panic was created in London by what was believed to be a new and dangerous crime called garotting. Garotting was an offence similar to what might now be called mugging, and , just as with mugging, it led both to a demand for severe measures to be taken against the offenders and to a search for an easily identifiable group upon which responsibility for these crimes could be fixed. It was popularly supposed that the garotters were convicts released on tickets-of-leave. Peter Bartrip has argued that too great an emphasis has to be laid on the role of the garotting scare in penal policy. Certainly measures for more effective law enforcement and administration had, as he says, been gradually introduced since 1853 because of the decline in transportation and the hulks, and because of a perceived increase in crime, but the London garotting scare was, at the very least, something which accelerated this process, and which, more importantly, seemed to confirm opinions that Jebb's system was too soft. Whatever the truth of this, 1863 saw the setting of up two inquiries into penal discipline: the Carnarvon Committee and the Royal Commission on Penal Servitude. Both of these had an important effect on penal policy.[30]

The Carnarvon Committee recommended an increase in severity, for, although paying lip-service to reformation, the committee clearly regarded the need for what it called 'due and effective punishment' as more important. Hence it dropped religious reformation as the guiding objective of prison discipline. The Committee adopted Jebb's view: 'I think that the deterring elements of the punishment are hard labour, hard fare, and a hard bed . . .' However, Jebb had qualified this statement by saying that a prisoner's life was so different from that of the free labourer that their respective lifestyles — for example, their diets — could not be compared.[31] This was by no means a new view; it had long been regarded as dangerous to use diet as a means of punishment, and as recently as 1843 the prison inspectors had criticised this idea. Indeed, both Rev Clay, a supporter of religious reformation, and Dr William Baly, a writer on prison diseases, had gone as far as to suggest that prisoners actually required more food than 'free' labourers because of the effect which the depression caused by imprisonment had on their health.[32] The Committee was less willing to compromise; they favoured the diet being less-eligible than that of the workhouse pauper, so that paupers might not commit crimes in order to be sent to prison.

The Committee said that there should be no relaxation of

discipline, a clear criticism of Crawford, Russell and Jebb: education and religion should, therefore, be restricted so as not to interfere with punishment. Separation, both by system and by architecture, was approved not because of its ability to achieve religious reformation, but rather because of its severity. Hence, the Committee wanted separation throughout the prison system and disapproved of the 'relaxation' introduced by Jebb in school, chapel and at exercise.

Work should be of the severest sort:

> . . . whilst industrial occupation should in certain stages form a part of prison discipline, the more strictly penal element of that discipline is the chief means of exercising a deterrent influence, and therefore ought not to be weakened, as it has been in some gaols, still less to be entirely withdrawn.

Harking back to the Penitentiary Act, the Committee suggested a precise definition of hard labour should be adopted: treadmill, crank and shot drill. Although industrial occupation might be allowed in the later stages of imprisonment, for the most part labour should be penal and irksome.

The Committee's general outlook can be summarised in one quotation. Having vigorously dissociated themselves from the views of Perry, one of the prison inspectors, the report continued that the Committee

> do not consider that the moral reformation of the offender holds the primary place in the prison system; that mere industrial employment without wages is a sufficient punishment for many crimes; that it is in itself morally prejudicial to the criminal and useless to society, or that it is desirable to abolish both the crank and the treadwheel as soon as possible.

The Committee did favour the use of grading in order to reward behaviour. As the term of imprisonment went on and so long as a prisoner's behaviour was good, then the work which that prisoner would be required to do would be made easier. However, this suggestion had little importance for the majority of prisoners in local prisons since the Committee did not wish this relaxation to apply before three months had elapsed and most sentences were under that period. The exclusion of short-term prisoners was deliberate since the main aim was to make a lasting impression.

Finally, the Committee suggested the closure of small prisons, and the withdrawal of Treasury funding from local prisons which failed to implement Home Office rules.

The reports not only of the Carnarvon Committee, but also of the Royal Commission, in effect amounted to a rejection of the approaches of Crawford and Russell, and of Jebb. Coincidentally Jebb died in 1863. The Prison Act 1865 (28 & 29 Vic., c. 126), which applied to all prisons, followed the basic recommendation of the Report that greater severity was required in prisons. The Act also took the view that conformity to certain modes of behaviour rather than internal reformation was all that could be hoped for from prisoners. Although Crawford and Russell had opposed both penalties and rewards because in their views they led to hypocrisy, a progressive stage system had been used in the colonies and was regarded as an important means not of reforming prisoners, but rather of maintaining control of them: for this reason it was adopted in the Act. This stage system had little importance for the majority of prisoners who were serving short sentences, and because of this cruder methods, mainly whipping, had to be used to maintain control.

In some respects the Committee's recommendations were toned down. The fear of injuring health led to equivocation on the question of prison diet. It was left to the discretion of the local justices. On the issue of prison labour, many never entirely gave up the idea of productive labour. However, in the main the prison regime increased in its severity during the 1860s and 1870s under the direction of Jebb's successors, first Henderson and then Du Cane.

Most radical of all were sections 35 and 36 of the Prison Act. The government's financial involvement in local prisoners was such that it felt able to allow the withdrawal of government funds from a prison, or even its closure, if the Act or Home Office rules made under the Act were not complied with. The Home Office did indeed write to those Quarter Sessions whose prisons were defective threatening to withdraw funds. At Brecon the visiting justices reported as early as 1866 that substantial alterations would be required to conform to the Prison Act, but the Quarter Sessions did nothing until the letter came from the Home Office in January 1868 threatening sanctions. Even so the alterations were not begun until 1869.

The next step, nationalisation, was urged by those who saw it as a means of achieving uniformity or of getting rid of underused prisons, but nationalisation actually came about as a result of a Conservative government's commitment to cut rates. Although for many the local prison was part of a town's civic dignity, others saw it simply as a drain on resources. Furthermore, legislation, especially the Prison Act 1865, had removed much of the justices' control over the prisons. When the Bill to nationalise the prisons was before the House of Commons it was welcomed by the Chairman of the Radnorshire bench as a saving of the rates; however it did not seem to occur to him that it might lead to the closure of the Presteigne County Gaol. Once the Prison Act 1877 (40 & 41 Vic., c. 21) became law putting the local prisons under the control of commissioners appointed by the government, the Home Office set about closing small prisons, including Presteigne. Locally this was opposed on the ground of the loss of civic dignity, but before representations could be made to the Secretary of State the order closing the prison as from 1 May 1878 went through.

The nationalisation of prisons cannot, however, be seen simply as an exercise in vote catching. By the 1870s central government had shrugged off much of its reluctance to intervene in society. Responsibility for the infrastructure, that is, the provision of essential services which private capital would be unable or unwilling to provide, had long been regarded as a proper area for government intervention. However, local government was less able to bear the cost of such services. The subsidies from, and eventual takeover by, central government of some of these services was largely, therefore, inevitable.[33]

Local Prisons

In addition to the older local prisons, the house of correction and the borough and county gaols, the development of the modern police force during the nineteenth century led to the erection of buildings which incorporated a police station, living quarters, and a lock-up cell designed to hold suspects.[34] The distinction between the houses of correction and the gaol was not formally abolished until the Prison Act 1865 (section 56). According to the Webbs this distinction had, for all practical purposes, vanished during the seventeenth century. This is not entirely true. Certain categories of offenders would not be sent to the house of correction, but would go to the county gaol: for instance, felons. The house of correction was, right up until its abolition, a place for minor offenders, hence late eighteenth-century prison reformers often regarded the house of correction as the first target for a more rigorous discipline, because there were imprisoned those 'whose habits are as yet unfixed'.[35]

In Radnorshire at the end of the eighteenth century the house of correction which up until that time had been in the same building as the county gaol and under the same gaoler, was moved to a different building and put into the care of a different gaoler, but by 1846 there appears to be only one gaoler for the two prisons.[36] Furthermore, the Gaol Act of 1824 (4 Geo. IV, c. 64, sections 2 and 5) required each county to have one house of correction — although it could be in the same building as, and administered in tandem with, the county gaol.

Despite the apparent decrease in gaol fever and the building of a number of new prisons, John Howard in 1789, Lord Loughborough in 1793 and Nield in a general survey of 1812, all found little overall improvement in prisons. Loughborough found it was still common practice for the gaoler to allow beer into the prison, but, more generally, the failure to replace fees with a salary for the gaoler meant the continuation of abuses which Howard had criticised so many years before. Loughborough felt that the defective state of the prisons was caused not so much by a 'want of GOOD LAWS, as from their INEXECUTION'. He, therefore, called for national reform, especially since the local improvements which had, in some places, occurred,

> have not yet produced all the benefit expected, nor can they, while the Reform is local, not general: one County gains little by the strictness of its Discipline, if in all the adjoining Counties there is a general relaxation.

J.J. Gurney, the Quaker brother of Elizabeth Fry, writing in 1819, felt that part of the problem lay with Howard's concentration on the alleviation of physical distress and a consequent lessening of the emphasis on moral improvement.[37]

For the most part the justices probably would have echoed the sentiments expressed by the Radnorshire Quarter Sessions when replying to Sir Herbert Mackworth who had sent them a plan for a Bill on prisons, they informed him 'that they have no Objection to the general plan of the Bill, only think it too extensive for Small Countys such as this'.[38]

However, the Gaol Fees Abolition Act 1815 (55 Geo III, c. 50), otherwise Bennet's Act after Grey Bennet who introduced it into the Commons, did have a crucial effect. Gaol fees had long been regarded as a source of abuse, indeed they were the reason for Howard's initial interest in prisons. The Act abolished gaol fees and substituted payments by the justices in Quarter Sessions. No matter how reluctant the justices had been to intervene in prisons in the past, the Act forced their involvement if only to ensure that the county's rates were being properly spent. It did not necessarily mean the introduction of gaolers' salaries: the Act allowed either a salary or compensation for lost fees, and the Radnorshire Quarter Sessions chose the latter for a few years.

Despite the Act, its re-enactment in 1839 (2 & 3 Vic., c. 56, section 6) and countless prison rules to the same effect, fee-taking continued into the 1840s at least in respect of debtors, even if it was dressed up in the form of hiring out furniture and so forth. 'Fees' seem, also, to have been paid in order to secure certain coveted prison jobs, such as prison cook.[39]

From 1815 mention of local prisons in the records of the Quarter Sessions becomes more frequent, a reasonable indication of their growing importance in county affairs. Chiefly such discussion centred upon expenditure, and questions of administration and discipline seem to have been left to the visiting justices who were appointed by the Quarter Sessions. Although visiting justices were used before, the Gaol Act 1823 formally required their appointment and that they reported back to the Quarter Sessions, who then made a report to the Secretary of State (4 Geo. IV, c. 64, sections 16-17 and 23-24). This was significant not so much because it gave government information about local prisons, since it is not clear if it did or if the Secretary of State made any use of the information, but rather because it gave a precedent for intervention in the administration of local prisons.

The Gaol Act was also an important first statement of central government penology in its requirement of classification, work and religion; it amounted to an acceptance of the view that vice was, like gaol fever, contagious. The Gaol Act seems to have been only weakly enforced.

The problem remained one of inefficiency: in the main, local prisons were too small and underused and justices had little interest beyond ensuring that expenditure was kept within reasonable limits. Yet despite the cost of the prison, most justices seemed to have regarded its maintenance as a matter of local civic pride: at Presteigne it was feared that if the local prison were closed then the town might also lose the assizes and hence its status. At the same time, the complex and often vague principles contained in the Gaol Act were devised mainly for the most serious offenders, and for large prisons, whereas most local prisons were small and their prisoners were both few in number and serving short sentences. These problems dogged the nineteenth-century penal debate, but were rarely faced up to until the 1860s and the 1870s because of the resistance of the justices.

After the Prison Act 1865 which imposed fairly rigorous requirements on the local prisons, the Radnorshire Quarter Sessions resisted the views of the Secretary of State, the inspector, J.F. Perry, the Surveyor-General of Prisons and even the visiting magistrates, all of whom regarded Presteigne County Gaol as too small to keep open; indeed it was shown to be cheaper to send prisoners to Hereford gaol. Despite the expense involved the justices were determined to maintain a prison at Presteigne since it was regarded as essential in maintaining the town's status.[40]

The practical effect on local prisons of penological theories, even those propounded by the prison inspectors, is difficult to gauge. As has been pointed out already, the question of expenditure was always a major factor: Clay met opposition from the justices on the grounds of cost when he sought to create a discipline based on the separate system at Preston House of Correction.[41] Leaving aside the question of cost, it has already been seen that such penological theories might often have seemed irrelevant to the needs of local prisons: religious reformation, for instance, seemed unlikely when most prisoners were serving sentences of no more than a few months. It is not surprising, then, that whilst the treadwheel was fairly rapidly and widely used, the separate system was never common.

DeLacy argues, in her paper on Lancashire prisons in the nineteenth century, that the authorities concentrated on health measures, such as bathing new arrivals, and that the main achievement of local prisons lay in their reduction of the death rate: for instance, Lancaster Castle and Preston prisons entirely escaped the cholera epidemic of 1832, and between 1838 and 1842 Preston prison had a death rate which was a sixth of that in the town itself. Furthermore, she seeks to demonstrate that the disciplinary regime was, on the whole, slack. For instance, in one prison in 1839 it was noted that

> The female Crown prisoners reported for having returned their cotton unpicked. I am quite sure that this is the result, not only of idleness, but of misapplication of time, for when I yesterday visited the penitentiary, the women were playing at blindman's buff in one shop, while those in the other were dancing.[42]

Another reason for the failure of the reform movement in the period before the 1823 Act, was the dependency on local initiative. It was very much a matter of whether or not there was an active and interested justice, who was capable of carrying his colleagues on the bench, and there were few such justices.

The Gaol Act 1823 and the Prison Act 1839 were of importance in extending government opportunities for intervention in local prisons, but these interventions relied more on persuasion than on effective sanctions. To a large extent, as has been seen, the justices were willing to defer to the advice of the inspectors. But some advice was consistently rejected.

On the other hand, the inspectors' reports and the regularisation of the system of visiting justices may have increased awareness of conditions in prisons; for instance, soon after the regularisation of visiting magistrates under the Gaol Act 1823, the visiting magistrates for Presteigne County Gaol made critical reports to the Quarter Sessions which eventually led to the construction of a new prison.[43] But whilst a new building might more readily be constructed in the nineteenth than in the eighteenth century, such construction work was unlikely to be prompted by penological theory; although once a decision to build had been taken then such theory would be used to assist in the design.

The Staff

At the start of the nineteenth century it was normal to have a prison looked after by a single gaoler who had no previous experience in the work; by the 1870s there were professional governors, warders, surgeons and chaplains. Here I will only have space to consider the gaoler/governor and the chaplain, both of whom played important and often conflicting roles within the prison during the nineteenth century.

The Gaoler/Governor

The staff have always had a crucial bearing on the administration of the prisons in which they work, and the most important member of the staff has always been the gaoler. The gaoler had been the main point of criticism at the end of the eighteenth century, and ultimately any system of discipline relied for its success upon the gaoler. However, the gaoler's concerns were often ordered rather differently from those of the justices or the inspectors or the theorists. The primary concern of the gaoler was to maintain some control, and it was this which governed the nature of their relationship with the prisoners. In 1822 at Exeter Borough prison one of the inmates, William Way, made 'a most hideous noise', upon which Gully, the gaoler, was clear in his response, 'When I found reasoning with him had no effect I used the cane which had effect what was desired — peaceable behaviour.'[45] Since the aim was control, religious and moral persuasion took a second place to physical methods which may have seemed to achieve their objectives more directly. One prison inspector complained of a Lancashire prison in 1839, 'If I am not greatly mistaken, there is a disposition to employ physical rather than moral means in the government of this establishment . . .'[46]

In any case, money was short, the staff was usually too small and untrained, and the prison buildings were inadequate so that the task of imposing a discipline such as the separate system was beyond most local prisons. Hence in 1835 Elizabeth Fry found conditions in local prisons — notably moral rather than physical conditions — were deplorable. She reported that prisoners

have no Instruction, no Employment, no Inspection, no Classification, and that they get into a most low and deplorable

State of Morals, and they may be truly called Schools for Crime; I would not say that all are in that Condition, but I fear many are.'[47]

Because of the difficulties facing the local prisons, rather than seeking to impose a particular theory of discipline upon the prisoners, the gaoler sought their co-operation, since without it control was largely impossible.[48] The reformers, on the other hand, wished to stop prisoners having a degree of self-determination. This was regarded as a part of the old abuses of prisons, where in exchange for fees prisoners could live almost as they wished. To the reformers, prisoners were rather like children who had no idea of what was good for them; or else, prison was regarded as a place in which people were confined in order to suffer punishment. Either way the prisoners were not to be consulted in the discipline.

The desire to break the gaoler-prisoner relationship became a recurrent theme in reform programmes; for instance, the abolition of alcohol sales and of fees, and the desire to close down small prisons. A longer term approach to this issue was the reduction of the gaoler's discretion through legislation which provided for regular reports, an increased supervision by the visiting justices and the inspectors, and laid down certain requirements as to internal organisation of the prison. However, the professionalisation of prison staff from about the middle of the nineteenth century — by which a group of 'experts' grew up in response to the demand for better gaolers — meant that the staff once again gained much of the control over prisons.

In many local prisons the attitude of the gaoler was regarded as the main stumbling block, and better systems of inspection had sought to do something about this, but inevitably such criticism meant that a new type of galoer was required. To some extent the justices may have been reluctant to replace a gaoler because employing a more skilled one might have reduced their control. Certainly rather dubious gaolers were still appointed in the nineteenth century. At Presteigne in 1812 Thomas Meredith replaced as keeper of the house of correction Thomas Sirrell 'who being confined a Prisr. within Gaol cannot attend the Duties of the Office of Keeper of the sd. House of Correctn.' The case of William George, governor of Caernarvon County Gaol, has already been mentioned. His final dismissal in 1848 may have been part of a campaign to clear out the old gaolers and to stop abuses which had never entirely disappeared. In 1847 William Went had been dismissed from the post of gaoler at Presteigne County Gaol for hiring a bed to a debtor for five shillings. His successor, Henry Verdun, was charged in 1849 with using prisoners' provisions for his own purposes, and censured in 1868 for being a party to a fraudulent bill of sale executed within the county gaol itself. Verdun, however, retired on a pension of £50 a year. Shortly after George's dismissal the governor of Beaumaris gaol was also sacked.[49]

Gradually, however, justices decided that to improve the quality of prisons it was necessary to improve the quality of gaolers. To raise the respectability of a post which had traditionally been stigmatised, the term 'governor' came to be adopted and larger salaries offered. To some justices appointing a respectable and, because of the salary, a financially dependent governor seemed the best way for the bench to take control of the prison. However, this policy led to the development of a professional body of prison governors with their own expertise gathered through working at several prisons; this in turn meant that the less knowledgeable justices were more likely to defer to the governor's superior skill.

This new breed of governors came initially from the services, sometimes from the police. This reflected the view that in practice the primary object of a governor, just as it had been with the gaoler, was control. On this point Whitworth Russell disliked such governors. He said that they were concerned with the notions of constraint and behaviourism, and were incapable of furthering the objective of religious reformation amongst prisoners. He, therefore, favoured those who had 'a similarity of objects, means, and principles with a good Chaplain'. Someone, in other words, like himself. Of course, he achieved his aim when Rev Daniel Nihill was appointed chaplain-governor of Millbank in 1839. As the notion of religious reformation faded and the severity typified by the Carnarvon report of 1863 replaced it, so the military governor became the model. Jebb and his successor Du Cane had both been in the Royal Engineers and both favoured the military governor, precisely because of those qualities which Russell disliked.[50]

The Chaplain

The Gaol Chaplains Act 1773 (13 Geo. III, c. 58) authorised the Quarter Sessions to pay a chaplain for the gaols, although it was not made obligatory until the Gaol Act of 1823. As has been seen already, the chaplain's role greatly expanded in importance at least in the national penitentiaries in the nineteenth century; it is less easy to generalise about the chaplain in local prisons.

In 1789 the Radnorshire Quarter Sessions appointed Rev Smith 'to do duty twice in each Week' at the county gaol. When Rev William Thomas was appointed in 1814 these duties were made a little more explicit. The duties were to be

> considered as similar to that of a Clergyman of Parish that he perform divine Service and Preach a Sermon every Sabbath day attend the Sick when necessary and all Criminals under the Sentence of death and at the time of Execution of the Sentence.

A later chaplain was castigated for his failure to visit two condemned prisoners. In addition to these duties Rev Smith was ordered 'to inspect the Gaol agreeable to Mr. Howard's plan', and a later chaplain, Rev John Grubb, was actually one of the justices.[51]

The chaplain's role in legitimising the prison discipline was widely accepted. This carried over from the clergymen who had gone into prisons to persuade a condemned prisoner to confess — often, as in the case of the Ordinary at Newgate prison in London, such a confession, real or imagined, was a source of profit to the clergyman. This function still continued even if the publication of last confessions ceased. Those whose lives were not about to be taken, but whose crimes were serious were also visited in order to obtain some sort of confession or acceptance of the justice of the sentence imposed. John Williams, chaplain at Brecon County Gaol, reported his visit in 1840 to John Jenkins who was about to be taken to the hulks:

> I spoke and reasoned with him on the subject of his past conduct and pointed out to him the advantage of amendment of conduct both with respect to the punishment to be inflicted which might be lighter by good conduct, and his situation be made more comfortable in every respect.[52]

The chaplain at Brecon sought out prisoners who were about to be released or who had been punished for an offence against prison regulations or, more interestingly, prior to their appearance at their trial.[53]

The typical chaplain's role in the prison discipline seems to have been subsidiary to that of the governor: at Brecon County Gaol, John Williams, the chaplain, resigned in 1842 following the unexplained refusal of 'the Turnkey' to allow him to read morning prayers. However, the chaplains did talk to the prisoners and get them to learn passages from the Bible.[54] The chaplains' lack of influence on discipline may have been due not only to their non-residence at the prison, but also to the local justices preferring physical control to moral and religious instruction, as has been seen. At the most the typical chaplain adopted an advisory role: for instance, in 1841 at Exeter Borough Prison, the chaplain wrote 'The Juvenile offenders, having refused from idleness and ungodliness to learn the religious lessons which I appointed them, I have requested the Governor to adopt some measures by which their attention might be secured . . .'[55] Even such an active chaplain as Clay found it difficult to force his views through at Preston since he was opposed both by successive governors and the justices.

Inevitably because of his strongly held views on prison discipline Clay came into conflict with both the successive governors and the justices. He clashed with Captain Anthony, appointed governor in 1827, over the question of religious reformation and the use of the separate system; Anthony preferred a system of military discipline. He pointedly remarked in his report to the justices in 1838 that the silent system, which was being used at Preston, depended on the quality of persons enforcing it for its effect. But the justices were reluctant to give up the profitable prison work of weaving which required association of the prisoners. It seems that only after Anthony's retirement in 1842 did Clay begin to take control — this was, of course, at a time when the chaplain and religious reformation through the separate system were in the ascendancy nationally. The depression in Lancashire in the 1840s, which meant that prison work was no longer profitable, may also have been responsible for a greater willingness on the part of the justices to listen to Clay's scheme. Clay justified his intervention in discipline on the grounds that reformation could be achieved not by work under the silent system, but only by religious instruction under the separate system. His answer to a question from the 1850 committee reveals his viewpoint: 'You look in point of fact, then, for the reformation or the deterring of prisoners, to moral means, rather than physical means? — Certainly.'[56]

The objectives which might have motivated a chaplain like Clay to get involved in prison discipline, were likely to be fundamentally different from those that might be sought by either a governor or a rates-conscious justice. It is, therefore, not surprising that against such opposition the chaplain was rarely going to be imortant in the prison discipline, even if he cared to involve himself in it.

However, as with much else in prison administration there was an increasing role for the chaplains during the nineteenth century. Certainly whilst the chaplains at Brecon County Gaol in the 1820s and 1830s only made very short reports to the Quarter Sessions recording that they had held services, those of the mid-1840s, following the appointment of Morgan Jones, were much more active. Jones visited daily, instead of weekly as had been the case before, and since part of his job was, as he stated it, to report 'on the religious and moral instruction of the prisoners with my observations thereon', he felt able to comment on the causes of crime and on any irregularities within the prison, and to make suitable recommendations. For instance, in 1845, he suggested the separation of those women who were in prison for deserting from service from those in prison for theft and prostitution; he reported on the state of the building; and he made a complaint against the governor and the turnkey. Significantly, whilst the justices acknowledged that there were defects in the building, they ignored his first suggestion and rejected the complaint against the officers.[57]

The Prisoners

Commonly, historians of the prison have avoided the most problematic, and yet potentially one of the most interesting, aspects of the prison, namely the prisoners themselves. A superficial examination of the texts on prisons — not just the secondary sources, but also the documents which the prison itself produced — might suggest that the prisoners were fairly passive, merely substances to be moulded according to the latest theory. To the penologist of the early nineteenth century the prisoner was raw material upon which the machine of the penitentiary was to work. Prisoners were not so much individuals as units, all identical, at once single and a mass. One theory would work equally well for all criminals. This, however, does not satisfactorily explain why these various theories have, apparently, never achieved their objective, be that reformation of the individual, or a general reduction in the level of crime through a severely punitive regime. Nor does it explain why the prisons never satisfactorily gained absolute dominance over the prisoners. It is perhaps significant that the only people who did recognise the role of prisoners were the gaolers and Elizabeth Fry: as has been seen, the gaolers were under constant attack and Fry's contribution was out of line with what might be called the mainstream of reform, that is, the search for a system of discipline which did not involve the prisoner.

The problem, then, is how do we hear the voice of the prisoner? True, various prisoners spoke to Parliamentary committees and others wrote 'autobiographies', but, whilst these sources are by no means to be written off, what they tell us cannot be accepted without some degree of caution. For instance, the 'autobiographies' seem to have been written generally by members of the middle class[58] and cannot, therefore, be taken as typical of the prison population, generally composed of the working class. Nor is the evidence of prisoners to committees to be greatly relied upon for obvious reasons. These sources have their uses, but they are one source, and of rather questionable reliability.

Different prisoners had different views about prisons, and reacted differently to prison discipline. Of Pentonville Ignatieff has written,

Some prisoners were broken by Pentonville, others were not. A few fought its discipline openly. From the punishment reports there appears a picture of continuous struggle between the 'incorrigibles' and the prison staff: . . . Most convicts gave up trying to fight Pentonville. They settled into the routine, kept out of trouble, and waited out their time. Some showed no apparent signs of being damaged by the silence and the solitude. But most prisoners bore its marks in some way.[59]

Certainly some served out their time quietly, although even in their silence we may hear dissent, a stubborn refusal to do any more than conform during their incarceration. Others reacted more positively. I wish to look briefly at these and suggest that in their reactions we may perhaps find the voice also of those who remained silent.

One form of reaction was to complain after release. Kidd Wake was one. The Gloucester discipline did not break him, he seems to have served his time fairly quietly and held back his resentment until he was released. Similarly, John McCormick made his complaint to *The Hereford Times* in 1855 about his treatment in Brecon County Gaol.[60]

The government prisons experienced great problems with the prisoners. In the earliest national penitentiary, Millbank, the prisoners, used to the more relaxed discipline of the county gaols, rebelled in 1818: they chanted in the chapel demanding better food; they broke up their cells; they assaulted the officers. This continued on and off until, in 1828, the authorities had to admit defeat and reintroduce whipping to try to regain control. Similarly, at Pentonville: some prisoners went mad, some committed suicide; but others fought back by tearing up bibles, smashing furniture and assaulting warders.[61] When, in about 1815, the authorities sought to introduce separation in the hulks, the prisoners tore down the bars which divided them from their fellows. The bars were not replaced.[62] Problems with the prisoners also occurred in the local gaols, although scanty documentation makes study rather more difficult.

The early enthusiasm for ventilating prisons in order to reduce the risk of gaol fever did not coincide with the prisoners' desire to stay warm and so they blocked the ventilation holes up. John Orridge, governor of Bury gaol, was at a loss to understand this stubborness; he remarked in 1819,

The mode of ventilation is by keeping every window open; there is a window in every cell and passage; that is rather an important object, for persons of this description generally consider there is a comfort in exclusion of air, and dirt; and it becomes a very important subject to keep them clean, and study the means of ventilation, and that is done solely by withholding their allowance till that is effected, and by keeping their windows open; . . .[63]

Prisoners separated from each other in Pentonville tapped messages through the thick walls and along the drainpipes, and Cold Bath Fields, which operated under the supposedly silent system, 'hummed with a secret language'.[64] At Exeter Borough Prison in 1822 it was discovered that 'the prisoners by means of a wire had made a hole through the wall into the female day room and . . . notes had been passed'.[65]

Prisoners commonly assaulted one another. Often these were as a result of niggling disagreements or racism. However, on occasion a prisoner was assaulted for doing too much work, as happened in 1845 to John Norbury, a weaver imprisoned at Lancaster Castle. Shortly after this another inmate refused to work following intimidation.[66] Some prisoners simply assaulted the staff: Kilgarland, a prisoner at Exeter in 1824, assaulted the gaoler, his son and the taskmaster. George Smith, imprisoned at Caernarvon in 1857, threatened the turnkey, swore and smashed his 'bed, bench and wall'.[67] Escaping work through illness seems to have been such a problem that it was often assumed that the illness was feigned.[68] Other prisoners tried to escape the prison altogether, an act which would be punished by ironing, or solitary confinement, or both.[69]

Some prisoners resented the chaplain's role within the prison, for in the guise of a prisoner's friend he was seeking to legitimise the disciplinary system. The chaplain of Brecon County Jail, John Williams, recorded one of his visits to a prisoner in 1840, 'Had a long conversation with David Lewis (alias Crispin) on the subject of Religion, & subordination to the Laws of this Land. I was sorry to find him still persevering in his former opinion.'[70]

The prisoners occasionally reacted in chapel, since the compulsion involved in attendance at the service symbolised the chaplain's hypocrisy. In 1844 the chaplain, Morgan Jones, at Brecon reprimanded Thomas Rees for irreverent behaviour in chapel and John Patrick for 'tearing a Bible, two prayer books and utterly destroying a Spelling Book'. The voice of Morgan Jones apparently carried little weight with the unfortunate Timothy Jones who was in solitary confinement in 1842 when the chaplain visited: 'As soon as the door of his cell was opened, he rushed out and neither myself nor any of the turnkeys could prevail upon him, by fair means, to go back.'[71] We are left to speculate upon the foul means that were used.

Single prisoners would conduct campaigns, the objectives of

which we can only speculate upon. John Edwards, a felony prisoner in Brecon, complained in June 1852 to the visiting magistrates that the potatoes served at the prison were bad. As with all such complaints at that time, the visiting magistrate sided with the governor and rejected the complaint. But this was only the start. The next day Edwards was brought before the visiting magistrate on a charge of 'general Insubordination and assaulting the Turnkey'; sadly the details are missing. He was given six days in solitary confinement on bread and water, with the promise of a whipping if he misbehaved again.

This threat may have had some effect since it was more than six months before Edwards appeared again in the visiting magistrates' journal. This time he complained of 'improper treatment', and again his complaint was rejected, the visiting magistrate merely noted that Edwards had been punished by the governor for 'cursing & swearing at the barber'. Three months passed. Then Edwards was placed in solitary confinement for refusing to work. Rather than being subdued, the visiting magistrate noted that 'he has been very boisterous, kicking the door & singing, & although spoken to by me on the subject five minutes ago, he still continues kicking.'

No doubt smarting from this rebuff, the visiting magistrate ordered that Edwards remain in solitary confinement for three days — the threatened whipping was apparently forgotten. However, Edwards was still there seven days later and still very disorderly. The visiting magistrate decided that Edwards was 'either deranged or pretending to be so', and he called the surgeon. There Edwards disappears from the visiting magistrates' journal.[72]

It was not just men who rebelled against the prisons. Newgate's women prisoners were infamous for smashing their cells prior to transportation before Fry ended this custom. In Brecon County Gaol the chaplain, Morgan Jones, recorded in June 1844 that

Winifred Morris behaved so irreverently in Chapel that I was under the necessity of reprimanding her. — This person ever since her imprisonment, seems to delight in doing things contrary to the rules of the prison.

In January of the following year, he felt compelled to admonish 'the Females with regard to their behaviour in prison'.[73]

This all too brief and geographically rather narrow look at prisoners' reactions does suggest that one reason for the failure of the new prisons lay in their assumption that prisoners were virtually passive, and that through architecture and regulations a particular form of discipline with a particular objective could be *imposed* upon prisoners.

The 'Achievements' of the Penitentiaries

As the earlier chapters of this book have shown, prisons were by no means invented in the nineteenth century; however, the penitentiary did serve an important role in this period. The penitentiaries had been suggested, and to some extent adopted, as an alternative to the death penalty and to transportation, and by the 1850s, with the hulks and transportation winding down, prisons had become firmly rooted in penal practice. Through their initial justification as alternatives to other forms of punishment, which, for whatever reasons, had become unacceptable, the prison had become permanently legitimised, so that although the form which the prison discipline took was open to question, the institution itself was not, nor was it likely to be in a society where similar institutions were so familiar: factories, schools, workhouses, hospitals and lunatic asylums, parts of what Foucault has called 'the carceral archipelago' in which the prison is 'a punitive model . . . at the limit of strict penality'.[74]

The penitentiary also had an important effect on the entire criminal justice system. During the eighteenth century the moral lifestyle of an accused felon had a great bearing on his or her ultimate fate. It was a consideration taken into account by the jury in making up their minds whether to acquit or to convict as charged or to convict of a lesser, non-capital, offence (this was possible because the capital nature of an offence often rested on the goods involved being valued at over a certain amount, so that by valuing the goods at a lesser amount the jury took the defendant out of the capital offence). Once a conviction had been secured in a capital case it was very much a matter for the judge and the Secretary of State to decide whether or not that person should hang, and they also considered the lifestyle of the accused, the crime and the support for a pardon.

The point was that in a criminal justice system built up around the gallows, it was necessary to ensure that only 'proper' victims were executed: hanging a first offender or a young child did little to enhance the values which the criminal justice system sought to underpin. What was needed was someone with a bad character whose life could be read — literally — as a warning not to fall into similar bad habits (typically, idleness and drunkenness). In the nineteenth century far fewer people were convicted of capital crimes because of the reduction in offences which had been largely completed by 1830. Gradually it was the penitentiary which, therefore, took on the weighing up of the criminal.

The court still judged guilt or innocence, but it was less involved with assessing the accused's character since his or her life was no longer at stake: gradually such issues became irrelevant and, under the developing laws of evidence, inadmissible. Of course, in sentencing character had relevance, but it was no longer so fundamental to the courts, it was not a part of the trial. To the advocates of prison reform the prisoner was not being looked at in terms of the crime committed, except in so far as that indicated character traits which might be relevant to assessing the means of obtaining a successful reformation. Under this system the penitentiaries were seeking not to punish for a crime, but rather to 'correct' a character defect of which the crime was merely a symptom, the causes lying in something earlier, usually a lack of religious education. The disciplines which sought a greater role for purely punitive objectives in prison were similarly seeking to act on the prisoner not on his or her crime. The courts were handing criminals over to those who were developing a penological expertise from which the courts were willingly excluded.[75]

Inevitably this concentration on studying the prisoner led to the construction of general theories to explain the motivation of criminals, and these also legitimised prison disciplines — Foucault indeed argues that the penitentiary and criminology developed together. In the Napoleonic period crime had been regarded as a symbol of alienation and of working-class radicalism. But during the nineteenth century it was argued that since not all the working class committed crimes then it could not be an act of rebellion; there must be something which marked out the criminal from the working class. Criminals were not rebels or symbols of a greater disaffection amongst the working class, but were abnormal, weak minded, morally degraded, irrational monsters. However, they were not beyond hope; through treatment they could be 'cured'.

The growing disillusionment in the late 1840s with religious reformation was taken as evidence that criminals were a sub-species who could not be educated. This categorisation was supported by the theory that they were in fact physically different from non-criminals. Thomas Carlyle wrote, describing prisoners in 1858, that they were

> Miserable distorted blockheads, the generality: ape-faces, imp-faces, angry dog-faces, heavy sullen ox-faces; degraded under-foot perverse creatures, sons of *in*docility, greedy mutinous darkness, and in one word, of stupidity, which is the general mother of such.[76]

They were a class of defective, barely human beings. This theory backed up the impression that the penitentiaries were failing to reform prisoners: because criminals were a sub-species, then there was no, or at least only a tenuous, link between penal practice and crime. But there were wider implications. The idea that criminals were a distinct class of irrational monsters was used to split up the working class as had the Poor Law Amendment Act 1834.[77]

This 'marking out' can be seen in the common belief amongst the upper and middle classes that there existed a class of professional criminals, in other words a 'criminal class'.[78] The newly formed police force had a clear target, the 'criminal class', and in the production of that 'criminal class' — whether image or reality — the penitentiary played a crucial role. Here was the justification not only for the penitentiary, even though it had apparently failed to reduce crime or to reform criminals, but also for the police and a whole set of disciplinary strategies. This also helps to explain the harsher punitive measures characterised by the Carnarvon report: those measures marked the prisoners out. They did not seek to return prisoners to society as citizens, but rather to inflict punishment with the aim of disciplining them; and they did not teach any skills which might enable a return to a society where the ability to do productive work marked out the citizen from the criminal and the pauper. All of these provided a counterbalance to 'libertarian' measures, such as the Factory

Acts, the legalisation of trade unions and the widening of the franchise in 1867 — measures which were won through struggle by the working class and which were, at the same time, concessions given in order to incorporate the working class within the existing structures of power. So although the penitentiaries failed in one undoubted aim, that of reducing crime, they had greater success in the aim of creating an image of a criminal class which was different from the 'respectable' working class, and which was, therefore, to be feared by that class as much as by the middle and upper classes.

In one respect, then, the question of which form of prison discipline was to be adopted — classification, separate or silent — was irrelevant, since the effect of all was the same. Hence, the approach adopted by the Carnarvon committee was, perhaps, the more honest: prisoners should suffer and be marked, since they had to act primarily as a deterrent to others. In many ways the penal system had changed little from the objectives of the eighteenth century when the gallows predominated. The prison was only acceptable if it was an effective deterrent, that is, if it created a proper impression. Those who advocated religious reformation always had to bear this in mind, even if they were more interested in the individual convict. Prisons, then, like the workhouse under the New Poor Law, were not primarily for locking up people, but about disciplining those who were not in prison. So, although the convicts might resist and obstruct prison discipline, their role in social control was assured simply by their existence. Bentham and Sydney Smith both recognised this objective — surprisingly few others did — and the principle infused the whole debate on prisons, although it is rarely discussed.

In purely material terms the new prisons might in some respects be regarded as successful. The buildings themselves, especially Pentonville's radial design, provided models for most future prisons. The bureaucratic arrangements demanded by the new systems of discipline laid down models for the future as well. The detailed requirements of the disciplines, even those which were principally punitive, led to the formation of a corps of prison officials whose 'expertise' enabled them to enjoy a large measure of autonomy.[79] Furthermore, there were certainly improvements in certain aspects of health; gaol fever was virtually wiped out. However, its replacements in the nineteenth century, insanity, scurvy and suicide, were no less unpleasant.

Notes

1. *Report from the Select Committee appointed to consider the Law Relating to Prisons: &c.*, Parliamentary Papers, 1822 (300), vol. IV, p. 3; Ignatieff, *Just Measure of Pain* (London, 1978), pp. 167-9. On Bennet's Act see section 'Local Prisons' below.

2. Rev. W.L. Clay, *The Prison Chaplain: A Memoir of the Rev. John Clay, B.D. late chaplain of the Preston Gaol, with selections from his reports and correspondence, and a sketch of prison discipline in England* (Cambridge, 1861), p. 164.

3. McConville, *A History of English Prison Administration* (London, 1981), pp. 256-9; *Report from the Select Committee on Agriculture*, Parliamentary Papers, 1833 (612), vol. V, p. vi; *Report of the Commissioners appointed to inquire into the Municipal Corporations in England and Wales*, First Report, Parliamentary Papers, 1835 (116), vol. XXIII, p. 42.

4. *Select Committee of the Lords*, Third Report, Parliamentary Papers, 1835 (440), vol. XII, pp. iii-iv; U.R.Q. Henriques, *Before the Welfare State: Social Administration in Early Industrial Britain* (London, 1979), pp. 66-116; P.W.J. Bartrip and P.T. Fenn, 'The Evolution of Regulatory Style in the Nineteenth Century British Factory Inspectorate', *Journal of Law and Society*, 10 (1983), pp. 201-22; McConville, *A History of English Prison Administration*, pp. 170-217, 250-4; E. Stockdale, 'A Short History of Prison Inspection in England', *British Journal of Criminology*, 23 (1983), pp. 209-28; *Report and Evidence taken before Mr. Russell, Inspector of Prisons, on the late Inquiry instituted into the Conduct of Mr. George, Governor of the County Gaol of Carnarvon*, Parliamentary Papers, 1843 (422), vol. XLIII; Caernarvonshire Record Office (CRO). Caernarvonshire Quarter Sessions (CQS), County Gaol Records, XQA/G 298-9, 3 April 1848, 4 April 1848.

5. Melossi and Pavarini, *The Prison and the Factory* (London, 1981), pp. 143-81; Foucault, *Discipline and Punish* (London, 1977), pp. 237-9; McConville, *A History of English Prison Administration*, pp. 116-22 and passim.

6. *Report of William Crawford*, p. 11 & pp. 16-19.

7. Foucault, *Discipline and Punish*, p. 318n.7; M. Zimmerman, *Solitude considered with Respect to its Influence upon The Mind and The Heart* (Dublin, 1795), p. 163 and passim; *Report of William Crawford*, pp. 12, 39-40; L.H. Butterfield, *Letters of Benjamin Rush*, 2 vols. (London 1951), I, p. 512.

8. Evans, *The Fabrication of Virtue*, pp. 318-45; *Report from the Select Committee on Prison Discipline* (Grey Committee), Parliamentary Papers, 1850 (632), vol. XVII, pp. 354-5.

9. *Report of William Crawford*, pp. 24, 37-9; *Select Committee of the Lords* (1835), p. 239.

10. McConville, *A History of English Prison Administration*, p. 243n.; [Rev J. Field], *Separate Imprisonment: Report read at the Berkshire Quarter Sessions by the Chaplain of the County Gaol and House of Correction, at Reading, Michaelmas, 1845* (Reading, 1845), p. 5.

11. McConville, *A History of English Prison Administration*, p. 164; Foucault, *Discipline and Punish*, pp. 236-9.

12. *Report of William Crawford*, pp. 37-41.

13. J.J. Gurney, *Notes on a Visit made to some of the Prisons in Scotland and The North of England, in company with Elizabeth Fry; with some general observations on the subject of prison discipline* (London, 1819), p. 98; Anon., *Thoughts on Prison Discipline. By a Looker-On* (London, 1837), pp. 79-80; *Select Committee of the Lords* (1835), pp. 101-2; Foucault, *Discipline and Punish*, pp. 244-6.

14. McConville, *A History of English Prison Administration*, pp. 129, 148; Melossi and Pavarini, *The Factory and the Prison*, pp. 154-5; Ignatieff, *Just Measure of Pain*, p. 75.

15. *Select Committee of the Lords* (1835), p. iv; Second Report, Parliamentary Papers, 1835 (439), vol. XI.

16. McConville, *A History of English Prison Administration*, pp. 160-9.

17. Grey Committee (1850), pp. 7-8; McConville, ibid., pp. 181-7.

18. Evans, *The Fabrication of Virtue*, p. 346; Ignatieff, *Just Measure of Pain*, p. 3.

19. *Report of the Surveyor-General of Prisons on the Construction, Ventilation and Details of Pentonville Prison*, Parliamentary Papers, 1844 (594), vol. XXVIII; Evans, *The Fabrication of Virtue*, pp. 346-67.

20. *Second Report of the Surveyor-General of Prisons*, Parliamentary Papers, 1847 (867), vol. XXIX; Evans, *The Fabrication of Virtue*, pp. 367-87.

21. Evans, *The Fabrication of Virtue*, pp. 384-7; Ignatieff, *Just Measure of Pain*, pp. 199-200; McConville, *A History of English Prison Administration*, pp. 207-8.

22. Clay, *The Prison Chaplain*, passim; Field, *Separate imprisonment*, passim; McConville, *A History of English Prison Administration*, pp. 207-10, 216n.

23. Grey Committee (1850), pp. 595-6; NLW, Breconshire Quarter Sessions (BQS), Brecon County Gaol, Q/AG, 1804-22/ 1826-50, Returns from Brecon County Gaol, Michaelmas 1849, The Chaplain's Report.

24. McConville, *A History of English Prison Administration*, pp. 177-81, 215-7; E. Stockdale, 'The Rise of Joshua Jebb, 1837-1850', *The British Journal of Criminology*, 16 (1976), pp. 164-70; *Report from the Select Committee of the House of Lords, on the Present State of Discipline in Gaols and Houses of Correction* (Carnarvon Committee), Parliamentary Papers, 1863 (499), vol. IX, pp. xiii-xiv.

25. Grey Committee (1850), p. 14 and pp. 9 and 12; Carnarvon Committee (1863), p. 110 and passim; *Second Report of the Surveyor-General*, pp. 6-7; H. Mayhew and J. Binny, *The Criminal Prisons of London, and Scenes of Prison Life* (London, 1862), p. 141; Stockdale, 'Joshua Jebb', passim; McConville, *A History of English Prison Administration*, pp. 181-7, 206-10, 396-414. Millbank had, of course, used the progressive stage system: see infra.

26. *Report from the Select Committee on Transportation*, Parliamentary Papers, 1837-8 (669), vol. XXII, p. xli; Bentham, 'Panopticon', IV, p. 58.

27. *Report and Minutes of Evidence taken upon an Inquiry Into the General Treatment and Condition of the Convicts in the Hulks at Woolwich*, Parliamentary Papers, 1847 (831), vol. XVIII; McConville, *A History of English Prison Administration*, pp.187-203; Shaw, *Convicts and the Colonies*, pp. 348 et seq.

28. McConville, *A History of English Prison Administration*, pp. 193-6, 440.

29. M.H. Tomlinson, 'Penal Servitude 1846-1865: A System in Evolution', in V. Bailey (ed.), *Policing and Punishment in Nineteenth Century Britain* (London, 1981), pp. 126-49; McConville, *A History of English Prison Administration*, pp. 187-203, 385-96, 439-41; Shaw, *Convicts and the Colonies*, pp. 335-60.

30. Compare J. Davis, 'The London Garotting Panic of 1862: a Moral Panic and the Creation of a Criminal Class in mid-Victorian England', in V.A.C. Gatrell, B. Lenman and G. Parker (eds.), *Crime and the Law: The Social History of Crime in Western Europe since 1500* (London, 1980), pp. 190-213, with P.W.J. Bartrip, 'Public Opinion and Law Enforcement; The Ticket-of-Leave Scares in Mid-Victorian Britain', in V. Bailey (ed.), *Policing and Punishment*, pp. 150-81; Carnarvon Committee (1863), passim; *Report of the Commissioners appointed to inquire into The Operation of the Acts (16 & 17 Vict. c. 99. and 20 & 21 Vict. c. 3) relating to Transportation and Penal Servitude*, Parliamentary Papers, 1863 (3190), vol. XXI.

31. Carnarvon Committee (1863), p. 125.

32. *Report Relative to the System of Prison Discipline* &c. *by the Inspectors of Prisons*, Parliamentary Papers, 1843 (457), vol. XXV, p. 3; Clay, *The Prison Chaplain*, p. 223; Dr W. Baly, *On the Mortality in Prisons, and the Diseases Most Frequently Fatal to Prisoners*, n.p. [1845], pp. 122-3. For the government's view see the letter from Sir James Graham, Home Secretary, to all quarter sessions, *The Law Times, and Journal of Property*, vol. I, no. 5 (1843), p. 122.

33. NLW, BQS, Brecon County Gaol, Q/AG 1844-78, letter from Home Secretary, 24 Jan. 1868, reports of the visiting magistrates 19 Feb. 1866 and 6 Mar. 1866, Quarter Sessions Order, Easter 1868; similarly see, CRO, Caernarvonshire County Gaol, XQA/G, 254, 13 Jan. 1868; McConville, *A History of English Prison Administration*, pp. 468-82. One local justice opposed the discarding of the idea of profitable labour on the grounds of finance clinging to the old idea of using prisoners' labour to help pay for the prison: Sir John Bowring, *On Remunerative Prison Labour, as an instrument for Promoting the Reformation and Diminishing the Cost of Offenders* (Exeter [1865]). W.K. Parker, 'Radnor County Gaol: The Last Decade, 1868-78', *The Transactions of the Radnorshire Society*, vol. LII (1981), pp. 35-46. J.C. Mansell-Pieydell, *The Milborne Reformatory, with Remarks upon Recent Legislation and other Measures for the Suppression of Crime* (Dorchester, 1872), pp. 5-7; W. Tallack, *The Problem of Diminishing Prevalent Destitution and Temptations to Crime*, n.p. [1869], pp. 3-12.

34. NLW, RQS, s. 3096, Police Committee Minute Book (1857-1889), passim.

35. S. and B. Webb, *English Prisons Under Local Government* (London, 1922), pp. 14-17; introductory essay by Capel Lofft in Dr J. Jebb. *Thoughts on the Construction and Polity of Prisons, with hints for their improvement* (London, 1786), pp. viii-ix. In a slightly different vein, but perhaps more typical of local feelings, is the comment of Sir Harford Jones, a visiting justice for Presteigne County Gaol, that 'It has long appeared to me, that the Commitment to the House of Correction in this County is thought but too lightly of by the Person committed . . .' NLW, RQS, S. 817, 17 Aug. 1819.

36. NLW, RQS, Order Book 1, 14 Apr. 1790; Order Book 9, 22 Oct. 1846, 7. Jan. 1847, 9 April 1847.

37. Lord Loughborough, *Observations on the State of the English Prisons, And the Means of improving them; Communicated to the Reverend Henry Zouch, a Justice of the Peace* (London [1793]), pp. 21, 24 and passim; Howard, *An Account of the Principal Lazarettos*, pp. 124-215; James Nield, *State of the Prisons in England, Scotland, and Wales* (London, 1812); Gurney, *Notes on a Visit*, p. 98; Ignatieff, *Just Measure of Pain*, pp. 153-6.

38. NLW, RQS, Order Book 1, 6 Oct. 1779.

39. NLW, RQS, Order Book 5, 18 Oct. 1815, see gaoler's 'account' for eleven pounds and ten shillings in 1816, ibid., 17 July 1816; McConville, *A History of English Prison Administration*, pp. 289-90; M.E. DeLacy, 'Grinding Men Good? Lancashire's Prisons at Mid-Century', in V. Bailey (ed.), *Policing and Punishment*, pp. 182-216, at p. 189.

40. Parker, 'Radnor County Gaol', passim; NLW, RQS, S. 1572-1573, S. 1575-1578.

41. Clay, *The Prison Chaplain*, pp. 195, 220-1.

42. DeLacy, 'Grinding Men Good?', p. 193 and passim.

43. NLW, RQS, Order Book 5.

44. J.E. Thomas, *The English prison officer since 1850: A study in conflict* (London, 1972).

45. W.J. Forsythe, *A System of Discipline: Exeter Borough Prison 1819-1863* (Exeter, 1983), p. 45.

46. DeLacy, 'Grinding Men Good?', p. 186.

47. *Select Committee of the Lords* (1835), p. 334.

48. DeLacy, 'Grinding Men Good?', p. 199.

49. NLW, RQS, Order Book 4, 8 Apr. 1812; Order Book 9, 21 Oct. 1847; Order Book 9, 4 Jan. 1849; Order Book 10, 3 July 1868.

50. McConville, *A History of English Prison Administration*, pp. 284-7, 315-8, 454-6; Thomas, *English Prison Officer*, pp. 47-50; CRO, County Gaol Records, XQA/G323, 18 April 1848, 352-67, 19 June 1868–28 May 1869; Llangefni Area Record Office, Anglesey Quarter Sessions, Beaumaris Gaol Records, W/QA/G, 816, 14 Sept. 1848, 829, 13 Jan. 1849.

51. NLW, RQS, Order Book 2, 15 July 1789; Order Book, 19 Oct. 1815 and 8 April 1818; Order Book 2, 15 July 1789 and 27 April 1808.

52. NLW, BQS, Brecon County Gaol, Chaplain's Journal, 20 July 1840.

53. For example, ibid., 27 June 1842, 15 Oct. 1841, 4 Aug. 1840, & passim.

54. Ibid., 6 Feb. 1842; see also, 9 Sept. 1842, 5 Oct. 1844; NLW, BQS, Q/AG 1804-22/ 1826-50, Michaelmas 1845, Chaplain's Report.

55. Forsythe, *System of Discipline*, p. 70.

56. Clay, *The Prison Chaplain*; Grey Committee (1850), p. 355; DeLacy, 'Grinding Men Good?', pp. 200-11.

57. NLW, BQS, Q/AG 1804-22/ 1826-50, Michaelmas 1845, Chaplain's Report.

58. A good example, which is useful for its detail of prison administration, is [William Thomson], *Five Years Penal Servitude, By One Who Has Endured It* (London, 1877).

59. Ignatieff, *Just Measure of Pain*, pp. 10-11, generally pp. 9-11.

60. Wake, *The Case of Kidd Wake*; NLW, BQS, Q/AG, Visiting Magistrates' Journal, 2 Nov. 1855.

61. Ignatieff, *Just Measure of Pain*, pp. 9-10 and 199.

62. G. Holford, *Statements and Observations concerning The Hulks* (London, 1826), pp. 16-18.

63. *Report from the Select Committee on the State of Gaols* (1819), p. 332.

64. Ignatieff, *Just Measure of Pain*, pp. 9, 178; J.G. Torry, *Chelmsford Prison* (Ipswich, 1980), p. 37.

65. Forsythe, *System of Discipline*, p. 44.

66. DeLacy, 'Grinding Men Good?', p. 193.

67. Forsythe, *System of Discipline*, p. 44; CRO, County Gaol Records, X/QA, 114, 16 May 1857.

68. Forsythe, *System of Discipline*, p. 45.

69. NLW, BQS, Q/AG, Visiting Magistrates' Journal, 6 Jan. 1853, 8 April 1853.

70. NLW, BQS, Q/AG, Chaplain's Journal, 13 April 1840.

71. Ibid., 15 July 1844, 5 Sept. 1844, 8 Oct. 1842; also Forsythe, *System of Discipline*, pp. 23, 70-1.

72. NLW, BQS, Q/AG, Visiting Magistrates' Journal, 15 June 1852, 16 June 1852, 6 Jan. 1853, 16 April 1853, 23 April 1853.

73. Ignatieff, *Just Measure of Pain*, p. 144; NLW, BQS, Q/AG, Chaplain's Journal, 16 April 1844, 5 Oct. 1844, 2 Jan. 1845; also NLW, BQS, Q/AG, Visiting Magistrates' Journal 22 Dec. 1856, 26 Dec. 1856; Forsythe, *System of Discipline*, pp. 23, 45, 70-1.

74. Foucault, *Discipline and Punish*, pp. 296-7.

75. Ibid., pp. 246-52.

76. Ibid., pp. 252-4; McConville, *A History of English Prison Administration*, pp. 328-9.

77. P. Golding and S. Middleton, *Images of Welfare: Press and Public Attitudes to Poverty* (Oxford, 1982), Part I.

78. Foucault, *Discipline and Punish*, pp. 264-92; McConville, *A History of English Prison Administration*, pp. 128-31, 278-9. On the 'criminal class', see J.J. Tobias, *Crime and Industrial Society in the Nineteenth Century* (Harmondsworth, 1972).

79. Thomas, *The English Prison Officer*.

PART FOUR

Modern Period, from 1877

7
THE ORGANISATION OF A STATE PRISON SYSTEM

It is open to argument when a modern period of imprisonment in this country could be said to begin, and in any case the term 'modern period' needs to be given some kind of definition. Essentially, what is being referred to is a distinctively new phase in the use of prisons: one in which a system of imprisonment, under the control and direction of the central government, figures significantly in a state penal and correctional system. That might be a fair description of the prison system in this country during the present century. The problem is to identify the stage in the nineteenth century when it takes on this character. It could be argued, for instance, that the Report of the Home Office Departmental Committee (the Gladstone Committee)[1] in 1895 was the single most important influence on the way in which the prison system was to develop during the twentieth century, so that 1895 would be a crucial date. Alternatively, looking at the matter in terms of administration rather than penal policy, the whole system was brought under direct central control in 1877 and so it may be said that that year, the date of nationalisation, was particularly significant. Or it would even be possible to go back further and see the beginnings of the modern period in the gradual demise of transportation and the establishment of the convict prisons in the middle of the nineteenth century.

Any one date will to some extent represent an arbitrary choice but if, for purposes of exposition, we need to start from a single point, then 1877 does have a useful significance. In that year there occurred the major official move to sort out the administrative muddle of an embryonic state prison system and for the first time a centrally directed penal philosophy was applied effectively to all prisons throughout the country. Moreover, once the state had committed itself so wholeheartedly to this penal method, the maintenance of the prison system developed into a significant problem of official policy. This was a problem which, within a hundred years of the nationalisation of the system, would assume crisis proportions. Growing attacks on the use of imprisonment in principle combined with an official loss of confidence in the system to produce, in the post-war period, an increasingly desperate search for alternatives. Yet it must be emphasised that, whatever the problems and doubts which have been experienced during the course of this century, imprisonment has consistently been at the centre of government policy in this area. This is so much the case that, by the 1970s and early 1980s, the adherence of the general public and of many sentencers to the use of imprisonment as a major and necessary penal response seems virtually unshakeable.

In discussing the state's commitment to the use of imprisonment, account should be taken of the changing context of crime, criminal law and general perceptions of crime and delinquency over the last century. From the later part of the nineteenth century until the outbreak of the Second World War there was, in terms of official statistics, an overall stabilisation of crime rates and, relatively speaking, a certain confidence about the ability of society to contain problems of social disorder and wrongdoing. During this period British society *appears* relatively stable and, despite some points of social and political tension, on the whole less prone to the influence of volatile forces compared to post-war society. In the latter period, however, there has been an escalation of crime rates and a massive increase in the prison population. In society as a whole there have been more rapid shifts in direction and a breaking down of homogeneous attitudes, all of which has undermined the foundations on which penal policy had been based since the last part of the nineteenth century. In very broad terms, the period up to 1939 is characterised by an optimism and a faith in institutional responses. In the post-war period there has been an increasing pessimism about what can be positively achieved through the use of the prison system and a growing critical detachment in some sections of society from the 'socialising' functions of incarceration. The striking fact, however, is that despite these changes there has been more, not less, use of imprisonment.

The development of the prison system may also be viewed in an institutional context. Prior to the mid-nineteenth century the use of state institutions as instruments of social policy had been largely centred around the problems of poverty and vagrancy. But a growing awareness of the complexity of social disorders, whether manifested in criminal or other forms of antisocial behaviour, or in forms of social inadequacy, stimulated a more 'scientific' approach to these problems, and, in turn, a variegated institutional response. Different institutional regimes were developed to cater for the criminal, the mentally disordered, the habitually inebriate and the young person in trouble, in addition to existing measures for the destitute and the feckless. This is not to say that 'community' responses to these problems were wholly ignored; indeed, during this period we can also see the state's interest in and acquisition of the probation system[2] which, like the modern prison system, had predominantly local and private origins. But probation has competed unsuccessfully with imprisonment and its off-shoots for the central ground in penal policy and has in any case been partly integrated into the prison system for purposes of aftercare and pre-release programmes. Penological enthusiasm for probation and other community-based measures has never been matched by popular support; there has been a tendency to regard such approaches as a 'soft' option. In more recent years when the effectiveness of imprisonment, institutions for young offenders and even mental health institutions has been seriously called into doubt, probation has had to vie with newly introduced non-custodial measures such as community service. Overall, there remains a popular scepticism towards community-based measures and this is probably reflected, at least to some extent, among the judiciary.

However, while observing this proliferation of institutions, it should be noted that they have not always existed in a clearly defined relation to one another, and care should be taken to avoid an oversimplified categorisation of the different social problems for which the state has gradually assumed responsibility and sometimes prescribed institutional treatment. Criminal conduct, which is the basic qualification for a sentence of imprisonment, is a legal rather than a pathological condition: what is criminal is that defined by the law as criminal. The reasons for involvement in criminal activity may include forms of social or mental malfunctioning such as mental disorder, habitual inebriation, drug addiction or even something as wide and elusive as social disadvantage or fecklessness, much of which could be best catered for in more specialist, non-penal institutions. During the last hundred years such institutions have existed, to a varying extent, alongside imprisonment and have sometimes been used for those who have come technically within the scope of the criminal law. The 1898 Inebriates Act, for example, allowed a court to order an offender to be held in a state inebriate reformatory instead of passing a sentence of imprisonment. The Mental Health Acts, 1959-83, enable a court to make hospital or guardianship orders in respect of mentally disordered persons convicted of offences. But at the same time, the drunk, the mentally disordered and the socially inadequate have found and still do find themselves in prison, because no specifically appropriate measure exists or is seen as suitable for their particular case. Again, petty persistent offenders have commonly been given prison sentences and those suffering from psychopathic disorder have in many instances been directed towards the prison system for want of a better alternative. Thus there has been in some areas both an overlapping and an inadequacy of institutional or alternative community treatment and this situation has contributed to the perception of the prison as a 'social dustbin'.

Having indicated that the essential area for discussion now is the use by the state of institutions and most importantly imprisonment, for penal and corrective purposes, it remains to say something in general about the underlying objectives of the prison system during this period. We shall see that the prison has retained to some extent its more purely custodial and punitive functions. But the main thrust of official policy much of the time has been to use imprisonment constructively to reduce criminal and antisocial behaviour. This policy, based on developments in penal theory from the later part of the eighteenth century onwards, was crystalised by the Gladstone Committee in 1895 in terms of the twin objectives of deterrence and reform. The prison authorities were then able to put these ideas into practice for a period of 50 years with virtually no legislative interference. The essential character of the prison regime during this time is perhaps best summed up in the idea of the prison as a 'training' institution; as the Prison Rules stated: 'the purpose of the training and treatment of convicted prisoners shall be to encourage and assist them to lead a good and useful life.'[3] The predominant idea was to make prisoners into good citizens.

The important analogy is surely with the education system, and one of the most significant institutions of the period, in terms of policy, was the borstal: actually part of the prison system, a kind of prison for older juveniles, but modelled in many respects on the English public school. But if the Gladstone Committee's report in 1895 can be seen as an important event in the beginning of this process, then perhaps a significant point in its demise was the publication in 1955 of the Mannheim-Wilkins prediction study[4] which cast doubt on the corrective value of long periods of custody. This contributed to the shattering of the borstal concept and indirectly to that of the idea of the prison as a viable training institution. Another event which may be seized upon to represent the terminal stages of penological optimism in the use of prisons is the Report of the May Committee in 1979[5] which argued that the prison regime should now be based on the idea of 'positive custody'. There is no doubt that the idealism of the early years of this century has surrendered its place to a bleaker realism and that, in many respects, the prison has reverted to an institution of custody, albeit with a veneer of humane confinement.

The Administrative Structure of the Prison System

What was already in existence in 1877, in broad terms, was a dual system of imprisonment. Alongside the 113 local prisons (still controlled by local authorities although increasingly but unevenly under the influence of central government policy) there had been established, as we have seen, a number of convict prisons, the successors to transportation and the hulks. It was in the convict prisons in particular that, in the middle years of the nineteenth century, the main elements of what was to emerge as a general prison regime were being worked out. We shall return to the nature of this regime in due course but first need to outline the administrative structure of the nationalised system which came into being in 1877.

The movement towards central governmental control of the whole prison system had been under way for some years. To recapitulate the central points: an important step in this direction had been the appointment of Home Office inspectors in 1835, and the Prison Act of 1865 attempted to generalise the uncompromisingly punitive and deterrent regime advocated by the Carnarvon Committee[6] in 1863. The uniform and monotonous system of prison labour which was a ubiquitous feature of

English prisons after 1877 was in fact already being demanded of the local authorities by the Home Office with some vigour in the later 1860s[7]; and in the period between 1862 and 1877, eighty out of the 193 local prisons operating at the earlier date were closed down. In a sense, therefore, the 1877 legislation merely confirmed a process already in motion. Ironically, it was Disraeli's Conservative government, opposed in principle to the trend towards central administration, which was directly responsible for the full nationalisation of the prison system. That government was committed to a reduction in rates. Although there were arguments about how much money would actually be saved, it made sense in theory at least to relieve ratepayers of the burden of supporting an unnecessarily large number of local prisons.[8] The Prison at Buckingham, for example, had no inmates at all when the 1877 Act came into force in 1878.

The main effect of the legislation in 1877 was to vest overall responsibility for the prison system in the Home Office. Actual administration of the prisons was delegated to a Prison Commission which was accountable to the Home Secretary and was to be assisted by an Inspectorate. The convict prisons, which had been administered by a separate Board of Directors, continued under this body but since the Chairman of this Board, Sir Edmund Du Cane, became the first Chairman of the Prison Commissioners, the two bodies were for many practical purposes merged together (the Board of Directors of Convict Prisons was officially incorporated with the Prison Commission under the Prison Act of 1898). It was the regime favoured by Du Cane, an officer in the Royal Engineers with a wide experience of penal administration, with its energetic commitment to a uniform regime of austerity and deterrence, which was to be used by posterity to characterise the first 20 years of the centralised prison system. Certainly Du Cane was a dominant figure and the changes introduced after his retirement have been interpreted partly at least as a reaction to his autocratic and uncompromising administration. The general view is that the Home Office found him a difficult man to deal with and that he dominated his fellow Commissioners, and also the Inspectors,[9] whose role was conceived as being much more independent under the 1877 legislation.

By the early 1890s, the deterrent and punitive regime being so efficiently applied throughout the whole prison system had produced a strong reaction of both public and informed opinion.

A result of this was the setting up of the departmental committee under Herbert Gladstone (then Under-Secretary at the Home Office), whose report in 1895 was to signal an important change of direction in penal policy, so as to elevate the reform of the criminal to a major function of imprisonment. Du Cane retired shortly after the publication of the Gladstone Report and was succeeded by his fellow Commissioner, Sir Evelyn Ruggles-Brise, who held the post until 1921. Ruggles-Brise, with his Oxford and civil service background and close relations with Liberal politicians, was very different from Du Cane in temperament and outlook: both more forward-looking and more conscious of wider developments, an active participant in international penal conferences and ready to visit institutions abroad. Ruggles-Brise was therefore a suitable agent for some of the changes advocated by the Gladstone Committee and was associated with some of the notable penal developments in the early years of this century, especially probation, borstal training and preventive detention.

At the turn of the century there also occurred an important shift in the ultimate responsibility for the prison system. The Prison Act of 1898 enabled the Home Secretary to make rules for all categories of prison and for 50 years, until the passage of the Criminal Justice Act of 1948, Parliament effectively delegated the business of imprisonment to the Home Office and Prison Commission. There is thus a significant executive imprint on prison policy and administration in the first half of this century and this was perhaps most notable in the period after Ruggles-Brise's retirement, during the 1920s and 1930s, which was dominated by the figure of Sir Alexander Paterson, one of the Commissioners though never the Chairman. Ruggles-Brise, for all that he reflected the values of a liberal reformer, was by the end of his term regarded by many within the prison system as autocratic and detached from some of the pressing practical problems of prison administration. (Rupert Cross says of him that he 'probably had as much of the determination to improve prison conditions as could be expected of a civil servant of his generation'.[10]) Paterson worked within a different tradition: another Oxford graduate, but one whose early concern took him straight into social fieldwork (the Oxford Medical Mission to Bermondsey) rather than a Whitehall office. He was a particularly influential figure within the prison system through to the late 1940s and he used his position to shift the emphasis to a general amelioration of conditions within prisons, the provision of aftercare for prisoners and the use of more constructive regimes of open imprisonment and borstal training. This was the essential period of penological 'optimism' when imprisonment as an institution of social reform was at its most viable and some of the ideals of the Gladstone Committee came closest to realisation.

In the post-war period, the administrative structure and pattern of policy has evolved differently. The prison system, for reasons that cannot always be identified with confidence, has steadily moved towards a state of crisis. After 1945 a new kind of professionalism emerged, different from the penal practice inspired by conviction which predominated in Paterson's time. There has tended to be a harsher view taken of penal achievement, paying more attention to statistical information and the findings of increasingly rigorous penological research. The changing character of the prison administration begins to make itself clear in the approach of Sir Lionel Fox, Chairman of the Commissioners from 1942 till 1960. Fox was closely involved in the preparation of the soul-searching government White Paper of 1959, *Penal Practice in a Changing Society*,[11] and displayed an approach which was perhaps more academic and certainly less assured about the potential of the prison system. There was also, in the early 1960s, an attempt to rationalise the prison administration and provide clearer central direction. In 1963, after some years of discussion, the Prison Commissioners were replaced by a Prison Department of the Home Office. There had been a Scottish Prison Department since 1928 and this had been presented as a useful model to be followed in England and Wales; after an unsuccessful attempt to carry out this change in the 1948 legislation, the Prison Commission was eventually abolished under the Criminal Justice Act of 1961. The arguments which won the day referred to the complexity of the tasks being carried out by the prison service and to the need for a more co-ordinated approach to the overall problem of dealing with offenders, under the central supervision of the Home Office. There was some feeling that more direct Home Office control would not be conducive to the best development of the prison system and a fear that the Prison Commissioners' willingness to engage in open discussion would not be so readily adopted by the new Prison Department. Indeed, it has been possible since that time to detect an emerging ambivalence in Home Office policy:

on the one hand, support for research into penal and related questions in order to improve the content of policy (the Home Office set up its own research unit in 1957, and has funded other research); yet at the same time exercising some control over research activities and also insisting on a certain level of secrecy about some activities and events within the prison system (evidenced, for example, by an unwillingness on the part of the Home Office to release to the public the findings of its own enquiries into prison disturbances).[12] Whatever the advantages or otherwise of the administrative changes in 1963, since that date the prison service in England and Wales has been under the control of the Prison Department of the Home Office and actually administered by a Prison Board.

The Penal Population: Prison Closures and Prison Building

To gain a clear picture of the development of the prison system over the last 100 years it is of course useful to have some idea of the numbers involved, the general character of the penal population and the effect of the size of the prison population on individual prisons. But at the outset, a general point should be reiterated: any rise or fall in the prison population ought not to be viewed in isolation. If, for example, there is a fall in the numbers held in prison (as there was in the late nineteenth century), it is important to ask whether there has been a diversion to other types of institution, or whether it is a reflection of an increased resort to non-custodial penal methods or even of a drop in the crime rate. In the 1880s, Sir Edmund Du Cane, having described the regime applied to those undergoing a sentence of penal servitude, went on to point out the reduction of those sentenced 'for serious crime', implying that the prison system was effectively contributing to a diminishing crime rate.[13] It was true enough that the daily average prison population, both in the convict and the local prisons, fell considerably during the time of Du Cane's administration. The daily average population under sentence of penal servitude, for example, fell from almost 10,000 in 1876-7 to under four and a half thousand in 1893-4 and there appears to have been some decrease in the amount of crime — all of this against a rising population. But it is doubtful whether Du Cane was justified in using these figures for the purpose that he desired. The Summary Jurisdiction Act of 1879 had widened the powers of magistrates to use measures other than imprisonment and during the period in question prison sentences became noticeably shorter, perhaps as a sentencing reaction to the tougher prison regime. In other words, the regime inside prison may have deterred the courts as much as the criminals. The availability of alternative institutional and other measures should be taken into account in this kind of examination. To what extent did the setting up of retreats and reformatories for habitual drunkards account for some of the decrease in the prison population in the later part of the last century and similarly a sentencing trend in favour of probation in the 1930s? Conversely, what effect does the unwillingness on the part of mental health institutions to deal with certain categories of disordered offenders in recent years have on the penal population? It is worth noting, for present purposes, the thesis put forward by Penrose[14] as far back as 1939: on the basis of a comparative study of European statistics he argued that, before the Second World War, those countries with a large psychiatric hospital population had a small penal population, and vice versa, so that the populations of prisons and hospitals seemed to be inversely related. Such a thesis could be tested against other institutions which provide an alternative to penal disposals and prison then emerges as just one institutional option for society in dealing with its problematical members.

What, then, has been the general pattern of the prison population in England and Wales since the 1870s? A broad picture of the fluctuating total prison population can be gained from a glance at the daily average population at certain regular points during the period between 1880 and the present. (The daily average population is a reflection of both the number of receptions into prison and the length of sentence: the population figure depends on both of these factors.) Figure 7.1 shows how the prison numbers fluctuated between around 17,000 and just over 20,000 in the last years of the nineteenth century; dropped sharply to under 10,000 by 1916; were maintained at between 9,000 and 13,000 or so in the years between the wars; and rose steeply in the post-war period to a figure in excess of 40,000 by the early 1980s. Space does not permit a detailed comment on these figures. However, it is worth noting that the drop in number in the period 1910-15 was no doubt linked, partly at

Figure 7.1: Daily Average Prison Population, 1880-1980

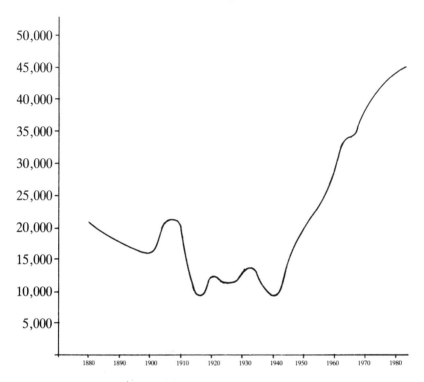

least, with some legislative action at that time. Section 8 of the Mental Deficiency Act of 1913 enabled courts to make an order for committal to an institution for mental defectives, rather than pass sentence, for those persons coming within the definition of mental deficiency under the Act; and section 9 also allowed transfer from prisons to such institutions. But of much more significance was the provision in section 1 of the Criminal Justice Act of 1914, which required magistrates to allow time for the payment of fines unless there were good reasons not to do so. The number of fine defaulters received into prison was around 85,000 in 1910 and had dropped to about 15,000 by 1921. The maintenance of the prison population at a relatively low level in the inter-war period reflects an increasing resort to non-custodial measures, especially probation. It should also be remembered that the carnage of the war itself reduced the younger male population from which many offenders would have been drawn. The increase in numbers since 1945 is notorious and explanations of the phenomenon are contentious. It remains a matter of official dismay that the introduction of more non-custodial measures and the system of release on licence have had such little impact on the swelling prison numbers.

As would be expected, policy as regards the closure and building of new prisons broadly reflects the fall and rise in the daily average population over the last century. When Du Cane took charge of the system in 1877, there was clearly a need to rationalise the collection of local prisons, since some of these contained very few prisoners; during his period of office, the number of local prisons was reduced from 113 to 56. After the First World War, another 18 were closed and the premises disposed of, while some others ceased to be operational and the buildings were held in reserve such as Chelmsford, used by the military authorities during the war and then closed between 1919 and 1930. In short, there was, until 1945, a surplus of accommodation. The most significant consequence of this was a legacy of mid-nineteenth century prison building and design which survives in many cases to the present day. The convict prisons date from the middle years of the nineteenth century and many of the local prisons had been redesigned in the first half of the century. Despite changing ideas about the nature of the prison regime after the 1890s, there was a strong economic disincentive to any prison rebuilding. Sir Lionel Fox was able to write in 1951:[15]

So it comes that in England there is only one prison building of the twentieth century, the former preventive detention prison built at Camp Hill in the Isle of Wight after the Act of 1908. Equally there is only one Borstal which was built as such — Lowdham Grange: and this was made possible only because it was built over a long period of years almost entirely by Borstal labour. . . To see a modern prison in Great Britain, one must cross the Border to Edinburgh.

By 1946 it had become clear that more accommodation was necessary and by 1950 the number of prison and borstal institutions had risen from 39 to 59. However, this need was partly met by reopening premises which had been closed but not disposed of, such as those at Canterbury and Reading, but especially by making use of existing accommodation which was not purpose-built, such as large country houses and services' premises, which could be used in particular for open prisons. It was not until the late 1950s that any prison building programme got under way. There has been a tendency to add to existing establishments, since it takes a number of years to progress from the design stage to the opening of a new prison and the rate of increase in the penal population made this an attractive short-term expedient. But there are limits in the case of many of the prisons to what could be done by way of extension and some of the problems of pressure of space may be compounded if the original premises are confined. Between 1958 and 1984, 27 new purpose-built prison establishments have become operational, 12 of which are closed prisons. Four of the training prisons opened since 1957 have been former RAF camps and all of the present open prisons for men are former service camps. By the 1980s the Prison Department therefore had a mixed estate: a number of nineteenth-century establishments (nearly all the local prisons were built before 1900); some converted premises, usually former service camps; and a minority of modern purpose-built prisons.[16] Despite the acquisition of new premises and the building programme, many of these prisons are now overcrowded. In 1982,[17] all of the local prisons and nearly all of the remand centres for male prisoners were seriously overcrowded; there was also overcrowding in a number of the training prisons and borstals, and especially in the detention centres. Accommodation has become, therefore, to put it mildly, a major problem for the Prison Department.

The Development of the Prison Service: Staff and Ancillary Personnel

The year 1877 may also be seen as an important date in the development of a national prison *service* — by which we mean a body of personnel, centrally directed in the implementation of a national policy for prisons. And in the same way that Du Cane, the Chairman of the Board of Directors of Convict Prisons, was placed in charge of the new Prison Commission, so the staff structure and ethos of the convict prisons was translated to the national system. In 1877 there was introduced into the local prisons a new staff professionalism, embodied in the so-called para-military staff structure and involving the frequent employment of ex-servicemen, and perhaps epitomised in the person of Du Cane himself, who retained his army commission long after his appointment to the prison service. The prison service having been established along these lines, however, there was soon to emerge an inherent conflict within the system after the Gladstone Committee had argued for a change in the nature of the prison regime. It has been argued[18] that the change in policy after 1895 proved to be an important factor in the stress which developed within the prison service during the twentieth century and in particular produced a problem of identity for the prison officer.

It had been clear to the new Prison Commission in 1877 that a national system required a restructuring of prison staff and a removal of the less professional kind of administration which continued, despite determined attempts at central control, in some of the local prisons.[19] Necessary reforms were therefore introduced: the employment of prisoners as clerks was brought to an end; the Commissioners sought to ensure that appointments and promotion within the service depended on merit rather than patronage; conditions of pay, service and allowances were standardised; and the para-military staff structure was introduced into the whole service.[20] The establishment of a single career structure for prison officers throughout the whole system should rank as one of Du Cane's most enduring achievements.

Thomas[21] identifies two salient characteristics of the para-military organisation: a pyramidical hierarchy of authority, and the wearing of uniforms. The need for this kind of staff structure is said to lie in a 'crisis' situation, inherent in the prison as a repressive institution, where a clear sense of authority is necessary in matters of administration. Such a staff organisation emphasises, of course, the element of *control* in imprisonment and control was naturally an important feature of the prison administration under Du Cane, when the objective was a disciplined and uniform regime for purposes of deterrence. There was some concern expressed at the development of the prison service along such militaristic lines[22] but this was in fact part of a wider development and a similar trend could be seen in other countries.[23] Certainly in Europe there remains to the present time a strong tradition of recruiting prison officers from the military.

It is now widely accepted[24] that the post-Gladstone policy posed problems for staff whose essential function had hitherto been one of discipline and control. Giving effect to the Committee's views about prison work necessarily required more association among prisoners and made the task of control more difficult (this had been one of the virtues of separate confinement from the point of view of the prison administration). Moreover, the emphasis on reform as one of the principal objectives of imprisonment led to difficulties of role for the prison officer who was to be concerned not only with the business of discipline and order but also of reformation of offenders. Thus in 1919 the warders became officially known as 'officers'. Although it was assumed at that time that such different roles could be performed by the same people, this is much less taken for granted now. The objective of reform also led to the introduction of different types of personnel into the prison system: at the level of governor, where direct entrants tended to be more concerned with penal theory than the everyday business of controlling inmates; then in the borstal institutions, introduced in 1908, where the regime was firmly grounded on ideas of training and improvement; and, at a later date, with the introduction of specially trained personnel — welfare officers, psychiatrists and psychologists.

It has not only been a problem of the prison officer's role and of a bifurcation of professional types within the prison service; conditions of employment have at different times been a matter of dispute. The Committee of Inquiry into the United Kingdom Prison Service (the May Committee) commented in 1979:[25] '. . . it is remarkable how frequently the questions with which [previous inquiries] . . . and now our present Inquiry, have had to deal have been the same.' As early as 1883 a Committee was set up under the Earl of Rosebury to look into the questions of pay, leave, hours of duty and grading of staff. There were further committees[26] established to examine questions of pay and work in 1891, 1923 and 1957 before the May Committee were asked to look at these questions again at the end of the 1970s. The latter Committee suggested that by that time causes of unrest among prison officers included a loss of confidence in treatment objectives, a distancing of staff and inmates as a result of overcrowding, a poor working environment, an increased emphasis on security and the introduction of specialist staff. Although a number of prison officers have been and are keen to develop a 'pastoral' role, increasingly the nature of their task makes this difficult and staff frustration was evidenced by industrial action at the beginning of the 1980s.

The role of the governor has also evolved since 1877. In particular, since the turn of the century the governor, and later on the new grade of assistant governor (which had its origins in the borstal system), were viewed as much as agents of reform as senior officials in an institution concerned with control. It also became more difficult for prison officers to secure promotion to the governor grade and this helped to widen the gap between the two levels of staff. However, the governors too began to feel a gulf opening up between themselves and their seniors, particularly after the abolition of the Prison Commission. The tendency, therefore, has been towards a more fragmented prison service, resulting in a collection of people with diverse functions (officers, governors, specialist training and 'pastoral' staff and Home Office officials) not always relating to each other very easily.

Finally, in discussing the personnel within the prison service, it is difficult not to feel that there has been a tendency over the last 100 years towards greater anonymity. Not surprisingly, in the middle of the nineteenth century, which was a period of innovation and controversy in penal matters, the character of individual chaplains, inspectors and other officials had an impact on the development of imprisonment. Even in the first half century after nationalisation of the prisons it could be said of some Commissioners and other figures — such as W.D. Morrison, the Chaplain of Wandsworth Prison — that their personality had a decisive effect on developments. However, both the expansion of the prison system and its later constitution as a department of the Home Office have led to a greater degree of impersonality. This is evident in the style of the later Prison Department Annual Reports which, while not uninformative, are reminiscent of company reports. Their bland tones suggest the sense of managerial remoteness which seems to be felt now in different sections of the prison service.[27] The problem, from the point of view of the prison officer, is summed up by Thomas:[28]

> The result of this increasing remoteness of the Head Office was a feeling of hopelessness on the part of officers, and a conviction that 'the people in London' did not know anything about prisons. Those who did, Inspectors and Commissioners, were powerless.

Such personnel and organisational problems cannot easily be disentangled from the development of the prison system as a response to changing social and other forces. It is to this that we should now turn our attention.

Notes

1. Report from the Departmental Committee on Prisons (Gladstone Committee), 1895, C. 7702. I.U.P. British Parliamentary Papers, Crime and Punishment, Prisons, 19.
2. On the development of the probation system generally, see Dorothy Bochell, *Probation and After-care, Its Development in England and Wales* (Scottish Academic Press, Edinburgh, 1976).
3. 1964 Prison Rules, Rule 1 : 1964 Statutory Instruments, 388.
4. H. Mannheim and L.T. Wilkins, *Prediction Methods in Relation to Borstal Training* (HMSO, London, 1955).
5. Committee of Inquiry into the United Kingdom Prison Services, 1979, Cmnd. 7673 (May Committee).
6. Report from the Select Committee of the House of Lords on the Present State of Discipline in Gaols and Houses of Correction, 1863, H.L. 499.
7. See, for instance, the study of Exeter Borough Prison in this period: W.J. Forsythe, *A System of Discipline* (University of Exeter, 1983).
8. For a discussion of the debates which preceded the nationalisation of the prisons, see J.E. Thomas, *The English Prison Officer Since 1850* (Routledge & Kegan Paul, London, 1972), pp. 19-24; Louis Blom-Cooper, 'The Centralisation of Governmental Control of National Prison Services', Ch. 7 in J.C. Freeman (ed.), *Prisons Past and Future* (Heinemann, London, 1978); Sean McConville, *A History of English Prison Administration* (Routledge & Kegan Paul, London, 1981), Vol. 1, Epilogue.
9. Jill Pellew, *The Home Office 1848-1914* (Heinemann, London, 1982), pp. 43-7; Peter Tibber, 'Edmund Du Cane and the Prison Act 1877' (1980), 19 *Howard Journal*, 9.
10. Rupert Cross, *Punishment, Prison and the Public* (Stevens, London, 1971), p. 28.
11. Cmd. 645.
12. Mike Fitzgerald and Joe Sim, *British Prisons* (Basil Blackwell, Oxford, 2nd ed. 1982), p. 10.
13. Sir Edmund Du Cane, *The Punishment and Prevention of Crime* (Macmillan, London, 1885), pp. 191-2.
14. L.S. Penrose, 'Mental Disease and Crime: Outline of a Comparative Study of European Statistics' (1939), *British Journal of Medical Psychology*, 8, 1-15.
15. Sir Lionel Fox, *The English Prison and Borstal Systems* (Routledge & Kegan Paul, London, 1952), p. 98.
16. See Appendix 2 : list of new prisons opened since 1958.
17. Annual Report of the Prison Department, 1982, Appendix No 3, Cmnd. 9057.
18. For instance, by Thomas, *The English Prison Officer*, p. 217 et seq.
19. See Forsythe, *Exeter Borough Prison*.
20. For details, see Thomas, *The English Prison Officer*, Ch. 3.
21. Ibid., p. 41.
22. Especially by William Tallack, the Chairman of the Howard Association. Generally, see Thomas, *The English Prison Officer*, pp. 48-9.

23. See the Report of the Gladstone Committee, Appendix 1 : Report on the Prison Systems of Foreign Countries, Answers to Question 6.

24. For instance, see the Report of the May Committee, paras. 2.17 and 2.21.

25. Ibid., at para. 2.11.

26. For details, see Thomas, *The English Prison Officer*, Ch. 5, and Report of the May Committee, para. 2.11 et seq.

27. See the view expressed by the May Committee, para. 5.9.

28. *The English Prison Officer*, p. 219.

8

TYPES OF PRISON SENTENCE AND THE PRISON REGIME

As we have seen, the significance of the 1877 legislation was that it brought all prisons in England and Wales, despite the continuing division into convict and local prisons, under a centrally directed regime, determined essentially by the Prison Commission. However, the use of convict and local prisons was related to different types of sentence and offender and since these distinctions continued well into the twentieth century, it is important to clarify what was involved in these different kinds of imprisonment.

Penal Servitude

The convict prisons (see Appendix 1) were for prisoners sentenced to penal servitude. In 1877 these prisons were the 'depots' at Millbank and Pentonville in London and the 'public works' prisons at Portland, Dartmoor, Portsmouth and Chatham; convict labour was later used to build new prisons of this kind at Woking, Wormwood Scrubs and Borstal. As already described in Chapter 6, the sentence of penal servitude, introduced in legisation of 1853, originated in the demise of transportation and in broad terms substituted, for the more serious offenders, a term in an English convict prison and then release on licence ('ticket-of-leave') in this country for performance of the sentence in an overseas penal colony (although for some years a small number of convicts continued to be sent to Bermuda, Gibraltar and Western Australia).

The important feature of the sentence was that it was staged.[1] The first nine months were spent in separate confinement in either a convict prison or one of the local prisons which catered for this class of convict and the prisoner was subject to first class hard labour for the first month (hard labour is discussed below and in Appendix 3). In the words of Du Cane:[2] 'The first stage is one of severe penal discipline, during which the prisoner's mind is thrown in upon itself . . . he becomes open to words of admonition and warning . . . he is put in that condition when he is likely to feel sorrow for the past and to welcome the words of those who show him how to avoid evil for the future.' In the second stage, the convict was put to associated but still 'silent' labour in a public works prison. This involved, typically, work such as farming, quarrying and land reclamation and such projects as the building of harbours at Filey and Dover. In this stage the prisoner progressed through four classes by means of a system of marks earned for exemplary industry and lost by bad conduct.[3] John Lee, in his autobiography,[4] recalls how the notoriously misconvicted Adolph Beck lost some privileges for a breach of the rules which forbade prisoners to talk to warders — Beck was trying to do a favour for another prisoner who was about to be released. Privileges with regard to such things as visits, letters and exercise were used as an inducement to good behaviour and promotion to a higher class and eventually perhaps remission. Finally, the prison authorities could determine the appropriate point at which to release the prisoner on licence for the rest of his term. The licence was primarily subject to a condition of good behaviour and was under a degree of police supervision (an account is presented by Joseph Conrad, in relation to his character Michaelis, the 'ticket-of-leave Apostle' in *The Secret Agent*). Any misconduct, not only the commission of a further offence, could lead to revocation of the licence. The length of the sentence of penal servitude was related to the former sentence of transportation — sentences would be for three (until 1864), five, seven, ten or fourteen years.

As already mentioned, Du Cane[5] had claimed that the prison regime at that time was effective in reducing the level of crime and in particular he drew attention to the reduction in the number of sentences of penal servitude between 1859 and 1884 and implied that there was a related decrease in the level of serious crime. The Gladstone Committee, however, were critical of the initial stage of separate confinement and argued that virtually the whole period of confinement should be served in association in a convict prison. When this change was implemented after 1898 the real distinction was not so much between penal servitude and other imprisonment as between a term in a convict prison and confinement in one of the local prisons. Those in the convict prisons were the more serious, longer-term prisoners, moving through the progressive stages system towards release on licence. But even the rationale of the progressive stages system, that privileges and remission should be *earned* in accordance with a mathematical score, eventually came under attack. Sir Alexander Paterson argued against the spurious 'scientific' basis of such penal evaluation:

> . . . when it is a question of deciding whether a man of many convictions for violence and robbery shall be let loose on the public, it may be well to distinguish between the man who is α− and him who is β− but it is hazardous to choose between a man who has in the estimation of the imponderables scored 1,800 and one who, by failure in lip service or boot polish has only registered 1,500.[6]

In the course of time many of the differences between penal servitude and imprisonment were whittled away so that when the sentence was formally abolished in the Criminal Justice Act of 1948 the main surviving distinction was the release on licence for those serving the former sentence. Sir Lionel Fox commented[7] that the legal abolition of the sentence was a recognition of a largely *de facto* situation (and the number of those sentenced to penal servitude had become very small — just over 1,300 in 1921, for example, with the result that Portland could be closed as a convict prison); but he added that it would have the beneficial result of removing the tradition among the convict class that they were 'the Horse Artillery of the convict world'.

Imprisonment, With or Without Hard Labour

This was the term used for prison sentences other than penal servitude. The majority of offenders sentenced to imprisonment were given shorter terms, to be served in local prisons, with or without hard labour (usually the former: in 1893, for example, there were over 109,000 sentences with hard labour as compared to 41,000 without). However, the term 'hard labour' was misleading. As Du Cane pointed out:[8]

. . . any prisoner sentenced to imprisonment should be, and is by law, required to labour, under specified conditions, suitable to his health and his capacity; and, in fact, excepting the specific kind of labour called 'First Class Hard Labour', defined in the 'Prison Act 1865', as 'crank, tread-wheel, etc. and other like kind of labour', the term 'hard' has no particular meaning, and its employment in the sentence makes no practical difference.

Therefore, by the 1880s, it was only the first class hard labour which was distinctively hard and the Gladstone Committee a few years later inveighed against the kind of useless labour involved in that regime, with the result that under the 1899 Prison Rules first class hard labour was abolished and all prisoners were to be employed on 'useful industrial labour' from the start of their sentence. Even so, the sentence with 'hard labour' still involved an initial period of 28 days separate confinement with hard bodily or manual labour, the prisoner then proceeding to associated labour of 'a less hard description'. It was difficult, however, to work out different degrees of hard labour and in practice the work done under separate confinement, contrary to the original intention, tended to be less rigorous.[9] The period of separate confinement was abolished during the First World War — in the public interest, it was necessary for the so-called hard labour prisoners to work as hard (and usefully) as the others — and thereafter there was a more or less single regime of prison labour in the local prisons. The surviving feature of the distinct regime of hard labour was the requirement that during the first fortnight of the sentence the prisoner should sleep on a plank, and this rule was not removed until 1945.

As far as imprisonment without hard labour was concerned, there was an attempt to introduce a structure into this sentence in the 1898 Prison Act, according to which the sentencing court could specify that the imprisonment be in the first, second or third division. Placement in these divisions affected the privileges and general creature comforts allowed to prisoners, the first division being reserved for 'political' and a few other prisoners not regarded as belonging to the typical criminal type and so deserving less harsh treatment. One of the most famous prisoners to sample an earlier version of the first division was the Editor of the *Pall Mall Gazette*, W.T. Stead, haplessly convicted of an offence involving the selling of children into prostitution and for whose introduction he himself had vigorously campaigned.[10] He was guilty only in a technical sense and this fact was acknowledged in his prison sentence. In his cell on E Wing of Holloway Prison he had papers, books and flowers, could continue to work as a journalist and received a stream of visitors: 'Never had I a pleasanter holiday, a more charming season of repose' he commented. But it was clear within a few years of the courts being given this power of classification that they were making little use of it, principally because most sentences were to be served with hard labour.[11] From 1900 the prison authorities used certain classifications for their own purposes, notably the use of the 'star' class for first offenders (a classification already used in the convict prisons) so as to separate the first and other offenders. Later on, prisoners between the age of 16 and 21 were placed in a distinct Juvenile Adult Class.

The Criminal Justice Act of 1948 abolished the sentences of penal servitude and hard labour and also the divisions of imprisonment without hard labour. Apart from the special regimes for preventive detainees and those sentenced to corrective training, discussed below, there has since that date been a single sentence of imprisonment for adult offenders, whatever the nature of the offence or antecedents of the offender.

Two things are striking about these attempts to systematise sentences of imprisonment. Firstly, the idea of providing a carefully worked out, almost scientific structure for these sentences lost much of its appeal in the post-Gladstone period. The progressive stages system built into penal servitude was cumbersome to administer and we have seen how it was eventually attacked in principle. It came to be argued[12] that a system which was based on the *earning* of privileges was essentially a negative approach, encouraging a servile attitude and working against a real rehabilitation of character. This approach was contrasted with that adopted in American prisons, where prisoners started their sentences with privileges which they forfeited through misconduct or idleness. Then again, the attempts to classify hard labour encountered practical difficulties which were compounded for some time by the insistence that there be some period of separate confinement. In retrospect, it is not so surprising that the whole system was gradually reduced to a general scheme of associated, though 'silent', useful labour.

This was probably inevitable once the implications of the Gladstone recommendations were fully worked out.

In the second place, the availability and use of these different regimes appears not to have been properly understood outside the prison service to a remarkable degree. In particular, sentencers seem to have been badly informed about what was actually involved in penal servitude and hard labour. There was a widely held but erroneous belief until 1950 that sentences of imprisonment for common law offences were subject to a maximum of two years.[13] Consequently, many sentences of imprisonment were for much less than two years (which no doubt contributed to the relatively low prison population). This misinformed view was related to the belief, which survived well into the twentieth century, that imprisonment with hard labour was a much tougher experience than penal servitude and so ought not, on both practical and humane grounds, be imposed for too long a perod. So in 1932, Ellis Cyril Jones, being dealt with at Middlesex Sessions for shopbreaking and other offences,[14] received a sentence of three years penal servitude rather than two years hard labour, since the latter would, in the view of the court, have been a more severe sentence. By that time there was little difference in fact between the two regimes, so that the court was inadvertently passing a heavier sentence than it had intended. This was pointed out by the Lord Chief Justice when Jones appealed against his sentence, and a sentence of two years hard labour was substituted. Such a situation was perhaps a reflection of the long period of executive control over prison development, whereby an absence of legislative intervention led to a judicial lack of awareness of what prison conditions were actually like.

The Single Sentence of Imprisonment

Since 1948 these different types of sentence have been merged into a single sentence of imprisonment and the sentencer's function has been limited to deciding upon the use of imprison-ment in the first place and determining the basic length of the sentence. It has been the role of the prison authorities to decide upon the placement and classification of prisoners. Leaving aside for the present penal institutions for offenders under the age of 21, four types of prisons have come into use since 1948: the local prison, as before, concerned with remand, allocation of convicted prisoners and those sentenced to shorter terms; 'training' prisons for longer term prisoners (a term brought into official use in 1969 to replace the terms 'central' and 'regional training' prisons used after 1948) — the successor to the convict prison, some of these being open prisons; a small number of prisons for female offenders; and, since 1967, a number of 'dispersal' prisons, which are training prisons with conditions of maximum security. Allocation to a particular prison depends on a number of factors but in particular, since the late 1960s, on a security rating: categories A, B, C and D, ranging between the two extremes of a maximum security dispersal prison (category A) and an open prison (category D).

At the level of sentencing, therefore, the important development over the last 100 years has been one of simplification, resulting in a single generic prison sentence. However, that statement leaves out of account the development of a number of sentences and institutions for younger offenders, best discussed separately, and tends to mask a complexity of classification once a person has been given a prison sentence. It is perhaps also fair to say that, despite the different types of sentence in existence during the last part of the nineteenth century, there was probably a greater uniformity of regime and prison experience than in more recent years, given the variable conditions of overcrowding and available facilities in present day prisons.

The Nature of the Prison Regime

Since 1877 the nature of the regime inside prison has been influenced more by major shifts in policy than by the legal denomination of the sentence of imprisonment — penal servitude, preventive detention, or whatever else. The prevailing idea of what imprisonment was intended to achieve has determined the main content of the prison experience and tended to override any distinction contemplated at the sentencing level. We have seen already that the original distinction between penal servitude and imprisonment and between hard and ordinary labour was gradually whittled away; and Rupert Cross remarks[15] about the idea of preventive detention (discussed later) under the 1948 Criminal Justice Act:

How was preventive detention distinguished from imprisonment in practice? . . . [There] were more or less significant difference to begin with, but they became less and less significant as the conditions of ordinary imprisonment improved.

The most important fact about the prison regime in the last 100 years is that, while in 1877 imprisonment was conceived mainly as a punitive and deterrent experience, from the end of the century the main thrust of official policy was to use prisons for reformative purposes. If reform was going to be at all meaningful in this context clearly there had to be some modification of the highly repressive regime in existence in the later years of the nineteenth century. The changes urged by the Gladstone Committee necessarily implied an abandonment of useless labour, a move away from separation of inmates and a general amelioration of living conditions within prisons. The changes in particular aspects of the prison regime will be considered in some detail, but firstly it would be helpful to trace the general shift in official policy over the period as a whole.

Policy Changes

In so far as imprisonment has been used in modern times for penal as opposed to more general custodial purposes, such as remand, there would seem to have been three major objectives. (Here, it should be noted, the infliction of punishment by means of a prison sentence is not being treated as an aim or objective of imprisonment.[16] So far as imprisonment has a repressive and punitive character, this is justified on the grounds that the offender has committed an offence and punishment is achieved in the fact of imprisonment itself. If the regime inside prison is described as punitive, what is really meant is that it is hard and unpleasant for (usually) deterrent purposes or (conceivably but unconvincingly) for reformative ends.) These primary objectives may be summed up as: deterrence, of the offender and other potential offenders; reform of the offender's criminal character; and protection of society from further offences by means of the offender's incarceration. This last objective is perhaps the least controversial. It is accepted by most people as necessary to some extent and what arguments there are centre around the problems of evaluating serious harm to others and predicting the likelihood of further offences, the two important factors in deciding upon 'protective' incarceration. But both deterrence and reform (the 'corrective' objectives) are inherently difficult, since the measurement of both the deterrent and reformative effects of imprisonment has proven consistently problematic. Indeed, the recent suggestion of 'positive custody'[17] as a central objective in prison policy reveals an unwillingness to claim faith any longer in either deterrence or reform. But over the last century, imprisonment has been an area in which the respective merits of deterrence and reform as objectives have been matched against each other.

Both 'deterrence' and 'reform' are, of course, general ideas which embrace a number of complex notions and these in turn resolve themselves over a period of time into different 'schools of thought'. The term 'reform', in particular, begs a number of questions: reform into what? Law-abiding people? But why do people not abide by the law? Sometimes perhaps they have a good reason not to.[18]

During the nineteenth century the concept of reforming criminals went through a number of forms; as we have seen the earlier 'evangelical' ideas of reform produced a reaction, epitomised in the Report of the Carnarvon Committee, in favour of punitive deterrence, which became the keynote of the prison regime under Du Cane. But already in the early days of the nationalised prison system new ideas of reform were being developed and were gradually taking root in the official consciousness. While in 1863 the Carnarvon Committee had urged that the regime in prison should consist of 'hard labour, hard fare and hard bed', seven years later the First National Prison Congress in Cincinnati issued a Declaration of Principles, the contents of which are in striking contrast:

> In prison administration, moral forces should be relied upon, with as little admixture of physical force as possible, and organised persuasion be made to take the place of coercive restraint, the object being to make upright and industrious freemen rather than orderly and obedient prisoners; moral training alone will make good citizens.[19]

Ironically, in 1877 when Du Cane took charge of the whole prison system in this country, the New York State Reformatory at Elmira was ready to be opened, an institution based on reformatory principles very much at variance with the penology espoused by the first Chairman of the Prison Commissioners (and even the second Chairman, to some extent: after Ruggles-Brise visited Elmira at a later date he had reservations about some of the regime in force there).[20] With such wider penological developments in mind, it is not surprising that Du Cane's regime should eventually crumble in the 1890s.

Changing ideas on deterrence and reform were not of course simply matters of fashion. Adherence to one approach or another sprung partly from different views of human behaviour and criminal tendencies. Du Cane, on the one hand, referred to 'classes of incurable criminals'[21] while the critic of his methods, the Chaplain of Wandsworth Prison, W.D. Morrison, noted that 'the personal, social and economic conditions which generate a criminal disposition and criminal habits of life are fostered to a very large extent by the herding together of the population in a few immense commercial and industrial centres'.[22] This last view, demonstrating a wider appreciation of the causes of criminality, points to the background to the ideas which underlay the Gladstone Committee's Report. The immediate reasons for the setting up of the committee lay in a vociferous public campaign in the early 1890s spearheaded by Morrison and the *Daily Chronicle* and highly critical of the existing prison regime. There seems also to have been a reaction in the Home Office against Du Cane's methods. By the 1890s a new breed of civil servant was emerging: university trained, appointed on merit rather than patronage and typified by Ruggles-Brise, a man both friendly with and in tune with the views of Liberal politicians such as Asquith and Herbert Gladstone. The emerging mood within the Home Office made it increasingly difficult to tolerate Du Cane's autocratic and military style of administration. But, personalities apart, there were probably more deep-rooted reasons for the Committee's arguments in favour of a more reformative approach, most importantly, an alteration in the philosophical and political climate.

By the close of the nineteenth century, the role of the individual in society was being revalued. At a superficial level, this appeared as a concern for individual rights and well-being, especially as regards the position of children. Popular literature in the middle of the century had focussed attention on the ill-treatment of children, in 1884 the NSPCC had been established and in 1891 the Humanitarian League was founded to promote 'a consistent, intellectual and well-researched protest against all forms of cruelty'. At the same time, some commentators pointed to a greater confidence about issues of law and order, at least at an official level, which prompted a more sympathetic response to instances of delinquency and some aspiration to search out and deal with the underlying causes. Sir Francis Powell remarked in 1897:[23]

> The diminution of sentences had arisen not only from a change of public feeling and increase of sympathy and consideration for the weaker brethren, but also from a feeling that crime had diminished, and that, therefore, there was not the same necessity for sharp punishment as a deterrent. There could be no doubt that judges and justices of the peace had diminished sentences, because they believed that there was now greater order in society than formerly, and that property was in greater security.

Moreover, as for imprisonment itself, in the later years of the century the experience of being imprisoned was being conveyed to the general public and to more informed opinion by a number of articulate prisoners, as diverse as Oscar Wilde and the collection of Irish Members of Parliament regularly imprisoned during this period: this effected some shift in the view of imprisonment, from that of society outside to that of the prisoner.

But the increasing willingness of the state to confront issues of juvenile delinquency and drunkenness and other social problems reflected more than simply an altruistic concern for the position of the individual in society. Ideas about 'reforming' delinquents and wrongdoers also sprang from a paternalistic concern about changing attitudes and a perceived social degeneration. However well-intentioned the motives of social reformers, we should not lose sight of the fact that many reforming measures (and this would increasingly include imprisonment and its analogues) were enforced, and that welfare policies could be given a dictatorial application. The shift from deterrence to reform in penal policy should be associated with the search for more constructive and effective measures to reinforce certain values and to contain degenerative influences. A graphic illustration of the type of concern which underlay these policies was the setting up in 1904 of an Inter-Departmental Committee on Physical Deterioration,[24] which was a response to more extreme fears then in circulation about a supposed deterioration in the physical and moral character of the British people.

It was in this climate of opinion that the Report of the Gladstone Committee inaugurated the modern era of the prison as a training institution. 'We think', the Committee stated in paragraph 25 of its Report,

> that the system should be made more elastic, more capable of being adopted to the special cases of individual prisoners; that prison discipline and treatment should be more effectually designed to maintain, stimulate, or awaken the higher susceptibilities of prisoners, to develop their moral instincts, to train them in orderly and industrial habits, and wherever possible to turn them out of prison better men and women, both physically and morally, than when they came in.

And this led to the well-known formulation of principle: 'that prison treatment should have as its primary and concurrent objects, deterrence and reformation' (paragraph 47). Overriding the doubts of Sir Godfrey Lushington,[25] 'I regard as unfavourable to reformation the status of a prisoner throughout his whole career', which have now found more recent echoes, these influential statements encouraged a climate of 'penological optimism' which has persisted for much of this century and has spawned a set of reformative and welfare institutions, such as borstal training, prison welfare services and aftercare of discharged prisoners, concerned with improving the material and moral well-being of those who come within the net of the criminal law.

An itemised discussion of particular aspects of the prison regime is problematic since many of these features of imprisonment are interdependent. However, it is possible to extrapolate certain crucial elements which have an important effect on prison design and conditions: association, labour and security. And despite the shift in emphasis towards the prison as an institution of reform, the development of activities such as education and industrial training have in many prisons been very much affected by the legacy of an earlier period with different concerns. This legacy resides in the major programme of building and rebuilding during the early and middle part of the nineteenth century to accommodate a theory of imprisonment which insisted on the separation of inmates and a system of hard, often useless labour. With a declining prison population in the earlier part of this century, it was difficult to justify, in economic terms, a rebuilding of the existing institutions.

While reformative ideas could be accommodated in some penal institutions, such as the borstals and open prisons, it was not until the 1960s that new prisons as such were being built (see Appendix 2) and by that time the idea of the prison as a training institution was losing much of its appeal and considerations of control and security had become dominant.

Separation Versus Association

The main inspiration for nineteenth-century prison design in this country was undoubtedly the 'model' of Pentonville, whose radial lay-out was intended to accommodate separate confinement and facilitate control of prisoners. Cellular confinement of prisoners was in origin punitive (solitary contemplation of own wrongdoing) and preventive (avoidance of criminal 'contagion') and simplified the warders' task of control. By 1895, however, the Gladstone Committee were aware of the psychological dangers of prolonged solitary confinement and did not favour an absolute application of what they regarded as 'unnatural' silent association. There followed a gradual reduction in the periods of cellular labour until in 1922, following the retirement of Ruggles-Brise, the Prison Commissioners reported that 'separate confinement is now being regarded as in the nature of a restraint, only to be used when necessary for the maintenance of discipline'.[26] Also at this time the Rule of Silence was substantially modified — it had in any case been very difficult to enforce and personal accounts from prisoners in the early years of the century made it clear that prisoners would inevitably find ways to communicate with each other, whether in their cells (Brocklehurst recounts how prisoners would talk down toilet waste pipes to each other)[27] or working together in conditions of silence. Arthur Harding's account[28] of the sentences he served in a number of different convict prisons between 1911 and 1922 reveals that he came to know a number of his fellow prisoners very well. More recently, problems of overcrowding have meant that it has for some time been the norm in local and in some other prisons for cells to be shared. This situation has attracted a good deal of criticism, principally on humanitarian grounds. But, as the May Committee were told,[29] the main objections are sanitary and many inmates seemed to prefer company rather than be entirely alone in a cell, particularly if opportunities for association outside cells are limited, as has been the case in many local prisons.

Thus the theory of separate confinement had in fact lost much of its appeal by the later part of the nineteenth century[30] and its practice has been substantially modified, despite the nineteenth-century lay-out of many present-day prisons, partly through the implementation of a 'training' regime, but also through force of circumstances. The new wave of prison building begun in the 1960s, for which the prison at Blundeston (near Great Yarmouth and the birthplace of David Copperfield) has been a model, confirms the reality of the departure from the separate system.[31] At Blundeston there is provision for both separate cells (grouped more 'intimately') and dormitory accommodation; a main objective is a reasonable standard of privacy and hygiene; and suitably sized association and quiet rooms have been provided. It is a pity, from the point of view of the viability of a reformative regime of imprisonment, that such radical design had to wait until the 1960s.

Prison Work

Throughout the modern period the assumption that prisoners should do work of some kind has never been doubted and since 1949 it has been a requirement stated in the Prison Rules for prisoners to engage in 'useful work'. This was no doubt originally an understandable reaction to the chaotic situation of idle inmates in the prisons of the eighteenth century. For practical reasons of control, too, a prison system cannot easily afford a large collection of idle prisoners. But the use of labour also had its more positive aspects. In particular, it could be punitive in nature and so fortify the deterrent effect of the experience of imprisonment. This was the idea of course underlying the concept of hard labour and especially the 'useless' first class hard labour. Useless labour was based on such devices as the treadwheel, the crank, the capstan and shot drill (see Appendix 3) and was carefully measured so that the maximum of effort could be expended on doing nothing useful. (In fact, some treadwheels were used to operate windmills for ventilation, or to draw water, but the labour remained useless from the prisoner's subjective viewpoint; unlike activities such as oakum-picking or mat-making, there was no concrete evidence of the results of the prisoner's labour.) Such labour tended to break both the body and the spirit and by the 1890s opinion was turning against it (see, for example, the evidence given to the Gladstone Committee by Captain Schuyler and Colonel Garcia).[32] It was roundly condemned by the Gladstone Committee: 'the strongest argument against this type of labour is that it keeps the prisoners in a state of mental vacuity, and this we regard as a most undesirable and mischievous result' (paragraph 48). Useless labour was subsequently abolished in the Prison Rules of 1899 and since then all prison work has been 'productive'.

There had in fact been a tradition of productive prison work throughout the nineteenth century. At the close of the previous century, as already noted in Chapter 5, a secular and utilitarian theory of reform, based around the writings of Beccaria and Bentham, had gained some support. It was argued that antisocial tendencies could be moderated by a regime of industry which would inculcate a greater self-discipline and sense of social responsibility. Bentham had favoured the idea of an industrial prison and in the early years of the nineteenth century there were some local prisons, such as Bury Gaol and the Preston House of Correction,[33] which instituted regimes of useful labour. The Prison Act of 1823 had prescribed a regime of 'Due Classification, Inspection, Regular Labour and Employment and Moral Instruction'. Although these developments were undermined during the 1820s by increasing unemployment which created fears about competition from prison labour, and rising crime rates which hardened public opinion against 'cheerful industry' in prisons, the idea of productive labour was absorbed into the regime of some overseas penal colonies. Alexander Maconochie, the superintendent of the penal settlement on Norfolk Island from 1840 to 1845, and Sir Walter Crofton, who was involved in the administration of the Irish convict prisons between the 1850s and the 1870s, developed the 'staged' sentence, the underlying objective in the words of Maconochie being to 'recover the man's self-respect, to gain his own goodwill towards his reform . . .'. The kind of labour developed under these regimes[34] then provided the model for the central part of the sentence of penal servitude: the term in a public works prison.

Four of these prisons were quickly established in the middle of the century. Portland was opened in 1849; the old prison on Dartmoor, originally built to hold American and French prisoners of war, was converted by convict labour from Millbank in 1850-51; Portsmouth was opened in 1851 and Chatham in 1856, these two replacing the hulks at Portsmouth and Woolwich and on the Medway. In addition, the Surrey County Prison at Brixton was taken over for female convicts in 1853. As noted already, convicts in these prisons were put to different types of outside work and the public work aspect manifested itself in projects of public utility: the dockyards at Chatham and Portsmouth were extended, the breakwater at Portland was constructed and the prisoners were used in the building of new prisons at Woking, Borstal and Wormwood Scrubs and for adding new wings to existing prisons (the tradition of using prison labour to build new prisons strikes an ironic note). Du Cane explained[35] that convict labour had three objectives: deterrence, of course; reform ('to instil into the convict habits of industry, to develop their intelligence by employing them on industrial labour, and to facilitate their entering the ranks of honest industry on their discharge, by giving them facilities for acquiring a knowledge of trades'); and finally, 'these objects are fortunately conducive to another very desirable result, viz. that of making the prisons self-supporting in various degrees.'

This was the kind of prison labour which was to become the norm throughout the prison system after the turn of the century, in local prisons, in so far as facilities allowed, as well as the convict prisons. Not surprisingly prisoners themselves compared public works labour favourably with the more monotonous, confined type of work which tended to be found in the local prisons, especially in the earlier part of this century. Arthur Harding remarks[36] of his time in Portland: 'I think I gained more in health, wisdom and learning in the two years I was there than I could possibly have gained anywhere else ; looking back I do not regret my stay although it was enforced. I wish the same could be said of Wormwood Scrubs.' Interestingly, Harding also pointed out: 'Discipline was very strict, the governor believed in punishment. . . The question of reformation never caused him the slightest anxiety, he never considered it a part of his duty'.[37] This suggests that talk of reform, and deterrence too, had a theoretical rather than a practical validity. For many prison staff, the overriding concerns have consistently been punishment and control; many prisoners, like Harding, have been appreciative of a healthy and disciplined regime which has returned them to society fit and well-trained but usually done little to dissuade them from further crime (indeed, proponents of 'lesser eligibility' would have found fuel for their arguments in Harding's remarks). What penal theory has tended to underestimate, perhaps, is the concern of those actually working and held in prison for the present rather than the future.

By the 1920s the idea of productive labour as a form of training had become part of penal orthodoxy. In 1922 the Commissioners stated[38] that they were aiming for a minimum of eight hours' associated work for all prisoners, although there were practical difficulties in achieving this in some of the local prisons. A Departmental Committee reporting on the employment of prisoners in 1935[39] considered that 'suitable employment is the most important factor in the physical and moral regeneration of the prisoner'. However, the ideal of suitable employment has not been so easy to achieve in practice. Account has had to be taken of the willingness, basic abilities and fitness of prisoners, the need to avoid competition with external labour and of the crucial fact that many prison sentences have been too short for training in any meaningful sense.[40] The excessive prison population of recent years has compounded the problem by placing further strain on the available facilities and stretching staff resources. For some time it has been generally true that the training prisons (as the name implies) are in the best position to carry out a programme of training work, since they are best equipped, the least overcrowded and hold longer-term prisoners. In the local prisons, work has tended to be of the more mundane kind, such as the proverbial sewing of mailbags.

Prison work is still viewed as an essential part of the prison regime, but the objectives have altered. The May Committee in 1979 urged that the 'rhetoric' of treatment and training should be abandoned and its discussion of prison labour is more in terms of the vital role that such work plays in maintaining the physical and mental well-being of the prisoner. The function of prison work seems therefore to have moved through a number of roles during the course of the last century: punitive deterrence, training and then, more negatively, minimising what are now seen as the necessarily adverse effects of removing the prisoner from society.

Security and Discpline

The third factor which has determined the everyday life of the prisoner since 1877 is the need for security. It is axiomatic that, in so far as prison holds people against their will and some of these are regarded as a danger to society, the institution must be able to contain many of its inmates securely. Moreover, the concept of penal incarceration in itself — enforced confinement as a punishment — is only meaningful if effective, and only effective if the temptation to abscond cannot be successfully realised. This obviously implied 'perimeter' security, but also, to enforce a system of separate confinement and for purposes of internal control and the protection of some categories of prisoners, security within the prison as well. In short, the term 'security' can be taken to comprise the totality of means by which the coercive nature of the institution is maintained.

The physical manifestation of this need for security may be seen in the paraphenalia of control which have become hallmarks of imprisonment: locked cell doors, high perimeter walls and fences, warders with jangling keys and a strict routine according to which the prisoners do certain things or go certain places at set times. Before the post-Gladstone changes, security was certainly facilitated by separate confinement and strict restrictions on association between prisoners. This did not, however, remove all problems of control. Warders were often exposed to the risk of assault and in 1882 Francis Peek, the Chairman of the Howard Association, had complained[41] to the Home Secretary about 'opportunities for intrigue and conspiracy' among convicts and urged greater measures of control. But with the increased association which was allowed to prisoners in the early years of this century, there was a more evident need still for new devices of control. It was recognised that the threat of punishment was to a large extent a self-defeating instrument of discipline since it promoted bad feeling and tension within the prison. The solution adopted was rather the opposite idea: incentives to good behaviour. Most importantly the 1898 Prison Act authorised the use of remission of part of the sentence for good behaviour and this quickly proved to be one of the most effective instruments of control for the prison authorities. As the Governor of Northampton Prison pointed out in 1908,[42] remission 'tends to strengthen a governor's hand in maintaining discipline, and gives him an alternative punishment to the "well worn" bread and water diet, for which I am thankful'. In 1898 the maximum amount of remission which could be earned was one sixth of the sentence (in the case of penal servitude, one quarter for men, one third for women); a flat rate of remission of one third was introduced during the Second World War.

The problems of security and discipline in prisons where inmates are allowed to associate with each other have been analysed by Thomas,[43] particularly in connection with the mutiny in Dartmoor in January 1932. (It is interesting, incidentally, to reflect on a change in terminology. What happened in 1932 was described as a 'mutiny'. In the 1970s people referred to 'prison riots' — an illuminating shift from a military to a civilian metaphor.) The Dartmoor munity, which was the first in this country when prisoners actually took control of the prison, for a short while, demonstrated the inherent problems in a situation where prisoners heavily outnumber staff in a tense, repressive environment. The mutiny was contained by police action on the outside and quelled by the use of firearms. The Du Parcq inquiry[44] into the mutiny refused to attribute the uprising to the more relaxed nature of the regime since 1898. Writing 40 years later, Thomas reaches a different conclusion: 'The origins of the mutiny lay in the social dynamics which association initiates'.[45] Clearly, an uprising of that kind would have been virtually impossible before 1898. However, the Prison Commissioners and the Home Office were able to resist any pressure for a toughening of the regime, and tightening of security and discipline was not to occur before the late 1960s.

In the post-war years the mood of the outside community was much less tolerant. In the 20 years or so after 1945 the escape rate progressively worsened. The prison authorities could point out with some justification that if it was hoped to reform criminals by the experience of imprisonment, the reintroduction of a general custodial priority would undermine this objective. However, there was understandable public concern at the escape of some prisoners regarded as dangerous, and some escapes from Broadmoor Hospital, although administratively not part of the prison system, helped to harden attitudes on the question of prison security. Inevitably, this kind of problem made good copy for media reporting on imprisonment and the Prison Officers' Association's increasingly vociferous criticism of the level of security fuelled the debate.

Problems of internal control matched those of perimeter security during the post-war years. Freedom of association between prisoners had by the 1950s fostered a complex inmate sub-culture and social structure which it was difficult for the prison authorities to manage. Accounts from this period of terrorism and bullying of prisoners by other prisoners, of homosexual practices and the activities of 'barons',[46] point to some of the merits of Du Cane's regime of tight control and discipline, which did at least minimise the level of abuse as between prisoners. The difficulties of the prison officer's position in terms of role and status, to which we have already referred, were exacerbated by the progressive resort by the prison authorities to inmate 'leadership' of other prisoners, as part of a regime of reformative self-discipline (typified by the systems of 'crews' of prisoners led by 'strokes' — the rowing metaphor is telling, once again — in Wakefield and Maidstone Prisons).[47] By the 1960s many prison officers were experiencing a sense of isolation in the wider community and their sense of the fragility of their position was perhaps emphasised to them by the abolition of corporal punishment in prisons under section 65 of the 1967 Criminal Justice Act. These developments made internal control, in reality, a more significant problem than external security. By the middle of the 1960s the problem of both had in fact reached a crisis level.

It is important in this discussion to bear in mind the way in which the prison environment had changed in the 60 years or so since the Gladstone Report. Undeniably, one factor in the developing problems of discipline and security was the official allegiance to a reformative regime. But other post-war developments should not be lost sight of. The prison population had swollen from around 15,000 to over 30,000 between 1945 and the mid-1960s, by which time a programme of new prison building was only just getting under way. Other developments combined to introduce a particularly explosive catalyst into the situation. The declining use and eventual demise of capital punishment put a rather different type of life sentence prisoner into the prison system — a 'no-hoper' who would not be responsive to a system of incentives and had no real prospect of release back into the community. At the same time, and rather ironically, more skilful police work was sending a greater number of professional criminals into the prisons and these brought their own dangers, not the least of which proved to be the organisation of escapes from outside. This last phenomenon brought into sharp relief the difficulties of control and security, especially with the organised escapes of two of the notorious 'Great Train Robbers', Charles Wilson in 1964, and Ronald Biggs in 1965.

Matters came to a head in October 1966 when George Blake, who had been convicted of serious spying offences in 1961 and sentenced to a total of 42 years imprisonment, escaped from Wormwood Scrubs. This in itself was a massive blow to prison security and the Home Secretary Roy Jenkins agreed to appoint an inquiry under Lord Mountbatten to examine this and other recent escapes and to recommend improvements in security. The Mountbatten proposals[48] concentrated on the need for more effective perimeter security and suggested a fourfold classification of prisoners for security purposes, which was adopted, and a single escape-proof maximum security prison for those whose escape would be dangerous to the community or the security of the state ('Vectis', to be located on the Isle of Wight). The last proposal was not implemented, preference being given to the establishment of a number of maximum security 'dispersal' prisons, on the grounds that a concentration of such prisoners inside one prison would prove unmanageable. Mountbatten also recommended some staff restructuring, most importantly the setting up of a distinct security service, with improved technical facilities (a revival, in modern form of the civil guard, which existed between the middle of the nineteenth century and 1919 to perform perimeter security).

The Mountbatten Report may be seen as another landmark in the development of prisons in this country. While nowhere near as wide-ranging in its discussion as the Gladstone Report, (or the subsequent May Report), it produced a change of mood within the prison system. The reimposition of custodial priorities disturbed the foundations of the reformative programme and while some of the control and security difficulties of the post-war period have been resolved, this has not been without its cost. The policy of dispersal of category 'A' prisoners, coupled with the use of 'segregation units' for prisoners regarded as troublesome, as recommended by the Radzinowicz Committee in 1968,[49] has produced points of tension within the prison system. There have been riots[50] at Parkhurst (1969), Hull (1976) and Gartree (1978) and in 1979 a peaceful protest at Wormwood Scrubs was inexpertly and violently dealt with by a squad of officers especially trained to deal with riots (so-called MUFTI: Minimum Use of Force Tactical Intervention). Such events have been accompanied by a a growing mood of secrecy, suspicion and repression exemplified by the use of 'control units'[51] between 1973 and 1975 for difficult and violent prisoners. These units involved a return to periods of solitary confinement and attempts to maintain a certain level of secrecy about their use only reinforced the sense of public disquiet at their introduction, which was eventually sufficient to persuade the Home Office to discontinue their operation (their legality was challenged, unsuccessfully, before the courts[52]). This harsher penal climate has also produced a backlash of informed opinion, resulting in an immense critical literature[53] on both the concept and practice of imprisonment and stimulating a significant prisoners' rights movement, involving pressure groups such as PROP (Preservation of the Rights of Prisoners) and an increasing resort to the European Convention on Human Rights to test the legality of certain aspects of imprisonment.[54] Such developments have further affected the morale of prison officers, who continue to feel embattled and there was a notable bout of industrial action on the part of the Prison Officers' Association in the early 1980s (which had the beneficial effect of temporarily reducing the prison population). While there has undoubtedly been a return in recent years to a more repressive system of prison discipline (at least for some categories of prisoner), the situation is significantly different from 100 years ago: this is a clamping down on a prison population which is more volatile and more articulate, and which has been encouraged by certain sections of informed opinion to refute the political premise on which the prison system is based. To attempt a return to an earlier system of discipline would be to risk a polarisation of attitudes and the creation of an explosive institutional environment.

Living Conditions

The preceding discussion of accommodation, work, security and discipline will have already given some idea of the everyday experience of inmates in English prisons during this period. In a general sense, prison life has become much less physically repressive and gruelling; however, less evident but equally disturbing pressures of a psychological character, arising for instance from the operation of inmate culture, or out of the loss of official confidence in reformative objectives, have come to the fore instead. It need hardly be said that reaction to the experience of imprisonment is in any case highly personal and will largely depend on the prisoner's own sensitivity, background and circumstances of conviction. As Richard Haldane remarked about the imprisonment of Oscar Wilde: 'I . . . was haunted by the idea of what this highly sensitive man was probably suffering under ordinary prison treatment'.[55] Therefore, despite the interesting accounts which have been presented by inmates and former inmates, it is not clear how safe it would be to generalise from such statements. Nonetheless, there are some general features of prison life which, although often determined by aspects of the regime already discussed and no doubt affecting individual prisoners in different ways, deserve to be enlarged upon.

The mid-nineteenth century idea of 'hard labour, hard fare and hard bed' had some real meaning in the earlier part of the period. 'Hard bed' was understood literally in connection with the sentence of hard labour, under which the prisoner was required, until 1945, to sleep on a plank for part of his sentence. 'Hard fare' was also given careful consideration in the Victorian prisons and diet became an important component of the sentence, designed to make life less eligible inside prison but also to maintain the prisoner at the necessary level of fitness and nutrition to cope with the demanding physical life imposed by the prison system. In the earlier part of the period, diets were classified according to the different types of sentence, stage of sentence and type of prisoner. The approach is typified in the recommendations of a Home Office Departmental Committee Report on Prison Dietaries in 1899:[56] that the distinction between hard labour and non-hard labour diets should be abolished in local prisons; that Class I-IV local prison diets should be abolished or superseded by new Classes A to C diets; that there should be a uniform hospital dietary for all prisoners; that there should be two dietaries for 'ill-conducted' and 'idle' prisoners, No. 1 (bread and water) and No. 2 (porridge); that men, women and juveniles have separate diets; and that the standard of foodstuffs and preparation should be improved. This complex system of dietaries disappeared as the distinction between the different kinds of sentence became less clear. Rationing during the Second World War made set meals difficult to prepare, and if anything the standard of meals improved at this time since a ration scale was drawn up for each prisoner to match the civilian ration scale.[57] The post-war Prison Rules required the food in prisons to be 'wholesome, nutritious, well prepared and served, reasonably varied and sufficient in quantity'.[58] By this stage, it could be said that in terms of diet at least, Alexander Paterson's prescription that men did not come to prison for punishment had been given effect.

At a psychological level, another aspect of prison life has been the question of dress and appearance. Along with the convict prison came the idea that the inmates should be dressed in a uniform and readily identifiable manner. There were admittedly some practical arguments in favour of this: in particular, it was in some cases advisable for sanitary reasons, and it facilitated security, in that an escaping convict would be easily recognisable. Prison dress was also used, in the case of penal servitude, to identify prisoners in the course of the progressive stages system (see Fig. 8.1). But there were other objectives associated with the prisoner's uniform with less practical justification. It is not difficult to detect, as with other aspects of the nineteenth-century convict prisons, a significant military influence: the convict uniform, with its arrangements of arrows, stars and chevrons, is suggestive of service ranking.[59] Moreover, the placing of prisoners in uniforms served a symbolic penitential purpose, stressing to the prisoner his changed status and loss of civil rights. Haircutting emphasised further this aspect of incarceration; this was not only a matter of cleanliness, military fashion or part of the inculcation of self discipline,[60] but could also serve as a ritual of humiliation. Sir George Onesiphorus Paul had argued, in the early years of the nineteenth century, 'so far as the shaving the head is a mortification to the offender, it becomes a punishment directed to the mind, and is . . . an allowable alternative for inflicting corporal punishment . . .'.[61] From a late-twentieth century viewpoint, the cropped hair and drab clothes imposed upon the nineteenth-century prisoner appears both depersonalising and stigmatising. It has certainly given to posterity the outmoded but persistent cartoon stereotype of the prison convict.

In 1889 a Home Office Committee of Inquiry[62] noted a 'general acquiescence in the wearing of prison dress . . . doubt-

Figure 8.1: Convict Uniforms

The Distinctive Dress of Various Classes of Convicts

All the clothing up to number 5 is yellow. Reading from left to right the clothing indicates:—(1) First stage (first twelve months); (2) second stage (two years), black stripes on cuffs; (3) third stage (three years), yellow stripes on cuffs; (4) fourth stage, intermediate man, blue stripes on cuffs, chevron on cap and arms; (5) star man, blue stripes on cuffs, star on each arm and on cap; (6) grey dress worn by long-sentence men who earn 2s. 6d. a month and spend 1s. 3d. on comforts; (7) blue dress for good character; (8) black parti-coloured dress worn as punishment for striking an officer; (9) yellow parti-coloured dress, the penalty for running away; (10) canvas dress for those who destroy the ordinary clothing of their class. *Reproduced by permission of the Proprietors of Lloyd's News.*

less due to its being accepted as a necessary incident of imprisonment' but added that it could hardly be doubted that such acquiescence 'should not frequently be accompanied by a repugnance to the dress as humiliating and degrading and tending to confound those guilty of slight offences with habitual criminals'. The Committee resisted any suggestion that the prison uniform should be relaxed, except so far as to distinguish those in prison for short periods or awaiting trial. In the early years of the century, the appearance of the convicts at Dartmoor made a forceful impression on Alexander Paterson: 'their drab uniforms were plastered with broad arrows, their heads were closely shaven . . . Not even a safety razor was allowed, so that in addition to the stubble on their heads, their faces were covered with a dirty moss, representing the growth of hair that a pair of clippers would not remove.'[63] Matters began to change in the inter-war period when more emphasis was *actually* placed on developing the prisoners' self-respect. Following Ruggles-Brise's retirement, a number of changes were made in the rules governing dress — the arrows and the cropped hair were abolished and while prison dress was still characterised by a drab uniformity it was much less the case that prisoners were, in Paterson's words, 'objects of ugliness and contempt'. After 1945, the climate of opinion had changed so far that the authorities were looking for a design of prison dress which, while uniform and re-usable, would help to stimulate self-respect; and Lionel Fox is complaining in the early 1950s that perhaps 'the reaction against the "convict crop" has gone too far, and . . . the pendulum could with aesthetic advantage begin to swing the other way.'[64] But, while at the present time the rules as to prison dress are much less rigorous than at the beginning of the century, the uniform remains an essential feature of the institution, as does the ritual of beginning a prison sentence: the stripping off of the prisoner's own clothes and the regulation bath and issue of uniform and prison number. It is not necessary to labour the point that such insistence on uniformity of clothing and appearance reinforces an authoritarian structure and serves to break down individual resistance to an imposed system. Significantly, other institutions, such as the armed services and even schools, have made a similar use of uniform dress.

By its very nature imprisonment entails the isolation of the prisoner from society and it is now widely felt that the deprivation of social contacts, which is taken for granted by most people, constitutes one of the most damaging effects of incarceration. Obviously, deprivation of sexual relations, the company of family and friends and the experience of responsibility for an independent way of life is likely to be socially disruptive, although justifiable if imprisonment is viewed in a purely penal sense and objectives of reform are left to one side. While it would be true to say that in some respects conditions have improved from the prisoner's point of view, it has to be remembered that 100 years ago many inmates would have been serving sentences which were short by present day standards so that deprivation of social contact would have been less noticeable on the whole.[65] Doubtless it can be said that the prison authorities have developed a more sympathetic approach to such matters as visiting arrangements and letter writing, but practice has often lagged behind policy announcements and the official position has tended to be defensive — changes to the Prison Rules in relation to prisoners' correspondence, for instance, have only been brought about through applications under the European Convention on Human Rights.[66] More provision was made for the social readjustment of prisoners when prison welfare officers were first appointed in 1955. These were trained social workers and since 1965 have been members of the probation service. More recently, home leave and pre-release employment hostels have been available for selected longer term prisoners approaching the end of their sentence. It is possible, however, to view such developments as a corollary of more people being in prison for longer periods and as a spilling over of community welfare and aftercare developments into the prison system. When all this has been taken into account, it remains true that the basic fact of social dislocation has been a dominant feature of imprisonment throughout the period. Perhaps one of the most significant developments for a large number of prisoners within the last 20 years has been one which has altered not so much the conditions of imprisonment but the prospects of release: the provision of parole,[67] or early release on licence, brought into force in 1968. This has become an important feature of contemporary imprisonment with its own institutional structure, centred on the Parole Board, which recommends cases for early release to the Home Office. But, once again, this is a development which has largely been a reaction to overpopulation in the prisons and longer sentences rather than a genuine attempt to modify the fundamental nature of imprisonment.

Education

For so long as the modern prison has been regarded as a kind of training institution, some provision of education has been regarded, in theory at least, as an important component of the regime. Prior to the Gladstone Report, education of prisoners was viewed as a privilege and Du Cane argued[68] that 'care ought to be taken that the education, whether literary or technical, should be carried out without sacrificing the great moral and disciplinary advantages of the separation of prisoners'. The rigidly applied system of separation was inevitably an impediment to effective education through class instruction. The Gladstone Committee noted that the existing rule, under which only prisoners who were serving a sentence of over four months received any teaching, excluded the large majority of prisoners from any education. A system of teaching in classes for all prisoners likely to benefit from it was therefore urged by the committee (paragraph 74) and education facilities were gradually developed in the following years. Another of the leaps forward after Ruggles-Brise's retirement was the introduction in 1922 of voluntary teachers from outside and the appointment of Educational Advisers to prison governors. Since 1945 teaching has been carried out by LEA teachers, usually on a part-time basis in evening classes.[69]

There have been, and remain, inherent difficulties in providing a system of education in a prison institution. In this context, a distinction has to be drawn between the institutions for younger offenders (discussed in the following chapter), which have been developed in a tradition beginning with the nineteenth-century reformatory and industrial schools, and those for adult offenders. In the case of the latter, there have been a number of basic problems: the particular difficulties involved in teaching adults, the need to fit any teaching into a basic routine of prison labour and the problems posed by a relatively high rate of illiteracy among those received into the prison system.[70] Obviously, longer-term prisoners are better placed to take the benefit of educational courses: one of the touching ironies of recent years was the transformation of John McVicar from 'Public Enemy No. 1' to sociology graduate and, after his release, pundit on penal affairs.[71]

Notes

1. A useful contemporary account is provided by Sir Edmund Du Cane, *The Punishment and Prevention of Crime* (Macmillan, London, 1885), p. 156 et seq.

2. Ibid., p. 157.

3. For details, see Du Cane, *Punishment and Prevention of Crime*, pp. 162-4.

4. *The Man They Could Not Hang: The Life Story of John Lee* (Arthur Pearson, London, 1908), p. 69.

5. *Punishment and Prevention of Crime*, pp. 191-2.

6. *Paterson on Prisons*, ed. S.K. Ruck (Frederick Muller, London, 1951), p. 88.

7. Sir Lionel Fox, 'The Criminal Justice Act and Prison Administration' in L. Radzinowicz and J.W.L. Turner (eds.), *Journal of Criminal Science Symposium on the Criminal Justice Act 1948* (1950), pp. 8-9.

8. *Punishment and Prevention of Crime*, p. 60.

9. See the discussion by Fox, *The English Prison and Borstal Systems* (Routledge & Kegan Paul, London, 1952), p. 60.

10. For a fuller account of Stead's imprisonment, see John Camp, *Holloway Prison* (David & Charles, Newton Abbot, 1974), pp. 47-53.

11. Sir Rupert Cross discusses this point in *Punishment, Prison and the Public* (Stevens, London, 1971), p. 108.

12. For instance, by Alexander Paterson: see *Paterson on Prisons*, pp. 88-9.

13. See Rupert Cross, *The English Sentencing System* (Butterworth, London, 1st ed. 1971), p. 34.

14. (1931 – 32) 23 Crim. App. Reports 208.

15. *Punishment, Prison and the Public*, p. 154.

16. For a discussion of the justification for and the aims of punishment, see H.L.A. Hart, *Punishment and Responsibility* (Oxford University Press, 1968), Ch. 1; Alf Ross, *On Guilt, Responsibility and Punishment* (Stevens, London, 1975), Ch. 3.

17. Committee of Inquiry into the United Kingdom Prison Services (May Committee), 1979, Cmnd. 7673, para 4.26.

18. For a useful study of working-class resistance to certain kinds of law and institutional treatment, see Stephen Humphries, *Hooligans or Rebels?* (Basil Blackwell, Oxford, 1981).

19. See Max Grünhut, *Penal Reform* (Oxford University Press, 1948), p. 91.

20. See Roger Hood, *Borstal Reassessed* (Heinemann, London, 1965), pp. 7-13.

21. In *The Punishment and Prevention of Crime*, p. 4.

22. *Juvenile Offenders* (T. Fisher Unwin, London, 1896), pp. 38-9.

23. 'Discussion of the Reverend W.D. Morrison's paper', *Journal of the Royal Statistical Society*, 60, pp. 25-6. At a more popular level, however, there was concern about law and order: see Geoffrey Pearson, *Hooligan: A History of Respectable Fears*, (Macmillan, London, 1983), Chs. 4, 5.

24. Report of the Inter-Departmental Committee on Physical Deterioration, 1904, Cd. 2175.

25. Quoted in the Gladstone Committee's Report at para 25. The Committee's optimism finds support in other contexts: Robert Baden-Powell, writing in *National Defence*, Vol. 4, August 1910, p. 440, said that 'hooligans . . . are really the fellows of character if you can turn them in the right way. . .'.

26. Annual Report of the Prison Commissioners for 1921.

27. *I was in Prison* (T. Fisher Unwin, London, 1898), p. 103.

28. Raphael Samuel, *East End Underworld: Chapters in the Life of Arthur Harding* (Routledge & Kegan Paul, London, 1981), Ch. 13.

29. At para. 6.55.

30. See Ursula Henriques, 'The Rise and Decline of the Separate System of Prison Discipline', *Past and Present* (1972), 61.

31. See A.W. Peterson, 'The Prison Building Programme' (1960 - 61), 1 B. J. Crim. 307.

32. In evidence to the Departmental Committee: Captain Shuyler, in answer to Question 3132; Colonel Garcia, in answer to Question 6502.

33. See Ursula Henriques, *Before the Welfare State* (Longmans, London, 1979), p. 163.

34. See Fox, *The English Prison and Borstal Systems*, pp. 41 and 45; Grünhut, *Penal Reform*, pp. 83-5.

35. *The Punishment and Prevention of Crime*, p. 170.

36. Samuel, *East End Underworld*, p. 163.

37. Ibid., p. 160.

38. Annual Report of the Prison Commissioners for 1922.

39. Report of the Departmental Committee on the Employment of Prisoners, 1933, Part 1, p. 64, Cmd. 4462.

40. See the discussion in Fox, *English Prison and Borstal Systems*, p. 180 et seq.

41. See J.E. Thomas, *The English Prison Officer since 1850* (Routledge & Kegan Paul, London, 1972), p. 80.

42. Ibid., pp. 132-3.

43. Ibid., p. 159 et seq.

44. Report on the Circumstances Connected with the Recent Disorder at Dartmoor Convict Prison, 1932, Cmd. 4010.

45. *The English Prison Officer*, p. 159.

46. See, for instance, Hugh J. Klare, *Anatomy of Prison* (Hutchinson, London, 1960), pp. 31-3.

47. See Fox, *English Prison and Borstal Systems*, pp. 151-2.

48. Report of the Inquiry into Prison Escapes and Security (1966), Cmnd. 3175.

49. *The Regime for Long Term Prisoners in Conditions of Maximum Security*, Report by the Advisory Council on the Penal System, 1968.

50. On riots generally, see J.E. Thomas and R. Pooley, *The Exploding Prison* (Junction Books, London, 1980), Ch. 1; Mick Ryan, *The Politics of Penal Reform* (Longmans, London, 1983), pp. 62-5.

51. See Ryan, *Politics of Penal Reform*, pp. 48-9. Only one unit was in fact set up, at Wakefield Prison.

52. *Williams* v *Home Office* (No. 2), (1981), 1 All E. R. 1211.

53. For instance: Louis Blom-Cooper (ed.), *Progress in Penal Reform* (Oxford University Press, 1974); Sean McConville (ed.), *The Use of Imprisonment* (Routledge & Kegan Paul, London, 1975); J.E. Thomas and R. Pooley, *The Exploding Prison*; Martin Wright, *Making Good* (Burnett Books, London, 1982); Mike Fitzgerald and Joe Sim, *British Prisons*, 2nd ed. (Basil Blackwell, Oxford, 1982); Stan Cohen and Laurie Taylor, *Prison Secrets* (NCCL, London, 1976).

54. Knechtl v U. K., 1970 *Yearbook of the ECHR* 730; Golder v U. K., Series A, Judgements and Decisions, Vol. 18, 21.2.1975; Silver v U. K., Vol. 4 (1983), *Human Rights Law Journal*, No. 2, p. 252; Campbell and Fell v U. K. (1983), 5 *European Human Rights Report* 207.

55. Richard Burdon Haldane, *An Autobiography* (Hodder & Stoughton, London, 1929), p. 177. Records have recently been made available concerning the experience and condition of Oscar Wilde in prison: *Guardian*, 24.Sept. 1984, p. 2.

56. C. 9166. I.U.P. British Parliamentary Papers, Crime and Punishment, Prisons, 20, 289.

57. See Fox, *English Prison and Borstal Systems*, p. 232.

58. 1949 Rules; c.f. Rule 21 of the 1964 Rules (1964 Statutory Instruments, 388).

59. See Michael Ignatieff, *A Just Measure of Pain* (Macmillan, London, 1978), at pp. 190-1 on the origins of the militarisation of prison discipline.

60. C.f. measures taken by Elizabeth Fry for women prisoners: see Ignatieff, *Just Measure of Pain*, p. 144.

61. Parliamentary Papers, 1810-11, 111, p. 44; Ignatieff, *Just Measure of Pain*, p. 101.

62. Committee Report on the Rules concerning the Wearing of Prison Dress, 1889, C. 5759. I.U.P. British Parliamentary Papers, Crime and Punishments, Prisons, 18, 401, at p. 406.

63. *Paterson on Prisons*, p. 11.

64. Fox, *English Prison and Borstal Systems*, p. 228.

65. For the experience of a long-term prisoner, on the other hand, see the account given by John Lee, *The Man They Could Not Hang*, Ch. 22.

66. Decisions in the cases of *Golder* and *Silver*, above, n. 59.

67. On the introduction of parole and its effects, see: *Parole in England and Wales*, H.O. Research Study No. 38 (HMSO, London, 1977); *Parole: Its Implications for the Criminal Justice and Penal Systems*, ed. D.A. Thomas (University of Cambridge, 1974).

68. *The Punishment and Prevention of Crime*, p. 81.

69. See generally, Fox, *English Prison and Borstal Systems*, p. 208 et seq.

70. See *Prisons and the Prisoner* (HMSO, London, 1977), p. 36.

71. John McVicar, *McVicar by Himself* (Arrow Books, London, 1979). McVicar spent eight years in prison, during which time he studied for a degree in sociology. Since his release in 1978, he has assumed the role of media critic of penal policy, been the subject of a feature film and has most recently been Professor Laurie Taylor's guide to criminal haunts: see Taylor's book, *In the Underworld* (Basil Blackwell, Oxford, 1984).

9

THE SOCIAL FUNCTIONS OF IMPRISONMENT

So far we have presented the development of imprisonment in this country since the later part of the nineteenth century by concentrating on its main form, the institution for adult offenders. In this form, imprisonment has at various times been a measure of custody not only for convicted offenders but also for other categories of person, such as those awaiting trial ('remand' prisoners) and the so-called 'civil' prisoners, such as fine and maintenance defaulters. These distinct classes of prisoner have, for obvious reasons and in so far as it has been practically possible, been subjected to a different regime from that applied to convicted offenders. At the same time, among the convicted prisoners have been groups who may not be regarded as conventional criminals but who have nonetheless for different reasons come within the reach of the criminal law: most obviously, some mentally disordered, habitually drunk and drug addicted persons, and a loose category of 'political' offenders. To a lesser extent, these types of prisoner have been distinguished for purposes of deciding upon an appropriate regime within prison, and there have been occasional attempts to divert some of them to more suitable institutions which, although distinct from the prison system, have possessed some of the repressive features of custody and control characteristic of imprisonment. Within the prison system itself, there has also, since 1895, been a tendency to separate those offenders whose criminal behaviour is persistent and who show themselves to be resistant to a wide range of penal and corrective measures — the habitual offender or 'recidivist' — in an attempt to apply to them a more effective corrective regime. Finally, there is an important group of delinquents who have been increasingly diverted away from the main prison system since the middle of the nineteenth century: the younger offender, under the age of 21. For this group there has been developed an important range of custodial institutions, some of which have been administratively related to the prison system.

236

To appreciate the wider social context of imprisonment over this period, it is necessary to examine the role of the prison as a receptacle for such different categories of the socially offensive or problematical, or in some cases the fact that imprisonment has been passed over in favour of another institution. What we have already seen of the central regime within the prison system first of all should help towards a clearer perception of more specialised institutional regimes both within and outside prisons. The main prison regime has been a kind of barometer of society's response to problems of crime and delinquency and it may be seen that the main shifts in objectives for imprisonment itself have either influenced or been paralleled in the development of these related institutions.

Prison Regimes for Habitual Offenders

Discussions of the problem of recidivism often begin with the seminal statements on the subject by the Gladstone Committee, but there had already been a number of calls in literature during the second half of the nineteenth century for a particular response to the problem. The anonymous author of 'Five Years Penal Servitude by One Who Has Endured It' (1887)[1] had argued in favour of greater severity in dealing with habitual and 'professional' criminals (the author was a first offender convicted of fraud). A few years later, Thomas Barwick Lloyd Baker, a Gloucestershire magistrate whose arguments in favour of a more reformative prison regime anticipated the Gladstone Report, also advocated a more savage regime for prisoners who were resistant to reform, by means of cumulative sentences for repeated offences and a special regime within prison.[2]

So the Gladstone Committee came to argue about recidivists (in paragraph 85): 'To punish them for the particular offence in which they are detected is almost useless; witnesses were almost unanimous in approving of some kind of cumulative sentence; the real offence is the wilful persistence in the deliberately acquired habit of crime.' The kind of offender being referred to here is the type classified at that time as the 'professional' criminal: fit, competent, often highly skilled and determined to make a good living from a life of crime. A distinction was drawn between this type and the 'habitual offender', who fell into a criminal way of life on account of environment, physical disability or mental deficiency rather than acting on a deliberate intention to plunder society. When in 1908 the Prevention of Crime Act was passed, it was made clear by Herbert Gladstone, by then Home Secretary, that the new measure of preventive detention under section 10 of that Act was intended to deal with the 'professional' criminal. The Act provided that, if someone was convicted on indictment of a crime (defined as any felony, and a few other specified offences) and he admitted to being or was found by a jury to be an 'habitual criminal', and the court decided upon a sentence of penal servitude, then it could *in addition* impose a period of detention of between five and ten years. The definition of habitual criminal (an unfortunately ambiguous term, as we shall see) was both factual and impressionistic: an offender with at least three convictions for a crime since the age of 16, and who was persistently leading a criminal or dishonest life. The court, in order to pass the sentence, also had to be satisfied that it would be necessary for the protection of the public.

It was hoped that the combination of penal servitude and preventive detention would be deterrent, reformative and protective. It failed in most of these aims. The regime of the detention was intended to be less rigorous than that of imprisonment:[3] a special prison was built at Camp Hill on the Isle of Wight and the 'detainees' had privileges such as association at meals and in the evening, were allowed to smoke and read newspapers and could even earn pocket money (wages for work were not generally paid until the late 1930s). There were log cabins outside the prison — so-called 'parole lines' — an early kind of pre-release hostel, and release on licence was possible. Despite hopeful statements in the Prison Commissioners' Annual Reports, it had become clear by 1932 when a Home Office Committee on persistent offenders reported,[4] that the measure was having little effect. Most of the detainees were reconvicted not long after being released. Moreover, increasingly little use was being made of the sentence (an annual average of 36 sentences in the previous ten years). This was considered at the time to be a reflection of the declining resort to penal servitude itself, but Cross argues[5] that it also reflected the distaste of the police, the DPP and the courts for a double-track system, which offended against widely held notions of proportionality in justice. The sentence also failed to protect the public in any real sense, not only because of the small numbers actually detained, but on account of the fact, reported by the 1932 Committee, that most of those held in detention were 'of the type whose previous convictions testify as much to their clumsiness as to their persistence in crime'[6] — that is to say the habitual rather than the professional criminal. While Herbert Gladstone may have been clear about the intention behind section 10, it seems that subsequently sentencers found it hard to give effect to this purpose.

The sentence of preventive detention was marked down for replacement in the 1938 Criminal Justice Bill, but its actual abolition had to await the post-war criminal justice legislation of 1948. Section 21 of the 1948 Act introduced a 'single-track' sentence of preventive detention for offenders over the age of 30 with a substantial penal record; a sentence of between five and fourteen years, if this was 'expedient for the protection of the public'. This was a staged sentence, reminiscent of penal servitude, which had just been abolished: an initial stage of between nine months and two years in a local prison, a second stage in which exceptional privileges (such as more common room association) could be earned, and finally a period in a prison hostel with day release. Once again, practice failed to live up to the theory and there is a sense of history repeating itself in 1963 when the Advisory Council on the Treatment of Offenders published a report[7] on the operation of preventive detention. Very few sentences were being passed; of those given the sentence, only a minority were graduating to the final stage in a hostel; and once again the sentence was being used to deal with a significant number of petty recidivists.

These attempts at dealing with the problem of recidivism were, to put it mildly, discouraging. A kind of junior preventive detention for the 21 to 30 years age group, a sentence of between two and four years known as corrective training, was also introduced in the 1948 Act. This did not involve a different regime but was simply an extended term intended to provide for more effective prison training. Like preventive detention, it proved to have little corrective effect and provides another instance of judicial misapprehension as to the nature of the regime — in 1962 the Lord Chief Justice issued a practice note[8] to make it clear that the main object of the sentence was not to enable the 'trainee' to learn a trade.

Both preventive detention and corrective training were abolished under the Criminal Justice Act of 1967, which instead provided for an 'extended term' of imprisonment, in cases where the need for public protection was felt to necessitate a longer than normal sentence of imprisonment. The qualifications for this sentence are complicated[9] and it has been little used by the courts, with justification. Cross has summed up these developments as 'the sad history of twentieth century English attempts to cope with recidivism'.[10] These special regimes were a characteristic product of a period dominated by executive penal policy and demonstrate how the agents' reformist assumptions failed to square with the concern for justice and proportionality which dominated the work of the judicial sentencer. The failure of preventive detention also produced an unintended self-parody of the prison as a reforming institution and doubtless contributed a good deal to the demise of the reformist ideology.

Institutions for Young Offenders[11]

As we have already noted, during the course of the nineteenth century there was a general movement towards greater protection of children and a concomitant trend to deal separately with the problem of juvenile delinquency. Thus the development of penal and reformative institutions for young offenders may be seen in the wider context of a paternalistic movement to curtail the exploitation and employment of children and make greater provision for their education and welfare.

From the middle of the nineteenth century through to the 1980s there has been a gradual limitation on the use of imprisonment itself for children and young offenders. There was an early move to separate young offenders within the prison system in 1838 when the old military hospital at Parkhurst on the Isle of Wight was used for persons under 18 sentenced to transportation, to subject them for a few years to a more reformatory regime. In the words of the Gladstone Committee, this institution 'died a natural death' when the reformatory schools were established in the 1850s. The introduction over the next 100 years of reformatory, industrial and approved schools, the borstal and detention centres was accompanied by increasing restrictions on the powers of the courts to send juvenile offenders to prison. Under the Children Act of 1908, children (under 14 years) could not be sentenced to prison and 'young persons' (14 to 16 years, raised to 17 years in 1933) could not be sentenced to penal servitude, nor to imprisonment unless certified to be 'unruly' or 'depraved'. Subsequently, the Criminal Justice Act in 1948 contemplated the removal of imprisonment for juveniles under the age of 15 and the use of alternative methods as far as possible for those between 15 and 21 (the same legislation introduced the attendance and detention centres for this purpose and envisaged an increased use of probation hostels and homes). A number of more complex restrictions on the sentencing of younger offenders were introduced by the Criminal Justice Act of 1961 and the Children and Young Persons Act of 1969 (certainly felt by some judges to complicate their sentencing task) until, under the 1982 Criminal Justice Act, it has been laid down that, except for purposes of remand for trial or sentence, 'no court shall pass a sentence of imprisonment on a person under 21 years of age or commit such a person to prison for any reason' (s.1(1)). So, the position has finally been reached where imprisonment may not be used as a penal measure for those under the age of 21.

Schools and Homes for Young Offenders

The earliest institutional developments in relation to younger offenders were characteristically the result of rather haphazard private enterprise and enthusiasm, led in this field by the pioneering work of such people as Mary Carpenter, Sidney Turner and Matthew Davenport Hill.[12] In 1849 the Philanthropic Society, whose object was to help criminal and destitute children, founded a school at Redhill in Surrey; in 1851 Carpenter and Hill convened a national conference which called for the establishment, with state assistance, of free day schools, day industrial schools and reformatory schools; and in 1853 a Select Committee on Criminal and Destitute Children recommended the setting up of reformatory schools, with a certain amount of state assistance, and that courts should be able to commit to such schools instead of sending children to prison. As a result, the Youthful Offenders Act of 1854 set up reformatory schools to which children under 16 could be sent following a prison sentence, for a period of between two and five years. These schools were linked to the prison system in that state aid was conditional upon inspection and certification by one of the Prison Inspectors. Legislation of 1857 established a similar system of industrial schools, although these were, until 1860, linked to the education system, before being brought within the umbrella of Home Office control. The original provision was that, following a conviction for vagrancy, children between the ages of 7 and 14 could be committed to such a school and kept there until the age of 15; and, initially at least, they had a distinctly more educational bias as compared with the reformative schools.

These schools were essentially private institutions, supported by state funds and supervised through Home Office inspection. Because there was no direct central control, there were recurrent problems in connection with funding and the standard of education. General formulation of policy for the schools was achieved in fits and starts and was characterised by inconclusive debates and comittee reports divided on basic questions of regime and management. After considerable argument, the period of imprisonment prior to reformatory school was abolished in 1899 and the general trend, in so far as it can be identified, was to a less regimented school environment, emphasising the role of education rather than discipline. Indeed, by 1880 the number of industrial schools exceeded that of reformatory schools by a proportion of three to one, and this remained the position 40 years later; but by 1922 the total population of the schools had fallen to 10,000, compared to a peak population of 19,000 in 1915. During this period the schools were considered to be relatively successful in diverting children from a delinquent way of life: it seems that at least two-thirds of the children sent to the schools could reasonably be claimed as 'successes' in this sense and the Gladstone Committee were able to assert (paragraph 29) that 'numbers of lads and girls have been permanently rescued by the industrial and reformatory schools'.

By the beginning of the 1930s the industrial school had developed into a forerunner of what was to evolve as the care order after 1969. Under the Children Act of 1908 a child under the age of 14 could be sent to an industrial school on a number of grounds, not only as was originally the case, after a conviction for vagrancy. These grounds included the situations where a child was found to be begging, wandering or destitute, where the child was in the care of parents with criminal or drunken habits, if the child was the daughter of a man convicted of sexual assault on her, if the child was frequenting the company of thieves or prostitutes, where a child was failing to attend school or was persistently misbehaving while in a workhouse, or finally if a child was simply beyond control. In more modern terminology, this described situations where the child was in need of care and supervision. The reformatory schools, on the other hand, had come to cater for the more clearly delinquent children. Under the legislation of 1908, a child between the ages of 12 and 16 could be committed to one of these schools if convicted of an offence punishable with imprisonment in the case of an adult.

The reformatory and industrial schools had a considerable impact in their time. We have already seen how the Gladstone Committee were concerned to deal with the 'headsprings of recidivism' by tackling the problem of the young offender and this philosophy licensed a determined assault on juvenile misbehaviour during the later years of the nineteenth century and the first decades of the twentieth century. Because of the absence of direct central control, the standard of training was variable and there was opportunity for abusive treatment of inmates — something which was more unlikely in the rigidly structured and supervised prison regime — and this is well documented in Humphries' study.[13] As in the schools system generally, there was a paternalistic justification for both the content of the training and the methods used and these schools provide a striking early illustration of a dictatorial 'welfare' approach. They were undoubtedly concerned with the inculcation of a respect for authority and the suppression of rebellious natures and were sometimes, though not always, effective in such aims (see Humphries).[14]

The schools were reorganised under the Children and Young Persons Act of 1932, following recommendations made by a Departmental Committee Report on Young Offenders in 1927,[15] as 'Schools approved by the Secretary of State'. During the 1930s the approved school population was made up largely of offenders: the 'deprived' as opposed to the 'delinquent' child was gradually catered for more by community-based welfare and education programmes and in particular by the developing probation service. The approved schools continued until the end of the 1960s as the general custodial institution for offenders between the ages of 10 and 17, or, more loosely, 'children in trouble', so as to include categories such as school truants and refractory children in the care of local authorities (after these had taken over the responsibilities of the poor law authorities). A majority of the schools were administered by voluntary agencies, and some by local authorities; but, as before 1932, ultimate responsibility lay with the Home Office, acting through an inspectorate. The regime in these schools was characterised by variety: generally there was a system of both formal and informal education, but the training themes ranged between those of the naval college and those of an agricultural camp. From 1943 a few of the schools were developed as 'classifying' schools — centres to which the children would be sent by the courts for allocation to an appropriate regime of training.

Alongside the approved schools there existed during this period, institutions known as remand homes. These doubled as remand centres for juvenile offenders, replacing the 'places of detention' set up for that purpose under the Children Act in 1908 (see below), and as a form of penal institution to which young offenders should be sent instead of being sentenced to imprisonment. The maximum period of detention for this purpose was one month.

The population of the approved schools went through two periods of steady increase, on either side of a fall in population in the 1950s, contrasting with the rising prison population of that period (over 8,000 in 1938; rising to a peak of over 11,000 in 1954; a steady decline to between six and seven thousand in 1956; followed by a rise to over 8,000 again in the 1960s). The nature of this population, however, seems to have altered during this period. In 1967 a statement from the Children's Department of the Home Office reported:[16]

> It is generally agreed . . . that the schools are now receiving an increasing proportion of boys and girls who are more highly disturbed, and less responsive to therapy, than were the most difficult children received 20, or even 10, years ago.

At the same time, in the late 1950s and during the 1960s, there was publicly expressed concern about the behaviour of staff and certain aspects of the regime in some of the schools. Two major inquiries, into Carlton School in 1959 and Court Lees School in 1967, revealed that the system of management and Home Office supervision was insufficient to prevent outbreaks of brutal treatment. This despondent picture was completed by a disappointing reconviction rate for pupils from approved schools during the 1960s. On average 63 per cent of those leaving in the period 1963-7 were reconvicted within three years of release. It may be that young people were on the whole less responsive to the training methods used, than had previously been the case. At any rate, there was, as in the case of the prison system, a loss of confidence in the reformative potential of the institutions.

In 1969 the Children and Young Persons legislation brought about a major reorganisation of the system. The residential training system of the approved schools and the system of remand homes was brought within the ambit of the new care order and responsibility for placement in such an institution was given to the local authorities' social services departments. The term 'approved school' disappeared, its successor being the kind of 'community home' with 24 hours a day residence and educational facilities (the CHE). The subsequent history of the CHE has been far from happy. Encouraged by the spirit of the 1969 legislation to become 'good parents' to the children placed with them, the community homes have displayed an increasing unwillingness to cater for the more obviously delinquent children, who have therefore tended to find themselves shunted into the borstal and detention centre systems which were more obviously penal in character. At the same time, local authorities have been, in the view of many commentators, over-ready to order placement at a community home at too early a stage of a young delinquent's career.[17] The net result has been a greater incarceration of children in trouble, involving an increase in the intake of borstal and detention centres as well. In the meantime, the community homes have suffered from local authority economic stringency and increasingly from an uncertain sense of their position within the overall system. In 1981 the National Union of Teachers argued:[18] 'We strongly oppose regarding CHEs as penal establishments, to take pupils who have committed offences, as opposed to pupils who are exhibiting "disturbed behaviour" or who are "at risk" in their local environment.' Existing as they do in an uncertain borderland between child care and the penal system, these institutions are now finding themselves particularly vulnerable in the recent climate of disillusionment with reformative techniques.

The Borstal System[19]

The Gladstone Committee had shown a particular interest in the age group 16 to 21, referred to quite usefully in present-day terminology as the 'young adult offender'. In the late nineteenth century this group was still catered for by the main prison system and, according to Du Cane's statistics, there were 2,236 persons between 16 and 20 years of age in the prison system in March 1884.[20] The Committee, referring to the 'headsprings of recidivism', stated that 'the most fatal years are 17, 18 and 19' and 'a most determined effort must be made to lay hold of these incipient criminals and to prevent them by strong restraint and rational treatment from recruiting the habitual class' (paragraph 29). In place of imprisonment for offenders of this age group, the Committee recommended the setting up of a penal reformatory, a half-way house between the prison and the reformatory school to be set in a rural location and to have a penal character but also a staff 'capable of giving a sound education, training the inmates in various kinds of industrial work, and qualified generally to exercise the best and healthiest kind of moral influence' (paragraph 84). This idea is at the heart of penological optimism — it embodies the idea that the young person is potentially a good citizen and that, by means of an appropriate institutional regime, any downsliding into criminal life can be successfully checked.

Ruggles-Brise was keen to follow up this idea and had been impressed by some of what he had seen in the State Reformatories for young men in New York and Massachusetts.[21] In 1901 an experimental reformatory was established in part of the then largely empty convict prison at Borstal, near Rochester in Kent. To emphasise the distinctive nature of the regime and to avoid confusing terminology such as 'Juvenile-Adult', the name Borstal was adopted for the new system. The early years of experimentation were sufficiently encouraging in their results to allow the system to be set up nationally under the Prevention of Crime Act in 1908. In its early form, the sentence of borstal training was an indeterminate sentence of between two and three years, with a year under supervision following release. In Ruggles-Brise's words the borstals were intended for 'young hooligans well advanced in crime' (such as the young Arthur Harding who was one of the first trainees at Borstal).[22] The original borstals were carved from existing institutions: two convict prisons were converted (Borstal and Portland), Feltham Borstal had been a local authority industrial school and a female borstal was established in the former State Inebriate Reformatory inside the women's prison at Aylesbury.

It was during the inter-war period that the borstal system experienced its apotheosis, under the lead of Paterson who emphasised a system of self-discipline as opposed to penal discipline and organised the borstal along the lines of a public school, with a 'house' system. The regime developed at that stage smacked very much of the boy scout ethos:[23] outdoor pursuits and summer camps and a physically invigorating environment, away from the criminal contamination in urban cities, which would inculcate self-respect and self-reliance. The inmates were referred to as 'lads' and the officers no longer wore uniforms. This whole movement was epitomised by the famous march in 1930 by a group of borstal trainees from Feltham to Lowdham Grange in Nottinghamshire where they camped on the hillside and built their own open borstal. Part of the way on the march they were accompanied by Paterson and also by Sir Harold Scott, the Chairman of the Commissioners. There is little else which provides such striking evidence of the faith in reform as a penal objective, which dominated policy so much in the mid-century years.

By the end of the 1930s the borstal system had achieved a real prestige and its supporters could point to encouraging reconviction figures. After 1945, however, this reputation was gradually chipped away until the sentence was eventually replaced, under the Criminal Justice Act of 1982, by the youth custody order, which is little more than a general longer-term custodial measure for offenders under the age of 21. A number of explanations may be put forward for the demise of the borstal concept. Its earlier success bred later difficulties: the 1948 Criminal Justice Act contemplated a wider use of the borstal sentence, in the hope that this would remove the need to imprison young offenders for longer terms. As a result a greater number of offenders less suited to the borstal regime were sentenced to borstal training and not surprisingly the success rates were much less impressive in the 1950s and 1960s as compared to the pre-war years. In addition, rising crime rates in the late 1950s tended to harden public opinion in favour of a more disciplinary regime, such as had been introduced in 1948 with the idea of the detention centre. More sophisticated research techniques were being developed during this period and the Mannheim-Wilkins prediction study[24] which investigated the effectiveness of borstal training and was published in 1955, suggested that long-term training regimes were no more likely to be successful than shorter terms. Section 11 of the 1961 Criminal Justice Act then reduced the minimum and maximum of the term of borstal training to six months and two years, respectively. But, more generally, as already suggested, it may be doubted whether the young people of the 1950s and 1960s were as responsive as the previous generation to the rather paternalistic methods employed by Paterson and his followers. Many of the values promoted by the system of training in borstal were no longer taken so seriously, in the same way that the spirit embodied in the boy scout movement had lost much of its appeal by that time. In order not to become outdated, the borstals had to shed some of their earlier ethos and in the process became less easily distinguishable from imprisonment.

Indeed, the conditions and regime in the borstals, especially in the closed institutions, eventually came to differ little from those inside prison. Significantly, a new purpose-built prison at Stoke Heath near Market Drayton was able to be quickly taken over and used as a borstal during the early 1960s. It had been accepted that there would still be a residual category of more serious and difficult offenders under the age of 21 who would be suitable neither for borstal nor the detention centre regime and would have to go to prison. From the early 1950s efforts had been made to separate 'young prisoners', as they were called, within the main prison system and special 'Young Prisoners' Centres' were set up at Wakefield, Lewes and Stafford Prisons. It was a sign of the times that it was these centres which began to attract public approval. In the House of Lords debates on the Criminal Justice Bill in 1961, Lord Denning remarked: 'I have looked at a centre for young persons under 21, with their strict regime. It is a very fine thing for bringing them back to sanity; and that, in effect, will be the general system of borstal training.'[25]

So the prison and borstal regimes drew closer together and by the late 1970s a borstal such as that for girls at Bullwood Hall in Essex was in a state of crisis comparable with that in some of the prisons.[26] And it is notable that the new youth custody centres have shaken off some of the former borstal trappings; symbolically, there has been a reversion to staff uniforms.

Detention Centres

One of the earliest indications of a retreat in post-war years from the policy of reform was the introduction, in section 18 of the 1948 Criminal Justice Act, of the detention centre. This institution provided a shorter term of custody for male offenders between the ages of 14 and 21, who were not considered to be suitable cases for either borstal or a prison sentence. The regime in the detention centres was to be 'firm and brisk' with an emphasis on discipline. As we have seen, this did reflect the trend of wider opinion in the late 1950s,and although the Children and Young Persons Act in 1969 contemplated the phasing out of these centres for offenders under the age of 17, events and opinion during the 1970s ensured their survival and even a growing official favour. In the early 1980s the regime at two of the centres, at New Hall and Send, was made ostensibly tougher still to accommodate a vociferous law and order lobby within the Conservative Party.

Both the detention centre and borstal populations increased significantly during the 1970s (the total in both types of institution rising from just over 3,000 in 1969 to over 10,000 ten years later) and since 1982 the detention centre has assumed the role of the general short-term regime for young offenders (between 21 days and four months). It is difficult to resist the conclusion that the borstal and detention centre have eventually evolved as institutions for longer and shorter terms of something similar to imprisonment for the younger offender and that the wheel has turned full circle since the Gladstone Report.

Mentally Disordered Offenders

Perhaps because they constitute a minority of offenders, albeit a significant minority, there has been much less of a history of specific custodial provision for mentally disordered offenders than has been the case with either the habitual criminal or the juvenile offender. Part of the explanation lies in the failure of the substantive criminal law to develop defences to criminal charges based on the fact of mental disorder at the time of the offence, which might otherwise have directed such offenders to a non-penal disposal. The conservative attitude of much of the legal profession, but especially the judiciary, helped to delay any substantial provision for offenders who were mentally disturbed until the introduction of the important Mental Health Act of 1959.

There had been a growth in public awareness of the social problems posed by the mentally disordered since the late eighteenth century, when a number of hospitals for the insane were founded and the gradual establishment of a system of county asylums got under way.[27] While it was possible for those accused of offences to be found unfit to plead and so be committed to an asylum, or even, after 1840, for convicted prisoners to be transferred to an asylum by order of the Home Secretary, there was from the middle of the nineteenth century a significant category of offenders who, even though mentally disturbed, were convicted and sentenced to imprisonment but were not so badly disordered while in prison to warrant transfer to an asylum. Between 1843 and 1956 the only criminal defence based on grounds of mental disorder was contained in the narrowly conceived M'Naghten Rules, which required a lack of knowledge which was in practice difficult to prove even in cases of severe disorder, such as schizophrenia.[28] In any case, a successful plea under the M'Naghten Rules resulted in compulsory and indeterminate hospital confinement and for that reason the defence was rarely attractive to defendants: mainly in cases where the charge was murder and there was a possibility of execution if convicted. Even the wider defence of diminished responsibility, introduced in section 2 of the Homicide Act of 1956, did not affect the position of many offenders, since it was restricted to those charged with murder and operated only to reduce liability to manslaughter.

The resulting situation posed both moral and practical questions. In the first place, was it morally tolerable for a person to be convicted and perhaps be confined in prison if his responsibility for the criminal act could be put in doubt on account of a condition of mental disorder? This was, and still is, essentially a dilemma for the substantive system of criminal law with its narrowly drawn defences in connection with mental disorder. Secondly, in so far as mentally disordered persons were being sentenced to imprisonment, this raised in many cases questions about appropriate conditions of confinement or even the possibility of treatment within prison.

The Mental Deficiency Act of 1913 diverted the so-called mental defectives (retarded persons) from the penal system: it was provided that if such persons were convicted, they could be placed in an appropriate institution, such as Rampton and Moss Side hospitals, or under guardianship. This approach provided the model for the wider system eventually adopted under the Mental Health Act of 1959. Section 60 of that Act enabled courts to order that convicted offenders be treated in a hospital, if there was evidence of mental disorder, as defined in the Act. Therefore, even though convicted, and perhaps in some cases the kind of persons who ought for reasons of public safety to be held in secure conditions, mentally disordered offenders could then be diverted straightaway from the prison system. The problem of the 'dangerous patient' was provided for in section 65, which enabled a court to couple a hospital order with a restriction order, the latter making release from hospital dependent on the Home Office's consent. Since 1959, the courts have become acclimatised to this different form of disposal, gradually coming to think in terms of treatment rather than punishment for such offenders. But the procedures laid down in the mental health legislation of 1959 and 1983 still leave certain categories of disordered person to be dealt with by the prison system. The disorder must be of a kind listed in the legislation (broadly, mental illness, retardation or psychopathic disorder) and must be susceptible to treatment. Moreover, some patients need to be held in secure conditions and there have been a limited number of secure hospital places (at Broadmoor, established in 1863, and Rampton and Moss Side, opened respectively in 1910 and 1919, although both catering mostly for the mentally retarded before 1959). As a result, some seriously disordered offenders may find themselves in prison, for reasons of security, if only temporarily. In addition, in recent years many hospitals have been unwilling to accept psychopathic offenders since it is open to doubt whether there is any effective treatment for many who suffer from this condition. For those psychopaths who are aggressive and violent, the prison system has been used to a large extent to provide a convenient form of secure institution.[29] It has therefore been necessary for the prison authorities to develop suitable accommodation and a certain level of psychiatric and therapeutic care, if not treatment.

In some respects the prison authorities have in the past been happy to take on such a role. In the earlier years of this century the reformist tradition in the penal system quite naturally took on board some of the methods of treatment being worked out in the fields of psychology, psychiatry and psychotherapy. In 1932 the Departmental Committees on Persistent Offenders commented that: 'there is reason to believe that certain delinquents may be amenable to psychological treatment. . . A medical psychologist should be attached to one or more penal establishments to carry out psychological treatment in selected cases.'[30]

In due course, psychiatric treatment became an integral part of the prison sentence for some categories of prisoner and in the post-war period staff with expertise in this kind of treatment were brought into the prison service and centres for psychiatric treatment were set up in some prisons, notably Wakefield and Wormwood Scrubs. For more seriously disturbed prisoners, a special prison was opened in 1962 at Grendon in Buckinghamshire, mainly to cater for the more moderate kind of psychopath, and comprising a therapeutic regime within conditions of maximum security. There is also a wing at Parkhurst Prison for the most seriously disturbed prisoners, where the object is to minimise violent and aggressive behaviour rather than apply a positive regime of treatment.

The prison system has therefore come to take on some treatment functions, despite the intention of the legislation of 1913 and 1959 to divert the mentally disordered to more appropriate institutions. This has come about more through the failure to develop suitable alternative institutions than through the conviction that a prison is the best place for some categories of disordered offender. A question remains, then: is an institution such as Grendon Prison, where the regime is conceived as therapeutic rather than penal, best described as a prison when Broadmoor, Rampton and Moss Side, which receive convicted offenders, are known as hospitals? Again, we appear to be faced with an interchangeability of institutions, at least in relation to some categories of person.

Problems of Drunkenness and Addiction

A certain amount of criminal activity has been related to the consumption of alcohol and to drug-taking and in many such cases it has been reasonable to suppose that the curing of these habits would remove or at least reduce the propensity to commit such offences, certainly those described as 'offences of drunkenness'. Drunkenness was seen as a particular problem in this country during the second part of the nineteenth century: offences of drunkenness and drunk and disorderly behaviour increased dramatically in the 1860s and 1870s and there followed a rise in the number of such offenders sentenced to prison (just over 4,000 in 1860, over 23,000 in 1876). The most notable reactions to these problems were the growth of the temperance movement and the introduction of licensing legislation to control the sale and consumption of alcohol.[31] There was also in the later years of the nineteenth century an attempt to deal more directly with offences involving drunkenness by means of a specific institutional regime.

In 1879, the Habitual Drunkards Act gave local authorities the power to licence the operation of retreats for habitual drunkards. This was a permissive system of treatment: it was up to the individual to apply for admission himself and the criteria for admission were dangerousness or incapacity, not the commission of a criminal offence. The idea of an institutional response was taken a stage further in 1898, with the provision for state inebriate reformatories under the Inebriates Act of that year. This allowed a court to commit an offender to an inebriate reformatory for a term of up to three years, if the offence was committed under the influence of drink or drunkenness was a contributing factor, and the offender either admitted to being or was found by a jury to be an habitual drunkard. A number of state reformatories were to be set up under this legislation and private reformatories certified and inspected by the Home Office could also be used. However, all of this appears to have had little effect on the problem. Although Arthur Harding recalled that his mother curbed her drinking habits for fear that she would be 'put away in a home',[32] a Departmental Committee reporting in 1908[33] revealed that little use had been made of the powers under the Act. Less than 1.5 per 1,000 persons convicted of drunkenness had been detained under the legislation; some magistrates did not know of the Act, or were unwilling to make use of it (indicating a certain degree of reluctance to interfere with liberty in this way); the definition of 'habitual drunkard' caused problems in practice; and the Report stated that, when the powers had been exercised, it was usually to commit for the maximum term of three years, which experience showed to be too long if the subject was amenable to treatment. The general problem of drunkenness was reduced, in the event, more through the introduction of licensing legislation, particularly restrictions on the opening hours of public houses, which were brought into force during the First World War and subsequently retained. Convictions for offences of drunkenness, which stood at almost 162,000 in 1910, were down to just under 96,000 in 1920 and 53,000 in 1930. The inebriate reformatories died a natural death: the conversion of the reformatory inside Aylesbury Prison into the first female borstal was indicative of their decline. By 1921, all 15 of the state reformatories had been closed.

As with the crime rate generally, convictions for offences involving drunkenness rose after the Second World War: as low as 44,000 in 1940, they had climbed to over 65,000 twenty years later. From the 1960s, as well, the problem of drug abuse was brought generally within the scope of the criminal law. By the 1970s, although the great majority of drunken offenders were being fined, the prisons were still receiving a certain number of alcoholic and drug addicted offenders. A Working Party on Habitual Drunken Offenders[34] was told in 1971 that magistrates sometimes resorted to imprisonment for such offenders because other methods of disposal were seen to be ineffective or inappropriate. Sentences for aggravated drunkenness were usually short — a month or less — and were served in local prisons, so achieving little more than short-term shelter and 'drying out'. Section 34 of the Criminal Justice Act of 1972 attempted to divert less serious drunken offenders from a penal disposal by authorising the police to take certain offenders to treatment centres, but in practice little use was made of these powers.[35]

Overall there seems to have been little enthusiasm in this country, compared to abroad, for the institutional treatment of the problem of drunkenness, at least in so far as it has also been a problem of the criminal law, apart from the late nineteenth century measures, which may be regarded as part of a wider reaction exemplified by the temperance movement. Although prisons have continued to receive some such offenders, this has often been via fine defaulting, and the preferred response during this century has been to use preventive measures, such as licensing, or community treatment.[36]

The Remand Function of Prisons

We have seen that historically this has been an important function of the prison and one which, theoretically at least, is distinct from the use of the prison as a penal institution. During the last 100 years, a number of penal institutions have been used for purposes of remand, a term which for present purposes can be taken to include remand in custody pending trial, remand after conviction while awaiting sentence and the period of custody pending allocation to a particular institution. In the last two situations there may be some overlap between the sentence of imprisonment as a penal process and the situation of being held in remand and there have been few distinctions drawn between the regime for such prisoners and that for ordinary inmates; the main exception has been in relation to the access to legal services provided to those awaiting sentence or appealing against sentence. But in the case of persons awaiting trial in custody, it would be clearly contrary to justice to impose a specifically penal regime.

The 1877 Prison Act required that a clear difference be made between the treatment of persons as yet unconvicted and that of convicted prisoners, and that the confinement of the former should be the least oppressive possible. Therefore, it has always been the case that unconvicted prisoners could keep their own clothes, be supplied with food at their own expense, have necessary communication with lawyers to prepare their defence and choose whether or not to work. But despite the differences of regime and attempts to keep remand prisoners separate, their lot has worsened in the post-war period. The May Committee noted[37] in 1979 that, the detention centre population apart, the rate of increase in the number of remand prisoners since 1945 was the highest for all groups of prisoners and that the length of the period of remand had been increasing. The 1976 Bail Act, which set up a statutory presumption in favour of bail, and the Criminal Law Act of 1977, which sought to reduce delays in the Crown Courts, seemed to bring about only a temporary reduction in the rate of remand. Prisoners on remand are kept in the overcrowded local prisons and so have shared the deterioration of conditions in those institutions. The recent situation has caused increasing concern in view of the fact that almost half of those remanded before trial do not eventually receive an immediate sentence of imprisonment and it may be possible in some cases to take a cynical view of remand as a form of *de facto* anticipatory punishment. A small number of people have been diverted from remand imprisonment by the introduction of some bail hostels during the 1970s.

For certain categories of younger offenders, for instance those awaiting placement at a particular borstal, remand centres were gradually established to avoid the use of imprisonment in such cases. Some of these, such as the borstal allocation centre at Manchester Prison, are attached to prisons; some make use of old buildings, such as the remand centre at Ashford in Middlesex, which was formerly a London County Council residential school; while since 1965 there have been some purpose-built remand centres (Risley, in Cheshire, for example). In an ideal system, all remand prisoners would be held in such separate institutions, although Hall Williams has commented[38] that in some remand centres 'the circumstances of the detention are so similar to imprisonment that it is hard to see the difference'.

An early version of the remand centre was the 'place of detention'. These institutions were set up under sections 95 and 108 of the 1908 Children Act to hold juveniles under the age of 16 who had been apprehended by the police and not released on bail; they were to be provided by the police authorities. This function was transferred to the newly established remand homes under section 33 of the Children and Young Persons Act in 1933, and eventually to the remand centres referred to above.

Civil Prisoners and Fine Defaulters

As with remand, the coercive or enforcement function of imprisonment was well established in 1877. This is another area in which a concentration on strictly penal objectives has resulted in a movement to exclude a category of prisoners, the view developing that other means would be preferable to enforce the payment of debts, arrears and even fines.

Imprisonment for non payment of debts,[39] such an important feature of the early nineteenth-century prisons, was partly abolished by legislation of 1869, the ironically mistitled — as it turned out — Act for the Abolition of Imprisonment for Debt. In principle this removed the sanction of imprisonment 'for making default in payment of a sum of money', but still allowed a defaulter to be imprisoned for up to six weeks for refusing or neglecting to make a payment if he had the means to do so. This exception led to a considerable number of debtors being imprisoned after 1869.

A Select Committee in 1873 recommended[40] that the power to imprison for debt be abolished altogether. Admittedly, there were the 'contumacious' debtors but the Committee pointed out that 'although the judges take pains to ascertain the facts . . . it constantly happens that the materials are wanting'.[41] However, this recommendation was rejected and the matter received very little attention again until the early 1960s. In the years prior to the outbreak of the First World War, the number of debtors sent to prison had reached an annual figure of nearly 10,000. Although this figure was subsequently reduced in the inter-war period, it rose again during the 1950s, no doubt fostered by the increase in credit trading, and was well over 60,000 a year in the early 1960s. The strain which this imposed on an already crowded prison system finally led to the setting up of the Payne Committee, on the Enforcement of Judgement Debts, in 1965. This time, the recommendation[42] to abolish imprisonment for this purpose was accepted and implemented in the Administration of Justice Act 1970, although it has still been possible since then to commit to prison for default in the payment of Crown debts and in maintenance payments.

There was no evidence that the use of imprisonment to enforce the payment of debts during this period was effective and there were some grounds for saying that it was unjust. In 1946 the Prison Commissioners' Report[43] stated that many prison governors were convinced 'that the fault lies as much or more with their wives as with them'; and that insufficient attention seems to have been given by the courts to individual circumstances and 'more patient attempts to investigate and advise . . . would perhaps avert much unfruitful hardship to both man and wife'. The Report also draws attention to the problems experienced by ex-servicemen, and to a lack of consistency in the terms of imprisonment ordered in respect of similar debts. In 1965, Paul de Berker, the Principal Psychologist at Brixton Prison, remarked[44] of the civil debtors there: 'permanent debt seems to be a way of family life' and was 'a facet of a much more generalised picture of social difficulty such as marginal employment, general incompetence in financial planning and the like.' The regime applied to debtors lay somewhere between that for untried and for convicted prisoners: they were required to work and received the normal prison diet, but were kept separate, so far as this was practicable, and could wear their own clothes and were entitled to more letters and visits than were convicted prisoners.

After 1970 there remained a significant number of maintenance defaulters being sent to prison (almost 2,900 in 1979, for example) and a lesser number of Crown debtors (default in payment of income tax and rates) and persons convicted for contempt of court. In the 1960s there had been a division of opinion as to the use of imprisonment to enforce maintenance payments and this was reflected in the Payne Committee's Report. Again, there is little evidence that imprisonment is effective for this purpose — on the contrary, a majority of such defaulters serve their full term without making any payment.[45]

The term 'civil prisoner' is also sometimes used (for instance by Hall Williams[46]) to include those imprisoned for non-payment of a fine, although fine defaulters are treated inside prison as sentenced prisoners. Here imprisonment is being employed as a supporting sanction to secure the effectiveness of the fine. Once more, there have been doubts about the effectiveness of imprisonment in this connection and also as to the penal justification for incarceration in a case where it had originally been decided to use a non-custodial measure. In the early years of the century, the annual number of commitals for fine defaulters was in excess of 80,000 (although it must be borne in mind that, on account of the short length of their detention, the effect on the daily average prison population is not as devastating as such a figure might suggest). The Criminal Justice Act of 1914 required magistrates to allow time for the payment of fines and this measure, coupled with a decrease in the level of drunkenness (a major factor in that period in fine defaulting), led to a reduction in the number of committals to 15,000 in 1921. A further reduction was brought about by the Money Payments Act of 1935, which required an enquiry as to means before committing a defaulter to prison. Yet by the late 1960s the number of fine defaulters in prison had started to rise again and by the early 1980s had gone over 20,000. No doubt this is related to an increase in the imposition of fines in the first place, but there is some feeling that fines are used too readily in relation to the socially inept where there is a real risk of non-payment and eventual imprisonment.

Political Prisoners

Finally, the prison system has been used during this period to hold various categories of what might loosely be described as 'political prisoners' in the sense that their confinement has resulted from a politically motivated act or is justified by wider political considerations. It is possible to identify three main groups among such prisoners. Firstly, there have been those who have committed conventional criminal offences, involving injury to person or property, which have been politically motivated (including those now referred to as 'terrorist' offenders), or serious offences affecting the security of the state, typically espionage and treason. Then, there has been a distinct group of 'protestors' whose offences have arisen from a passive resistance to certain policies or whose protesting activities have involved them in offences against public order. Notable categories of 'civil disobedience' prisoners during this period have included pro-testors against the levying of the Education Rate under the 1902 Education Act, objectors to vaccination, conscientious objectors during the First World War, and peaceful demonstrators, particularly in connection with nuclear disarmament, convicted of public order offences. The third group has comprised persons who have been detained at times of emergency for the security of the state and who often have not been criminal offenders as such.

For certain 'political' offenders, convicted of offences of sedition and seditious conspiracy and libel, there was a practice, originating in the Prison Act of 1865 and re-enacted in the legislation of 1877 and 1898, of using imprisonment of the 'First Division', which entailed a much less rigorous regime with more privileges — something akin to the regime for unconvicted prisoners. Such prisoners were allowed to wear their own clothes, not to work if they so wished, were given superior cells and could have food, books, newspapers and writing materials or other means of occupation sent in, and could work at their normal vocation or employment as far as prison discipline and security would allow.[47] This special regime for seditious offenders was removed in 1972 in view of the obsolescence of the offences of sedition. But it was, during the course of 100 years or so, applied to some significant categories, such as suffragettes in Holloway Prison, after 1908[48], and Sinn Fein offenders during the First World War.[49]

Politically motivated offenders convicted of offences other than sedition have usually been subjected to the normal prison regime (the suffragettes being an exception). Some of these offenders have of course committed serious crimes and a few have been executed (for instance, Sir Roger Casement at Pentonville in 1916 and William Joyce at Wandsworth in 1946) and a number sentenced to very long terms, such as the spy George Blake (who escaped from Wormwood Scrubs in 1966). In recent years, a significant number of IRA terrorists have been held in dispersal prisons and some of these were involved in a battle between prisoners and officers in Albany Prison in 1976. At the same time, 'civil disobedience' prisoners have, strictly speaking, come within the terms of the normal prison regime.

The detention of certain categories of person in the interest of national security during the two world wars created, temporarily, a related type of institution: internment. Enemy aliens were interned in camps such as that at Knockaloe on the Isle of Man; and under Defence Regulation 18(b) of 1940, members of organisations controlled by persons sympathetic to the enemy, notably Sir Oswald Mosley and other members of the British Union of Fascists,[50] could be detained and were held in prison, at Brixton, Holloway and Liverpool and at camps at Ascot and the Isle of Man. Conditions of detention were similar to those under the 'First Division' of imprisonment, and husbands and wives were eventually allowed to cohabit in Holloway Prison. This kind of detention has its more recent version in the use of prisons to hold persons awaiting deportation or extradition and those detained as illegal immigrants. In all of these cases the function of custody is clearly non-penal and it follows that the regime for such detainees should be analogous to that for unconvicted prisoners on remand.

An important practical consequence of the imprisonment of various kinds of political offender, has been the impact on public opinion of articulate and forceful accounts of prison conditions and the experience of imprisonment, which have sometimes been published after the prisoner's release. The imprisonment of a number of Irish Members of Parliament under the Crimes Act in the later part of the nineteenth century produced an important lobby in Parliament in favour of prison reform and accounted for the presence of the Irish MP Arthur O'Connor on the Gladstone Committee. The imprisonment of conscientious objectors resulted, in particular, in the Labour Research Department's inquiry into the prison system, set up in 1919, and the publication of Hobhouse and Brockway's indictment of imprisonment under the Ruggles-Brise administration, in *English Prisons Today* (1922). Some of the autobiographical accounts of well-educated 'political' prisoners have revealed an uneasiness on the part of the prison authorities when accepting such charges.[51] Such prisoners, although numerically a small group, have made an important contribution to the growing sense of disillusionment with imprisonment as a penal and corrective process during the course of this century.

Notes

1. First published in 1877, recently reissued by Garland Press.
2. *War with Crime: Being a Selection of Reprinted Papers on Crime, Reformation, etc.* (published by Longmans, London, 1889, reissued by Garland Press).
3. A useful discussion of the regime can be found in Rupert Cross' *Punishment, Prison and the Public* (Stevens, London, 1971), p. 147 et seq.
4. Cmd. 4090.
5. *Punishment, Prison and the Public*, p. 151.
6. Cmd. 4090, para 138.
7. *Preventive Detention*, Report by the Advisory Council on the Treatment of Offenders (HMSO, London, 1963).
8. (1962) 1 All E. R. 671.
9. See s. 28 of the Powers of Criminal Courts Act 1973.
10. *Punishment, Prison and the Public*, p. 163.
11. See generally, Gordon Rose, *Schools for Young Offenders* (Tavistock Publications, London, 1967). For a critical view of developments in the period 1889-1939, see Stephen Humphries, *Hooligans or Rebels?* (Basil Blackwell, Oxford, 1981).
12. On the development of the reformatory and industrial schools, see Rose, *Schools for Young Offenders*, Ch. 1.
13. *Hooligans or Rebels?*
14. Ibid., Ch. 8.
15. Home Office, 1927, Cmd. 2821.
16. H. C. 603, 1967, p. 53.
17. See, for instance, Andrew Sutton, 'Theory, Practice and Cost in Child Care: Implications from an Individual Case' (1978) 26 *Howard Journal*, 159.

18. National Union of Teachers, 1981: Closures of Community Homes.

19. See generally, Roger Hood, *Borstal Reassessed* (Heinemann, London, 1965).

20. *The Punishment and Prevention of Crime* (Macmillan, London, 1885), p. 201.

21. Hood, *Borstal Reassessed*, pp. 7-12.

22. Raphael Samuel, *East End Underworld: Chapters from the Life of Arthur Harding* (Routledge & Kegan Paul, London, 1981), p. 74.

23. It is interesting to compare the various quasi-military youth movements as methods of dealing with unruly young people; see Humphries, *Hooligans or Rebels?*, p. 134-5.

24. H. Mannheim and L.T. Wilkins, *Prediction Methods in Relation to Borstal Training* (HMSO, London, 1955).

25. H. L. Debates, Vol. 230, col. 1121, 1 May 1961.

26. 'Keep Out', Bulletin No. 1, 10.2.1982: Spotlight on Bullwood Hall Borstal.

27. For a convenient summary of the development of institutions to cater for the mentally disturbed, see Nesta Roberts, *Mental Health and Mental Illness* (Routledge & Kegan Paul, London, 1967), Chs. 1, 2.

28. A useful critical study of the M'Naghten Rules is to be found in the Report of the Royal Commission on Capital Punishment, 1953, Cmd. 8932, paras. 244-50.

29. See the Report of the Committee on Mentally Abnormal Offenders (Butler Committee), 1975, Cmnd. 6244, Ch. 5.

30. Quoted in Fox, *The English Prison and Borstal Systems* (Routledge & Kegan Paul, London, 1952), p. 242.

31. G.P. Williams and G.T. Brake, *Drink in Great Britain, 1900 to 1979* (Edsall, London, 1980), Chs. 1-4.

32. Samuel, *East End Underworld*, p. 64.

33. Cd. 4438 (1908).

34. Report of the Working Party on Habitual Drunken Offenders (Weiler), HMSO, London, 1971.

35. See David Farrier, *Drugs and Intoxication* (Sweet & Maxwell, London, 1980), p. 188.

36. See the discussion in Farrier, *Drugs and Intoxication*, pp. 169-70.

37. Report of the Committee of Inquiry into the United Kingdom Prison Services (May Committee), 1979, Cmnd. 7673, at para. 3.66.

38. J.E. Hall Williams, *The English Penal System in Transition* (Butterworth, London, 1970), p. 307.

39. See generally, O.R. McGregor, *Social History and Law Reform* (Stevens, London, 1981). Ch. 5.

40. Select Committee on Imprisonment for Debt, Report, C. 348 (1873).

41. Ibid., at p. vi.

42. Report, Cmnd. 3909 (1969).

43. Annual Report 1946, Cmd. 7271, pp. 29-30.

44. 'Impressions of Civil Debtors in Prison' (1965), 5 B. J. Crim. 310, p. 313.

45. See Martin Wright, *Making Good* (Burnett Books, London, 1982), p. 86. In 1975, 76 per cent of maintenance defaulters spent virtually their whole term inside prison without paying.

46. *English Penal System in Transition*, p. 69.

47. See the 1964 Prison Rules (1964 Statutory Instruments, 388), Rule 64; and Fox, *English Prison and Borstal Systems*, pp. 288-93.

48. See John Camp, *Holloway Prison* (David & Charles, Newton Abbot, 1974), p. 64 et seq.

49. Fenner Brockway, *Towards Tomorrow* (Hart-Davis MacGibbon, London,

1977), Ch. 5. In fact, De Valera and some others escaped from Leicester Prison in 1917.
  50. Sir Oswald Mosley, *My Life* (Nelson, London, 1968), Ch. 21.
  51. Fenner Brockway, *Towards Tomorrow*, Chs. 4, 5.

DISCUSSION AND CONCLUDING REMARKS

We have seen in the preceding chapters how the institution of imprisonment took on a number of different forms and served a variety of functions over a period of several hundred years. Does this kind of historical examination provide us with some understanding of society's sustained resort to a policy of incarceration and explain its continuing appeal, despite enormous changes of social context, or enable us to envisage a future without prisons and like institutions?

In attempting this kind of general comment, there is an inevitable risk of falling prey to neat theorisation and the temptation to reduce the complexities of the subject to a more simple and easily communicable picture. A priority, then, is to beware of any fallacies of historical analysis. Robert Roth warns against the adoption of a model which would be given the force of 'a basic myth: the trap of generalisation threatens the users, who run the risk of obscuring the contours of their field of investigation the better to impose a model selected as an indisputable frame of reference'.[1]

To start with, there is what has been referred to as the 'evolutionist illusion', the suggestion of a progressive development of imprisonment over a period of several centuries. In one sense there have obviously been developments. Prisons have become institutions of some technical and organisational sophistication compared to the situation some hundreds of years ago. But to say that, is to do little more than point out the obvious material and technological developments in society over that period. However, we should resist the pat notion that there has been a progressive and consistent institutional evolution, a general movement away from more primitive custodial objectives to a sophisticated system of penal correction. There is too much theoretical certainty, for instance, in Durkheim's description of transition from a repressive to a rehabilitative penal system,[2] which glosses over an overlapping of objectives which is revealed

264

by a closer attention to historical fact. While it would be fair enough to assert that, in the medieval period, custody of offenders while awaiting trial and coercion of debtors were important functions of incarceration, we have seen that it would be misleading to exclude penal elements from the prison experience of that time. Similarly, despite the significant corrective aspirations of the nineteenth and twentieth centuries, the prisons during this later period have retained custodial and coercive functions: in quantitative terms, remand remains an important function of the present prison system while a coercive role is tenaciously preserved for maintenance and fine defaulters. Moreover, to see imprisonment in terms of a general progressive development leaves out of account an actual reordering of objectives and practices in relation to incarceration. This is particularly true when talking about the corrective role of imprisonment. The House of Correction, in its earliest form, as the name suggests, had clear corrective objectives, which were subsequently obscured in seventeenth-century practice, then to experience some revival from the end of that century,[3] particularly within the institution of the workhouse. Ideas of reformation which developed in the later part of the eighteenth century were given a sporadic application and these fits and bursts of reformist penology died away in the middle of the nineteenth century, while another ideology of reform, involving different justifications and methods, came to the fore at the close of that century. The overall picture, therefore, suggests a number of consistent basic objectives which have been shifted around each other over a period of time in response to changing pressures.

If the endurance of such an important social institution ought not to be viewed in terms of the evolution and refinement of its functions, is there any other single constant which will clarify its continuing appeal? It is at this point that we should perhaps confront the 'dustbin' theory concerning the role of imprisonment and relegate it to its proper position. Admittedly, it is possible to see the attraction of a line of argument which explains imprisonment in terms of a dumping ground for a varied collection of society's undesirables. But further reflection will show that this does little more than to state the obvious and beg further questions. For instance, why were some of these undesirable members not imprisoned, or consigned to different institutions? Moreover, the 'dustbin' analysis does less than justice to the conscious planning and innovation which has preoccupied successive generations of social and penal theorists. It misses the point that, much of the time, prisoners have not been regarded as human waste, but as material which can be worked upon and improved, or, at least, used as an object lesson to others.

A more careful examination of prisons over a considerable period suggests, rather, a complex but responsive institution of social control. In fact, imprisonment could be viewed as a number of institutions, increasingly brought within a common organisation as the apparatus of state itself becomes more refined over the centuries. Gaols, houses of correction and hulks are eventually brought together as institutions of imprisonment and the modern prison system has been a grouping of training and local prisons, borstals, detention centres and remand institutions, while some hospitals and educational establishments have served analogous functions. The constant is a bundle of penal, corrective, coercive, protective and administrative functions, which together have dictated the need for incarceration.

The forms taken and the regimes adopted for these purposes have been responses to forces of both an external and an internal nature. Most obviously, wider movements, not necessarily restricted to this country, in social organisation, economy and religious thought have influenced the character of the prison institutions at different points in time. Such broad historical changes as the demise of feudal organisation and the industrialisation of society have clearly contributed to the substance of the need for carceral institutions. It is particularly helpful to view imprisonment in its various forms in the context of the changing nature of social control. During the medieval period, the feudal organisation of society and the restraints which derived from dominant religious thought provided a large measure of social control. That a deprivation of liberty, and importantly its concomitant material discomforts might be used to punish is clear, but its use was restricted. At a time when individual freedom is not an abstract right but a relative privilege, when the correction of an evil nature is the task of the Church and when man's own capacity both to judge and to punish is but an imperfect reflection of God's proper function, the use of incarceration as a penal sanction must have been very differently viewed.

It is with the subsequent development of a capitalist and industrialised society, with its emphasis on individual performance and self improvement, that the deprivation of liberty becomes an especially meaningful instrument of penal policy and a potential vehicle for corrective processes. In more recent and contemporary society, the restrictions on personal freedom inevitably contained in a sentence of imprisonment constitute an important tool of social control. When the individual's role in a capitalistic, industrialised society is taken together with the humanistic enlargement of personal liberty, imprisonment appears as an appropriate final sanction in the process of moulding the behaviour of society's members. On such an analysis, it is difficult to foresee any significant reduction in the resort to imprisonment without radical (and for the most part improbable) changes in the organisation of society.

The consolidation of imprisonment as a social institution may also be related to wider political processes involving the centralisation of government and the increasingly incursive role of state agencies. While the organisation of prisons remained local rather than national and innovation was as much a matter of private initiative and individual expedience as governmental policy, the prisons had a limited pontential as instruments of social control. But as society became more complex and there was a resultant need for closer regulation of personal activities, it is possible to trace the development of the paraphernalia of law, enforcement action and sanctioning in which the use of imprisonment has become an important final control. With these imperatives of societal regulation in mind, it becomes easier to make sense of the shifts and turns in the use of imprisonment at particular times: why, for example, the Bray Committee's ideas for solitary confinement, which we have seen were not acceptable at the beginning of the eighteenth century, had become attractive by the end of the century, given radical changes in economic, political and religious thought.

However, imprisonment has not only responded to external influences. The institution has been increasingly sustained by its own internal forces and acquired a distinctive momentum of its own. These internal forces will include the expectations of the actual prisoners, for no matter that they have seemed at times mere pawns in someone else's game their own reaction, actual or perceived, to changes, accomplished or contemplated, has necessarily had an effect on the maintenance and planning of the system which confines them. Similarly this internal dynamic will comprise the self interest of those charged with the custody of the prisoners. At an early point this self interest is seen in a most basic form, the institution is run as a source of profit. An increase in uniformity together with a professionalism which thereby develops within the prison staff, now seen as a defined class rather than a disparate assembly of individuals, leads to a different formulation of this notion of self interest. The practical experience of the men who work within the prisons combines with and affects their own perceived goals and those which they regard as appropriate for their institutions. A more articulate professional grouping will be able also to allow such ideals and experiences to be communicated. In many respects, this internal tradition has been resistant to changes pressed upon the prisons by external developments. So, in the middle years of the last century, gaolers of some small municipal prisons naturally found it difficult to accommodate the demands for more professional gaolership made by government inspectors, who were concerned to implement a more carefully structured regime of discipline in the local prisons.[4] In recent years, there have been signs that the direct control of the prison system by the Home Office has committed the prisons to a programme of expansion initiated by that government department's policy objectives, in spite of wider pressures in society for a reduction in the scale of imprisonment.[5] In short, over a period of time, the continuing existence of the complex of institutions we now refer to as the 'prison system' has generated a self interest in the maintenance of some kind of carceral process.

But it would be wrong to present the internal tradition within the institution of imprisonment as merely conservative on account of a natural resistance to changes urged from the outside. It has also generated its own momentum towards change in certain areas. Notably, for example, the emergence of a profession of prison officers over the last hundred years has made a significant contribution to the revival of a commitment to security and control by the late 1960s and the pressures from within the prison system for such policy changes predated much of the public concern with such issues. There can be little doubt that the whole edifice of state incarceration is now a firmly entrenched social institution. Even such a severe critic of penal practice as Baroness Wootton, who would jettison the process of blame and punishment, concedes that there remains a need for some form of incarceration: instead of prisons, she would have 'places of safety'.[6] To be sure, the protective function in such a scheme replaces the penal objective, but the carceral principle remains securely imbedded in such arguments. And, in fact, the enduring quality of the notion of incarceration is physically demonstrated by a continuity of building and siting, despite changes in the more specific aspects of the institutions. A number of present-day prison establishments are housed in buildings or built on the site of former penal institutions in the same way that hospitals, as another example, have sometimes been erected on the site of workhouses. Undoubtedly this might be explicable in terms of pragmatic considerations of land utilisation, but it may perhaps also be seen as a kind of incarnation of the institutional tradition.

This leads to another important general point, concerning the way in which institutions of incarceration and their components are described. The turnkey, it will have been noticed, became successively the prison warder and then the prison officer; in the late eighteenth and early nineteenth centuries, prisons were built which were referred to as 'penitentiaries', a term which subsequently went out of vogue in this country (though not in North America); and the term 'borstal' was adopted specifically to indicate that the institution was unlike other prison establishments. Clearly, the adoption of certain names or terms reflects the perceived function of the institution. Thus 'house of correction' and 'reformatory' imply the ideology of reform; 'penitentiary' suggests a process of rehabilitation and personal redemption through punishment; 'penal servitude' connotes the idea of punishment and reformation through enforced labour. 'Officer' indicates the move away from the simple custodial function associated with 'warder', and 'inmate' conveys the ambivalence of modern penal policy in a way that the more graphic word 'prisoner' cannot do. An examination of terminology is therefore helpful in achieving an understanding of the policy and ideology of those making use of the institution.

On the other hand, we should bear in mind the fact that the use of different descriptions may obfuscate the practical operation of institutions and lead to a certain level of self-deception on the part of officials and wider society. So to call an institution a 'reformatory' may lead us too easily to believe that it is both reformative in purpose and effect, whereas it may be neither and (like the latter day borstal and some of the houses of correction) indistinguishable in its practical manifestations from a conventional prison. Of course, institutions concerned with compulsory detention have to be given some name for purposes of identification. But the history of imprisonment illustrates well the process of using descriptive language to relate the institution to its underlying ideology and how such language may become inappropriate, misleading or deceptive. The Scandinavian writer, Nils Christie, makes the point: 'In my opinion, on the whole, the best protection is afforded to the weakest party in a system employing compulsory measures if these measures are given their harshest names'.[7] The whole problem of the description given to an institution, its perceived function, its actual impact and the possible manipulation of these factors, is to be seen in the relationship between remand and penal incarceration. Remand while awaiting trial has been officially considered as non-penal, yet some practical aspects of the treatment of remanded persons, such as the high level of cellular confinement, and their own view of the experience may suggest a penal process,[8] while there remains a risk of manipulation: a court may, for example, use a refusal of bail as *de facto* punishment to offset the possibility of non-conviction, a principle certainly in operation in the Middle Ages.

Perhaps one of the most useful lessons to be learnt from a historical investigation of the use of imprisonment is that the institution has been largely reactive: a response to the changing demands and pressures within society and also to its own internal needs. As Maclachlan remarks,[9] penal reform has never been wholly empirical, not least because the causes of delinquency and rule-breaking have been imperfectly understood. When it is realised, from a historical enquiry, that the character of imprisonment has been largely determined by the action possible to each successive generation, then we may be better placed to understand the present state of the prison system and its possible future. It is obviously instructive to see how successfully the different functions of incarceration have been fulfilled in the past. But the study should also produce a range of helpful moral and practical questions. Moral: to what extent and for what purposes is society justified in limiting in this way individual freedom and self determination? Practical: given the state of society at any time, to what extent is the carceral solution a feasible policy for dealing with those problems which justify intervention on the part of the state? The answers to such questions will themselves inevitably, now that prisons serve a role primarily devoted to the confinement of crime, be based on ideas of criminality. So, to take some very basic examples, if crime is equated with sin, a redemptive approach is the more easily justified; in so far as it is equated with disease, a policy of treatment would appear more appropriate. Yet such all-embracing theories of criminality now seem to be out of favour, indeed comparatively recently a current of opinion has arisen which suggests that crime, in at least some of its manifestations, is inevitable. The role of the prison in years to come will depend upon the views of policy-makers, interest groups and the general public. Certainly over the last thousand years the prison has become well entrenched within our society; it would be naive to assume that it will cease to exist, at least in the near future.

Notes

1. Sixth Criminological Colloquium of the Council of Europe, 1983: *Historical Research on Crime and Criminal Justice* (Council of Europe, Strasbourg, 1984), PC-CC (84), 2, at p. 82.
2. Emile Durkheim, 'Deux lois de l'évolution pénale', *Année sociologique 1899 – 1900*, 1V, 65; c.f. R.D. Schwartz and J.C. Miller, 'Legal evolution and societal complexity', 1964 *American Journal of Sociology*, 159-69; and see Peter Grabosky, 'Theory and research on variations in penal severity' (1978) 5 *B. J. Law and Society*.
3. James Gardner, unpublished thesis, University of Wales, 1985: 'Justices of the Peace in Denbighshire, 1660 – 1699', pp. 181-90.
4. See W.J. Forsythe, *A System of Discipline — Exeter Borough Prison 1819-1863* (University of Exeter, 1983), Ch. 6.
5. See Andrew Rutherford, 'Deeper into the Quagmire: Observations on the Latest Prison Building Programme' (1984), 23 *Howard Journal of Criminal Justice*, 129.
6. Barbara Wootton, *Crime and the Criminal Law* (Stevens, London, 2nd ed. 1981), p. 82.
7. 'Utility and Social Values in Court Decisions on Punishment', in Roger Hood (ed.), *Crime, Criminology and Public Policy* (Heinemann, London, 1974), p. 281.
8. See Paul Robertshaw, 'The Political Economy of Bail Reform' (1983) 7 *Contemporary Crises*, p. 329.
9. Noel McLachlan, 'Penal reform and penal history: some reflections', in Louis Blom-Cooper (ed.), *Progress in Penal Reform* (Oxford University Press, 1974), 1 at p. 23.

REVIEW OF
LITERATURE AND SOURCES

Introduction

This is designed as a guide to further reading for those who wish to follow up particular aspects of the subject in more detail. It is not intended to be a comprehensive bibliography: much fuller listings are available elsewhere, for example, in Sean McConville's study. For the most part, this survey concentrates on items which should be readily available in an average university or equivalent library and so concentrates on secondary materials, rather than original sources which may not be easily accessible.

Part One: The Middle Ages

The use of medieval source material presents obvious problems for the general reader in terms of access to the subject-matter and the palaeographical and linguistic problems associated with it. A certain amount of the materials within the Public Record Office is available in print, however, some as translated calendars, others in the original Latin. Within these collections of official rolls are to be found many references to prisons and imprisonment. Similarly the cases and materials collected within the volumes of the Selden Society give many insights, as do the materials in the Councils and Synods volumes in the area of canon law. References to this type of material may be gathered from the notes to the preceding chapters but will not be given here. Included in the following list, however, are the titles of the leading medieval monographs which discuss imprisonment in any detail, although in none of these is there a protracted discussion. The reader may, however, wish to read more about the legal system as a whole as described by these authors, although some background knowledge is an advantage in any such attempt. All these texts are in translation and are listed by the name of their modern editor. Statutory provisions are found in the *Statutes of The Realm* collections.

As for secondary material one book stands out as a definitive technical monograph, Ralph Pugh's scholarly and impressive *Imprisonment in Medieval England* which is filled with factual detail. Articles by the same author on the subject may be similarly recommended. Bassett's work on the early history of Newgate and the Fleet is also very useful although the danger of generalisation from the records of these London prisons (a danger to which Bassett never succumbs) has been adverted to in the text. With the exception of these texts little has been written on medieval imprisonment *per se*, although McConville's work on the English system and Cameron's on the Scottish both contain introductory chapters. The reader must seek further information about imprisonment in works which deal more generally with the social or legal background of the times. Bellamy's *Crime and Public Order in the Later Middle Ages* contains a useful chapter on 'Prison, Punishment and Pardon' whilst the book as a whole, together with Hanawalt's detailed local researches, published as *Crime and Conflict in English Communities 1300-48*, gives a picture of the level and nature of medieval criminal activity. Hurnard's *The King's Pardon for Homicide Before 1307*, although more limited in its scope does contain material on matters not discussed elsewhere, as does Gabel's *Benefit of Clergy in the Later Middle Ages*. Specific matters are also considered in Plucknett's *Legislation of Edward I* while Summerson's work on 'peine forte et dure' is a rare attempt to explain this curiosity. The early history of bail is discussed by De Haas whose book contains worthwhile record evidence but is rather difficult to use.

For the wider social context of medieval imprisonment the picture has to be drawn from rather more diffuse sources and the reader's attention is drawn to the notes which accompany the text for specific guidance. Worthy of general note perhaps are Clay's work on the medieval hospital and Tierney's on the theory and practice of poor relief in this period.

Select Bibliography of Monographs and Articles

Bassett, M: 'The Fleet Prison in the Middle Ages', *University of Toronto Law Journal* (1943-4), Vol. 5, pp. 383-402.

—— 'Newgate Prison in the Middle Ages', *Speculum* (1943), Vol. 18, pp. 233-46

Bellamy, J: *Crime and Public Order in England in the Later Middle Ages* (Routledge & Kegan Paul, London, 1973)

Cameron, J: *Prison and Punishment in Scotland: From the Middle Ages to the Present* (Cannongate, Edinburgh, 1983)

Clay, R.B.: *The Medieval Hospitals of England* (Frank Cass, London, 1909), reprinted 1966

De Haas, E: *Antiquities of Bail* (AMS Press, New York, 1940), reprinted 1966

Gabel, L.C. *Benefit of Clergy in England in the Later Middle Ages* (Octagon Books, New York, 1928-9), reprinted 1969

Hanawalt, B.A: *Crime and Conflict in English Communities, 1300-1348* (Harvard University Press, London, 1979)

Hurnard, N.D: *The Kings Pardon for Homicide before A.D. 1307* (OUP, Oxford, 1969)

McConville, S: *A History of English Prison Administration Vol. 1 1750-1877* (Routledge & Kegan Paul, London, 1981)

Nichols, F.M(ed): *Britton* (Clarendon Press, Oxford, 1865)

Pugh, R.B: 'The King's Prisons before 1250', *Transactions of the Royal Historical Society*, 5th Series, Vol. 5 (1955), pp. 1-22

—— 'Some Reflections of a Medieval Criminologist', *Proceedings of the British Academy* (1973), Vol. LIX, pp. 83-104

—— *Imprisonment in Medieval England* (CUP, Cambridge, 1968)

Plucknett, T.F.T: *Legislation of Edward I* (OUP, Oxford, 1962)

Richardson, H.G. and Sayles, G.O. (eds.): *Fleta*, Selden Society, Vols. 72 and 89, for 1953 and 1972.

Summerson, H.R.T: 'The Early Development of Peine Forte et Dure', in Ives and Manchester (eds.), *Law, Litigants and the Legal Profession* (Royal Historical Society, London, 1983), pp. 116-26

Thorne, S.E. and Woodbine, G.E. (ed.): (translation and revision): Bracton, *de Legibus* (Harvard University Press, Cambridge, Mass., 1968-77)

Tierney, B: *Medieval Poor Law* (University of California Press, Berkeley, 1959)

Whittaker, W.J.(ed.): *The Mirror of Justices* Selden Society volume 7 for 1893.

Part Two: The Early Modern Period

The early modern period is not well covered by detailed studies of imprisonment and it is to be hoped that a future writer will attempt to bridge the gap between Pugh's study of the medieval period and the mass of material which is available on developments since 1750. The introductory chapters of these later studies are however often valuable and particular mention should be made here of Ignatieff's *Just Measure of Pain*, the Webbs' *English Prison Under Local Government*, and the first volume of McConville's *History of English Prison Administration*. Of these McConville's book, the product of a decade of research, is particularly valuable. Some coverage of the subject is also provided by Holdsworth's *History of English Law*, although for such a comprehensive work this is on occasions surprisingly thin in its treatment. *The History of Penal Methods* by Ives may also be mentioned; this is based on a mass of original sources but as Knafla observes is difficult to use and evaluate. Two theses by Dobb and Sheehan provide a useful overview of the prison system, at least in London, and between them cover most of the period. Dobb's work has been summarised elsewhere in a short article, but Sheehan's conclusions should perhaps be treated with some caution as other writers have not always agreed with them.

When we come to consider works on the history of crime and criminal procedure we are on stronger ground and the last ten years have seen a number of important studies in the area, particularly on developments in the eighteenth century. The literature in the field which appeared before 1975 was surveyed by Knafla in the critical bibliography which he provided for *Crime in England 1550-1800* edited by Cockburn, whilst Sharpe's recent study entitled *Crime in Early Modern England 1550-1750* also provides an overview of the field. Both studies are valuable in their own right. A more traditional view of the issues from a legal standpoint is to be found in either Holdsworth or Radzinowicz. This is not the place to enter into a discussion on the relative merits of other recent studies, suffice it to say that work by Beattie, Bellamy, Brewer and Styles, Foucault, Gattrell and Parker, Hay, Knafla, Langbein, and E.P. Thompson should also be noted. A couple of more popular surveys of the Elizabethan underworld should also be mentioned; Salgado provides a general anecdotal overview, while Judges reprints important contemporary pamphlets by Hutton and Fennor amongst others.

Contemporary theories of punishment are dealt with by Heath in *Eighteenth Century Penal Theory* and Radzinowicz who summarises the views of many propagandists of the period. More detailed coverage of the Commonwealth period is provided by Veall's *Popular Movement for Law Reform*, whilst some limited insight into sixteenth-century views is to be found in an essay by Rose which is included in *Tudor Rule and Revolution* edited by Guth.

As far as developments in penological practice are concerned, J.H. Langbein's *Torture and the Law of Proof* provides an insight into the use of galleys and transportation in Britain and Europe. More detailed studies of transportation are available and mention may be made especially of work by Sweeney and Shaw. The House of Correction occupies a central position in any discussion of punishment in the early modern period, but various writers have noted that we lack any adequate history of the institution, although work by Innes may soon fill this gap in the literature. Tudor attitudes to vagrancy and poverty have been studied by Pound and Beier, among others, whilst religious attitudes to the problem have been considered by A.J. Little. It is, however, unfortunately true that no major work on poor relief has been produced since Leonard's study in 1900. The history of Bridewell hospital was chronicled by O'Donoghue in a two volume work which appeared in the 1920s but this has been the subject of some criticism. The House of Correction was also studied by Passey in the 1930s, but his thesis may not be readily available. Sharpe provides some limited coverage of the institution in the seventeenth century in his Essex study, while Innes presented an important paper on the subject at Warwick in 1983. Marxist historians have ascribed a central position to the Bridewell in the development of imprisonment and important contributions to this debate have been made by Rusche and Kirchheimer and more recently Melossi and Pavarini.

We are fairly well served by studies of imprisonment for debt. A short overview of the subject was recently provided by J. Cohen in the *Journal of Legal History* while Innes has provided an important study of the King's Bench prison in the eighteenth century. Some useful insights into the imprisonment of debtors in the early seventeenth century are provided by Shaw in an article published shortly after the war. There are many contemporary accounts of imprisonment for debt provided by Dekker and others; one which should be mentioned since it is likely to be fairly readily available is T. Fennor's *Counter's Commonwealth* which was reprinted in Judges' study of the Elizabethan underworld. The subject of madness and incarceration has been considered by Foucault and Scull.

Any survey of the organisation and conditions within the prison system must begin by mentioning McConville's seminal work although useful material is also to be found in other general studies like the Webbs'. London's prisons in particular have come in for much attention; mention has already been made of Dobb's thesis, individual prisons have also been covered, Bassett dealt with the Fleet and Newgate in the Middle ages, Burford surveyed the Clink, and many writers have been attracted by Newgate, ranging in their scope from a two volume study by Griffiths in the nineteenth century, which is still useful, to a recent nicely illustrated volume by Rumbelow. Some accounts are primarily anecdotal, others, incuding Innes' study of the King's Bench, contain more of substance. As far as contemporary accounts are concerned mention must be made of John Howard's work, although strictly speaking it lies outside the period under review. Two contemporary accounts which are particularly useful on the vexed subject of prison finance are provided by Fennor, and the gaoler Harris in his *Oeconomy of the Fleet*, whilst the subject of charitable gifts for prisoners was touched upon by Kirkman Gray.

It is difficult to know where to begin when considering studies of daily life in prison. Many contemporary accounts are not easily accessible, although fictional renderings by H. Fielding in *Amelia* and T. Dekker are noteworthy. Modern studies by Sheehan and Linebaugh in Cockburn's book are interesting and McConville is as always reliable. On the ever-present problem of gaol fever Creighton's *History of Epidemics* may be found useful.

Reform of the prison system was generally limited in extent and ineffectual at this time. Apart from the general works already noted some assistance may be provided by Clay's study of the prison chaplain and Kirkman Gray; both are useful on the religious groups behind reform. For parliamentary action, particularly at the time of the Oglethorpe enquiry, the *House of Commons Journals* are invaluable (see note references for more detail) and much material is also contained in the *State Trials*.

Some of the more important matter has been collected by D. Thomas in a two volume compilation under the title *State Trials*. Statutory material is accessible through the series of *Statutes of the Realm* which is always to be preferred to other sources.

Beattie, J.M. 'The Pattern of Crime in England', 1660-1800, *Past and Present*, vol. 62, 1974

Beier, A.T. 'Vagrants and the Social Order in Elizabethan England', *Past and Present*, vol. 64, 1974

Bellamy, J.G. *Crime and Public Order in England in the Later Middle Ages* (Routledge, London, 1973)

Brewer, J. and Styles, J. (eds.) *An Ungovernable People* (Hutchinson, London, 1980). See especially, Innes, J. 'The King's Bench Prison in the Later Eighteenth Century'

Burford, E.J. *In the Clink* (New English Library, 1977)

Clay, W.L. *The Prison Chaplain: A Memoir of the Rev. John Clay* (Macmillan, Cambridge, 1861)

Cockburn, J.S. (ed.) *Crime in England 1550-1800* (Methuen, London, 1977). See especially, Sheehan, W.J. 'Finding Solace in Eighteenth Century Newgate', and Linebaugh, P. 'The Ordinary of Newgate and His Account'

Cohen, J. 'The History of Imprisonment for Debt', *Journal of Legal History*, vol. 3, 1982

Creighton, C. *The History of Epidemics in Britain* (Frank Cass, London, 1965), 2nd ed.

Dobb, C. *Life and Conditions in London Prisons 1553-1643*, unpublished B.Litt., Oxford, 1952

—— 'London's Prisons', in *Shakespeare in His Own Age*, ed. A. Nicoll (CUP, Cambridge, 1965)

Foucault, M. *Discipline and Punish* (Payne, London, 1977)

—— *Madness and Civilisation: A History of Insanity in the Age of Reason* (Tavistock, London, 1967)

Gattrell, V., Lenman, B. and Parker, G. (eds.) *Crime and the Law: The Social History of Crime in Western Europe Since 1500* (Europa, London, 1980)

Gray, B.K. *A History of English Philanthropy* (Cass, London, 1967)

Griffiths, A. *The Chronicles of Newgate* (Chapman, London, 1884)

Harris, A. *The Oeconomy of the Fleete* Camden Society, vol. 25 n.s, 1879

Hay, D. (ed.) *Albion's Fatal Tree: Crime and Society in Eighteenth Century England* (Allen Lane, London, 1975)

Heath, J. *Eighteenth Century Penal Theory* (OUP, Oxford, 1963)

Holdsworth, W. *History of English Law* (Methuen, Sweet and Maxwell, London, 1972), 17 vols.

Howard, J. *The State of the Prisons* (Professional Books, Abingdon, 1977)

Ignatieff, M. *A Just Measure of Pain: The Penitentiary in the Industrial Revolution, 1750-1850* (Macmillan, London, 1978)

Innes, J. *English Houses of Correction and Labour Discipline 1600-1780*, unpublished paper at Warwick Conference, 1983

Ives, E.W. 'English Law and English Society', *History*, vol. 66, 1981

Ives, G.A. *A History of Penal Methods, Criminals, Witches, Lunatics* (Stanley Paul, London, 1914)

Judges, A.V. *The Elizabethan Underworld* (Routledge, London, 1965)

Knafla, L.A. (ed.) *Crime and Criminal Justice in Europe and Canada* (Waterloo, Wilfrid Laurier University Press, 1981)

Langbein, J.H. *Prosecuting Crime in the Renaissance: England, Germany, France* (Harvard University Press, Cambridge, 1974)

—— *Torture and the Law of Proof* (University of Chicago Press, Chicago, 1977)

Leonard, E.M. *The Early History of English Poor Relief* (CUP, Cambridge, 1900)

Little, D. *Religion, Order and Law: A Study in Pre-Revolutionary England* (Harper & Row, New York, 1969)

McConville, S. *A History of English Prison Administration, vol 1, 1750-1877* (Routledge, London, 1981)

Macfarlane, A. *The Justice and the Mare's Ale* (Blackwell, Oxford, 1981)

Melossi, D. and Pavarini, M. *The Prison and the Factory: Origins of the Penitentiary System* (Macmillan, London, 1980)

O'Donoghue, E.G. *Bridewell Hospital, Palace, Prison, School* (John Lane, London, 1923-9)

Passey, W.E. *Houses of Correction in England and Wales*, unpublished MA thesis, Liverpool, 1936

Pound, J. *Poverty and Vagrancy in Tudor England* (Longmans, London, 1971). See also *Past and Present*, v. 71, 1976

Radzinowicz, L. *A History of English Criminal Law* (Stevens, London, 1948-68)

Rumbelow,D. *The Triple Tree* (Harrap, London, 1982)

Rusche, G. and Kirchheimer, O. *Punishment and Social Structure* (Russell and Russell, New York, 1968)

Salgado, G. *The Elizabethan Underworld* (Dent, London, 1977)

Scull, J. *Museums of Madness* (Allen Lane, London, 1979)

Sharpe, J. *Crime in Early Modern England 1550-1750* (Longmans, London, 1984)

—— *Crime in Seventeenth Century England: A County Study* (CUP, Cambridge, 1983)

Shaw, A.G. *Convicts and the Colonies* (Faber, London, 1966)

Shaw, P. 'The Position of Thomas Dekker in Jacobean Prison Literature', *PMLA*, Vol. 62, 1947

Sheehan, W. *The London Prison System 1666-1795*, unpublished Ph.D. thesis, University of Maryland, 1975

Sweeney, C. *Transported in Place of Death* (Macmillan, Melbourne, 1981)

Thomas, D. (ed.) *State Trials, vol 2, The Public Conscience* (Routledge, London, 1972)

Thompson, E.P. *Whigs and Hunters: The Origins of the Black Act* (Allen Lane, London, 1975)

Veall, D. *The Popular Movement for Law Reform, 1640-1660* (OUP, Oxford, 1970)

Webb, S. and Webb, B. *English Prisons Under Local Government* (Longmans, London, 1982)

Weisser, M. *Crime and Punishment in Early Modern Europe* (Harvester, Hassocks, 1979), new ed. 1984

Part Three: The Period 1750 to 1877

(Note: in this essay reference is made to secondary source material; mention should also be made of the Parliamentary Papers, many of which have been reproduced by the Irish University Press, and of various contemporary books and pamphlets to which I have referred in the text. All these materials must be used with caution: for instance, it is for the researcher to judge the reliability of statements made by convicts appearing before Parliamentary Committees; however, much reading-between-the-lines may be done.)

The period covered by this part of the book has long been written about by historians — political, economic and social —

although only comparatively recently has much significant work been done on the criminal justice system. Leon Radzinowicz *History of the English Criminal Law* (4 volumes, London 1948-68), provides a description of certain reforms. However, this work is best used as a reference book for finding out what was said by those most directly involved in the debate, rather than as a work of history since there is little attempt to relate the reforms to their context, and since Radzinowicz is essentially a Whig historian. For instance, in volume I, he sees the debate on capital punishment as largely between the 'goodies' (the reformers, epitomised by Romilly) and the 'baddies' (the opposition, epitomised by Lord Eldon), with victory inevitably going to the 'goodies' because theirs is a truth which cannot be denied. Of course, the debate did not split so evenly, nor can it be understood purely in terms of levels of humanitarianism. At the end the reader is left happy, perhaps, that the 'goodies' have won, but rather uncertain as to why the reforms occurred at the time they did, or why the reformers won (the only explanation offered for this was that their opponents, who are portrayed as very much out on a limb, simply gave in or died), or even why, if reform was such a good thing, it did not happen much earlier.

On the same subject as volume I of Radzinowicz's book is J.N.J. Palmer's excellent, but largely ignored, article, 'Evils Merely Prohibited', *British Journal of Law and Society* (vol. 3(1976), pp. 1-17). This provides a useful discussion of some of the central issues in the debate on capital punishment. He argues that property offences were of secondary importance in comparison to issues of authority. Change to the criminal law was opposed on the grounds that although it might safeguard property, it would endanger authority. Finally, the major theories of those involved in the capital punishment debate are summarised in J. Heath, *Eighteenth Century Penal Theory* (Oxford, 1963), although his selection tends to lean rather too heavily to the 'reformers', implying that their opponents had little or no theory.

On crime in general much has already been said in praise of the books that emerged from Warwick University in the 1970s: D. Hay *et al.*, *Albion's Fatal Tree* (London, 1975) and E.P. Thompson, *Whigs and Hunters* (London, 1975). In addition, there is J. Brewer and J. Styles (eds.), *Ungovernable People? The English and their Law in the Seventeenth and Eighteenth Centuries*

(London, 1978). These books emphasise not only that crime is something committed by individuals for very individual reasons, a truism too often ignored in grand criminological theorising, but also that crime can be a form of political action by those who have no 'legitimate' political channels for their dissent. If nothing else, these books have ensured that crime has taken its proper place in the study of social history. Worth particular mention, however, is Douglas Hay's essay 'Property, Authority and the Criminal Law' in *Albion's Fatal Tree*. In this essay he argues that in the eighteenth century the criminal law was an important means of maintaining the authority of the ruling gentry since its flexibility meant that it was up to individuals to prosecute or not, and to support an application for a pardon or not. This discretion could be used to reinforce the relationships of dominance and deference. The reader of this essay must, however, bear in mind the importance of the poor: their potential for disruption played an important part in the eighteenth century; they were no mere tools of the ruling class. This is implicit in Hay's essay. Hay does tend to elide the gentry's interest in preserving their property and their interest in preserving their hegemony. The gentry were interested in both: on an individual level when faced by a particular crime which touched them or their interests, the gentry were interested in that crime and that criminal; whilst on a class level, they were concerned to maintain their hegemony.

On nineteenth-century crime there has been a gradual growth of literature. J.J. Tobias, *Crime and Industrial Society in the Nineteenth Century*, is useful as a source of middle and upper class perceptions of crime, it is not a social history of crime. An excellent work in the 'Warwick' vein is David Philips, *Crime and Authority in Victorian England: The Black Country 1835-1860* (London, 1977). Also useful is the collection of essays, by D.V. Jones, published collectively as *Crime. Protest, Community and Police in Nineteenth-Century Britain* (London, 1982).

With respect to prisons themselves, there are three outstanding books to which, as the reader will have seen, I have been greatly indebted in my two chapters. Sean McConville, *A History of English Prison Administration, Volume 1 1750-1877* (London, 1981), is an excellent piece of research, if rather tiring to read because of endless sub-headings which break up the flow of the .text. The difficulties of writing a comprehensive book on prison history are immense because of the need to try and run several different, and apparently contradictory, themes alongside one another. This is *the* source book for further reading on prisons, especially since it includes a fairly full bibliography. M. Ignatieff, *A Just Measure of Pain: The Penitentiary in the Industrial Revolution, 1750-1850* (London, 1978), is a more readable and thought-provoking account with a much more explicit theoretical basis. He argues that the prisons reflected the class relations within society as a whole, so that a study of the former necessarily becomes a study of 'the moral boundaries of social authority in a society undergoing capitalist transformation' (p. xiii). This task is not so easy, since although one might expect prisons to be a society stripped bare of all its comforting and comfortable ideologies, in fact, of course, prisons are veiled in the half-truths of 'humanitarianism', 'reformation', 'treatment' and 'deterrence'. Importantly, he seeks to introduce the prisoner into the history of prisons, just as other historians working in the study of crime have introduced the 'criminal'. Finally, Michel Foucault in his book *Discipline and Punish: The Birth of the Prison* (London, 1977), uses a discussion of the history of prisons as a case study for inquiring into the relationship between power and knowledge. For Ignatieff and Foucault 'deviance' is a construct of the social sciences and of the prisons. Foucault, in 'Prison Talk' (in C. Gordon (ed.), *Power/Knowledge: Selected Interviews and Other Writings 1972-1973*, pp. 37-54 at pp. 47-8), argues that criminology was constructed as a justification for punishment in order to replace the old notion of punishment as justified in terms of revenge for an act which threatened the sovereign. Once crime is regarded as 'deviant' behaviour, that is, as evidence of a psychological disturbance or of a poor environment, then punishment is justified as treatment, and treatment requires an even more exact observation of prisoners.

Robin Evans' popular Ph.D. thesis has recently been turned into an excellent, if rather expensive, book: *The Fabrication of Virtue: English Prison Architecture, 1750-1840* (Cambridge, 1982). He concentrates, as the title suggests, on design, since this was regarded as a crucial part of prison discipline in the period up to the middle of the nineteenth century. In theory, a properly designed prison would be a largely automatic mechanism which would mean that no prisoner could resist the discipline, and no member of the staff could abuse it. It, therefore, promised almost certain reformation. Architecture, as Bentham sought to show, could be the key which turned theory into practice.

Ultimately, the conclusion one arrives at is rather obvious. Prisons were acceptable in Victorian society because they represented, albeit in an extreme form, the norm of that society, rather than because of any specific penological theories. Factory, school, hospital and prison are all governed by inspection, regularity and time.

Ignatieff does not fall into crude economic determinism — the idea that the form which punishment takes is a direct reflection of the dominant mode of production. However, Foucault's work is guilty of a certain degree of determinism and of seeking to obliterate the 'author'. The middle way lies between a view of history which sees it as a procession of Great Men and Women (Radzinowicz tends to this) and one which sees it as an inevitable product of processes outside the individual's control. Marx's famous dictum that men make history, but not in the ways which they choose, provides the compromise. Individuals played a crucial role in the development of the modern prison, but it developed in ways which Howard, for instance, could not have predicted, and this was because of structural pressures within society: the obstruction of local justices, the constraints of finance, the dogmatism of other individuals such as Crawford and Russell, the resistance of prisoners, the development of an industrialised society, and the birth of a working class.

Part Four: The Modern Period, from 1877

Not surprisingly, there is an abundance of both basic source material and commentary and critical literature for this most recent period in the study. The increased involvement of central government with all aspects of imprisonment, the further development of scientific study in the fields of sociology and criminology and a more informed level of public debate have naturally fostered an expanding body of literature. This can perhaps be usefully divided into the following main categories: (1) government publications, most importantly in the form of reports of committees of inquiry and commissioned research, and to a lesser extent in policy documents; (2) critical and explanatory literature, emanating in the earlier part of the period from those actually working within the penal system but increasingly, as time goes on, produced by people within reform movements, such as the Howard League, and by an emerging class of academic writers and researchers; (3) autobiographical, anecdotal and general literature which, while not so formally rigorous in its discussion, does provide some insight through personal experience and detailed illustration; and (4) empirical research into the operation and effectiveness of the prison system, more especially in the period after 1945, with an increasing interest being shown within universities and the setting up of bodies such as the Home Office Research Unit.

The accessibility of this literature is variable. Some of the official publications have been brought together in convenient collections such as the Irish University Press series of British Parliamentary Papers and the Chadwyck Healey microfiche series, while on the other hand some of the older reports may only be available in original form in a few libraries. Again, while it may not be easy to find monograph discussions of imprisonment, even those published relatively recently, there has been a certain amount of reprinting by some publishers (a notable project is Garland Publishing's series of 30 titles on Crime and Punishment in England, 1850-1922), although these may be quite highly priced. It is important to bear in mind that many of the monographs referred to in this book are out of print, a factor of the fast-changing topicality of their subject-matter and of their relatively specialised readership, so that their availability even in university libraries should not be taken for granted. Research literature will generally be more readily available. It is usually of more recent origin and often in periodical form, and such items will frequently be found in the holdings of academic libraries. The availability of the fourth type of work will depend very much on the status and popularity of the author. References to the penal system in the work of Charles Dickens are easy to come by. On the other hand, a book such as John Lee's 'popular' autobiography is a rare find.

For those coming to the subject for the first time, there are few 'overviews' of the whole period. Lionel Fox's *The English Prison and Borstal Systems*, which takes us as far as the early 1950s, is a rare example of a detailed summary but even so it is concerned as much with contemporary as historical matters. Some of the more general works tend to take the perspective of penal reform (as the titles of Rose's *The Struggle for Penal Reform* and Grünhut's

Penal Reform suggest) while some of the most incisive discussions, such as Rupert Cross' *Punishment, Prison and the Public*, are necessarily selective in their treatment of the subject. The serious student of this subject inevitably has a large bookshelf to work from but on starting would be well advised to consult Sean McConville's bibliographical discussion in Martin Wright's *Use of Criminology Literature* (Butterworths, 1974).

Official Publications

For those researching in this area and seeking out material, it is useful initially to consult a general guide to such publications, such as P. and G. Ford's *Guides or Lists of Parliamentary Papers*, covering the period 1833 to 1974. A useful collection of reprinted parliamentary papers is contained in the Irish University Press series, which has 21 volumes on *Crime and Punishment: Prisons*, which covers most of the nineteenth century, although mainly the period prior to 1870. Volumes 18 and 20 contain a number of reports on conditions and discipline, Volume 21 has reports on Treason-Felony convicts and Volume 19 comprises the Report and Minutes of Evidence of the important Departmental Committee under Herbert Gladstone. From the beginning of this century, many reports concerning the prison and penal systems have been published as command papers. Amongst the most relevant of these and other official publications on the prison system may be listed the following:

Report from the Departmental Committee on Prisons (Gladstone Committee), 1895, C. 7702

Report from the Departmental Committee on Inebriates and their Detention in Reformatories and Retreats, 1908, Cd. 4438

Report from the Departmental Committee on Reformatory and Industrial Schools, 1913, Cd. 6838

Report from the Departmental Committee on the Treatment of Young Offenders, 1927, Cmd. 2831

Report by H. Du Parcq on circumstances connected with the disorder at Dartmoor Prison, 1931-32, Cmd. 4010

Report from the Departmental Committee on Persistent Offenders (Dove Wilson Committee), 1932, Cmd. 4090

Report from the Committee on Discharged Prisoners' Aid Societies, 1953, Cmd. 8879

Royal Commission Report on Capital Punishment, 1953, Cmd. 8932

Penal Practice in a Changing Society (Government White Paper), 1959, Cmnd. 645

War Against Crime in England and Wales (Government White Paper), 1964, Cmnd. 2276

Preventive Detention, Advisory Council on the Treatment of Offenders, 1963, Home Office

Report from the Committee of Inquiry under Lord Mountbatten into Prison Escapes and Security, 1966, Cmnd. 3175

Report on the regime for long-term prisoners in conditions of maximum security, Advisory Council on the Penal System, 1968, Home Office

Report on Detention Centres, Advisory Council on the Penal System, 1968, Home Office

People in Prison (Government White Paper), 1969, Cmnd. 4214

Report from the Working Party on Habitual Drunken Offenders, 1971

Report from the Committee of Inquiry into the United Kingdom Prison Service (May Committee), 1979, Cmnd. 7673

In addition, much useful information may be gleaned from the Annual Reports of the Prison Commissioners, up to 1962, and of the Prison Department of the Home Office since 1963 (all published as command papers).

Critical and Explanatory Literature

Much of this kind of work in the latter part of the nineteenth century and earlier twentieth century was produced by those working within the prison system. Towards the middle of this century there was an increasing contribution from writers working under the aegis of reform movements, while most recently the major input has been from academic commentators. Amongst the most useful monograph publications are the following:

Sir Edmund Du Cane, *The Punishment and Prevention of Crime* (Macmillan, 1885, reissued by Garland Publishing): informative detail and also useful in providing some idea of Du Cane's penal philosophy.

W.D. Morrison, *Juvenile Offenders* (1896, reissued by Garland):

gives some insight into the penology of a notable critic of Du Cane's prison regime.

Sir Evelyn Ruggles-Brise, *The English Prison System* (Macmillan, 1921, reissued by Garland): historical account and penological theory.

S. Hobhouse and A. Fenner Brockway (eds.), *English Prisons Today* (Longmans, 1921, reissued by Garland): critical account of the prison system under Ruggles-Brise, produced by the Prison System Enquiry Committee, set up in 1919 by the Labour Research Department.

Max Grünhut, *Penal Reform* (OUP, 1948): theoretical penological work, with a comparative discussion of British, European and American systems.

Sir Lionel Fox, *The English Prison and Borstal Systems* (Routledge & Kegan Paul, 1952): very full account of the contemporary prison system with a fair amount of historical material; quite a useful retrospective account.

S.K. Ruck (ed.), *Paterson on Prisons* (Frederick Muller, 1951): selected penological writings of the influential Prison Commissioner of the 1920s-40s.

Gordon Rose, *The Struggle for Penal Reform* (Stevens, 1960): historical account of change in the prison system during this period, largely from the perspective of the Howard League for Penal Reform.

Roger Hood, *Borstal Reassessed* (Heinemann, 1965): very useful account of the development and demise of the Borstal system.

Gordon Rose, *Schools for Young Offenders* (Tavistock, 1967): similarly useful treatment of reformatory, industrial and approved schools.

Sir Rupert Cross, *Punishment, Prison and the Public* (Stevens, 1971): published version of Hamlyn Lectures, containing some incisive though selective discussion of aspects of the prison system over the last hundred years.

J.E. Thomas, *The English Prison Officer since 1850* (Routledge & Kegan Paul, 1972): despite the rather narrow scope suggested by the title, this is a thought-provoking and informative penological history, unusual in its adoption much of the time of the prison officer's perspective.

Stephen Humphries, *Rebels or Hooligans?* (Basil Blackwell, 1981): interesting and illuminating investigation of juvenile delinquency and related subjects in the period 1889-1939, with a useful final chapter on reformatory schools.

Robin Evans, *The Fabrication of Virtue: English Prison Archi-tecture 1750-1840* (CUP, 1982): although strictly speaking outside the period, useful to consult for an understanding of the architecture of many present-day prisons.

Mick Ryan, *The Politics of Penal Reform* (Longmans, 1983): condensed but informative account of developments in the prison system since 1945.

Biographical, Anecdotal and Occasional Literature

These materials are very scattered and vary in their usefulness. References to the prison system not infrequently occur in the works of popular authors — Charles Dickens most readily comes to mind — and these must be viewed in the context of the work in which they appear: they may, for instance, be included for dramatic effect or part of a propaganda effort in favour of reform. Autobiographical works and collections of reminiscences may contain interesting material, but this of course is based on subjective experience and caution should be used in generalising too far from such accounts. Amongst such works may be mentioned the anonymous *Five Years Penal Servitude By One Who Has Endured It* (1877, reissued by Garland); Frederick Brocklehurst, *I Was In Prison* (T. Fisher Unwin, 1898), John (Babbacombe) Lee, *The Man They Could Not Hang* (Arthur Pearson, 1908); and the reminiscences of Arthur Harding, in Raphael Samuel, *East End Underworld: Chapters in the Life of Arthur Harding* (Routledge & Kegan Paul, 1981). There are a number of more local studies of individual institutions which may be included in this category: for instance, John Camp's *Holloway Prison: The Place and the People* (David & Charles, 1974).

Periodical Literature and Occasional Papers

Again, this is a scattered source and more often comprises contemporary comment which is subsequently of historical interest (such as the series of articles in the April 1961 issue of the *British Journal of Criminology* on prison architecture) rather than historical study in itself. Occasional papers sometimes surface in published collections: for instance, Louis Blom-Cooper's discussion of the centralisation of the prison system in Blom-Cooper (ed.), *Progress in Penal Reform* (OUP, 1974).

Worthy of special mention, however, are two papers which put forward reappraisals of the historical study of the prison system: Noel McLachlan's article, 'Penal Reform and Penal History', in Blom-Cooper, *Progress in Penal Reform, op. cit.*; and Sean McConville's 'Future Prospects of Imprisonment in Britain', in McConville (ed.), *The Use of Imprisonment* (Routledge & Kegan Paul, 1975).

Empirical Research

As already stated, most of this work is relatively recent and so not of such obvious historical interest. But it may be fair to single out the research by H. Mannheim and L.T. Wilkins, *Prediction Methods in Relation To Borstal Training* (HMSO, 1955), which probably had an important impact on policy. Other earlier research tended to concentrate on the problem of recidivism, notably Norval Morris, *The Habitual Criminal* (Longmans, 1951), a comparative account of methods of dealing with persistent offenders with some detailed studies of preventive detainees under the 1908 Prevention of Crime Act, and W.H. Hammond and E. Chayen's *Persistent Criminals* (Home Office Research Unit, 1963), a study of preventive detainees in 1959. The bulk of such research will be of interest to those examining the most recent period in the history of imprisonment.

CHRONOLOGICAL TABLE

892-3	Law of Alfred mentions imprisonment
925-39	Reign of Aethelstan
1020-30s	Law of Cnut on imprisonment
1066	Norman Conquest
1166	Assize of Clarendon orders building of County Gaols
1176	Assize of Northampton
1219	Henry III's ordinance on imprisonment of suspect felons
1237	Mention of Chapel and separate accommodation for women at York
1247	Foundation of Bethlehem Hospital
1275	Statute of Westminster I overhauls aspects of, and makes considerable use of, imprisonment
1283-4	Statute of Acton Burnell ⎫ Imprisonment for
1285	Statute of Merchants ⎭ mercantile debt
1285	Statute of Westminster II — imprisonment for defaulting accountants
1295	Statute of Breaking Prisons
1215-17	Famine
1330	Gaol delivery process reviewed
1348	Arrival of Black Death
1349	Ordinance of Labourers
1351	Statute of Labourers
1377	Warden of Fleet liable for debts of straying prisoners
1381	Peasants' Revolt
1419	Ludgate prisoners temporarily transferred to Newgate
1423	Death of Richard Whittington — will provides for rebuilding of Newgate
1450	Jack Cade's Revolt
1463	Exercise Yard built in Ludgate
1503	Sheriffs' powers to keep gaols confirmed. Negligent escapes penalty
1531	Act concerning construction of gaols and Justices' powers

1544	First appointment of prison clergyman to visit Newgate
1547	Punishment of vagabonds by slavery
1556	Bridewell receives its first inmates
1572	Act for punishment of vagabonds. County bread allowance
1575	Houses of Correction to be provided
1596	Establishment of Rasphuis in Amsterdam
1597	Act for punishment of vagabonds, allows transportation and galleys
1605	Charges for conveyance of offenders to gaol
1609	Houses of Correction to be provided in all counties
1619	Mutiny in Fleet
1620	King's Bench revolt. First full-time chaplain in Newgate
1649	£5 Act to relieve insolvent debtors
1666	Act for the relief of poor prisoners and setting them to work
1670	Act for the release of poor distressed prisoners for debt
1679	Habeas Corpus Act
1681	Regular inspection of Newgate prison commences
1692	Surgeon from St Bartholomew's starts to visit Newgate
1696	House of Commons Committee under Pocklington investigates abuse in Fleet
1699	Act enables JPs to build and repair gaols. Report on abuse in Fleet
1701	House of Lords Committee reject bill to reduce Fleet overcrowding
1702	SPCK report on Newgate and Marshalsea
1703	Act allows military service for insolvent debtors. Clement XI gaol at San Michele
1716	Act details Sheriffs' powers and control of sale of gaoler's office
1717	Act permits transportation of felons
1719	Act covering prison building and JPs' power to send offenders to House of Correction
1728-9	Act allows for relief of debtors in prison. House of Commons report on Marshalsea and Fleet. House of Lords report on insolvent debtors. Trial of Huggins

1737	Act for relief of poor prisoners
1744	Justices' powers in relation to House of Correction increased
1751	Sale of spirits in gaols forbidden
1752-3	Further report on the King's Bench by Oglethorpe and Calvert
1767	Publication in Britain of Beccaria's *Of Crimes and Punishments*
1771	Publication of Eden's *Principles of Penal Law*
1773	Howard appointed High Sheriff of Bedfordshire
1774	House of Commons' Committee on Gaols leads to Discharged Prisoners Act and Health of Prisoners Act
1775	Horsham's House of Correction built
1776-83	Loss of American colonies: temporary halt to transportation
1777	Publication of Howard's *The State of the Prisons*
1779	Penitentiary Act passed
1782-4	Gilbert Acts passed
1784	Transportation Act passed
1785	Beauchamp committee recommends transportation, but still nowhere to send the convicts
1787	First convict ship to Botany Bay, Australia
1787-91	Bentham draws up plans for the Panopticon prison
1789	Petworth House of Correction and Gloucestershire Penitentiary completed: both incorporating separate cells
1793-1815	French Wars
1810	Holford Committee recommends the building of a national penitentiary
1815	Gaol Fees Abolition Act passed
1816	Millbank Penitentiary opened in London
	Elizabeth Fry begins her visits to Newgate prison
1817	Society for the Improvement of Prison Discipline formed
1821-2	Sydney Smith's attacks on prisons published
1822-3	Scurvy at Millbank following a cut in the diet
1823	Peel's Gaol Act passed, seeks to prevent moral contamination
1834	Crawford's report on American prisons published
1835	Prison Act passed: establishes a prison inspectorate.

	Crawford and Russell amongst those appointed.
1837	Appointment of a chaplain-governor at Millbank
1837-8	Molesworth Committee recommends the abolition of transportation
1839	Prison Act passed: incorporating ideas of religious reformation. Appointment of Jebb as advisor to the Home Office on prison building.
1842	Pentonville Penitentiary opened
1843	Millbank becomes an assessment depot
1847	Deaths of Crawford and Russell
1848	Public works prison opened at Portland
1850	Jebb appointed head of the new Directorate of Convict Prisons
1853	Penal Servitude Act ends short terms of transportation
1857	Last English hulk goes out of service. Abolition of transportation as a judicial sentence
1863	Garotting scare. Carnarvon Committee recommends tougher prisons. Jebb dies
1865	Prison Act
1867	Formal end of transportation
1877	Prisons Act. All prisons brought within central government control and Prison Commission set up. Sir Edmund Du Cane appointed first Chairman of the Commissioners
1879	Summary Jurisdiction Act: increased the availability of non-custodial measures
1887	Probation of First Offenders Act: a further diversionary measure
1895	Report of the Gladstone Committee. Resignation of Du Cane and appointment of Sir Evelyn Ruggles-Brise as Chairman of the Prison Commissioners
1898	Prisons Act. Legislative commitment to the recommendations of the Gladstone Committee. Home Office given power of regulation of prisons
1901	First borstal institution set up on an experimental basis in the convict prison at Borstal in Kent
1907	Probation of Offenders Act: probation made generally available
1908	Prevention of Crime Act: sentence of preventive detention introduced, and borstal system made

fully operational

Children Act: restriction on the imprisonment of children

1913 Mental Deficiency Act: diversion of mentally deficient persons from the prison system

1914 Criminal Justice Administration Act: restriction on the imprisonment of fine defaulters

1922 Ruggles-Brise retires as Chairman of the Prison Commissioners. Report of the Prison System Enquiry Committee (Labour Research Department)

1930 March of borstal trainees to Lowdham Grange and the building of the first open institution

1932 Prison disturbances and mutiny at Dartmoor convict prison

1933 Children and Young Persons Act: reformatory and industrial schools replaced by 'approved' schools

1936 First adult open prison established at New Hall, near Wakefield

1948 Criminal Justice Act: penal servitude and hard labour abolished and new sentences of preventive detention and corrective training introduced. Detention centres established

1959 Mental Health Act: hospital and guardianship orders introduced

1963 Prison Commission replaced by the Prison Department of the Home Office

1964 Probation service made responsible for prison welfare

1966 Escape of George Blake and others. Mountbatten Report on prison security

1967 Criminal Justice Act: attempts to reduce prison population by introduction of suspended sentence and release on licence (parole). Abolition of preventive detention and corrective training and corporal punishment within prisons

1968 Parole becomes operational

1969 Children and Young Persons Act: introduction of care and supervision orders and replacement of approved schools and remand homes by community homes

1970 Administration of Justice Act: removal of imprisonment for debt

1972	Criminal Justice Act: introduction of further non-custodial measures, in particular community service
1979	Report of the May Committee on Prison Services, following a number of disturbances during the 1970s and a lowering of staff morale. Advocates a policy of 'positive custody'
1982	Criminal Justice Act: removal of sentences of imprisonment for all persons under 21. Borstal training replaced by youth custody

APPENDIX 1
STATE CONVICT PRISONS IN THE NINETEENTH CENTURY

(Prisons distinct from county or borough gaols, houses of correction and local prisons)

Millbank, London	1816	Later a 'depot' prison for those under sentence of penal servitude. A local prison from 1883. Closed 1890
Parkhurst, Isle of Wight	1838	Special prison for juvenile offenders until 1863. Used for female convicts until 1869, then male convicts
Pentonville, London	1842	Built as a 'model prison'. Used as a local prison after 1885
Portland, Dorset	1848	Public works prison (for penal servitude). Borstal after 1921
Dartmoor, Devon	1850	Formerly used for prisoners of war. Public works prison
Portsmouth, Hampshire	1852	Public works prison. Closed in 1895 and transferred to the Admiralty
Chatham, Kent	1856	Public works prison, with a smaller prison at Chattenden, 1877-86. Closed in 1893 and transferred to the Admiralty
Borstal, Kent	1874	Public works prison. Fully operational as a borstal 1908
Dover, Kent	1885	Public works prison. Used as a borstal after 1953
Woking, Surrey	1860	Used for invalid and lunatic convicts, and for female convicts from 1888 until 1895, when it was

		transferred to the War Department
Brixton, Surrey	1853	Formerly the Surrey House of Correction. Used for female convicts until 1870. Rebuilt in 1880 and then used as a local prison
Fulham, Middlesex	1856	Refuge for female convicts until 1888
Wormwood Scrubs, Middlesex	1883	Replaced Millbank as a convict establishment. Replaced Millbank as a local prison in 1890
Aylesbury	1895	Took female convicts from Woking

APPENDIX 2
PURPOSE BUILT PRISON ESTABLISHMENTS OPENED SINCE 1958

(Note: This is intended to provide some idea of the extent and location of the prison building programme in recent years.)

YCC: Youth Custody Centre (the institution known as the Borstal until 1982).

1958	Everthorpe, Humberside (YCC)	Built as a prison
1961	Hindley, Lancashire (YCC)	Built as a prison
1962	Grendon Psychiatric Prison, Buckinghamshire	Adjacent to Spring Hill Prison
	Bullwood Hall, Essex (YCC for females)	
1963	Blundeston, Suffolk	
	Swinfen Hall, Staffordshire	Built as a borstal
1964	Stoke Heath, Shropshire (YCC)	Built as a prison
	Wellingborough, Northants (YCC)	
1965	Brockhill, Worcestershire	Remand centres
	Thorp Arch, Yorkshire	
	Winchester, Hants	
	Low Newton, Durham	
	Pucklechurch, Avon	
	Risley, Cheshire	
1966	Gartree, Leicestershire	
	Whatton, Nottinghamshire (Detention Centre)	
1967	Albany, Isle of Wight	Partly converted from army barracks; adjacent to Parkhurst
1968	Eastwood Park, Avon (Detention Centre)	Built by inmate labour
	Onley, Warwickshire (YCC)	Built as a prison

| 1969 | Coldingley, Surrey | Built as an 'industrial prison' |

1971 Long Lartin, Worcestershire
1974 Channings Wood, Devon
1976 Featherstone, Wolverhampton
1979 Wymott, Lancashire
1980 Cookham Wood, Kent
       (Women's prison)
1981 Frankland, Durham
1982 Hollesley Bay, Suffolk
1983 Highpoint North, Suffolk

Prisons at the design or building stage, 1984

Wayland (Norfolk), Castington (Northumberland) and Stockton (Leicestershire), under construction; Full Sutton (Humberside), Garth (Lancashire), Swalehill (Kent), Bovingdon (Hertfordshire) and Woolwich (London — to be a local prison), at design stage.

At present 14 new institutions (three to be local prisons, the first to be built this century) are planned for the end of this decade. For a discussion of this building programme, see Andrew Rutherford, 'Deeper into the Quagmire: Observations on the Latest Prison Building Programme', 23, *Howard Journal of Criminal Justice*, 1984, 129.

APPENDIX 3
A NOTE ON HARD LABOUR IN NINETEENTH-CENTURY PRISONS

The idea of hard labour was a pervasive element in nineteenth-century prison discipline but was never defined in legislation with any precision. The Criminal Law Act of 1776 provided for convicted felons not transported to be set to hard labour dredging the River Thames or 'other such laborious services'. The 1779 Penitentiary Act was more specific in its proposals for two penitentiaries in which hard labour would figure as an important component in the regime: 'Labour of the hardest and most servile kind, in which drudgery is chiefly required . . . such as treading in a wheel or drawing in a capstan for turning a mill or other machine, sawing stone, etc., etc., or any other hard or laborious service', with less demanding types of labour for those who were unfitted by age or sex for the heavier work.

The nature of hard labour in practice depended largely on the kind of confinement which was used. Under the system of separate cellular confinement, limitations of space dictated the forms of labour so that a hand-crank or hand-loom could be used, but not a treadwheel. Labour involving the treadwheel or shot drill necessarily involved association, even if in conditions of silence. From the middle of the nineteenth century, the important practical distinction lay between 'useful' or 'productive' and 'useless' or 'unproductive' work. Even so, 'productive' work such as oakum picking or quarrying could be of a very monotonous and gruelling nature, as is demonstrated by accounts of the conditions of labour in some of the public works prisons.[1] The 1865 Prison Act differentiated First Class Hard Labour, defined in terms of heavy, generally unproductive work, and undefined though less physically demanding Second Class Hard Labour. As time went on (and this is pointed out by Du Cane[2]), the distinction between the two classes of hard labour lost much of its meaning, although perhaps labour of the first class involved greater psychological stress in that its uselessness could be more dispiriting. It may be useful, however, to provide some account of what was involved in the main types of unproductive labour, before it was discontinued under the terms of the 1898 Prison Act in response to its condemnation by the Gladstone Committee.

The Treadwheel

This instrument of hard labour was first used in Brixton Prison in 1817, having been invented by Mr Cubitt, 'the engineer of Lowestoft . . . a gentleman of science, of extensive professional connections, and of gentle and pleasing deportment', in response to the request of a magistrate outside the Suffolk county gaol at Bury St Edmunds: 'I wish to God, Mr Cubitt . . . you could suggest to us some mode of employing these fellows!'[3] The treadwheel was subsequently developed into a labour instrument of some sophistication. Mayhew and Binney give a description of the wheel at Coldbath Fields House of Correction in London, on which 12 men were put to work at any one time for 15 periods of 15 minutes per day, with the same interval of rest between each stint on the wheel. 'Each wheel contains 24 steps, which are eight inches apart, so that the circumference of the cylinder is sixteen feet. These wheels revolve twice in a minute, and the mechanism is arranged to ring a bell at the end of every thirtieth revolution, and so to announce that the appointed *spell* of work is finished.'[4] It was officially calculated that each prisoner would ascend 7,200 feet on this wheel per day. Its use was controversial: there was evidence presented from time to time concerning its ill effects (it could produce varicose swelling, cause severe weight loss and aggravate pulminory and rheumatic complaints.)[5] There is a treadwheel preserved at Beaumaris County Gaol, on Anglesey, now a museum.

Crank Labour

This involved work on a machine consisting of an iron drum on legs, with a handle on one side to be turned (10,000 times at Coldbath Fields[6]) by the prisoner. The handle operated a number of cups inside the drum which scooped up sand and emptied it again 'after the principle of a dredging machine'. It was usually employed as a punishment or as a test of feigned sickness.

Shot Drill

An open air exercise, which involved the lifting and passing of cannon balls down a line of prisoners at the shouted command of a warder, for a period of an hour or more (for a description, see Mayhew and Binney's account[7]: 'although not larger than a cocoa-nut, it required a considerable effort to lift it').

Other instruments of labour which could be used, although these could often serve a 'useful' purpose (as indeed could the treadwheel) were pumps and capstans. By the time evidence was being submitted to the Gladstone Committee in 1895, the forms of 'unproductive' labour listed are just the treadwheel and the crank.[8]

Notes

1. See Sean McConville, *A History of English Prison Administration* (Routledge & Kegan Paul, London, 1981), Vol. 1, pp. 397-8.
2. *The Punishment and Prevention of Crime* (Macmillan, London, 1885), p. 60.
3. Quoted in Henry Mayhew and John Binney, *The Criminal Prisons of London and Scenes of Prison Life* (Griffin, Bohn & Co., London, 1862), p. 288.
4. Ibid., p. 303.
5. See Robin Evans, *The Fabrication of Virtue* (Cambridge University Press, 1982), pp. 303-9.
6. Mayhew and Binney, *Criminal Prisons of London*, p. 308.
7. Ibid., pp. 308-9.
8. Report of the Departmental Committee on Prisons, 1895, C. 7702, Appendix 4 (p. 542 of the Report).

INDEX

Acton Burnell, Statute of 13, 28
Aethelstan, King of England, Laws
    of 7, 8, 36
alcohol, sale of in prisons 41, 91, 119,
    144, 162, 167
Alfred, King of Wessex, laws of 7, 8,
    18, 28
American War of Independence 111,
    120
Auburn Prison 146, 147
Ayenbite of Inwyt 15

Bacon, Francis 94-5
bail 4, 5, 27
    see also remand
Bambridge, Thomas 83, 86, 98, 101
Beccaria, Cesare 109-10, 127, 219
Beauchamp Committee 110-11
Becher, Rev. Thomas 131
behaviourism 128-9, 131, 146, 151,
    155
benefit of clergy 6, 10-12, 59
Bentham, Jeremy 114, 155-6, 179,
    219
Bethlehem Hospital 23, 37, 83
Bishops' Prisons 10, 11, 18-19, 23, 28
    see also benefit of clergy
Black Death 9, 14, 29, 39
Blackstone, Sir William 117
Boethius 16, 22, Plate 1
Borstal 191, 246-9
Boniface, Archbishop of Canterbury
    12
boroughs, medieval prisons within
    19-20, 39
Bracton, Legal Treatise 6, 18
Bray, Thomas 56, 99, 100, 267
Brecon County Gaol 169-171, 174-5
Bridewell Palace 67-9, 85
    see also house of correction
Britton, Legal Treatise 24
Bromyard, John 25-9
Burdett, Sir Francis 126
Burke, Edmund 113
Bury Gaol 137, 173, 219

Cade's Revolt 26
Calvin, John 67
capital punishment 6-10, 24, 57-60,

109-10, 121, 125
Carlyle, Thomas 178
Carnarvon Committee, Report of
    154, 158-60, 168, 178, 191, 213
Castlereagh, Lord 125
central government funding,
    withdrawal of 145, 160
chapels in prisons 45, 119
chaplain, prison 87, 144, 149, 151,
    169-71
charitable donations 29-30, 41, 48,
    66, 89
Chester Gaol 21, 38
Chidley, Samuel 62
children,
    see young offenders
Clarendon, Assize of 4, 5, 21, 26
Clay, Rev. John 83, 96, 99, 101, 153,
    158, 164, 170, 171
Clink, prison 82
Cnut, King of England, laws of 3
Coke, Edward 61, 63, 69, 72, 96, 97
Coldbath Fields, House of
    Correction 125-6, 174, 302
Commmission for Poor Prisoners 81
Community homes 245
Control units 226
Conwy (Conway) Gaol 21, 39, 42
Cooper, R. A. 130
Corrective training 239-40
Convict Prisons, Board of Directors
    of 154, 156, 192, 205-7, 211,
    Appendix 1
Counters, London 20, 27, 78, 84
Crank labour 218, 302-3
Crawford, William 126, 130, 135,
    139, 143-54, 159, 160
Crime levels 57-9, 120-1, 125, 136,
    139, 143, 157-8, 188, 195-6
'Criminal class', creation of 178-9
Criminal justice, effects of on
    penitentiary 176-7
Criminal Justice Act 1948 193, 207,
    209, 211, 239, 241, 247, 249
Criminal Justice Act 1967 224, 240
Criminology 14-15, 177, 214
Crofton, Sir Walter 219
Cromwell, Oliver 62
Cubitt, Thomas 138, 302

Dalton, Michael 72
Dartmoor Mutiny 223
debt, imprisonment for 12-14, 24, 25, 28, 39-40, 48, 64, 78-81, 89, 92, 134, 256-8
Dekker, Thomas 55, 62, 78
Delacy, Margaret 164-5
De Montfort, Amaury 16, 39
detention centres 249
Dialogus de Scaccario, Treatise 13
diet 41-2, 89, 90, 118, 138, 158, 160, 227-8
   see also starvation
Directorate of Convict Prisons
   see convict prisons
disease 37
   see also Black Death, gaol fever, hospitals, prisoners' health
divisions of imprisonment, without hard labour 208-9, 259
dress 118, 123, 228-30
drunkenness 91, 252-4
Du Cane, Sir Edmund 160, 192-3, 195, 200, 206, 207-8, 213, 214, 220, 232

Edward I 8, 13, 16, 17
Edward III 11
Eden, William (Lord Auckland) 109-10, 117
education 11, 232
Edwards, John 175
Ellwood, Thomas 71, 85
Elmira State Reformatory, New York 213-14, 246
escapes
   see security in prisons
Exeter Borough Prison 166, 174

feet, putrefaction of 23
fees 23, 27-8, 41, 43, 44, 47, 49, 88-91, 114, 115, 162, 163, 167
   see also finance, prison
Fennor, William 78, 88, 90, 91
Fielding, Henry 58, 70
finance, prison 26-30, 88-91, 93
   see also central government funding, fees
fine defaulting 197, 258-9
First National Prison Congress, Cincinnati 213
Fleet Prison 16, 20, 25, 29, 40, 44, 80, 82, 85, 86, 88, 92, 98, 100, 101, 134, 135

Fleta, legal treatise 16, 24, 46
Fothergill, Dr. 116, 118
Foucault, Michel 56, 83, 176, 177
Fox, George 62, 100
Fox, Sir Lionel 194, 207, 230
franchisal prisons 17-18, 24, 26, 84
Fry, Elizabeth 135, 138, 166-7

galley fleets 64
Gaol Act 1823 143-4, 149, 150, 163-4, 165
Gaol Fees Abolition Act 1815 143, 163
gaol fever 93-6, 99
   see also disease
gaolers 10, 11, 17, 27, 45-7, 84-7, 114, 115, 126-6, 128, 129, 166-8
garnish 90-1, 93
George, William 145-6
Gilberts Acts, 1782 and 1784 119
Gladstone Committee, Report of 187, 190, 193, 201, 206, 208, 212, 216, 217, 232, 237, 240, 242, 243, 246, 302
Gloucester Penitentiary 122-4, 125, 131, 136, 149
governor
   see gaoler, prison staff, after 1877
Grendon Psychiatric Prison 252
Grey Committee 150, 151
Grosseteste, Robert, Bishop of Lincoln 45
Gurney, I. J. 162
Giffard, Humphrey 99

habitual offenders 237-40
haircuts, prison 11, 123, 228-30
Hall, John 90, 92
Hanawalt, Barbara 6
Hanging, Not Punishment Enough 55, 60, 63
hard labour 207-9, Appendix 3
Harding, Arthur 217, 220, 253
Harris, A., Warden of Fleet 80, 90, 92
Hay, Douglas 120
Henry II 4, 10
Henry III 9, 10, 29
heresy 17, 18-19, 39, 44
Hext, Edward 58, 69
Holford Committee 119, 129, 131-4
Home Office, and prison system 192, 194-5, 214
Horsham House of Correction 116

hospitals 17, 23, 30, 37, 48, 66, 67, 83
House of Commons
    Committee on Gaols 1774 115-16
    Enquiry into Fleet 1696 100
    Enquiry into Fleet and
        Marshalsea 1729 55, 56, 90,
        101
House of Lords Committee 1835 145,
    150
houses of correction 65-73, 76, 77,
    82, 83, 87, 97, 119, 161-2, 265
Howard, John 76, 78, 84, 91, 112-16,
    117, 118, 122, 128, 138, 146, 162
Huggins, John 78, 87, 98, 101
hulks, 118, 119, 156, 220
Hurnard, N. 36

Ignatieff, Michael 70, 73, 77, 112,
    152
inebriate reformatories 190, 196, 253,
    254
inmate sub-culture 90-3, 224
inspectors, prison 43, 99, 145-54, 165,
    191, 192
irons 22-3, 24, 27, 37, 46
Islip, Simon, Archbishop of
    Canterbury 28

Jebb, Joshua 151-3, 154-6, 158, 160,
    168
juveniles
    see young offenders

King's Bench Prison 21, 26, 78, 80,
    81, 85, 87, 92, 94, 100

labour, regulation by statute 27, 38
    see also Black Death in prisons
    see work, in prisons
Langbein, John 63
Lee, John 206
Levellers 62, 80
lock-ups 19, 161
Lollards
    see heresy
Loughborough, Lord 162
Lowdham Grange Open Borstal 198,
    247
Ludgate Gaol 20, 27, 30, 42, 48
Lushington, Sir Godfrey 216

Maconochie, Alexander 219
McVicar, John 232
Mandeville, T. 91

Marshalsea Prison 26, 55, 89, 91, 93,
    100, 101
maximum security dispersal prisons
    211, 225
May Committee, Report of 191, 201,
    221, 255
mentally disordered offenders 36-7,
    83, 190, 197, 249-52
Merchants, Statute of 1285 13, 25, 28
mesne process 79
military, recruitment of prison staff
    from 192, 200
military service 64
Millbank Penitentiary 126, 134, 135,
    138, 144, 151, 153, 205, 220, 297
Mirror of Justices, legal treatise 8, 17,
    46
monks, monastic imprisonment 16,
    19
Montreuil-sur-mer, Treaty of 1275
    13
Monson, Sir William 64
More, Thomas 55, 61
Morrison, W. D., Chaplain of
    Wandsworth Prison 202, 204
Mountbatten Inquiry 225
Mynshul, G. 89, 94

nationalisation of prisons 161, 187,
    191-2
Newgate Prison 20, 22, 24, 27, 28,
    29, 30, 39, 40, 41, 43, 45, 46, 48,
    64, 76, 82, 84, 85, 86, 87, 89, 91,
    95, 98, 99, 100, 115, 135, Plate 2
Nield, James 94, 115, 162
Nigel, Richard, son of, imaginative
    escape attempt by xiii, 22
Northampton, Assize of 1176 4
nuns, imprisonment of 19

Oglethorpe, James, 56, 100, 101
overcrowding within prisons
    see prison population

Paley, William 60
Panopticon 126-31
parole 231-2
pardons 10, 15-16, 25, 36
Paterson, Sir Alexander 193, 207,
    230, 247
Paul, Sir George Onesiphorus 122-3,
    136, 228
Peasants' Revolt 26
Peel, Sir Robert 143

penal servitude, sentence of 156-7,
  205-7
Penitentiary Act 1779 117-18, 122,
  129, 130-1
Pentonville Prison 127, 151-3, 156,
  172-3, 179, 205, 217, 260, 297
Perkins, William 67, 69
Petworth House of Correction 119,
  136
Philadelphia Prison 146-8
philanthropy 111-12
  see also charitable donations
Pitt, William 86, 98
Pole, Cardinal 61
politic debtors 28, 44, 80
political prisoners 38-9, 81-2, 259-61
poorer classes 190, 121-2, 125, 178
  see also working class
Powell, Sir Francis 215
Presteigne County Gaol 111, 124,
  161, 164, 165, 167-8, 169, 182 n.
  35
Preston House of Correction 137,
  164-5, 170-1, 219
preventive detention 211-12, 238-40
Price, David 154
Prison Act 1839 150-1, 163, 165
Prison Act 1865 160, 161, 164, 191
Prison Act 1898 192-3, 208, 222, 239
prison architecture 21, 130, 152, 179,
  218
  building programmes 4-5, 198-9,
    218, Appendix 2
  closures 20, 161, 164, 198
  Commission 192, 194
  Department of the Home Office
    194-5
  forte et dure 10, 47-8
  population 40-1, 76-83, 195-8
  staff, after 1877 199-203
prisoners, association together 134,
  150-1, 201, 217-18
  classification of 16-17, 39-40, 43,
    116, 144, 150, 208, 209
  punishment of 24, 118, 224
  rights of 226, 231
prisons, health 93-6, 114, 115, 116,
  144, 158, 164-5, 179
  see also disease
  moral corruption 16-17, 39, 44,
    91, 92, 114, 116, 144, 217
probation 189
progressive stages system 118, 134,
  159, 160, 205-7

public works prisons 155, 156-7,
  205-6, 219-20
punishment by labour 61-2

Quakers 85, 100, 135, 147

Radnorshire Quarter Sessions 124,
  161, 162-3, 169
recidivism
  see habitual offenders
religious reformation 15-16, 123,
  131-4, 148-9, 151, 155, 156,
  158-9, 162, 213
remand before trial 3-6, 77, 255-6
regulations, in medieval prisons 23,
  27, 43
remission 118, 222
Richmond, Duke of 116, 119
riots in prisons 26, 89, 225-6
  resistance by prisoners 156-8,
    172-6
Romilly, Sir Samuel 130-1
Ruggles-Brise, Sir Evelyn 193, 214,
  246
Rules, King's Bench Prison 92
Russell, Rev. Whitworth 126, 139,
  143-54, 159, 160, 168

San Michele Prison 99
schools
  approved 243-5
  industrial 240-3
  reformatory 240-3
security in prisons 21-6, 86, 222-6
  see also escape
segregation units 225
sentencing by courts 210
separate system 118, 119, 126, 144,
  148, 150, 151, 152, 155, 166,
  217-18
  see also solitary confinement
shot drill 218, 303
silent system 147, 148, 206, 217
Smith, Rev. Sydney 136-8, 148, 179
Society for the Improvement of
  Prison Discipline 130, 135, 138,
  143
solitary confinement 23, 40, 99, 123,
  125, 126, 129, 137-8, 144, 147-8,
  151, 226
Southwell House of Correction 119,
  131
S.P.C.K.
  see Bray, Thomas

sponging houses 85, 90
starvation in prisons 41
Stead, W. T. 208-9
stocks 9, 18, 19, 23

Taylor, John, 'The Water Poet' 60, 74, 84
Thatched House Society 89
toads, attack by 43
Tower of London 20, 43, 44
training prisons 211
transportation 63-5, 110-11, 114, 117, 121, 153, 155-7, 187, 205
treadwheel 33 n. 68, 138, 218, 302
Tun, London 20

Utopia 55, 61

vagabonds, vagrants 11, 37-8, 67-73
villeins, villeinage 7, 14, 18, 26, 37
visits 44-5, 231

Wake, Kidd 123-4, 173
'wandering abroad' 44
Wesley, John 100
Westminster I, Statute of 1275 5, 8, 9, 10, 16, 27, 47
Westminster II, Statute of 1285 13, 25
Whiston, James 88, 100, 101
Whittington, Richard 30, 34 n. 101
Wilde, Oscar 215, 227
women prisoners 39-43, 175-6, 211, 220, 248
work, in prisons 48, 218-21
    as punishment 117-18, 129, 137-8, 159
    as a reformative regime 117-18, 124, 128, 131-4, 148, 156, 219-21
    for profit 128, 129, 131-4, 149, 160
    unproductive, condemnation of 218-19
    see also crank labour, punishment by labour, shot drill, treadwheel
workhouses 73, 119, 124, 179
working class 124, 125, 177-8
    see also poorer classes

young offenders 35-6, 240-9